MIDNIGHT
AT THE
PERA PALACE

ALSO BY CHARLES KING

Odessa

Extreme Politics

The Ghost of Freedom

The Black Sea

The Moldovans

Nations Abroad (co-editor)

MIDNIGHT AT THE PERA PALACE

The Birth of Modern Istanbul

Charles King

W. W. NORTON & COMPANY

New York • London

Photo credits: Frontispiece courtesy of Pera Palace Hotel Jumeirah. All other
photos courtesy of Yapı Kredi Bank Selahattin Giz Collection.

For information about permission to reproduce selections from this book,
write to Permissions, W. W. Norton & Company, Inc.,
500 Fifth Avenue, New York, NY 10110

For information about special discounts for bulk purchases, please contact
W. W. Norton Special Sales at specialsales@wwnorton.com or 800-233-4830

Manufacturing by Courier Westford
Book design by Ellen Cipriano
Production manager: Louise Parasmo

Library of Congress Cataloging-in-Publication Data

King, Charles, 1967–
Midnight at the Pera Palace : the birth of modern Istanbul / Charles King.
— First edition.
pages cm
Includes bibliographical references and index.
ISBN 978-0-393-08914-1 (hardcover)
1. Istanbul (Turkey)—History—20th century. 2. Istanbul (Turkey)—Social
life and customs—20th century. 3. Istanbul (Turkey)—Social conditions—
20th century. 4. City and town life—Turkey—Istanbul—History—20th
century. 5. Pera Palas Oteli (Istanbul, Turkey)—History—20th century.
6. Social change—Turkey—Istanbul—History—20th century.
7. Cosmopolitanism—Turkey—Istanbul—History—20th century. I. Title.
DR731.K56 2014
949.61′8024—dc23
2014012360

W. W. Norton & Company, Inc.,
500 Fifth Avenue, New York, N.Y. 10110
www.wwnorton.com

W. W. Norton & Company Ltd., Castle House,
75/76 Wells Street, London W1T 3QT

1 2 3 4 5 6 7 8 9 0

Frontispiece: The main entrance to the Pera Palace Hotel, on the corner of
Graveyard and Thugs Streets.

For

Cătălin Partenie,

teacher and friend

CONTENTS

Pera / Beyoğlu circa 1935

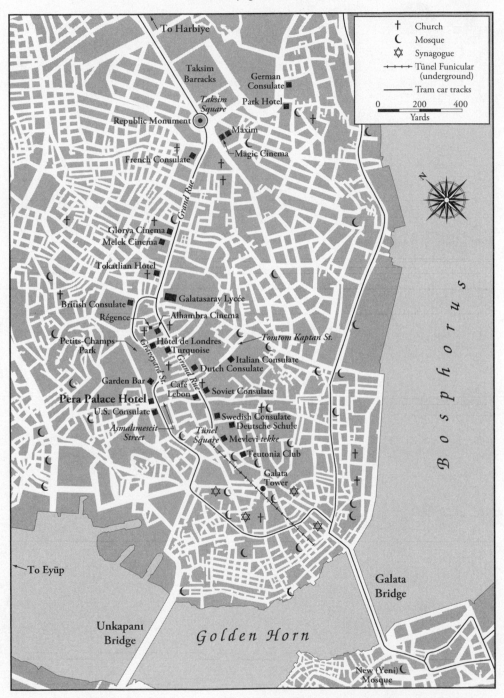

Legend:
- † Church
- ☾ Mosque
- ✡ Synagogue
- ┼┼┼┼ Tünel Funicular (underground)
- ── Tram car tracks

0   200   400
Yards

To Harbiye

Taksim Barracks

German Consulate

Park Hotel

Taksim Square

Republic Monument

Maxim

French Consulate

Magic Cinema

Glorya Cinema
Melek Cinema

Tokatlian Hotel

Grand Rue

British Consulate

Galatasaray Lycée

Régence

Alhambra Cinema

Petits-Champs Park

Hôtel de Londres

Tomtom Kaptan St.

Turquoise

Graveyard St.

Italian Consulate

Dutch Consulate

Garden Bar

Grand Rue

Café Lebon

Soviet Consulate

Pera Palace Hotel

U.S. Consulate

Swedish Consulate

Deutsche Schule

Asmalımescit Street

Tünel Square

Mevlevi *tekke*

Teutonia Club

Galata Tower

To Eyüp

Bosphorus

Galata Bridge

Unkapanı Bridge

Golden Horn

New (Yeni) Mosque

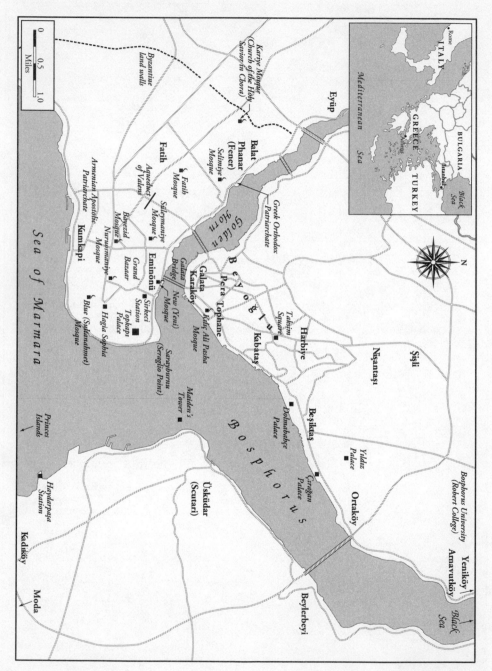

Istanbul Today

AUTHOR'S NOTE

In writing about a complex past, inconsistency of language is inevitable. I use the name "Istanbul" throughout this book, even though before 1930 or so, many locals and most foreigners knew it as a version of "Constantinople." I use the word "Muslims" to describe people who would have used that label in the Ottoman era, regardless of their level of religious devotion. Many of these people would later come to call themselves Turks. People of Greek Orthodox heritage in Istanbul have long distinguished themselves from Greek-speakers who live in Greece, and I make a similar distinction in English. I call the former "Greeks" and the latter "Hellenes." I refer to the present İstiklâl (Independence) Avenue as the "Grande Rue," a term that many people continued to use in the interwar years, even after the street had officially been given its current name.

I generally spell Turkish words in the Turkish fashion. I make exceptions for idiosyncratic spellings found in written sources, which I have left unaltered, and for terms and names that have English equivalents (hence, pasha rather than *paşa*). I refer to some historical characters—especially Turkish Muslims—by one or more given names up until the time they adopted an inheritable family name, around 1934. Before then, individuals were normally referred to by a first name plus an honorific, such as "Pasha" for generals or senior administrators, "Bey" or "Efendi" for men of rank, and "Hanım" for similarly placed women. "İsmet Pasha" would therefore be the equivalent of "General İsmet," while "Halis Bey" would be something like "Mr. Halis."

I mainly use the cardinal directions to describe the layout of Istanbul, even though a glance at a map will show this to be inaccurate; there are few geographical features that run strictly east–west or north–south. The hilltop neighborhood once called Pera can be subdivided into many different subsections today, and most of them are now contained within the municipal district of Beyoğlu.

Of course, if a reader is trying to track down the characters and locales in this book, these finer points of usage need not be a hindrance. Istanbul is, after all, a very forgiving place.

But Istanbul is so vast a city, that if a thousand die in it, the want of them is not felt in such an ocean of men.

EVLİYA ÇELEBİ,
Seyahatname (Book of Travels), seventeenth century

The palace is empty, its fountain silent,
The ancient trees have grown brittle and dry . . .
Istanbul, Istanbul! The last dead encampment
Of the last great migration.

IVAN BUNIN,
"Stambul," 1905

Constantinople and the narrow straits upon which it stands have occasioned the world more trouble, have cost humanity more in blood and suffering during the last five hundred years, than any other single spot upon the earth. . . . It is not improbable that when Europe in her last ditch has fought the last great battle of the Great War, we shall find that what we have again been fighting about is really Constantinople.

LEONARD WOOLF,
The Future of Constantinople, 1917

Midnight
at the
Pera Palace

PROLOGUE

A bartender pouring a glass of raki at an
Istanbul establishment.

WHEN I FIRST SAW THE Pera Palace, nearly twenty years ago, you had to have a rather specific reason for being in that section of Istanbul, like getting a lamp rewired or calling on a transgender prostitute. The old hotel was squat and square, wrapped in dirty, green-plastered marble. Its faded fin-de-siècle grandeur was out of place amid the seedy mid-rises that had grown up pell-mell in the 1970s and 1980s. Inside, the red-velvet chairs in the Orient Bar were always empty. The bartender seemed surprised whenever I stopped in for a cocktail and a bowl of stale *leblebi*, tooth-cracking roasted chickpeas.

Things had once been different. The Pera Palace was established in 1892 to service clients arriving on the Orient Express in the capital of the Ottoman Empire. For decades afterward, it was the obvious place for out-of-towners to stay. The wood-and-iron elevator, which rose up like a birdcage through the marble staircase, had been only the second one installed in Europe (after the Eiffel Tower's). A baroque dining hall stood next to a lounge of faux-marble inlay and filigreed screens, covered by a soaring glass canopy. Beyond the building's stately façade lay Pera, Istanbul's most fashionable neighborhood. A short walk along the main street, known to many Istanbullus in the nineteenth century and after as the Grande Rue, led to the embassies of most of the major world powers. Next door to the hotel, American diplomats shared the street with both the YMCA and legal brothels, and not far away, the

British, Russians, and Germans could entertain government officials in gilded restaurants and dark clubs.

The Pera Palace was meant to be the last whisper of the Occident on the way to the Orient, the grandest Western-style hotel in the seat of the world's greatest Islamic empire. Like Istanbul itself, the hotel was Europeans' first major port of call when they went east into a traveler's fantasy of sultans, harems, and dervishes. But before the Pera Palace had celebrated its twentieth year in business, all of that had begun to change.

A revolution deposed a long-reigning Ottoman sultan and ushered in more than a decade of political turmoil and communal violence. The First World War brought military defeat and foreign occupation. And in 1923, in one of modern history's most profound exercises in political self-creation, Turks made a purposeful break with their Ottoman past, rejecting an Islamic and multireligious empire and declaring in its place a secular, more homogeneous republic. Turkey's new leaders shifted their capital two hundred miles to the east, to the wind-whipped hills of Ankara, far from the corrupting memories of the old center.

A young reporter named Ernest Hemingway saw the beginning. "From all I had seen in the movies, Stamboul ought to have been white and glistening and sinister," he wrote in the *Toronto Daily Star* in the late autumn of 1922. He had arrived from the Balkans by train, rolling past brick-red Byzantine land walls and children splashing in the water, into a tumble of small mosques and wooden houses with dusty domes and sprung clapboards rubbed gray by salt and wind. He had seen roads choked with colorfully dressed peasants trudging behind muddy, bristle-haired water buffaloes. Queues of migrants in damp overcoats snaked around foreign embassies. Demobilized officers strutted in frayed tunics. From a plaza near the Pera Palace, he looked through a spyglass at refugee families pressed tight against the railings of a steamer spewing ash. Everything white was dirty white, he observed, and the mood was hopeless and resigned, like the feeling of waiting while a doctor and nurse are upstairs with someone you love.

Veils and harems, fezzes and frockcoats were disappearing. The sultan and the caliphate—the institution that embodied Muslims' understanding of God's will on earth—would soon be declared defunct. Hours and dates would be reckoned the way they were in Paris or New York, not as in Mecca and Medina. Ministers and generals were moving to Ankara. Foreign embassies and their entourages would follow. Istanbul was settling into a self-absorbed sense of *hüzün*, the hollowed-out melancholy that Turkish intellectuals said infused the crumbling walls, tumbledown mansions, and rotting seaside villas.

But between the two world wars, displacement and disorientation opened up a set of opportunities that no one could have foreseen. Loss was also a serviceable kind of possibility. The antidote to *hüzün* was what the Turks called *keyif*: a sense of joyful abandon, of singing to avoid crying, the willful summoning of mirth as an answer to horror. A different kind of Istanbul was already rising. Buffalo carts shared the streets with electric trams and automobiles. Circles of radical nationalists held meetings in the same districts where socialist agents plotted world revolution. New music drifted up from quiet neighborhoods: orchestral jazz, slithery and daring; the staccato plectrum work of a blind Armenian lute player; the torch songs of the Levantine underworld. You could have a drink at Maxim, a club owned by a black Russian American, or dance to the Palm Beach Seven playing nightly at the Garden Bar.

The minarets and dervishes were still there, but Istanbul was becoming a novel version of an Islamic city: an island of outcasts and the self-made, the cosmopolitan ex-capital of an Islamic empire that dreamed itself into a nation-state, and a place that—then as now—was struggling to shape its own way of being Muslim and modern at the same time. In these years of movement and change, if you squinted into the winter sun setting low over the Grande Rue, past the beggars and grifters, it was not hard to dream up a different kind of country and a different kind of life—one that, by force of will and dint of circumstance, you got to remake.

For more than half a millennium, the West's image of the Islamic world has been shaped by its encounter with Istanbul: the grandeur of its golden age, the swiftness of its decline, the apparent choice between the bad alternatives of authoritarian rule and religious extremism. But in the interwar years, Istanbullus embraced Western ideals with a zeal that no one could have imagined. The city whose very geography united Europe and Asia became the world's greatest experiment in purposeful reinvention in the Western mold.

In the process, the former Ottoman capital came to reflect both the best and the worst of what the West had to offer: its optimism and its obsessive ideologies, human rights and the overbearing state, the desire to escape the past and the drive to erase it altogether. When visitors complained that the old Istanbul seemed to be slipping away, what they meant was that Istanbul was coming to look more and more like them. "[W]e civilised people of the West," wrote the historian Arnold J. Toynbee on a visit to Turkey in the 1920s, "glance with pity or contempt at our non-Western contemporaries lying under the shadow of some stronger power, which seems to paralyse their energies by depriving them of light. . . . Yet if we paused to examine that dim gigantic overshadowing figure . . . we should be startled to find that its features are ours."

Europeans who came to Istanbul understood the dark side of their own civilization precisely because many of them were its victims. After the First World War, in the parallel universes created by the collapse of empires across Europe and the Near East, Westerners were sometimes the needy immigrants and Easterners their reluctant hosts. Wave after wave of Europeans landed in Istanbul in ways they could never have imagined—not as conquerors or bearers of enlightenment but as the displaced, impoverished, and desperate. They wandered Istanbul's streets and were shooed away from the Pera Palace's doorstep: drunken sailors and ruined businessmen; former nobles flogging family silver and moth-eaten furs; unwanted ethnic minorities cast off by some European government; the losers of a civil war, palace intrigue, or world-changing revolution.

No one understood this history better than a man who turned out to be an unexpected traveling companion in my journey into the thicket of the hidden Islamic jazz age. I first came across Selahattin Giz in a series of limited-edition Turkish photograph albums published in the early 1990s. He was a bootstrap newsman whose job was to record daily life as he saw it, often in blurry, motion-filled detail. When I visited his archive, now owned by a Turkish bank, I found that one of the biggest collections of images was filed under the category *"Kaza"*—Accident. They included the grisly and sensational photos you would expect to see on the front page of any newspaper eager to shift copies: car wrecks, pedestrian deaths, and the aftermath of a nightmarish day when the cable on the Tünel funicular snapped, sending the wooden carriage careening through the front of the downhill station. There were also the private experiments of a man with a camera on some lazy afternoon: alley cats, interesting shadows, some tentative erotica.

As I made my way through Giz's collection, I realized that I had stumbled upon the person who had helped chronicle the vanished world I wanted to understand. I also knew that his own life mirrored the story of exile and rejuvenation that defined his adopted city.

Giz was born to a Muslim family in Salonica (modern Thessaloniki, Greece) in 1914. His hometown was Greek by origin, largely Sephardic Jewish by population, and—until just two years before he was born—Ottoman by government. Salonica passed to Hellenic control as a

result of the Balkan Wars, a kind of regional dress rehearsal for the devastation of the First World War, and the new government worked hard
to erase the centuries of multiculturalism that had defined urban life
there. Minarets were pulled down. Mosques became churches. Muslim
homes and businesses passed to Christian ownership.

The Giz family joined hundreds of thousands of other Muslims
pushed out of southeastern Europe. They settled in the Beylerbeyi
neighborhood of Istanbul, on the Asian side of the Bosphorus, an area
whose Greek Orthodox, Jewish, and Armenian inhabitants replicated
the mixed world the Gizes had known in Salonica. But the young Selahattin spent most of his life and career on the other side of the water,
amid the cinemas, street performers, and cabarets of Pera. An uncle
gave him a camera on the occasion of his *sünnet*, the Muslim circum-
cision ceremony typically performed a few years before a boy reaches
adolescence. As a student at the prestigious Galatasaray Lycée in the
late 1920s, he threw himself into photography, wandering the city
with his Zeiss Ikon and talking his way into the darkroom of the city's
largest daily, *Cumhuriyet* (The Republic). He formally joined the newspaper's staff in 1933 and spent the next forty years as one of its premier
photojournalists. He died, at eighty, in 1994.

Looking at his photographs—and those of many unknown photographers that he slipped into his collection—is like visiting an Istanbul
that few people, whether Turks or tourists, can imagine ever existed.
There are towheaded Russian chorus girls, arms flailing and cheekily
self-aware. There is a meeting of the alumni association of the eunuchs
of the sultan's imperial harem. A crowd of Muslim men sacrifices two
rams to bless a trolley car. There are firemen in otherworldly gas masks
during an air-raid drill and schoolgirls caught up in a frenzy of grief
on the death of Mustafa Kemal Atatürk, Turkey's founding president.
Grown women skip rope to the delight of a child or zip down a street
on a bicycle, their dark hair and summer dresses blowing in the breeze.
And there is Giz himself, smiling, snapped by a friend in an Istanbul

Selahattin Giz in an Istanbul winter.

winter, the wet snow piling up on the brim of his fedora. If journalism is the first draft of history, it is also sometimes a salutary shock: a way of forcing us to recall a mode of being that made sense at the time, of lives lived messily among neighbors who prayed and ate differently— Muslims, Christians, and Jews; religious and secular; refugees and natives—with everyone, in one way or another, starting over.

Istanbul is today a global city, a sprawling urban space of more than thirteen million people, making it more populous than Greece, Austria, or Sweden—larger, in fact, than two-thirds of the world's countries. Old fishing villages have become fashionable suburbs, and old suburbs have become city centers in their own right, with glass-clad skyscrapers rising above new mosques and malls. Even during Muslim holy days, the Arabic-language call to prayer competes with Turkish-language pop music pounding through the thin walls of café-bars. In an afternoon, you can visit the universal seat of the Greek Orthodox faith, a headquarters of the Armenian Apostolic Church, the office of Turkey's chief rabbi, and the mausoleum of one of Muhammad's closest companions. It is home to people who feel their first identity to be Turkish and others who might list Kurdish, Alevi, Armenian, or Circassian, and who are now more freely confident in doing so than at any time in recent history.

Istanbul's rise began with the journey away from a place that visitors often knew as Constantinople. The new city was the product of immigrants as well as emigrants—women and men who, by choice or necessity, had come to Istanbul as well as those who had left it, the first generation of republican Istanbullus or the last generation of imperial Constantinopolitans. In an era of leave-taking and restlessness, a time we now call the interwar years, the Pera Palace was not the only place where these transients and newcomers began their reinvention. But for wave after wave of refugees, migrants, and exiles, the storied old hotel was a symbol of the transition from a past age to a new one—a place that embodied the ties between East and West, between empire and republic, and between nostalgia and experiment in the only place on earth to have been the epicenter of both Christendom and global Islam.

GRAND HOTEL

Pigeons in flight: The Golden Horn with the sixteenth-century mosque complex of Sültan Süleyman the Magnificent (or the Süleymaniye) in the background.

"AS FOR THE SITE OF the city itself, it seems to have been created by nature for the capital of the world," wrote Ogier Ghiselin de Busbecq, a Flemish diplomat and traveler, in the sixteenth century. Istanbul had been founded as Byzantium, perhaps in the seventh century BC. It became New Rome when the Roman emperor Constantine the Great inaugurated it as his capital in 330 AD. In 1453, Ottoman Muslims wrested it from Constantine's political descendants, the Byzantines. Turkish-speakers knew it officially as *Kostantiniyye*, a name derived from the popular Greek term *Konstantinoupolis*, or "Constantine's city." Local Jews borrowed the first two syllables from the Greeks and called it *Kushta*. Local Armenians borrowed the last two and called it *Bolis*. Slavs used *Tsarigrad*, or "Caesar's city."

Coming upon Istanbul from the sea is still one of the most breathtaking experiences on earth—seductive and romantic, with the old city's pointed skyline shimmering above whitecaps and treetops. No other place can claim to be more perfectly situated. But a hidden truth of the modern city—the city of boulevards, Parisian-style shopping arcades, and tramcars, rather than the one of Byzantine basilicas and Ottoman mosques—is that arriving by land has always been something of an anticlimax. The twisting streets, crowded highways, and small hills chockablock with buildings, all unrolling in patches of red and brown like an Anatolian carpet, are poor substitutes for a first sighting from aboard ship. One way to preserve the enchantment, advised a visitor in 1910 emphatically, was simply *"Never step ashore."*

Unlike other great cities, Istanbul even hides its central railway terminal. Sirkeci station is squeezed into the hillside below Sarayburnu, or Seraglio Point, near the spot where Byzantine emperors and Ottoman sultans chose to site their royal households. "I am willing to run the rails through my body if it means a railway will be constructed in my domain," the reforming Sultan Abdülaziz was believed to have said in the 1860s. When the station was built more than two decades later, it did require running the rails through the territory of one of his successors, Sultan Abdülhamid II. Bits of the Byzantine sea walls and the tiered gardens of the sultan's Topkapı Palace were removed to accommodate the tracks. A visitor might have thrilled at the sight of smoke enveloping the sultan's palace in marvelous white clouds and think all this the height of Oriental fantasy until it was pointed out that the mist was being produced by a steam engine rounding the headland.

Sirkeci was opened in 1890, but even in its heyday, few remarked on the experience of reaching it. In London's St. Pancras or Budapest's Keleti, a rail journey ended with a crescendo and a cymbal crash. There, carriages creaked to a halt inside soaring halls that gave way to even grander streetside façades. Sirkeci, however, was more like a coda. Trains slowed to a crawl once they reached the Ottoman border—going from an *allegro con furore* to a definite *legato*, observed Agatha Christie on one of her journeys aboard a transcontinental express—because of inferior rails and poorly serviced lines. The Sea of Marmara gradually came into view as the carriages jerked between windswept hills and the rocky coast, before rounding the cape at the mouth of the Golden Horn and stopping with a final sigh from the steam engine. When the American novelist John Dos Passos arrived in the summer of 1921, he initially thought his train had stopped at a siding, waiting for another engine to pass. "Is it? No, yes, it must be . . . Constantinople," he finally decided.

Istanbullus embraced the timetables and all-weather predictability of rail travel only reluctantly. The reason was a matter of geography. According to the ancient historian Herodotus, when Greek colonists from the Aegean first settled the area, they planted themselves on the eastern side of the Sea of Marmara at Chalcedon. A Persian commander visited the area some time later and denounced the Chalcedonians for their poor planning. Only a blind man, he said, would willingly choose to place a colony there rather than on the strategic headland just across the water. Later builders were savvier. Greek settlers moved across the Bosphorus and founded Byzantium, a rather minor trading center but one well situated on the sea route linking the Mediterranean with other Greek outposts on the Black Sea to the north.

Nearly a millennium later, the Roman emperor Constantine the Great was obscure about the reasons for naming Byzantium his new capital, citing only the commands of the Christian God he had embraced as his empire's exclusive deity. But Byzantium did have the advantages of being well away from the barbarians of the West and unsullied by the pagan traditions of the old capital. *Nova Roma*, as it was first called, grew to encompass the cape as well as the hills to the west and, centuries later, the highlands to the north. Over time—from the collapse of the western empire through the rise of Constantine's political successors, the Byzantines—locals came to inhabit the sea nearly as much as the land, scuttling back and forth between two continents and three water systems: the brackish Golden Horn, rising from two small streams in the west of the city; the saltier Bosphorus, constantly exchanging water with the Black Sea; and the Sea of Marmara, which leads on via the Dardanelles strait to the Mediterranean.

Byzantine legal codes enshrined the right to a property owner's sea view, and the expectation that daily affairs should naturally involve both land and water remained central to urban life throughout the Byzantine Empire's existence. Sitting astride a north–south sea route also allowed the Byzantines to build a local economy based on taxing shipping between the Mediterranean and the Black Sea. The emperor

Justinian I, in the sixth century, established customs houses along the Bosphorus, with magistrates paid from imperial coffers. But according to the contemporary chronicler Procopius, officials were also free to charge ship captains whatever price they wished. Merchants frequently complained that they were being bled dry when their vessels passed the imperial capital. The spectacular growth in the city under Justinian's reign, with new churches and private houses rising on the hills stretching out from the old quarter of Byzantium, was in part fueled by what would now be called extortion.

Much the same approach to water and land characterized the inheritors of the empire. The Ottomans had been in constant contact with the Byzantines for roughly two centuries. Their distant roots stretched back to Turkic tribal groups in Central Asia, pulled and pushed westward in several rounds of migration, but by the early modern era they were as culturally and genetically mixed as the Byzantines themselves: a patchwork of nomads, warriors, converts, and natives united mainly by their loyalty to the sultan, the Ottomans' supreme ruler. When Sultan Mehmed II took the city in May 1453, he issued a special decree mandating that shipbuilders and sailors not be harmed, and from that point the Ottomans developed a well-regulated and infinitely complex system of rules and etiquette governing the use of the city's waterways.

Rowed caiques ferried passengers from shoreline to shoreline, connecting the waterside summer villas, or *yalıs*, that Ottoman grandees built amid fishermen's cottages along the Bosphorus. The number of oars on each caique was strictly regulated according to rank: eighteen for the commander of the navy; ten for the grand vizier (prime minister), the *şeyhülislam* (chief Islamic cleric), and foreign ambassadors; eight for regional governors and heads of major cities; six for mid-ranking military officers and leading citizens. Watchmen along the water were on guard not only for capsized boats but also for transgressions of oar-related propriety.

The grandest caiques were reserved for the sultan's flotilla, which featured twenty-four oarsmen, a gold-fringed canopy supported by gilded poles, a prow with a gilded falcon, and a dais at the stern for the sultan himself. During the summer months, when the sultan and his retinue took to the water for the *selâmlık*, the weekly procession to Friday prayers, the spectacle could be transporting. According to Charles White, one of the most insightful nineteenth-century observers of the city:

> [T]he limpid freshness of the waters, crowded with vessels and craft of all sizes and countries—the beams of a mid-day sun, gilding the countless domes, minarets, and palaces, and illuminating the rich and varied landscape—give to this spectacle an air of fairy splendour, unequalled in reality, and not to be surpassed in the imagination but by the creations of Aladin's enchanted lamp. . . . It is the only regal spectacle in Europe where the points of attraction perfectly harmonise with surrounding objects.

It was not difficult to see, White said, why Bosphorus boatmen were widely regarded as perfect specimens of Ottoman manliness and reputed by locals to be Istanbul's most skillful lovers. By his day, there were some 19,000 registered boatmen on the lower Bosphorus, mainly Greeks and Armenians, in charge of 16,000 craft, as well as several thousand more in the villages stretching toward the Black Sea. That number trailed off later in the century, as steam-driven passenger ferries came to replace rowboats. But foreign sailors could still watch from their ships as Ottoman royalty used caiques to cross back and forth between their palaces on the European and Asian shores. With gold-uniformed oarsmen in the royal barge, and wives and concubines following in less ornately carved boats, all churning up small wakes in the shadow of modern cruisers, it was like an old world silently passing a new one on a calm sea.

Getting around the city required knowledge of not only streets and squares but also quays, docklands, and ferry stations. A ferry ride was needed to get from one rail terminus to the other. Sirkeci station serviced points west—Thrace and the Balkans—while Haydarpaşa station, built on the Asian shore in 1908, led on to points east—Anatolia and Syria. It is a cliché that Istanbul is the world's only city sitting on two continents (joined by two automobile bridges in 1973 and 1988, with another under construction), but one only appreciates the implications of that statement on the short sea journey from one railhead to the next. The situaton changed only in 2013, when a sub-Bosphorus metro line was inaugurated. It was the first time in history that anyone was able to make the intercontinental journey entirely on dry land.

"Do not suppose that every man understands the sea," warned the great Ottoman seafaring manual, the *Kitab-ı bahriye*, of the sixteenth-century naval commander Pirî Reis. Storms can turn the water black, with whitecaps lashing against the sea walls and ferries slamming against their berths. The standing waves and notorious currents on the Bosphorus, which whip around headlands at speeds that make the strait seem more like a river than an extension of the sea, frustrated sailors and rowers in earlier times. Even in an age of satellite-assisted navigation, the Bosphorus can still make harbor pilots and ship captains nervous.

Life on dry land was no less treacherous. Sited near one of the world's most active seismic zones, Istanbul rarely saw more than a decade without a devastating earthquake. Byzantine chroniclers recorded the first major one in 402 AD; after that, both minor and cataclysmic events were common. In 557, multiple churches were destroyed and the dome of Hagia Sophia was extensively damaged. In 989 and 1346, the dome collapsed. The Ottomans created a special government administration dedicated to post-earthquake reconstruction, and officials were kept busy. Massive earthquakes in 1489, 1509, 1557, 1648, and 1659 leveled thousands of houses and snapped stone minarets like matchsticks. In a huge series of earthquakes and aftershocks in the summer of 1766, the domes of the magnificent Fatih and Kariye mosques collapsed. The damage inflicted on Topkapı Palace caused Sultan Mustafa III to flee the city for safer quarters. In 1894, most major public buildings saw extensive damage, including the Grand Bazaar.

Under the Ottomans, regulations requiring wooden construction rather than stone for private residences were intended to reduce the deaths caused by earthquakes, but the solution to one problem abetted another. In the warren of narrow streets leading down to the water, large-scale fires were frequent and periodically devastating. A flame from a lamp or heating brazier might end with entire neighborhoods laid waste. Rebellious janissaries—the sultan's corps of elite troops and bodyguards—might take out their frustrations by deliberately reducing thousands of houses to ash, leaving iron fixtures twisted, stone foundations exposed, and a third or more of the city in ruins. For much of the nearly five centuries of Ottoman governance, an Istanbullu could expect to experience at least two cataclysmic blazes in a lifetime. It was all so familiar that "fire epics"—long poems that narrated the terror of fire and the wonders of fate—have been part of Istanbul's folk literature since the seventeenth century.

"As soon as it gets dark, the town may be relied upon to burst into flame at some point or another on the European or Asiatic side," wrote one observer. Huge fires occurred in 1569, 1633, 1660, 1693, 1718, 1782, 1826, 1833, 1856, 1865, 1870, 1908, 1911, 1912, 1915, and 1918, not counting those limited to individual neighborhoods. The destruction of newer buildings sometimes would reveal treasures from the ancient past. "I have walked over the burnt districts many times and with many archaeological friends," noted a resident of the city in 1908, "because we soon found that places which we had read of and had not been able to identify had now, in their stony strength, survived this and doubtless other conflagrations and gave us the information we wanted. The aspect . . . even now in many parts reminds me strikingly of Pompeii."

Brigades of firefighters, or *tulumbacıs*, were forced to negotiate the narrow and hilly streets on foot, running along with water canisters hoisted aloft like a pasha on a litter. Their cries of "*Yangın var!*"—"There's a fire!"—became part of the soundscape of the city, as predictable as the Muslim call to prayer or the nighttime mewling of alley cats. On his first visit to the city, the adventurer Aubrey Herbert was chased down the length of the Grande Rue by a mob of screaming, half-dressed madmen, no doubt bent on hammering an infidel, he thought. It was only when he arrived breathless at his hotel that someone explained that the mob was in fact a unit of firemen on their way to a blaze. Even then, for individual property owners, the cure was sometimes worse than the disease. The *tulumbacıs* were outfitted with a hand pump, which was useful for putting out small house fires, but for anything larger, their standard technique was to use hooks and chains to pull down adjacent structures before the fire could spread. A fair amount of the damage inflicted by Istanbul's frequent fires was in fact wrought by the firemen themselves.

Despite the fire danger, migration from the countryside fueled urban growth, so that by the early nineteenth century the city inside the old Byzantine walls had very little open space. The doorways of private houses opened directly onto the street and families managed to squeeze out additional living space by projecting bay windows from the upper stories, which turned the streets into dark tunnels. Even the Divanyolu, the grandest thoroughfare south of the Golden Horn and the major processional route from the western gates to the sultan's palace at Topkapı, was only about twenty feet across at its widest. Most of the old city's seven hills were taken up by monumental mosque complexes, such as the Baroque-style Nuruosmaniye mosque on the second hill, the majestic Süleymaniye on the third, and the Selimiye on the fifth, and this in turn reduced the space available for housing the city's burgeoning population. A small fire could easily snake through these overcrowded districts and, growing street by street, lay

it to waste. Photographs from the time of one of the last great fires of
the Ottoman era, in 1912, show crowds of newly homeless Istanbullus
gathered with bedrolls and stacks of wooden furniture around ancient
stone obelisks near the Sultanahmet (or Blue) mosque.

These disasters also provided unique possibilities, however. They
leveled entire swaths of the city with such frequency that urban planners, real estate speculators, and government administrators were able
to reshape the landscape according to their own grand designs. By the
1860s, the Ottoman government had formed a commission to regularize streets, create new public spaces, and install drainage systems.
In fire-ravaged sections, small parks and squares replaced shop-lined
alleys and irregular wooden houses with their characteristic bay windows. Today, tourists can get lost in the maze of passageways around
the Grand Bazaar, but the streetscape there is in fact the product of
Ottoman attempts to regularize the map a little more than a century
ago; the neighborhood is neat and gridlike compared to what came
before. The airy, open vistas around some of the signature monuments
of the old city, such as the Sultanahmet mosque and the Hagia Sophia,
are likewise the result of the frequent devastation suffered by earlier
generations.

Like other empires, the Ottoman government had long practiced a
policy of what it termed *sürgün*, or forced resettlement. Mehmed II had
used it as a way of repopulating Istanbul after the conquest of 1453,
and his successors applied it for purposes ranging from punishment
against a rebellious village to moving craftspeople or shepherds into
areas of the empire that needed their skills. But natural disasters were
probably responsible for the regular displacement of more Istanbullus
than state policy, war, or economic migration. In June 1870, a massive
blaze swept across the heights north of the Golden Horn and reduced
parts of Pera to rubble. By that stage, however, monied classes and foreign investors were beginning to understand the profitability of this

periodic rearrangement of Istanbul's cityscape. Their plans depended on another transformative innovation—and the reason that Sirecki station had been built in the first place: the coming of the age of rail.

On a Sunday evening in October 1883, a short train pulled out of the Gare de l'Est in Paris. Under new electric lighting strung throughout the station, huge crowds gathered to witness the departure. Hauled by a powerful steam locomotive, the train consisted of a luggage car, two sleeping wagons, and a brightly lit dining car, with a second baggage car for steamer trunks and other oversize gear bringing up the rear. The passengers were settling in for a trip covering eighteen hundred miles across the breadth of Europe. It was the inaugural journey of the train that had been christened the Orient Express.

The journey was a publicity stunt organized by Georges Nagelmackers, a Belgian engineer. His nemesis—and, in a way, the reason for the journey—was a man named George Pullman. To railway enthusiasts, Nagelmackers is a well-known figure in the history of trans-European travel, but Pullman's fame was genuinely worldwide. Pullman's innovation had been to develop carriages designed for sleeping—the famous Pullman cars. His design, unveiled in the United States in the early 1860s, featured twenty berths per carriage, arranged in upper and lower rows. It was now possible for passengers to make long journeys by train in the comfort of something approaching a real bed, even if the rail car was really no more than a bunkhouse on wheels.

Pullman's idea might have taken some time to catch on—after all, getting undressed and sleeping amid strangers was a novel idea for the time—had it not been for the fortuitous use to which his experimental carriage was put in 1865. When John Wilkes Booth assassinated Abraham Lincoln, a grand journey seemed the only proper way to commemorate the death of a president. A week later, a black-draped train departed from Washington, DC, and crawled to Springfield, Illinois, carrying Lincoln's body and offering mourners a chance to see the president on his final journey. Pullman cars were hitched to the back of the train, allowing family members and scores of attendants to make the trip along with the presidential cadaver. Even in the middle of a national tragedy, Pullman had shown that a train ride could be more than a dusty, cinder-strewn ordeal. It could also be, in the words of one railway historian, "a means of travel which could be memorable (and therefore profitable) as an example of gracious living on wheels."

Within only a few years, Pullman cars were beginning to take over not only the American market but also the European one. Nagelmackers had visited the United States in 1870 and returned to Europe determined to edge out Pullman's model and install himself as the leading manufacturer of sleeping cars in Europe. He relentlessly pursued railway companies and governments to convince them of the usefulness of his version of the sleeping car, or *wagon-lit* in French. He incorporated a new German-designed suspension system, known as a bogie, which cradled the cars on separate, removable-axle assemblages and served as a kind of shock absorber, providing an easier ride and potentially a more restful sleep.

In December 1876, Nagelmackers formally incorporated his Brussels-based firm. A few years later, he unveiled a logo that would become synonymous with luxury long-distance travel on the continent: the intertwined calligraphic letters *WL*, supported by lions rampant and surrounded by the company's French name—*Compagnie Internationale des Wagons-Lits et des Grands-Express Européens*. No one before had imagined that a single rail company could operate lines running across the entire continent. Railroads were not only symbols of national prestige. They were also critical parts of the national security infrastructure of European kingdoms and empires, and allowing a foreign train—especially one also filled with foreigners—to navigate across the continent with only minimal interference from passport and customs officers was something of a novelty. But having secured the patronage of Belgium's King Leopold II, the Wagons-Lits service managed to connect Paris with Vienna by the early 1880s, with plans for moving on to Bulgaria. The addition of yet another of Nagelmackers's innovations—the dining car—meant that long journeys could be completed without having to depend on the offerings of faraway stationmasters or the unorthodox foodways of strangers. The cars themselves were works of art, full of polished brass and wood inlay, wing chairs and leather banquettes, with the designs for foldaway tables and hidden compartments modeled on the tight-space solutions worked out by naval architects.

By 1883, the inaugural expedition of the Orient Express was meant to showcase how far the Wagons-Lits Company had come in only a few short years and to look toward the next great goal of extending the service all the way to the edge of Europe itself, to Istanbul. Nagelmackers invited a who's who of minor European dignitaries to go along for the ride: travel writers and essayists, French and Belgian ministers, German newspapermen, the first secretary of the Ottoman Embassy, Austrians and Romanians, a correspondent from the London *Times*. At the frontier between Austria-Hungary and Romania, a troupe of eleven musicians joined the group, set themselves up in the dining car, and played waltzes and other songs as the train sped toward the Black Sea.

The first journey only made it partway, however. The travelers had to alight in the Bulgarian port of Varna and then travel the rest of the way to Istanbul by ship. The entire journey took eighty-one hours and forty minutes, including fifteen hours steaming on the Black Sea. The reason was that Nagelmackers's ambition had outstripped the realities of Ottoman infrastructure.

By 1850, the Ottoman Empire had not a single mile of track, compared with more than eight hundred in Austria-Hungary and around six thousand in Great Britain. A burst of railway construction came later in the century, but even then the focus was on connecting outlying parts of the Ottomans' vast empire with each other, not on connecting the capital to European centers. Still, despite its inauspicious beginnings, Nagelmackers' project had its desired effect. Within five years, Ottoman railway projects had extended full service to Istanbul and connected trunk lines with the European network. By the time Nagelmackers died, in 1905, it was possible to board a train in Paris and not relinquish your sleeping berth until you reached the sultan's capital. When the Simplon Tunnel opened through the Alps a year later, it became easier than ever to get from the heart of Christendom to the heart of the Islamic world by rail. Passengers were deposited only steps from the geographical limit of Europe and a short walk from the major historical and tourist sites in the city. It was, said an observer at the time, "the annexation of Constantinople to the Western world." Even for seasoned continental travelers, the excitement of approaching the train in a French station never dulled. "I am going by it! I am *in* it! I am actually in the blue coach with the simple legend outside: CALAIS-ISTANBUL," wrote Agatha Christie of one of her frequent journeys by rail.

The first Orient Express travelers had been lodged in a string of hotels in Pera, the normal destination for visiting Europeans, but the overall quality and the paucity of available space in many of them provided both a problem and an opportunity for the Wagons-Lits Company. The firm had acquired a plot of land at the edge of the territory scorched by the great Pera fire of 1870. The site looked out on a municipal garden called Les Petits-Champs, which city planners had created after the blaze. The park had a somewhat grisly past. It was sited on top of a former cemetery, as were several of Istanbul's public parks. But within a few years, the street had become the city's newest hotel row, with a range of Parisian-style buildings overlooking the green space. Few visitors were aware that the exotic-sounding street to which they were directed by their guides and interpreters—Kabristan—actually meant Graveyard.

In 1892, the Wagons-Lits Company decided to build its own

hotel there, at the intersection of Kabristan and Çapulcular, or Thugs, Streets. The property had once belonged to a Muslim religious foundation established through a benefaction from the sultan. In 1881 it had been purchased by a family of Armenian merchants and bankers, the Esaians, whose roots lay in both the Ottoman and Russian Empires. The Esaians might well have regretted selling to the Wagons-Lits firm, because when the Pera Palace finally opened a few years later, business was brisk.

The hotel had a considerable advantage over the other first-class facilities nearby, such as the Hôtel de Londres, the Bristol, the Continental, the Angleterre, and—its perennial rival—the Tokatlian, situated right on the Grande Rue. It was the only hotel that was part of a pan-European network owned and operated by a single company. Its sister establishments in Nice, Monte Carlo, and other cities offered unprecedented luxury to a new generation of trans-European travelers, and staying at each of the Wagons-Lits facilities became a collect-them-all game, at least for those wealthy enough to afford it. Like the Four Seasons and Ritz-Carlton hotels of later eras, the Pera Palace provided an exclusive experience not because it was wholly unique but precisely because it was part of a chain—a grand community of properties such as the Avenida Palace in Lisbon or the Odyssée Palace in Paris that promised luxury, safety, and a certain degree of predictability in major destinations, all built to a similar style and standard. As the *Guide Bleu* later noted, the Pera Palace was equipped with "all the modern comforts: elevator, bathrooms, showers, radiator heat, and electric lighting, with a magnificent view over the Golden Horn."

Insurance maps from the period—one of the best sources for understanding Istanbul's changing landscape—show whole tracts of European Istanbul in ruins, the result of old fires that had never given way to rebuilding. The Pera Palace, however, stood at the center of the city's new commercial and financial district created in the wake of the Pera fire. A string of four- and five-story buildings, many constructed by local Greek and Armenian business leaders and financiers, gave a radically new look to the neighborhood. Their well-proportioned façades and expansive windows would have been at home in contemporary Paris. They faced Petits-Champs Park and looked out on the western outskirts of the city, making them among the best places to watch the sunset, when the blazing late-day light made the marble façades glow bright and otherworldly. Architects had also made sure the buildings were connected with Pera's traditional promenade, the Grande Rue, through a series of internal passageways.

Few people could have foreseen that, in only two decades after the Pera fire, the neighborhood would have not one but two prominent avenues, the Grande Rue and the newer Graveyard Street, both sporting horse-drawn trolleys and knitted together by the city's most splendid internal passages and arcades. When Le Corbusier visited in the first decade of the twentieth century, he found the relatively new streetscape on the heights above the Golden Horn to be a revelation. Istanbul now had, he pronounced, its own kind of *allure new-yorkaise*.

THE GRAY FLEET

A water view: A man and woman cross the Bosphorus on one of Istanbul's iconic ferries, with the old city and Galata Bridge in the background.

A T THE TIME THE PERA PALACE was founded, signs of progress and optimism were abundant in the Ottoman capital. Steamships carried passengers across the city's waterways. Luxury goods from Europe were displayed behind gilt vitrines along the Grande Rue. The new soccer clubs of Beşiktaş, Galatasaray, and Fenerbahçe—the teams that would later come to define some of the fundamental divisions within Istanbul's citizenry—sponsored gala matches and league championships. A Greek shipper, a Jewish cloth merchant, an Arab pearl diver, a Kurdish caravan master, and an Armenian financier could all regard themselves as subjects of a single sovereign, the Ottoman sultan.

But no future had a longer past than that of the Ottoman Empire. Its demise was the most overanticipated event in diplomatic history. Arguing over how other countries and empires might profit from its end was one of the fixtures of great-power diplomacy for much of the nineteenth century. Russia's Tsar Nicholas I was credited with labeling the empire "the sick man of Europe," and, in strategic terms, the Ottomans had in fact been in slow retreat since 1683, when the sultan's armies were pushed back from the gates of Vienna. But virtually any Ottoman official—from the sultan's senior advisers to regional governors on restive frontiers in the Balkans, Anatolia, and the Arabian Peninsula—could sense that the decline was accelerating.

Since the 1850s, the so-called Eastern Question—a conglomeration of territorial disputes, nationalist movements, and international standoffs—had roiled the empire and sparked muscular diplomacy and armed interventions by Britain, France, Austria-Hungary, Germany, and Russia. In the early 1860s, Russian attacks on Muslim highlanders in the Caucasus sent hundreds of thousands of Muslim refugees pouring across the frontier to seek the sultan's protection. In 1877–1878, a devastating war involving the Ottomans, Russia, and the Balkan states led to a peace settlement that removed Ottoman control from much of southeastern Europe, an area that Istanbul had ruled for centuries. More than half a million Muslim migrants again sought refuge in the sultan's shrinking domains. An entire generation of new Ottoman subjects, many concentrated in Istanbul, came directly from these consecutive waves of forced migrants, or *muhacirs*. Untroubled about their own Muslim subjects and citizens whom they had put to flight, Christian governments remained concerned about Christian coreligionists still inside the empire. They pressured the Ottomans to exempt Greeks, Armenians, and other non-Muslims from local criminal and civil law.

By the beginning of the twentieth century, no major power—not even European monarchs who worried about instability in their own overseas empires—faced the near-constant uprisings, rebellions, and guerrilla campaigns that confronted the aging Sultan Abdülhamid II. He had begun his reign in the 1870s as heir to the Tanzimat, the great midcentury Ottoman reform movement that sought to catch up to European powers by streamlining the state administration, instituting modern schooling, building new roads and railways, and modernizing the army and navy. But he had since retreated into reaction and suspicion. He owed his state budget to foreign creditors, his military power to British and German advisers, and his sense of personal security to a network of domestic spies whose written reports flooded daily into his Yıldız Palace complex, nestled in a forest overlooking the Bosphorus. The number of informants was so great that a sign in the Pera Palace reportedly requested government agents to yield seats in the lounge to paying guests.

In 1908, a conspiracy of military officers known as the Committee of Union and Progress, also called the Unionists or Young Turks, forced Abdülhamid to accept a constitutional monarchy and restore the imperial parliament, which he had earlier abrogated. The Unionists were part of a new generation of Ottoman officers painfully aware of the gulf that separated their own empire from the great powers. Many hailed from families who had been displaced in the Balkan territorial changes of the 1870s. Their movement for change had emerged in the western city of Salonica, an outpost of liberal ideas that had long been the empire's window onto the rest of Europe. The Unionists had witnessed one military defeat after another and had watched as their empire succumbed to crippling foreign debt. They were the first wave of the revolutionary impulse that would shake many countries over the course of the twentieth century, a revolt of ambitious majors and colonels against an establishment of decrepit generals and flaccid politicians. They were convinced that the restored constitution would return the empire to the faded ideals of the Tanzimat era.

For several months, Istanbul was full of optimism and a sense of relief. "The motley rabble, the lowest pariahs, were going about in a sublime emotion, with tears running down their unwashed faces, the shopkeepers joining the procession without any concern for their goods," recalled Halide Edip, a Muslim writer and feminist. "There seemed to be no thieves and no criminals. . . . It looked like the millennium." But newfound liberties soon became an excuse for license of all kinds. Newspaper workers demanded higher wages, citing the constitution. Smugglers openly sold tobacco in the street, pointing to the constitution as justification for breaking the state monopoly. Young boys threw rocks at passing automobiles, yelling *"Hürriyet var!"*—"There's freedom now!" Socialists and nationalists of every stripe—Armenian,

Kurdish, Arab, Albanian, Turkish—advocated transformation of the empire into a multinational monarchy, its breakup into sovereign countries, or its evolution into a nation-state for ethnic Turks.

In 1909, a counter-coup attempted to undo the constitutional changes, but the Unionists struck back, sending military units marching on Istanbul to defend the reforms. Abdülhamid—thin, stooped, and weary, the emblem of the dwindling empire that his own conservatism had helped to unmake—was placed on a train and exiled to Salonica, where he could be easily monitored by Unionist sympathizers. His brother, Mehmed V, was elevated to the throne, and Unionists eventually took control of key ministries, government departments, and regional administrations. Factions ranging from staunch monarchists to political elites in favor of a decentralized empire vied for influence in Istanbul, but in time a triumvirate of three Unionist leaders—the military officers Enver and Cemal, along with the civilian Talât—emerged as the effective power behind the throne.

With Istanbul consumed by domestic upheaval, opposition movements and foreign powers began to pick away at the edges of the empire. Bulgaria declared its independence under a self-styled king. Austria-Hungary annexed Bosnia-Herzegovina, an Ottoman territory it had administered under an international mandate for the previous three decades. In the autumn of 1911, Italy announced that it would extend its territory across the Mediterranean by annexing the Ottoman province of Tripolitania (now in Libya). In 1912 and 1913, two wars in the Balkans led to the independence of Albania, the loss of Macedonia and Crete, and the almost complete withdrawal of Ottoman power from continental Europe. The frontlines were little more than twenty miles from Istanbul, and windows rattled from the boom of artillery fire along the earthwork defenses on the landward side of the city. Muslim refugees flooded in from the countryside, pushed out by local reprisals and bivouacking soldiers.

By the summer of 1914, Ottoman subjects had already experienced

more years of war, civilian flight, and economic crisis than the inhabitants of any other great power. In the brewing conflict in Europe, the
sultan at first expressed neutrality, but economic disputes with Britain
and inducements from Germany pushed ministers and commanders
loyal to the Unionists toward the German camp. The Ottoman army
was restructured by a German adviser, Otto Liman von Sanders, who
assumed operational control. Two German cruisers, the *Goeben* and
the *Breslau*, steamed into the Sea of Marmara as the core of a newly
modernized naval force, captained and crewed by German personnel.
In October, the warships sailed across the Black Sea and launched a
preemptive bombardment of Sevastopol, the seat of Russia's southern
fleet. Within days, the Allied governments of Russia, France, and Britain declared war on the Ottoman Empire, which now fell into the
camp of the Central Powers alongside Germany and Austria-Hungary.
In turn, Mehmed V, in his role as caliph—the purported leader of
global Islam, a title his predecessors had carried for more than four
centuries—declared *jihad* against the Allies. It was the last time that a
universal Islamic ruler would be in the position to issue a call to holy
war on behalf of all Muslims.

In later years, Ottoman subjects would come to regret the slide
toward what became known as the First World War, blaming it on the
machinations of the Unionists and the prodding of Berlin. But war
fever and a wave of patriotism swept through the imperial capital.
Ottoman soldiers were mobilized on all fronts as the Allies laid plans
for a two-pronged attack on the empire: a rush through the Balkans to
threaten Istanbul and a push westward from the Russian Caucasus to
engage Ottoman positions in eastern Anatolia. Initial engagements on
both fronts produced no lightning victories for either side. The tumble
toward war quickly became a scramble for new allies, as the warring
parties sought to persuade neutral countries—Greece, Bulgaria, and
Romania—to enter on their side.

The Allies and the Central Powers alike used the promise of territory and postwar freedom as levers to win and keep support. The Arabs would be free of the sultan's control, the Allies declared. Russia would be awarded Istanbul and strategic access to the Mediterranean via the Bosphorus and Dardanelles Straits. Britain, France, and Russia would divide up much of eastern Anatolia, Syria, and Mesopotamia. Greece would have a share of the Aegean coast. For average Ottoman soldiers, these prospective territorial arrangements—made in secret but abundantly clear to everyone at the time—quickly turned the war into a struggle for survival. The potential costs were apparent: the end of the Ottoman Empire, the dismemberment of the state, and perhaps even the loss of the imperial capital itself.

"Ayesha, angel of beauty," an Ottoman infantry captain wrote to his wife a few months after the war began.

> We are bombarded here by the English. No rest we receive and very little food and our men are dying by hundreds from disease. Discontent is also beginning to show itself among the men, and I pray God to bring this all to an end. I can see lovely Constantinople in ruins and our children put to the sword and nothing but some great favor from God can stop it. . . . Oh, why did we join in this wicked war?

The letter was found on the captain's body after the fighting between Ottoman and British imperial forces in the campaign at Gallipoli, down the western peninsula from Istanbul. Gallipoli had been intended as the first phase of an Allied march on the capital, an effort to secure control of the Dardanelles and slowly choke off Istanbul from resupply via the Mediterranean. But for much of 1915, poor planning and heavy resistance by Ottoman field commanders kept Allied soldiers pinned down in ravines and scrubland along the coast, sometimes only steps away from their initial landing sites. When the Allies finally called a halt to the operation, the victory was a substantial one for the Ottomans, but it was extracted at a brutal cost. As many as three-quarters of a million men on both sides had been engaged at Gallipoli, and the grueling fighting illustrated the vulnerability of the capital to land and sea attack. Mines had been floated in the Straits, bringing the normally vibrant sea trade to a halt. The carcasses of Allied battleships poked out of the water and clogged the sea-lane.

Throughout the war, the Unionists, working inside the Ottoman state administration, sought to provoke Muslim revolts abroad, using the sultan's role as caliph to inspire Muslims in the Russian Caucasus, French North Africa, and British India to rise up against their governments. The British tried to do the same among the sultan's Arab subjects, most famously through the exploits of the adventurer T. E. Lawrence. None of these projects fully succeeded, but the connection between domestic politics and foreign intrigue remained a particular concern of Unionist leaders. Officials were intent on uncovering alleged fifth columns sympathetic to the Allies' territorial goals. In eastern Anatolia, military units and irregular militias organized the roundup and deportation of entire villages of Armenians and other Eastern Christians who were thought to be potentially loyal to Russia. Armenian revolutionary groups had in fact organized uprisings in Armenian-populated areas of the empire; some had even operated openly in Istanbul and, in 1896, had staged a spectacular raid on the Imperial Ottoman Bank, just downhill from the Grande Rue. But the military and political establishment around the leaders Enver, Cemal, and Talât, especially the so-called Special Organization within the Committee of Union and Progress, responded with a mass campaign of death.

The Special Organization's chief task was to organize paramilitary units under the command of the army and eliminate potential enemies of the state. Once Ottoman forces began to experience major defeats on the eastern front, especially after the decisive battle with Russian forces at Sarikamish in December 1914–January 1915, the Special Organization and its sympathizers moved to eliminate Armenians who were thought responsible for undermining the war effort. By March, Unionist leaders had taken the decision to kill or deport hundreds of thousands of Armenians in sensitive border regions and to arrest or assassinate key civic and political leaders within the Armenian community. The Unionist sons of Muslim refugees from the Balkans, pushed out of former Ottoman lands in the 1870s, now orchestrated a similar fate for Ottoman Christians. On the night of April 24–25, 1915, more than two hundred Armenian intellectuals and community leaders were deported from Istanbul to the Anatolian countryside. Some were already refugees from anti-Armenian violence in the east and had come to the capital to seek refuge and redress with the central government. Grigoris Balakian, an Armenian priest, recalled sitting in the central prison with many of the major figures in Istanbul's Armenian community—parliamentarians, editors, teachers, doctors, dentists, and bankers—along with average men and boys caught up in the frenzy of violence. He was soon sent to central Anatolia, where he began a long odyssey of forced marches, imprisonment, and abuse. He managed to return to Istanbul three years later but then only in the disguise of a German soldier.

Balakian compiled a record of his sufferings and the fates of friends, victims, and collaborators. He was among the fortunate ones, he said, who, "thanks to large bribes or powerful and influential connections, succeeded in returning to Constantinople and were saved." Many of the others perished. Even for the escapees, however, scars remained. Gomidas Vardabed, the premier Armenian liturgical composer and choral master, was allowed to return to the capital, but he soon fled to Paris and, year by year, descended into madness. He died in a French psychiatric hospital.

Meanwhile, more roundups followed in Istanbul. Tripod scaffolds were set up outside the grand Kılıç Ali Pasha mosque near the Bosphorus, where Armenians and others were hanged for sedition as crowds of men, women, children, and a few German soldiers looked on. In the end, it was perhaps only because of pressure from German officials—who feared the impact that disorderly lynchings and deportations would have on the war effort—that the rest of Istanbul's Armenian population was spared from removal. However, over the course of the war, anti-Armenian violence and deportation policies led to the near-wholesale elimination of the Armenian presence in Anatolia and the deaths of somewhere between six hundred thousand and more than a million Ottoman Christians.

The genocidal attacks were meant to facilitate a new wave of Ottoman battlefield victories, but military losses over the next three years whittled away at Ottoman positions. New offensives against Greece in the Balkans and Russia in the Caucasus ground to a halt. To the south, in Mesopotamia and Palestine, Ottoman armies were in disarray, facing the loss of Damascus and outgunned by British imperial troops. Germany was bogged down on the western front, besieged by a new Allied offensive there.

In Istanbul, raids increased on houses belonging to British and French expatriates. The harbor remained empty, with shipping blocked by the effective closure of the Dardanelles and Russian patrols on the Black Sea. Coal was scarce, and the gasworks were closed, often leaving the city in blackness at night. Police permits were required to buy more than one loaf of bread per day, and fights frequently erupted at bakeries. Even then, the loaves on offer were sometimes made from a rank mixture of flour and straw. An infestation of venomous lice sickened thousands and kept people out of crowded tramcars or other enclosed spaces.

Earlier in the war, the empire's neighbor to the west, Bulgaria, had opted to join the Ottomans on the side of the Central Powers. But in September 1918, Istanbul newspapers carried stunning news. Facing its own battlefield losses and hemmed in on nearly all sides, Bulgaria agreed to sign a separate armistice with the Allies. The Ottomans' western shield was now gone, and Istanbul lay within easy marching distance of the Hellenic border, where Allied troops were already massed. The Ottoman government soon approached the British with a desire to negotiate an end to hostilities.

Over three days in October, representatives of the British War Office met with their Ottoman counterparts on the battleship *Agamemnon*, anchored off Mudros in the Aegean Sea. On October 30, they signed the armistice that ended the fighting between the sultan's empire and the major Allied powers. Just under two weeks later—at the eleventh hour, of the eleventh day, of the eleventh month—Germany signed an armistice as well, bringing the First World War to a close. News of the full cessation of hostilities raced through the streets of Istanbul, but locals barely had time to contemplate what lay ahead for their defeated country. The Allies had arrived to tell them.

On the overcast morning of November 13, 1918, a fleet of steel-hulled battleships sailed into the Bosphorus from the south. Large naval ensigns, specially unfurled for the event, flew from their mainmasts. At the front came the British flagship *Superb*, followed by the *Temeraire*, *Lord Nelson*, and *Agamemnon*, along with five British cruisers and several destroyers. French dreadnoughts followed close behind, while Italian cruisers and Hellenic destroyers brought up the rear.

As far as one could see, the water was choked with gray ships. "The grand sight of the combined British-French-Italian and Greek Naval Squadrons slowly and majestically steaming into the Bosphorus, thus breaking (I trust for ever) Turkish tyranny—men and women met and shook hands but could not speak—the joyous excitement was immense amongst the Christian population," wrote a British eyewitness. It was the largest and deadliest contingent of armed foreign vessels ever to reach the city.

Around 8:00 a.m., admirals and captains ordered the anchors dropped. Sailors on board looked out and saw the impressive line of coastal guns and other defenses behind the ancient sea walls. Although the ships were within easy artillery range of four of the sultan's palaces, they met no resistance.

The victors were now making a show of force against their former opponent, steaming straight into the heart of the Ottoman city. None of the other enemy capitals in the war—Berlin, Vienna, Sofia—played host to so much Allied firepower. The newcomers saw themselves not just as winners but as liberators, sent on a providential mission to unburden the people of Istanbul of their benighted government and free the Christians of the city from Muslim rule. "It was a sight one was glad to have been privileged to see," said Able Seaman F. W. Turpin, a gunner aboard the *Agamemnon*.

Not everyone agreed. Musbah Haidar, the daughter of the emir of Mecca, joined the tens of thousands crowding the heights above the Bosphorus to witness the arrival of the Allied force. She was a relative of the imperial family, and her father was the official guardian of the holiest city in Islam. She watched from her family's mansion as the Hellenic flagship *Averoff* sailed right up to the imperial quay at the sultan's Dolmabahçe Palace. Local Greek Orthodox inhabitants "were in an ecstasy of excitement," Musbah recalled, while Muslims like herself "looked on dazed . . . their empire broken."

Muslim refugees fleeing from fighting in the Balkans had built a shantytown around the footings of the ancient Aqueduct of Valens. Families had flattened discarded oilcans and used them to build walls and roofs against the winter rains, making entire neighborhoods look like giant advertisements for Standard Oil. Grigoris Balakian, the disguised priest who had been deported from the city during the Armenian genocide, crossed the Bosphorus in a rowboat just as the ships were entering the strait. "Effendi, what bad times we're living in!"

said his Muslim boatman. "Who would have believed that a foreign fleet would enter Constantinople so illustriously and that we Muslims would be simple spectators?"

Over the following days and weeks, French officers in blue-corded kepis marched down the streets of the old city beside British comrades in khaki field dress and steel helmets. Senegalese infantrymen and Italian *bersaglieri*, the long plumes on their hats blowing in the breeze, patrolled the Grande Rue. General George Milne, the senior officer in the British contingent, took up residence at the Pera Palace before moving to a waterfront house in the suburb of Tarabya requisitioned from Krupp, the German steel conglomerate. Later, the French commander, General Louis Franchet d'Espèrey, made a ceremonial entry into the city on a white horse, only to discover that British General Edmund Allenby had trumped him by doing the same thing the previous day. He consoled himself by moving into an exiled pasha's residence in the pleasant village of Ortaköy. "It was . . . like having two prima donnas on the stage together," recalled Tom Bridges, a British liaison officer, "and the play went much better if we could keep one in her dressing room."

The city was soon divided into zones of control headed by representatives of the principal Allied powers. The British were to oversee Pera and Galata, the French the old city south of the Golden Horn, and the Italians the Asian suburbs in Üsküdar. A combined force assumed control of the city's police. Allied high commissions would later be appointed to try criminals, oversee port activity, inspect and maintain the prisons, provide for public sanitation, govern hospital and convalescence facilities for Allied troops, and supervise the demobilization and disarmament of Ottoman soldiers.

By the time the Allies steamed into the Bosphorus, the Unionist triumvirate of Enver, Cemal, and Talât had already fled the capital aboard a German submarine. None would be around to witness the occupation. Three years later, Talât was gunned down by an Armenian assassin on the streets of Berlin, an act of revenge for his role in the genocide. Cemal was killed the following year in Tbilisi, also by an Armenian, while Enver died attempting to rouse Muslims against the Bolsheviks in Central Asia.

By the time the *Superb* dropped anchor, the Ottoman Empire had existed for six hundred nineteen years. When the Allied fleet sailed into port, the sitting monarch, Sultan Mehmed VI—who had ascended the throne upon his brother's death in July 1918—counted himself the thirty-sixth member of a dynastic line running back to its founder, Osman (from which Westerners had derived the mispronounced label "Ottoman"). He shared his name with both the fifteenth-century conqueror of Constantinople, Mehmed II, and the Prophet Muhammad. His distant ancestors had been Turkic tribal leaders and Circassian slaves, but around the world, hundreds of millions of Muslims looked to him as successor to the Prophet and the earthly leader of the one true faith.

Istanbul had long been "the principal storm center of Europe and Asia," declared a briefing book for American naval personnel, who soon arrived in the city as part of the Allied contingent. Muslims had "misguided the city through a colorful and turbulent career, . . . giving it a more or less malodorous reputation in international affairs." Now it would be supervised by benevolent Western powers until a final peace settlement could be reached and the fate of the powerless Ottoman Empire determined.

As Allied officers worked to set up their administration, the coldest winter in living memory descended on the city. The Spanish flu began to sicken locals and foreigners alike. Looters ransacked unguarded mansions. A Turkish-speaking Muslim, Ziya Bey, witnessed the first months of the occupation. He was relatively new to Istanbul, but he would in no sense have put himself in the same category as the refugees and Allied soldiers who were streaming into the city. He was born in Nişantaşı, the fashionable district to the north of Pera, surrounded by quiet avenues and ornate, fin-de-siècle apartment buildings. His family spent summers on the Princes Islands in the Sea of Marmara, an easy ferry ride from the docklands of central Istanbul and a traditional summering spot for Greeks, Armenians, and the few Muslims who were able to afford property there.

When Ziya was still a boy, shortly before the First World War, his father collected the family and decamped for New York to look after his export businesses. In America, Ziya met a young woman, originally from New Orleans, and fell in love. The two were married a short time later. With the war over and trade beginning to pick up again, new opportunities called the family back to Istanbul. The political future was still uncertain, but Ziya must have reckoned that being around for the beginning of whatever kind of country would replace the old empire was a reasonable bet, especially for an ambitious, cosmopolitan young man seeking to move out from under his father's shadow.

Istanbul was not the same city he had left, however. "Greedy or inviting glances" followed him everywhere. Civilian refugees, skinny and often clothed in little more than rags, mixed with maimed Ottoman soldiers, some still wearing uniforms and battle decorations. Destitute people sold old wooden toys, artificial flowers, candies, and newspapers to passersby. On one corner, a young mother, sad-looking and visibly pregnant, leaned against a wall and held out a bouquet of multicolored balloons. Children slept on curbs and in doorways before being moved along by an Allied patrol.

At first Ziya took lodgings for his family in Pera, but they rather quickly shifted to the other side of the Golden Horn, to a house near Topkapı Palace. Pera might have offered more spacious accommodation, but the district's foreign embassies were like magnets for refugees seeking jobs, visas, or food. "Prostitution, dishonesty, misery and drunkenness are openly flaunted in this section of the city," he recalled, "which revives all the vices of Byzance coupled with those of Sodom." Ottoman police officers had been restricted to dealing only with traffic matters in that part of the city, while Allied soldiers marching along in multinational platoons were believed to favor foreigners over locals when a dispute arose.

By Ziya's estimate, no more than one out of every fifteen people on the street was a Muslim. The Allied troops were the vanguard of what was intended to be a permanent international force that would usher in a new era of good governance in the defunct Ottoman capital. The Ottoman Empire still existed in theory. The royal house would in fact outlast many of its historic friends and rivals. The Romanovs had already fallen in the Russian Revolution, and the Hohenzollerns and Habsburgs would soon be ousted by the creation of republics in Germany and Austria. Mehmed VI, still the acknowledged head of state, sat in enforced silence in the dilapidated Yıldız Palace complex, surrounded by retainers and turbaned cavalrymen. "[W]hat will happen to Constantinople if all these foreigners . . . remain here and spread their propaganda of discontent, restlessness and lawlessness?" a local Muslim asked Ziya. No one—neither the occupiers nor the occupied—was quite sure what was supposed to come next.

OCCUPATION

A group of men in a small Istanbul café, some smoking a traditional water pipe.

"PERA HAS THREE THINGS to curse," went an Istanbul saying, "plague, fire, and interpreters." In the Middle Ages, Italian merchants and financiers had been given wide-ranging commercial rights in the Byzantine Empire. The Genoese had governed a string of overseas trading centers around the Black Sea from the heights of Pera and the slopes of Galata. They enclosed portions of the neighborhoods behind thick, crenellated walls. These defenses decayed under the Ottomans, but even centuries later, when Greek, Armenian, Jewish, and Muslim proprietors supplanted the Italians, businesses still operated in the shadow of the imposing Galata Tower, a remnant of the old Genoese fortifications. French—the language of diplomacy and international commerce—came to fill the district's street signs, window placards, and hotel advertisements. By the winter of 1918, with Allied powers making Pera the center of their growing administration, Istanbul looked more than ever like a foreign city within a native one. The former—which seemed to be welcoming invaders rather than standing against them—was winning out.

The newer avenues and promenades, populated by non-Muslim minorities and foreign administrators, were a world away from the older districts south of the Golden Horn around Topkapı Palace, the Grand Bazaar, and the soaring imperial mosque complexes. Muslim refugees from the Balkans and Anatolia tended to concentrate in the south, among the traditional bazaars and commercial houses, or *hans*, where goods from the countryside were bought and sold. But the sultan himself had long ago decamped to new residences north of the inlet. Palaces such as Yıldız, a collection of small European-style pavilions, and Çırağan and Dolmabahçe, both grand piles of carved marble, reflected the sense of optimism and modernity that rulers had once hoped to impress into the city's landscape. Along the coast road, mosques and clock towers in a version of Ottoman Baroque copied the excesses and curlicues of their European counterparts, minus the winged cherubs.

"To catalogue completely the different types of humanity to be found in a half-hour stroll would take pages," M. M. Carus Wilson, a British lieutenant, wrote to his father in England. "A walk is a continual kaleidoscope of the nations. . . ," he added, as he described the scene:

> Among the representatives of the Allied forces, for instance, passing over the common ruck of British, French and Italian soldiery, we may fasten upon the white combination hat of the American sailor and the white skirt-kilt of an occasional Greek warrior as being specially worthy of notice. . . . Without the war influx, of course, the streets present a sufficiently diverse spectacle, drawn from the various races, Turks, Armenians, Greeks, Jews and many others who form the permanent population and form about as homogeneous a whole as a mixture of oil and water. Many of these are dressed like a London crowd, though the Fez with the European lounge suit strikes a different note. Amid the straw hats and flappers' frocks, however, move strange figures: bearded porters, with turbans and sashes two feet broad, staggering along beneath incredibly mountainous loads; mysterious green robed mullahs clicking their rosaries as they deign to accept the contributions of the faithful; kaffedjis armed with brightly polished brass coffee urns . . . ; the black-garbed Turkish women shrouded in veils of various efficacy, some dutifully quite opaque, others

the merest apology of a whisp [*sic*] or possibly non-existent; and finally and perhaps the most diverting of all the whiskered jovial Greek monks and priests in their long robes stretching to their feet and sometimes . . . wearing such curiously incongruous headgear as a Homburg or a Panama.

Each Friday the *selâmlık*—the sultan's public procession to a mosque for prayer—featured gilded carriages and horse guards clopping past pious onlookers. Prayers at an imperial mosque could attract ten thousand worshippers, with the bespectacled Mehmed VI arriving on a white horse surrounded by torchbearers. Among the city's non-Muslim residents, the Hissar Players staged plays with a multicultural cast of Armenian, Greek, and other Christian young ladies. The annual Yuletide recital was held at Robert College, an illustrious institution founded in 1863 by Protestant missionaries and situated on a beautiful hilltop overlooking the Bosphorus, with piano performances of Bach and seasonal carols. Its sister institution, the American College for Girls, held commencement exercises featuring an address by the American high commissioner, Admiral Mark Bristol, on "The Life Work of Women" and music provided by the band of the British flagship *Iron Duke*.

General George Milne presided over the city like a latter-day proconsul dispatched to govern a rebellious province. The king he served, Britain's George V, had almost by accident become de facto ruler of the world's two largest Muslim empires: by perceived right, his own—which included the vast Muslim populations of the Indian subcontinent—and by might, that of the Ottomans, which still stretched in theory from Thrace to Arabia. Milne and his French and Italian colleagues were now cast in a role that no foreigners had enjoyed since 1453: coequal governors of ancient Constantinople. Allied soldiers underscored the point by patrolling three abreast, one from each of the occupying powers.

Milne was a dutiful soldier, a cliché of a British officer in jodhpurs and carefully trimmed gray mustache, but much of his career had been a sideshow. He had commanded troops on the battlefields of France and arrived in the Balkans to try to recoup the losses his country had sustained three years earlier in the disastrous Gallipoli campaign. He had most recently led a ragtag outfit known as the Salonica Army, whose exploits had helped win the war on the eastern front but were just as quickly forgotten.

All this was poor preparation for governing a postwar city. The economy was in ruins. Inflation was rampant. Speculation and hoarding of scarce goods, from coal to food, were widespread. Disgruntled Ottoman soldiers were pulling weapons from arms depots or dragging their feet on complying with disarmament orders. The restive fringes of one empire came into bizarre contact with those of another. A British Punjabi detachment might be sent to guard a cache of weapons against a raiding party of Ottoman volunteers. French-uniformed Moroccan cavalry might struggle to remove the bolts from rifles before criminals could lay their hands on the decommissioned weapons. Istanbul was the capital of a country that still existed on paper but in reality seemed to have blown away like an Anatolian dust storm.

On the same day the Allies began their occupation, an Ottoman field commander named Mustafa Kemal checked into a room in the Pera Palace. At the time of the armistice, he had found himself in southern Anatolia in command of an army group arrayed against British forces pressing northward from Palestine. With the fighting over and his units preparing to be demobilized, he decided to make the long train journey to the capital. He hoped to convince the Ottoman ministry of war to mount an underground resistance to the Allies or perhaps even to appoint him as war minister. At a minimum, he might offer himself as an agent for organizing military units in eastern Anatolia, a region where the reach of the Allies barely extended.

He arrived at Haydarpaşa station and, with his aide-de-camp, took the short ferry ride to the European shore. En route, he could look out on the choppy Bosphorus and see the strait full of Allied warships and launches unloading men, horses, and equipment. He had lived in Istanbul as a young man and knew the city well. Three years earlier, as commander of a frontline division at Gallipoli, he had fought hard to save it. Now, in defeat, the empire had given up the very prize that he and hundreds of thousands of "Little Mehmeds"—the Ottoman version of British Tommies and American Doughboys—had vowed to keep out of foreign hands.

Born at some point in the winter of 1880–1881—his birth date, like that of many Ottoman subjects of the era, was uncertain—Mustafa Kemal was a native of the liberal and multicultural city of Salonica, the birthplace of the 1908 revolution. He was part of the younger generation of Ottoman officers schooled in professional military colleges and shaped by the experience of the Unionist movement that had deposed Abdülhamid II. Older officers within the Unionist ranks could recall a time when the empire had embraced modernization and reform, but Mustafa Kemal's generation had known little besides violence and defeat. By the time the First World War began, he had already fought the Italians in Libya and the Bulgarians in Thrace. In each instance, he had seen the empire whittled away by the nationalism of religious and ethnic minorities, often abetted by foreign powers. Now, after the Mudros armistice, he and his brother officers were witnessing its wholesale destruction.

Mustafa Kemal's credentials as a reform-minded and patriotic soldier were impeccable, if not exceptional. If he needed convincing of how much Istanbul had changed since his last visit, the Pera Palace provided ample evidence. Always filled with foreign guests, the lobby and restaurant were now overrun with British and other Allied officers in uniform. Members of foreign delegations, travelers, and local women, including unveiled Muslims, congregated at the Orient Bar. Even Grigoris Balakian, the Armenian priest and genocide survivor, found the streets around the hotel to be a shocking testament to Istanbul's newfound libertinism. "The rich, having made money easily during the war, ate, drank, and enjoyed life to the hilt, buying properties and spending recklessly," he recalled. "The ridiculous styles and dress of the women with their made-up faces, half-exposed breasts, and immodest manners occupied my special attention. . . . [T]he Turkish capital had become a Babylon."

General Milne was staying in the hotel while he waited for more permanent accommodation, and even defeated German officers such as Otto Liman von Sanders—who had discreetly moved a short distance away to the Hôtel de Londres to avoid any unpleasant meetings in the Pera Palace's lounge—could be seen walking along Graveyard Street. The Allies and the Central Powers were no longer in a state of war, even though no permanent peace treaty had been signed, and custom demanded that belligerents accord one another the standard military courtesies.

A later story told of Mustafa Kemal's encounter with a group of British officers enjoying a drink in the hotel. When the officers invited him to their table, Mustafa Kemal refused. A host should not be in the position of going to the table of a guest, he said, and the officers could come to him if they wanted to share a drink. The account was probably apocryphal, designed to show a young officer's vigilant resistance to British rule. But Mustafa Kemal was at base a pragmatist, and evidence suggests that he went to the Pera Palace precisely because it was the epicenter of the Allied occupation.

G. Ward Price, a correspondent for the British *Daily Mail*, had arrived in the city on board the *Agamemnon*. He caught up with Mustafa Kemal a few days after he checked in—or, rather, Mustafa Kemal caught up with him. Price received a note from the hotel manager saying that an Ottoman officer wished to speak with him. Price had never heard of Mustafa Kemal but agreed to have a conversation. When they met, Price found that the Ottoman officer had left behind his military uniform and appeared in a frock coat and fez, the standard civilian attire for well-to-do Ottoman men—"a handsome and virile figure, restrained in his gestures, with a low, deliberate voice," Price recalled.

Mustafa Kemal complained that the Ottomans had chosen the wrong side in the war and had mistakenly turned against their old friends, the British, largely because of the baleful influence of Enver and other pro-German leaders among the Unionists. He imagined that the Allies would choose to divide up Anatolia among themselves, and his wish was for Britain to play a major role. The British were likely to be friendlier to Muslims than the French, who had their own rocky history with governing Muslims in North Africa. In that event, the British would need experienced natives like himself to help manage the situation. "What I want to know," Mustafa Kemal said to Price, "is the proper quarter to which I can offer my services in that capacity." Price reported his conversation to British officers at the Pera Palace, but the response was dismissive. Few people seemed to know who this Mustafa Kemal was, and in any case Ottoman officers were coming out of the woodwork to offer help to the Allied cause. "There will be a lot of these Turkish generals looking for jobs before long," responded a senior intelligence officer.

Later historians skipped over the incident or claimed that it was an effort to undermine the British from within. But the fact remains that Mustafa Kemal spent much of the next six months behaving like a man in search of a future. He moved out of the Pera Palace and rented a house farther north in Osmanbey. He met with virtually anyone who would receive him: military officers, cabinet ministers, disgruntled parliamentarians, and on four occasions Sultan Mehmed VI himself. What he found was a great deal of dissatisfaction with the Allies but very little unity among their opponents. The occupation had sharpened divisions among various factions in the city—the palace, the parliament, businessmen, and the army's general staff—with each group seeking mainly to avoid a wrong move rather than to strike out boldly and shape their country's fate.

Although the triumvirate of leading pashas was no longer in the city, they had left behind an underground organization, *Karakol* (Sentry), which might have provided the germ for organized resistance. But Mustafa Kemal found that Karakol was only one of a number of subversive groups then operating in the city, with little coordination among them. Once the British began to arrest and deport suspected Unionist militants, in the spring of 1919, secret plots became an even less sure way of realizing the liberation of the city and the old empire. That same spring, the Ottoman government, pressed by the occupation authorities, began arresting and trying members of the Committee of Union and Progress who had been involved in the Armenian massacres. Any officers like Mustafa Kemal who might have once been part of the Unionist cause now had an incentive to distance themselves from that legacy and find routes other than secret meetings and underground plots to press their case.

The house in Osmanbey became one of the centers for informal gatherings of officers searching for a way both to reverse the Allied occupation and to steer clear of the Ottoman government, which seemed prepared to imprison any military men who were perceived as internal threats. The sultan's loyalists were keenly aware of the fact that the Allies were the real power in the city, and the palace was disinclined to have upstart soldiers spark a crackdown that might well end with the sultan's being packed off to Malta, where the British had already sent prominent Ottoman officials and potential troublemakers. But dissension among the Allies was also acute in a city that had been divided into geographical thirds, each governed by a separate Allied military command. From officers' messes to the rank and file, Allied soldiers' disdain for local Muslims was matched only by their suspicion of each other. Italians passed intelligence to the Ottomans. The French countermanded British orders. The British kept crucial information from them both.

Frustrated by the squabbling among the underground opposition and the bumbling Allies, Mustafa Kemal managed at last to secure an official position as inspector of the Ottoman armed forces in eastern Anatolia. The job was largely nominal, given that much of the Ottoman army was in disarray, with widespread desertions and no unit at full fighting strength. His task was to assist in the orderly implementation of the Mudros armistice, in effect supervising the dismantling of what remained of the imperial army. The post at least afforded him the one thing that most Ottoman officers coveted at that stage: an actual job, reporting to virtually the only government official whose existence was not yet in question, the sultan. His energetic job hunt had also made his name much better known than when he first arrived in Istanbul. By early 1919, Mustafa Kemal seems finally to have come to the attention of Allied authorities, with plans put in place to arrest him and deport him to Malta as a subversive endangering the armistice.

Before the order could be executed, however, he managed to leave the city. With his letter of appointment from the sultan in hand, he boarded the steamer *Bandırma* on May 16, 1919, and headed for the Black Sea port of Samsun, a logical place to begin the overland journey toward the remnants of Ottoman forces in the east. Few people noticed his arrival in the provincial city on May 19, but today every Turkish schoolchild can name the date. It marked the beginning of what would come to be called the war of independence, and it was the first step on Mustafa Kemal's journey toward becoming the founding president of the Turkish Republic.

No one really knew how many people were living in Istanbul at the time the Allies assumed control. The most recent prewar census had commenced in 1906 but was never completed, given the turmoil caused by the Young Turk revolution. Just before the First World

War, statisticians estimated that the city had around 977,000 people, of whom perhaps 560,000 were Muslim by religion, 206,000 Greek Orthodox, 84,000 Armenian Apostolic (or Gregorian) Christian, along with smaller numbers of Jews, Roman Catholics, and other minorities. Nearly 130,000 people were classed as foreign subjects, most of them non-Muslims, working mainly in trade, manufacturing, and finance. While Muslims had a slim majority over non-Muslims, the foreign presence was already pronounced even before Allenby and Franchet d'Espèrey paraded into the city on their chargers.

During the long Ottoman era, Muslims and non-Muslims had lived within an administrative patchwork that established communal privileges and regulated the relationship between confessional communities and the state. Individual religious communities, known as *millets*, were granted self-government in such matters as canon law, public order, contract enforcement, and other legal, social, and economic areas. All Ottoman subjects owed loyalty to the sultan, and Christians and Jews were required to pay special state taxes that Muslims were able to avoid, but in general people were born, wed, and died according to legal codes that were unique to their specific religious category, the exact number and nature of which changed over the centuries. In theory, it was impossible to be outside the *millet* system if one were a subject of the sultan. The assumption was that, at every stage of life, one would turn most frequently toward the appropriate religious authority, not the state, for resolving matters ranging from registering a birth to executing a will.

The entire hierarchy of state administration was built around this stovepiped system of confessional self-rule, even if there were also plenty of ways to transgress it. As caliph, the sultan stood at the top of the religious hierarchy for Muslims, but he governed his non-Muslim subjects only indirectly, working through established religious leaders such as the Greek Orthodox patriarch, the Armenian Apostolic patriarch, and the *hahambaşı* (chief rabbi) of the Jews. This arrangement in turn reinforced the power of these earthly religious rulers over their flocks.

The *millet* system was a management strategy for handling a religiously diverse empire, and it lasted in various forms for more than half a millennium, a track record far longer than that of liberal democracy or the nation-state. All three of the major non-Muslim *millets*—Greeks, Armenians, and Jews—had roots that stretched back to the earliest precursors of the modern city. Greeks had an unbroken presence in Istanbul that went back to the seventh century BC, even though it was difficult for any individual family to demonstrate such a long pedigree. From his expansive cathedral in the Phanar (Fener) neighborhood south of the Golden Horn, the Greek patriarch served as the administrative head of the local Greek Orthodox community as well as the spiritual pole of the entire Greek Orthodox world, stretching across the Mediterranean and beyond. When Greeks abroad thought of the center of their cultural and religious life, they turned naturally to Istanbul—or Konstantinoupolis—the place where Greek schools were most renowned, Greek churches most resplendent, and Greek businesses most vibrant.

Armenians likewise had an ancient existence in the city and formed a similar bulwark in the worlds of commerce and banking. The Balian family, for example, had produced some of the empire's most revered architects, designing public buildings ranging from ornate ferry stations to the sultan's palaces at Beylerbeyi and Dolmabahçe. The Abdullah Frères photographic studio, owned by an Armenian family, provided the literal face of the empire, serving as court photographers to Abdülhamid II and memorializing the empire's signature educational institutions and government buildings via thousands of glass-plate images. By the 1890s, the rise of Armenian nationalism, which sought a separate homeland for Armenians in eastern Anatolia, both divided the community and brought down the wrath of the imperial government.

Pogroms rocked Istanbul's Armenian population, irrespective of age or position, just as the later Armenian genocide emptied villages and put more than a million people to flight in parts of Anatolia. Still, despite the deportation of key community leaders in April 1915, thousands of Armenians found Istanbul something of a refuge from the devastating violence that engulfed other parts of the empire.

Jews, too, had historically found the city to be a haven—not from local massacres but rather from the congenital antisemitism of Christian Europe. Jews had lived in Istanbul since the Byzantine era, and after the Ottoman conquest of 1453, the new Muslim rulers generally perceived the Jewish community as being friendly to Ottoman interests. Synagogues and other communal facilities were left unmolested or allowed to expand. What sparked the transformation of community life was not so much the Muslim invasion as a new Jewish one. Most Byzantine-era Jews, known as Romaniotes, had spoken Greek and maintained traditions shaped by centuries of coexistence with Eastern Christianity. But in 1492, on the other side of the Mediterranean, Spain gave local Jews the choice of converting to Christianity or leaving the kingdom. Many chose to decamp for the Ottoman lands, where Jews were admitted into the sultan's realm as protected subjects. Over the next century, with the arrival of thousands of Jews from the Iberian Peninsula, the community more than doubled in size and became largely Sephardic in its traditions and practices. Ladino, or Judeo-Spanish, replaced Greek; Spanish surnames soon appeared on gravestones; and the Jewish foodways of the western Mediterranean—Spanish *bizcochos*, North African meatballs, preserved lemons—made their way east.

In the early twentieth century, most Istanbullus still experienced their city not as a grand whole—an urban environment that sprawled over seven hills south of the Golden Horn, through countless valleys and ridges to the north, and up the steep hills of the Asian suburbs east of the Bosphorus—but rather as an archipelago of hundreds of distinct neighborhoods, or *mahalles*. Each had its own more or less self-contained local economy and way of life, all lodged inside bigger concentric circles that tied individual *mahalles* to wider neighborhoods and districts. The traditions of the *mahalle* reinforced the distinctiveness of communal life but also ensured that Muslims and non-Muslims were still connected in a network of mutual dependence and welfare.

In Balat, for example, one of the major Jewish neighborhoods on the south shore of the Golden Horn, neighbors might share gossip in Ladino, Greek, Ottoman Turkish, or some combination of them all. Down a winding street, Persian shopkeepers sold spices, Bulgarians supplied milk and *kaymak* (sweet clotted cream), and Albanians dipped up tins of *salep*, a hot, thick drink made from orchid root that was good for dulling a winter chill. The doors of local bakeries were crowded with young boys sent by their mothers with copper trays of homemade pastries to be fired in the bakeries' ovens. Lines formed at public bathhouses on Friday mornings before the start of the Jewish Sabbath, and even longer lines would later spill out of the National, a cinemahouse that showed new releases on Sunday mornings. Greeks and Armenians would pass through on their way to services in the churches clustered in the nearby Phanar neighborhood. Families might decamp to the heights above Eyüp for afternoon tea at the Pierre Loti Café, with its panoramic view, or picnic along the waters of Kağıthane, both of which were also frequented by Muslims. Men, women, and children would sit on the grass in chatty clusters, re-creating Istanbul's patchwork demography in miniature.

In the modern era, the minority *mahalles* were never self-contained. They had already begun to weaken by the end of the seventeenth century, when Muslims moved into the propertied classes and, with their expanding wealth, into districts that formerly had been mainly Christian or Jewish. But the idea of keeping to one's own sphere remained one of the unwritten rules of Istanbul urbanity down to the end of the empire. "Ni a fuego, ni a pleto," Jews said in Ladino—"Don't go to a fire or to a fight." The structure of Istanbul's *mahalles* was not just a result of the natural clustering of religious communities around mosques, churches, and synagogues. It was also a survival strategy: a way of minding your own business, keeping your head down, and leaving the grand issues of politics and economics to the powerful. Lintels with their distinctive mezuzahs in Balat, the florid cross on an Armenian church in Kumkapı, or a Greek family name inscribed on an apartment building in Beyoğlu marked the geographical boundaries of daily life in the city, but they also traced the contours of power among communities that, until the Allied occupation, could all count themselves subjects of a single emperor.

Non-Muslims were the warp and weft of Istanbul's economy and popular culture. They were its barkeeps and bankers, its brothel owners and restaurateurs, its exporters and hoteliers. As late as 1922, Greeks still owned 1,169 of 1,413 restaurants in the city, compared with 97 owned by Muslim Turks, 57 by Armenians, and 44 by Russians. That social position also made non-Muslims natural rivals. Greeks and Armenians "got along like cats and dogs," recalled the Jewish memoirist Eli Shaul, "that is, they avoided each other, looked for opportunities to make fun of each other, and sometimes got into fights." A popular joke illustrated the wary circling and one-upmanship that characterized Istanbul's minority groups. Salomon, a Jewish boy, goes to an Armenian church. "I've committed a terrible sin," he explains to the priest, who is surprised to see him there. "I've slept with a girl and want to ask forgiveness."

"Which girl was it?" the priest asks warily.

"I'm too ashamed to say, Father," says Salomon.

"I know. It must have been Hagop's daughter!"

"No, not her."

"Then Mugerdich's sister?"

"No, not her."

"Wait, it must have been Sirapian's young wife!"

"No, not her."

Frustrated, the priest sends him away. Salomon's friend, Mishon, sees him leaving and asks what in the world he was doing in an Armenian church.

"Getting three referrals," Salomon replies.

In this complicated world, an Armenian family might be Catholic, Protestant, or Apostolic Christian. They might profess deep loyalty to the sultan or work secretly on behalf of a national liberation movement, which might in turn lean in either the liberal direction or the socialist one. They might be subjects of the sultan or enjoy citizenship of another country, even if they had lived in the city for generations. Jews were likewise divided among the Sephardim, descendants of immigrants from Spain, and the Ashkenazim of eastern Europe, who moved into the city in increasing numbers in the nineteenth century. Each might in turn identify as Zionists, socialists, or liberals, and as either Ottoman subjects or foreigners.

Under the Ottomans, a non-Muslim subject could enjoy a spectacular array of economic privileges as long as he could convince a foreign government to take him under its protection. This so-called Capitulations system had been part of the empire's administrative structure from the beginning of the Ottomans' reign, a result of muscular negotiation by foreign powers ranging from the Genoese to the British and French. It effectively exempted local employees of international firms from Ottoman law and provided foreign businesses with direct, protected access to the Ottoman economy. Over time, however, the Capitulations system came to define the domestic economy as well as foreign trade. Both were largely in the hands of foreign "colonies," as they were often called, which amassed substantial wealth from their grand compounds and business offices in Pera, Galata, and other areas north of the Golden Horn.

The most notable Greek families in particular were in the unusual position of working on behalf of a foreign power while living and making their fortunes inside the Ottoman domains. Individuals could use the complex system of being in—but not of—the Ottoman state to their own advantage, which could in turn work to the detriment of the state itself. Basil Zaharoff grew up in Tatavla (Kurtuluş), a neighborhood to the north of the Pera Palace, and despite his Russian-sounding name, his family was Greek and of modest means. He spent his youth as a tour guide, milling around the popular Café Lebon and offering visitors his expertise in negotiating the streets and alleys of Pera. He may have made money on the side as a paid arsonist for *tulumbacıs*, setting fires that the roving firemen could then put out for a fee gratefully paid by their wealthy victims. In time, he transformed a familiarity with foreigners and an eye for the double deal into incredible success. From an initial contact with a Swedish arms dealer, he took French citizenship and set himself up as one of Europe's foremost traders in weaponry, largely through the British-owned Vickers munitions company. He reaped a fortune by selling to both sides in one after another European conflict and offering the latest technology, such as the newly invented machine gun, at prices too good for any country to pass up. During the First World War, he reckoned that history was on the side of nationalism, not Ottoman imperialism, and he spied an opportunity to profit from the empire's changing fortunes. He was instrumental in pulling Greece into the conflict on the Allied side and almost single-handedly armed the Hellenic army against the Ottomans. A globe-trotting roué and an instantly recognizable name to every war ministry in Europe—with a good claim, in his day, to being the most interesting man in the world—he exemplified for many the seamier side of Istanbul's cosmopolitanism.

After 1918, many Muslims felt that the Capitulations and the tradition of freewheeling, minority-run commerce had reached their nadir, with non-Muslims now preparing to carve up the empire among themselves with foreign assistance. Allied officials had a clear preference for Greeks and Armenians when filling jobs ranging from typists to auxiliary police, who typically patrolled the streets in British uniforms distinguished only by special armbands. After all, the Allies saw part of their mission to be liberating Christians from the Muslim yoke, and they expected that a future peace treaty would explicitly protect local Christians and force the sultan to accept some degree of international oversight in the running of his own country. "The Hellenic and Christian character" of Istanbul, said a petition signed by Greek and Armenian leaders in 1920, "is confirmed today, even after so many centuries of slavery, by the incomparably greater number of its Greek and Armenian population [compared to Muslims] . . . and the earth that once contained the bodies of our emperor-kings and the remains of our patriarchs." The Christian leaders' statistics may have been questionable, but to Muslims, the power dynamic was clear. Charles Furlong, an American eyewitness in Istanbul in the spring of 1920, recorded a list of grievances that his Muslim informants had expressed against the Allies and against Istanbul's non-Muslims:

> The best Turkish homes commandeered, often with all their furnishings, for the use of allied officers; evidence pointing to the commandeering of these homes for the purpose of eventually looting their contents; there are no Turkish prostitutes on the streets of Constantinople, but I was informed on good authority that on the entrance of the allies, Greek and Armenian women donned the costume of the Turkish women in order to defile them in the eyes of the allies; Greeks mocked the Muezzin when he called to prayer from the minarets, and in the presence of Moslems, loudly call to strange street dogs—"come here Mohammed"; every few weeks great conflagrations were set in Constantinople, wiping out in a single fire sometimes thousands of Turkish homes, while Greek real estate dealers were sometimes on the

spot before the ashes cooled; thus has been going on under the
truce, the expulsion of the Turk from Constantinople.

For average Muslims, the city seemed to have been turned on its
head. Terrible stories were passed along from house to house. Senegalese soldiers in the French contingent would attack women on the
street, it was said, or roast Muslim babies for their evening meals.
Muslim women were pushed roughly out of tramcars. British soldiers
would scream at children in the street, knock the fezzes from men's
heads, or tear off women's veils. Much of this was the folklore of resistance, common in societies resentful of foreign rule, but if any Muslims
needed a living symbol of the link between occupation and the city's
non-Muslim minorities, they had only to speak with the new person
overseeing the check-in desk and entertaining arrivals at the Pera Palace. At the end of the war, the hotel had undergone a striking change
of ownership.

RESISTANCE

A jumble of old wooden sailing boats on the Golden Horn,
with the Süleymaniye in the background.

S VELTE AND WELL-DRESSED, with a tiny mustache and balding pate, Prodromos Bodosakis-Athanasiades—or Bodosakis, as he was generally known—was the very image of the urbane and confident Istanbullu Greek. He had taken over the Pera Palace from the Wagons-Lits company in 1919, in circumstances that remain unclear even in the Ottoman property records. The timing turned out to be excellent, however. British officers, disaffected Ottoman soldiers, and French and German businessmen found in Bodosakis a proprietor willing to accommodate just about any kind of guest. According to the memoirist Ziya Bey, the Pera Palace quickly established itself as a place where "foreign officers and business men are fêted by unscrupulous Levantine adventurers and drink and dance with fallen Russian princesses or with Greek and Armenian girls whose morals are, to say the least, as light as their flimsy gowns."

Born to a Greek Orthodox family of modest means, and with barely a primary school education, Bodosakis had started his working life as a small-time trader in Adana and Mersin, two regional commercial centers along the Mediterranean coast. After the First World War, he came to Istanbul, throwing himself into the rough-and-tumble world of shipping and industry and carrying with him a considerable record as a wartime entrepreneur. As an Ottoman subject, he had moved relatively freely inside the empire; as a Greek-speaker, he had immediate entrée into the city's commercial and financial elite. He also had family connections. He was married to the daughter of an Austrian engineer who in turn was related to Otto Liman von Sanders, head of the German military mission in Turkey. Von Sanders had helped run the war effort on behalf of the Ottoman army, and at least some of Bodosakis's early wealth seems to have come from his role as a supplier to the army's quartermasters. Even after the German and Ottoman defeat, knowing important people was still the first step in furthering an already successful business career, especially in a city crawling with foreign soldiers and émigrés.

Bodosakis had managed to thrive by negotiating several different economic and political worlds, but for many local Greeks, the arrival of the Allies posed more questions about the future than it answered. While the patriarch was the spiritual leader of Greek Orthodox Christians, there was a competing political authority emanating from Athens—the government of the Greek mainland, or the Kingdom of the Hellenes—that was now asserting its influence east of the Aegean Sea. The Hellenic presence among the Allies was relatively small: four warships out of dozens in the entire fleet, a few foot soldiers on patrol, and a detachment of Cretans guarding the Greek patriarchate in Phanar. But the presence of troops from Greece raised the fundamental issue of the future relationship between Istanbul's age-old Greek community and the relatively young Hellenic state.

Less than a century earlier, the territory of Greece had itself been part of the Ottoman Empire. In the 1820s, a revolt on the Greek mainland sought to throw off Ottoman power and create an independent country. Hellenic revolutionaries were often little different from other anti-imperial movements of the era—a combination of liberal politicians, overblown romantics, and profiteers looking to rid themselves of a faraway sovereign—but sympathizers in Europe saw them as living relics of the glorious Athenian past: the noble, freedom-loving ur-source of Western civilization as a whole. Philhellenism—support for Hellenic culture and the political cause that sprang from it—swept across Europe and aided the revolutionaries in creating their own state in 1832. The new country eventually expanded to include neighboring areas populated by Greek-speakers as well as by Slavs, Albanians, and Turkish-speaking Muslims.

King Constantine, the reigning monarch at the outbreak of the First World War, was well aware of the British and French interest in pulling his country to the Allied side. Greece's strategic position in the Mediterranean would be critical to the Allied war effort in the Balkans and the Near East. But as a brother-in-law of Kaiser Wilhelm II, he chose the middle path of keeping Greece neutral. As the war wound on and a German victory appeared less secure, however, pro-Allied factions within the Hellenic parliament rose against the king and, in 1917, forced him from the throne and into exile. Constantine's son, Alexander, was elevated to the monarchy, and Greece entered the war on the Allied side. The war seemed at last to provide an opportunity to realize the *Megali Idea*, or "Grand Idea," dear to pan-Greek nationalists: the dream of retaking Istanbul and restoring the Byzantine Empire under a Hellenic crown.

The power behind Alexander's throne was Prime Minister Eleftherios Venizelos, an experienced politician who had stage-managed the royal transition in order to bring Greece into the war. Venizelos was both visionary and pragmatic, and he saw clearly that an Allied victory would be in the long-term interests of Greece. To press its case for acquiring Ottoman territory, the Hellenic government launched its own occupation farther down the Aegean coast. On May 15, 1919, Venizelos's troops marched into the major Ottoman port of Smyrna (Izmir). The British and French offered tacit support, mainly as a way of keeping the city out of the hands of the Italians, another Allied power with designs on Ottoman territory. But unlike the Allies' arrival in Istanbul, the landing in Smyrna was a disaster. Disorder swept through the city as local Muslims tried briefly to fight off the occupiers. Stores were looted and the city's many religious communities—Greek,

Armenian, and Muslim—briefly descended into violence before Hellenic soldiers imposed martial law.

For local Greeks as well as Hellenes on the mainland, the seizure of Smyrna was a triumph, the first step toward the *Megali Idea*. (There were, in fact, more ethnic Greeks in Smyrna than in Athens at the time.) When news of Smyrna's capture reached Istanbul, the streets of Pera were draped with the blue-and-white flag of the Hellenic kingdom, and a huge portrait of Venizelos was unveiled in Taksim Square. For Ottoman Muslims, however, it was a heart-stopping tragedy. Not only was the imperial capital now administered by the Allies, but in clear contravention of the Mudros armistice, Hellenic forces had seized the empire's most important Aegean port. Unlike Milne's troops in Istanbul, the Hellenes seemed intent on annexing, not just administering, their prize.

While Bodosakis was weighing up his own possible futures in the wake of the Hellenic advance, Mustafa Kemal, the Ottoman field commander, was on his way to Anatolia. He had arrived in Istanbul on an inauspicious day—November 13, 1918, the moment when Allied ships sailed into the city—and he departed for Samsun the following May 16, only a day after the Hellenes took Smyrna. Both events galvanized the growing opposition movement that he managed to organize in the east.

Abandoning the pretext for his army inspection tour, Mustafa Kemal set about rallying officers and field units dissatisfied with the inaction of the Istanbul government. Within a few months of reaching Samsun, he had enlivened colleagues among the Ottoman officer class. He had also helped stage two large-scale congresses in the eastern cities of Erzurum and Sivas, where delegates from military units and other sympathizers rallied around the anti-occupation cause. The congresses denounced the Hellenic invasion and proclaimed the creation of a national resistance to the Allies. By the end of 1919, Mustafa Kemal had established his headquarters in Ankara, a town in central Anatolia that was far enough away from Allied positions to be defensible and, with its own railway station, in easy contact with the remnants of the Ottoman armies still regrouping after the armistice. For the Allies, Mustafa Kemal's expanding forces were a new and unexpected addition to an already complicated strategic and political environment.

With Ankara now becoming a rival pole to Istanbul, Allied observers came to describe the growing resistance movement as "Kemalists" or Turkish nationalists. The idea that Turks represented a distinct nation, rather than just part of the governing elite of a multinational empire, had been part of the Unionist cause earlier in the century, but under Mustafa Kemal, the nationalist message was married to the concrete political and military program of resisting the occupation and bucking up the enfeebled sultan. The Kemalists first turned their attention to the east, launching attacks on Armenians and other armed groups returning to areas from which they had been deported by the Unionists during the war. Over the next year and a half, violence spread to central and western Anatolia as well. Hellenic forces moved out of their enclave around Smyrna and extended their zone of control along the Aegean Sea. The sultan's government looked on these events with powerless detachment. While Mehmed VI was still the legal authority in Istanbul and the wider empire, he watched as his officers and soldiers organized their own defense of the fatherland without royal aid or sanction. Muslim politicians and intellectuals soon flocked to Ankara. Thefts from arms depots in Istanbul and smuggling of guns to the Kemalists increased.

The feckless Ottoman parliament, which continued to meet through the spring of 1920, wavered between tacitly supporting the Kemalists and seeming to acquiesce to the Allied authorities, who still recognized the sultan and parliament as the only legitimate government. The preferences of Muslim Istanbullus were clear, however.

In February 1920, a rally in the Sultanahmet district brought out perhaps 150,000 people to demand that the Turkish heartland remain part
of a unified state with guaranteed control over Istanbul and the Straits.
Later in the month, in its boldest act to date, the parliament adopted a
declaration known as the National Pact, which set out the Ottomans'
core demands vis-à-vis the Allies—ranging from asserting the freedom
and independence of the sultan's state to insisting that the future status of controversial border regions be settled by referendum. Crucially,
it was the first document produced by the Ottoman government that
used the word *Türkiye*—Turkey—for the country previously known as
the Ottoman Empire.

The growing disorder—as well as the fear that the sultan's government, the Kemalists, and Istanbullus might eventually unite against the
occupation—pushed the Allies into a fateful decision. On March 16,
1920, General Milne extended full military occupation over the city,
a technical change to the status that Allied forces had enjoyed since
1918. In a move not sanctioned by the Mudros armistice, the new
arrangement subjected all civilian and military institutions to Allied
oversight. British soldiers walked down the Grande Rue with bayonets
fixed and swords drawn. They were prepared for resistance, but in most
instances detachments of Allied guards simply walked into government
ministries and stood post outside office doors. Local police and military units were disarmed. Villages in outlying districts were searched
for weapons caches. Further rounds of uncooperative Ottoman bureaucrats were shipped to British-controlled Malta.

The occupation came as no surprise to anyone. Rumors of it had
circulated in the Pera Palace bar, and the French had shared the plans
with select Ottoman officials, who were able to leave the city rather
than face arrest or deportation by the British. But it was a rash decision
and ultimately a foolhardy one. Mustafa Kemal's associates in Anatolia
could now argue that they represented the only truly national government, since the sultan had stood by quietly as Allied troops launched

their formal seizure of the capital. In Ankara the next month, the nationalists opened their own parliament, the Grand National Assembly, which included some representatives from the defunct Ottoman parliament in Istanbul. Mustafa Kemal was elected its first president, becoming in effect the head of government of an as-yet-unrecognized country. The assembly issued a proclamation declaring that it had no intention of deposing the sultan, but, as with the Unionists' attempt to save the Ottoman state from itself in 1908, relations were tense between the established regime and its alleged saviors. The Ankara assembly prescribed execution for anyone who challenged its legitimacy, while the sultan proclaimed the same punishment for Mustafa Kemal and his closest supporters.

The Allies had taken over Istanbul because of the threat posed by a unified Turkish Muslim front, but within only a month, the prospect of a multisided, fractious, and internationalized civil war seemed closer than ever. Ottoman loyalists denounced the Turkish nationalists. Turkish soldiers targeted religious minorities, believing that all Greeks and Armenians were potential supporters of the Allied occupation. Hellenic troops clashed with armed Turks. Brigands and local warlords threw their weight behind whoever seemed to be on top.

A continent away, diplomats were meeting in the Paris suburb of Sèvres to create a document that was intended to transform the shaky Mudros armistice into a lasting peace. In May 1920, Allied negotiators presented Ottoman officials with the draft of a final peace treaty. The terms were shocking. Syria, Mesopotamia, and Palestine were to be taken away from Ottoman control, paving the way for a system of mandates that would administer these territories under the French and the British. Much of eastern Anatolia was to be divided between an independent Armenia and a future Kurdistan. Egypt and Cyprus were confirmed as free of Ottoman control. Portions of the Aegean coastline around Smyrna were ceded to Greece. Istanbul and the Straits were to be governed by an international commission composed of representatives from Britain, France, Italy, Japan, Russia, Greece, the United States, and other countries.

These were precisely the arrangements that Allied representatives in Istanbul had urged negotiators not to put forward. The American high commissioner in the city, Admiral Mark Bristol, had sent a raft of telegrams and memoranda arguing that the partition of the country would inflame local sentiment against the occupation and provide yet another specific cause around which the nationalists could coalesce. It would also ensconce Britain as the dominant power in the region, to the exclusion of the other Allies and to the detriment of the Turks themselves. "The United States entered the war and sacrificed men and money to overcome the imperialism of Germany," he wrote to Washington from his office next to the Pera Palace. "I must call attention to the evident imperialistic tendencies of Great Britain." Allied negotiators, however, saw themselves as playing a continual game of catch-up, drafting terms of a final peace that were moot almost as soon as they were proposed, given the fast-changing military situation across Anatolia. The Hellenes were carving up the old empire already, and there seemed little hope of reversing that course. The best outcome, negotiators reasoned, would be a treaty that would at least bring some order to the Ottoman breakup and give its various pieces a kind of international blessing.

In August 1920, the sultan reluctantly accepted the deal. The occupation had dismantled the country de facto, but Sèvres divided it up de jure. Like the Byzantine Empire it had displaced nearly half a millennium earlier, the Ottoman state was now whittled down to a tiny, insignificant, and largely demilitarized power at the edge of Europe. News of the Sèvres accord had precisely the effect that Admiral Bristol and others had predicted. It was one thing for Ottoman officials to give up the outlying parts of the empire—letting the Arab lands go, for example—but agreeing to the effective partition of Anatolia and the elimination of local control over Istanbul and the Straits was a monumental concession. The Allies were no longer temporary occupiers seeking to ease the transition from armistice to peace. They had become acquisitive victors dividing up the spoils of war, all with the sultan's blessing.

Lines on maps, international mandates, orderly population movements, and grand schemes for reforming governance were debated and redrafted by diplomats with little understanding of what was happening in the Ottomans' old domains. After the Sèvres accord, Mustafa Kemal's supporters were bolder and more convinced than ever of the justice of their cause. Hellenic troops continued to advance, pressing toward Istanbul overland through Thrace and up the Aegean coast from Smyrna. Each side—British, French, Italian, Hellenic, and Turkish—worked to create facts on the ground before the treaty could be fully implemented. The outcome, however, would be shaped by a bizarre event that unfolded more than three hundred miles away, in a garden outside of Athens. It turned out that Istanbul's fate, and the Ottoman Empire's, hung on a monkey bite.

Many people saw the affair as a bizarre form of cosmic justice, and it was wrapped up in one of the most complicated royal successions of the era. In early October 1920, King Alexander of Greece—the monarch who had ousted his father, led his kingdom to victory in the First World War, and now oversaw the troops marching toward Istanbul and Ankara—went walking with his German shepherd on his royal estate in the suburbs of Athens. Along the way, the dog leapt on a Barbary macaque, a monkey that belonged to one of the palace gardeners. Another monkey rallied to the defense, and the king ended up with a severe bite. He thought little of it at the time, but within a few days the bite had turned septic. The king took to his bed and died before the month was out.

"It is perhaps no exaggeration to remark that a quarter of a million persons died of this monkey's bite," Winston Churchill later observed. The political effects were enormous. With Alexander dead, the losers of the 1917 palace coup invited Constantine to return from exile and resume his reign. New elections were called, and in the political bargaining that followed, Venizelos was dismissed as prime minister. The turmoil in Athens was felt most deeply across the Aegean, but the results were not what anyone might have predicted at the time.

Given the turbulent politics of Constantine's sudden return, the momentum behind Hellenic advances in Anatolia might have dissipated; grand plans for seizing the coastline and eastern Thrace, and perhaps even pressuring the other Allies to hand Istanbul over to the Hellenic government, might have fallen away. But in this critical moment, Britain, the major occupying power, remained resolute. Islamophobic and philhellenic in equal measure, the British broadly endorsed Hellenic ambitions, tacitly urging Constantine to finish the job begun by Alexander and Venizelos. There was now a formal treaty in place—the Sèvres accord—and London dispatched a new commander, General Charles Harington, to take over from General Milne and implement the treaty that the sultan's government had approved. The French and Italians, by contrast, wary of the return to power of the pro-German Constantine, began to pull back their support for the Hellenic cause. These fissures within the Allied side emboldened the newly restored Hellenic monarch, who was eager to display his ability to win the peace by winning yet another war. Newspapers in Athens featured pictures of Constantine slaying a Turkish dragon and marching into a reclaimed Constantinople, flanked by his namesake, the long-dead Constantine XI Palaeologus, the last Byzantine emperor.

More than ever before, Turkish nationalists now had a mission: preventing the Hellenic soldiers from threatening the core areas in central Anatolia, blocking their march on Ankara, and gradually pushing them back toward the coast. In January 1921, Kemalist troops, led by the talented tactician İsmet Bey, defeated Hellenic forces at the first battle of

İnönü, south of the Sea of Marmara. Another Turkish victory followed on the same spot in April. In response, the Hellenic army launched a major offensive in the late summer, but that too was repulsed, this time at the Sakarya River near Ankara.

Turkish fighters were beginning to see the conflict as their own war of liberation—ironically, following the example that Hellenes, Bulgarians, Albanians, Arabs, and other non-Turks had already set in their drive for freedom from the Ottoman Empire—and Sakarya became the signature moment of that struggle. The victory also propelled Mustafa Kemal, who had assumed the role of commander in chief of Turkish forces, to the position of unrivaled leader of the nationalist movement. It allowed him to outmaneuver other potential contenders, such as the successful general Kâzım Karabekir, whose credentials as a member of the Istanbul elite and a seasoned field commander outshone virtually all others. Mustafa Kemal was elevated to the rank of marshal and given the honorific title of *gazi*, a term formerly applied to the most illustrious of Islamic holy warriors. "The retreat that started in Vienna," said a Turkish observer in 1921, referring to the zenith of Ottoman incursions into Europe in 1683, "stopped 238 years later."

British diplomats tried desperately to salvage what remained of the Sèvres treaty, but the Allies were by now largely spectators to the unfolding violence. The cost of continued occupation was outstripping any strategic benefits. By the summer of 1921, the Italians made a separate deal with the Turkish nationalists and removed their troops from Anatolia. The French followed suit in October. Late the next summer, Turkish nationalists began an offensive against the remaining Hellenic positions, with the spearhead of the advance pointed toward the key redoubt of Smyrna, the city from which Greece had launched its bid for dominance three years earlier. The two forces were roughly equal in size—some 225,000 Hellenic troops against 208,000 Turks—but Hellenic emplacements were stretched across virtually the breadth of Anatolia, with nothing behind them but the sea.

Hellenic military detachments fled toward the coast. They left behind rubble-strewn villages, burned croplands, and toppled minarets. "The atrocities perpetrated by the Greeks, since they landed in Smyrna, exceed all similar crimes recorded up to now in the annals of history," declared a Turkish report. "There is not the slightest doubt that the savageries committed by the Greeks of Greece and by that section of the indigenous Greeks, who sided with them, have been deliberately planned and carried out under orders proceeding from the Commanders of the various Greek military units."

It took only days for the Turkish troops to reach Smyrna. On September 9, 1922, Turkish nationalists marched into the city and began pushing out the last remnants of the foreign army. Local Greek Orthodox Christians, fearing reprisals from the nationalists as well as from their Muslim neighbors, rushed to join the Hellenic soldiers in retreat. Refugees crowded the docklands. Mobs ruled the streets. The Greek archbishop was lynched by a Muslim crowd whipped up by the Turkish commander in the city. A fire broke out in the Armenian section of Smyrna and roared through other neighborhoods, turning the sea the color of burnished copper and pushing even more people toward the waterfront. In the panic and disorder, thousands died before Hellenic and Allied ships arrived to ferry the survivors to the Greek mainland. Some 213,000 people, mainly Greek Orthodox and Armenian families who had lived in Smyrna for countless generations, left it for good. Three-quarters of the city was in ruins.

As news of the Smyrna catastrophe reached Istanbul, locals and Allies worried that it might well turn out to be a dress rehearsal for what could happen in the old capital: a Turkish nationalist attack followed by the chaotic emptying of the city's minorities and a dash for the door by the Allies. "Foreigners are nervous . . . remembering the fate of Smyrna," Ernest Hemingway reported from the scene, "and have booked outgoing trains for the weeks ahead." Processions of Turkish Muslims marched through the streets shouting, "Down with the

English." Portraits of Mustafa Kemal appeared in Muslim-majority districts throughout the city. Gone were the Hellenic flags and blue-and-white streamers that had once adorned the storefronts of Greek-owned businesses. "A fear of the future sits heavily upon these poor people now," a British lieutenant wrote in a letter home. "What will become of them when we leave?"

A year before the fall of Smyrna, Allied generals had issued a directive in Istanbul reminding Turkish soldiers that they were required to salute uniformed officers of the Allied contingent. A special commission had been created to study the problem of whether an Allied officer was required to salute back. Now, power had clearly shifted to the Turkish side. General Harington, the British commander, was reduced to issuing more and more strident—and less and less effective—declarations to Istanbul's civilian population. Possible death sentences were authorized for people found guilty of illegal possession of firearms, firing on Allied troops, destruction of telephone or telegraph lines, receiving stolen Allied goods, or "any other act or thing inimical to the interests or safety of the Allied Troops." Few people believed the sentences could be carried out.

The British, as the lead partner in the dwindling Allied force, faced a common dilemma among occupiers. Their friendliest local partner—the sultan—was the least legitimate among the native population, while the most legitimate—the Kemalists—were making plans to march on Istanbul and send the occupiers running. Mehmed VI was weak and unpopular, as were the remaining ministers and advisers around him. Their acceptance of the Hellenic occupation of Smyrna and the Treaty of Sèvres had diminished the prestige of the old regime and made the Ottoman establishment even less credible as a future government for post-occupation Istanbul. The Allied powers had painted themselves into a corner.

Before the Smyrna offensive, Istanbul had been the only place in Turkey where troops still loyal to the Ottoman government outnumbered the nationalists: 1,200 Ottoman troops against 1,000 Kemalists. Over the coming months, however, that balance shifted dramatically in favor of Mustafa Kemal. In late September 1922, fresh from the fighting in Smyrna, Turkish nationalist forces entered a neutral zone that the Allies had established along the Straits. British and nationalist troops squared off across their own entrenched positions, exchanging potshots that threatened to destroy the armistice, which by now had dragged on for nearly four years. "I know somebody will let his rifle off cleaning it, and then there will be another European war!!!" wrote Billy Fox-Pitt, an officer in the Welsh Guards, from the trenches.

The British government was inclined to stand up to the nationalists and ordered General Harington to prepare to fight, but Harington astutely ignored his direct orders. He proceeded with plans to meet Turkish negotiators at Mudanya, a small town on the Sea of Marmara, to draft a new agreement that would take into account the radically changed military situation. "No humbler setting could have been chosen for the negotiations of an agreement upon which depended the issue of peace or war between the Allied Powers and the Turkish Nationalists," wrote G. Ward Price, the *Daily Mail* correspondent who covered the talks. The British delegation arrived in force on the flagship *Iron Duke*. The Turks were led by İsmet, the hero of the earlier battles of İnönü against the Hellenes. İsmet had emerged as one of the key military leaders under Mustafa Kemal and now held the rank of pasha, or senior general. In driving rain and high winds, on October 11, 1922, Harington and İsmet Pasha crafted an accord that, in a roundabout way, saved Istanbul from destruction.

The Mudanya document governed the evacuation of Hellenic troops from eastern Thrace and their replacement by soldiers of the Grand National Assembly, essentially providing a way for Turkish troops to surround Istanbul on all sides in an orderly and peaceful manner. Mudanya in 1922 was in many ways the bookend to Mudros in 1918—the moment when the political and military advantage shifted from the Allies to the Turks, with the latter now in a much stronger position to influence the terms of a final peace. In a city that had seen rather few real heroes for some time, the levelheadedness of Harington and İsmet prevented Istanbul from repeating the horrors of Smyrna. The Sèvres treaty—signed but never implemented—was now dead, and a new set of concerns began to occupy both Harington in Istanbul and Allied diplomats farther afield: how to end the occupation and turn over control of the city to the de facto rulers, the Kemalists, who had marched steadily westward out of Anatolia over the previous three years. Almost as soon as he left Mudanya and returned to Istanbul, Harington was faced with a direct challenge to the embattled ruler he had been trying to prop up: the Ottoman sultan.

General Charles Harington—or Tim, as he was known—was a professional soldier of cool judgment and, like his predecessor, General Milne, of considerable experience. But where Milne had the distinction of superintending the Ottoman capital on behalf of Britain and the Allies, Harington's role was to figure out how to give it up.

Harington appeared at official functions in Sam Browne belt and beribboned tunic, the image of duty and resolve with his swagger stick and pencil mustache. Trained at the Royal Military Academy at Sandhurst, he had served in the King's Regiment during the Boer War. After the First World War, he was personally appointed by Winston Churchill, then Britain's secretary of state for war, to manage the delicate situation in Istanbul. To foreigners and non-Muslims in the city, he had a reputation for keeping a stiff upper lip in the face of rapid change and near-miss calamities.

"Life went on gaily, especially at night," Harington recalled in his memoirs. Ceremonial parades featured infantry march-pasts and gun salutes from ships on the Bosphorus. The British drank to the health of

King George V on his birthday and held seven-a-side rugby matches on weekends. "There was something for everyone: hunting, polo, shooting, fishing, yachting, golf, cricket, hockey, tennis, squash, etc., a good club and good cafes." The hounds ran at Maslak, in the European suburbs, chasing any animal worthy of sport. A small bear, Mishu, had been liberated by British soldiers from the Caucasus mountains and entertained the troops with acrobatics. When officers helped him down a glass of port at Christmas, Mishu attempted to walk along a railing at the edge of the Bosphorus and promptly toppled into the water. He was rescued by fishermen stunned at the odd catch they had drawn up from the swift current.

But the Allied occupiers, as well as the sultan, were living on borrowed time. "[T]he main preoccupation of the Allied Governments," reported G. Ward Price, "was to withdraw their troops from Turkey with the minimum of humiliation." The indecision regarding the final status of Istanbul and the empire, coupled with the devastating terms finally forced on the sultan's government at Sèvres, had contributed to the disorder in Anatolia. Britain's support had emboldened King Constantine and sealed the fate of Smyrna.

The Turkish nationalist government was in a stronger position than ever, with both the control of territory and the demonstrated military power to press its advantage. Turkish soldiers were encamped east and west of Istanbul, with Allied naval power the only obstacle to their taking the city by force. In Ankara, the Grand National Assembly was increasingly assertive, acting like the confident governing parliament of a real country, even if no major power accepted it as such. The assembly retroactively declared that Istanbul had ceased to be the capital from the moment the Allies took control of it. On November 4, 1922, Refet Pasha, a representative of the Grand National Assembly, arrived in Istanbul with the news that he would be assuming control of the city's gendarmerie and police, customs houses, public sanitation, and other municipal functions. Allied officials expressed frustration at the rapid erosion of their authority, but they remained powerless to stop it as long as the city was surrounded by thousands of Turkish troops whose presence was protected by the Mudanya accord. "Measures now being taken by Nationalists simply aim at gradual extraction of our means of control at every turn and reducing of our occupation to a farce," a British official cabled to London.

That was precisely what Refet Pasha, acting on behalf of Mustafa Kemal, had in mind. "It certainly came as a surprise to us when we realised we were passing through a revolution," said Harington. Later in the month, the Ankara government began the fundamental reorganization of the state itself. The sultan had acquiesced to the occupation, signed a paper treaty that would have apportioned his lands to Greece and the Allies, and watched helplessly as the nationalists took the lead in pushing back the Hellenic invaders. The monarchy was now formally abolished. The emerging country was to be a republic.

This news was a particular problem for Mehmed VI, who remained ensconced in Yıldız Palace. On November 16, 1922, almost four years to the day after Allied troops first stepped ashore, General Harington received a visit from the chief bandmaster of the sultan's household. Harington knew that the maestro was more than a court musician. He was in fact the sultan's most trusted confidant, and he carried startling news. Given the Grand National Assembly's recent declaration ending the monarchy, the sultan was convinced that his life was in danger and that plans were afoot to murder him during the next *selâmlık*. The Kemalists had done away with the sultanate; now he feared they were preparing to do away with the sultan, too.

Harington realized that the story, if true, would mark a turning point not only in the occupation but also in the history of the Ottoman Empire. He insisted on having the request in writing. Some time later the bandmaster returned with a note. "Considering my life in danger in Constantinople," Mehmed wrote, "I take refuge with the British Government, and request my transfer as soon as possible from

Constantinople to another place." Harington and his senior officers were on the brink of achieving something that no foreign power in five centuries had dreamed possible: They were going to kidnap—at the monarch's own request—the head of the Ottoman Empire and caliph of the world's Muslims. Working with a small group of commanders, Harington devised a daring scheme to spirit Mehmed away from the city.

On Friday morning, November 17, the general rose at four o'clock and downed a breakfast of bacon and eggs. The late autumn rains had already descended on Istanbul, so the officers and men of the Grenadier Guards grumbled when Harington informed them that they would be conducting a predawn drill in the barracks yard near Yıldız Palace. Around six o'clock, the sultan, his son, and a small group of servants took an early morning walk in the garden. When they reached the section of the garden adjacent to the barracks yard, the servants threw open the back gate, exposing the garden to the drilling guardsmen.

A select group of British soldiers who had been briefed on the mission quickly bundled the sultan and his retinue into two waiting ambulances, which accelerated out of the parade ground. A nest of machine gunners covered the departure, while the rest of the surprised Grenadiers stood at attention. The ambulances raced down the hill toward Dolmabahçe Palace and pulled up at the quay. A small British naval detachment, supposedly on an early morning drill, sat waiting.

The sultan was transferred to the boats and then to the dockyards farther down the Bosphorus, where Harington stood waiting in his personal launch. From there, Mehmed joined the British commander for his last crossing of the Bosphorus, a short ride to the British battleship *Malaya*, and a long sea journey toward voluntary exile. Harington had hoped the sultan would give him a small token to commemorate the event—a cigarette case, perhaps—but Mehmed instead entrusted him with looking after his five wives, whom he had left at the palace. For some time thereafter, Harington acted as a messenger between the sultan and his family. They were eventually reunited in a haven for ousted monarchs and erstwhile nobles, San Remo on the Italian Riviera.

Later that day, thousands of people came out as usual for the *selâm-lık* and waited patiently for the sultan's carriage to appear. Hours went by, and the crowds eventually dispersed, left to wonder why the ruler had skipped the Friday service. The story of what had really happened soon spread through the city. The sultan had abandoned Istanbul and the empire. A few days later, the Grand National Assembly named the crown prince, Mehmed's cousin Abdülmecid, as caliph but without the additional title of sultan. The roles of universal Islamic leader and imperial ruler were now separated for the first time in centuries. The dynasty of the House of Osman, which had governed an empire for more than six hundred years and had commanded Istanbul for four hundred sixty-nine, was no more. The sultan himself had become a refugee.

MOSCOW ON THE BOSPHORUS

Floor show: Two young women, probably Russians,
working as dancers in an Istanbul club.

GENERAL CHARLES HARINGTON HAD ARRIVED in Istanbul at what would turn out to be a decisive moment in the fading history of the Ottoman Empire. His tenure had begun with the Kemalist advance westward, and he was on hand both to witness the fall of Smyrna and to spirit away the last Ottoman sultan. At the time, however, it was hard to see these events as part of a single grand narrative of imperial collapse and national revolution. Harington was troubled by a more immediate set of concerns.

The fact that would have most impressed anyone living in Istanbul at the time was that it was a city teeming with refugees, military deserters, and out-of-work state employees. Some had been there since the early weeks of the First World War. Others had arrived after fighting flared between Hellenic troops and Turkish nationalists. Despite the Unionists' deportation of Armenian community leaders and intellectuals several years earlier, the influx of Armenian refugees fleeing the warfare in Anatolia meant there soon would be more Armenians in Istanbul than in all the rest of Turkey. They now shared space with displaced Muslims—more than 400,000 in Istanbul and western Anatolia combined—who had arrived from Greece and the Balkans since 1912.

Caring for many of these people naturally fell to the Allies, the only officials capable of wrangling adequate food, clothing, and medical care. The Allies had agreed that the French forces would be responsible for dealing with refugee issues, but the problem was so great that other countries quickly joined in. The US Navy set up a canteen in the yard of Sirkeci station, with open-air ovens and boilers turning out bread and hot cocoa. Members of Britain's Hampshire Regiment gave up their personal rations, including locally requisitioned milk that was needed for thousands of refugee children. Private charities ramped up their efforts. Within weeks of his arrival, Harington organized his own program for housing and feeding multitudes, even devising a ticket system to sort out the massive numbers seeking assistance. Colored chits were issued that corresponded to colored tubs from which families could retrieve soup and other meals. By the end of 1920, Allied soup kitchens were feeding 165,000 people a day, nearly a fifth of Istanbul's prewar population.

Among the needy were local Christians as well as Muslims, individuals pushed out of their homes in Thrace and Anatolia and now turning to the one place that seemed relatively calm and secure amid the growing violence in the provinces. But those who occupied most of Harington's time—and who came to define the refugee condition in Istanbul in the early 1920s—were not natives at all. Like the Turks who surrounded them, they had lost an empire, and its demise had not been of their own making. Yet it was difficult for them to imagine a new country precisely because they had not given up the idea of winning back their old one. They clung to memories of a place called the Russian Empire and a monarch called the tsar, and they were the exiles whose presence in the Ottoman capital was the most unexpected. The influx of Russians would also turn out to have a profound effect on the culture of their adopted refuge.

Turks and Russians had both experienced revolutions of a sort, and both found ways of remembering them that treated the losers as not just morally wrong but also deeply inconsequential. The triumphalist

version of Soviet history cast the Bolsheviks as predestined winners of
the universal struggle between the working class and its exploiters. A
popular revolt in February 1917 toppled the tsar and installed a provisional government, which in turn gave way to a workers' revolution
in October. But what began as a Bolshevik coup, a quick seizure of
power intended to quash the provisional government in advance of
parliamentary elections, evolved into a long and bloody civil war that
raged across the entire breadth of the Russian Empire. It was all "a salad
of warring communities and factions," Tom Bridges, the British liaison
officer in Istanbul, reported at the time. Homes were burned, people
were put to flight, and livestock was left to wander masterless along
village roads, no matter the cap badges or ideologies.

In the autumn of 1917, the anti-Bolshevik opposition was concentrated along the Don River, where Cossack communities refused to
accept the authority of the new socialist government in Petrograd. The
Cossack uprising turned out to be a magnet that attracted disaffected
imperial officers, old aristocrats, Russian nationalists, and adventure-
seeking schoolboys committed to turning back the Reds. They formed
the so-called Volunteer Army, a small force with no more than four
thousand men under arms at the outset. It grew to become the largest and most powerful of several opposition groups opposing Vladimir
Lenin, Leon Trotsky, and other Bolshevik leaders. Where the Bolsheviks had unity of mission and ruthlessness of execution, however, their
opponents—collectively known as the Whites—had only a vague program: restoring the old order, protecting their traditional privileges,
and denying a revolution that seemed to have the wind of history at
its back. By February 1920 the Whites were in full retreat, withdraw-
ing to the shelter of the Black Sea coast. Russian subjects streamed
out of ports such as Odessa and Sevastopol, which were soon overrun
by Bolshevik troops. The commander of the Volunteer Army, Anton
Denikin, was forced into a chaotic evacuation from his redoubt in the
port of Novorossiisk.

Charles Strafford, a British naval aviator on board the warship *Pegasus*, was part of the Allied contingent dispatched to cover Denikin's retreat. The tsar's empire had been an ally during the First World War, and British, French, and American forces made a halfhearted attempt to assist Russia's struggling loyalists against the socialists. Strafford was appalled by the scenes of desperation and disorder. The docks were covered with Russian soldiers and their families, all wearing a mix of uniforms and civilian clothes caked with mud. The night sky glowed from fires raging through the docklands, the searchlights of British and French vessels, and the flash of naval and shore artillery. Cossack cavalry unbridled their horses and turned them into the hills. As the fleeing army steamed away on a flotilla of evacuation vessels under Allied escort, the Cossack horses reportedly galloped into the sea, swimming toward their old masters on the departing ships. From the railings, people watched the foamy wakes subside as the horses drowned in the deep water.

As soon as the Novorossiisk refugees were safely in Crimea, an area still under White control, Denikin stepped down in disgrace. "The things in Russia are now very, very bad. Everybody who can is running away, but we stay here," seventeen-year-old Katya Tenner, a Russian in Crimea, wrote to Strafford. Individuals were weighing up the costs and benefits of leaving. Families of means could tilt fate in their favor, but everyone faced the common problem of planning for uncertainty. Twenty-year-old Vladimir Nabokov, the future novelist, had been packed off to Crimea by his father, a prominent Petrograd lawyer and minister of justice in Denikin's government. The family cook had prepared a knapsack of caviar sandwiches for the journey, and the family eventually settled on the grounds of the tsar's summer home, the Livadia Palace, near Yalta. Nabokov's father was able to secure places aboard a freighter carrying a cargo of dried fruit, calling briefly at Istanbul and then Piraeus. Next came a long journey by train and ferry to London, where the family began a new life as émigrés.

Tens of thousands of others were less fortunate. The remnants of the Volunteer Army were wedged onto the Crimean Peninsula, hunkered down between the mountains and the coast. The army was now under the leadership of Pyotr "Piper" Wrangel. His nickname referenced his love of Piper-Heidsieck champagne, but in the field he was ramrod-straight. Tall and lithe, in his early forties, he was usually clad in an exotic Cossack uniform, with a *cherkeska* tunic and fuzzy astrakhan hat. He exuded the martial pedigree that extended through an ancestral line of imperial field marshals.

On Wrangel's estimate, his men were outnumbered more than three to one, with the Bolsheviks counting as many as 600,000 men under arms. By early November 1920, the Bolsheviks had pushed into Crimea, threatening the coastal cities where Wrangel's civilian administration and army were concentrated. On November 11, 1920, facing a bitterly cold winter, Wrangel issued a proclamation from his headquarters in Sevastopol, the old seat of Russia's southern naval force. The unequal contest was lost, he said, and the last remnant of Russia on which law and order still prevailed was to be evacuated as quickly as possible. For weeks, he had been collecting ships in the Crimean ports for exactly this eventuality.

On a calm sea, Wrangel stepped aboard his flagship, the cruiser *General Kornilov*. It was soon joined by the French cruiser *Waldeck-Rousseau*, which fired a twenty-one-gun salute; the massive transport ship *Don*, its decks a fuzzy mass of fur hats and horseflesh; and other coastal steamers, icebreakers, cargo vessels, and warships of all tonnages—one hundred twenty-six ships in all. As seagulls wheeled overhead and a pink haze veiled the coast, Wrangel gave his last order in Russian waters: Make for Istanbul.

Three days later, the flotilla limped into port and set anchor near Moda, on the Asian side of the city within sight of Topkapı Palace. Since Russians and Turks had been on opposite sides of four wars over the previous century, this was not exactly the way generations of tsarist strategists had dreamed of a Russian navy's arrival in the Ottoman capital. Nor was it the way that generations of Ottomans had expected to receive them. But times had changed. The Russians were now refugees and the Turks were under foreign occupation.

"The plight of those poor people was indescribable," recalled General Harington. Some of the larger ships carried thousands of passengers, crammed onto decks and below, with no awnings or other covers to keep off the wind and rain—"like cattle ships," reported Admiral Bristol, the American high commissioner. No one had adequate food or water. When a small group of caiques and patrol boats approached from shore, women threw their fur coats and pearls overboard in exchange for bread.

Harington boarded one of the vessels and found "a starving mass of humanity." Lice and vermin were common. Counting Wrangel's flotilla, the largest single group of evacuees, some 185,000 people had arrived from Russia during the civil war, swelling Istanbul's population by as much as twenty percent. The harsh winter, the paucity of resources, and the potential threat to public order posed by the influx—more than a hundred thousand of the refugees were White Army soldiers, eager to regroup and launch a new war against Bolshevism—prompted some diplomats to suggest sending the Russians even farther southward, perhaps settling them in North Africa. But as the ships sat off Moda, it was clear that, at least for the time being, the only place the Russians were going to colonize was Istanbul.

Representatives from the Pera Palace and other hotels were on hand when the ships arrived, hoping to snag a few well-to-do patrons. The hotel owners seemed more than willing to evict their existing guests (including entire bands of prostitutes whose business was booming with so many foreign soldiers and sailors in the city) in order to charge even higher prices to the desperate Russians. Less fortunate migrants had to rely on the makeshift canteens and bunkhouses set up by occupation authorities. Istanbul was probably outfitted with more barracks than any city in the world, noted a British diplomatic report, but there had been so many waves of arrivals that some people were forced to sleep rough on the street or curl up in disused foxholes dug during the First World War. Dead bodies sometimes went uncollected for days. There was barely time to disinfect an old barracks or tent encampment before the next group struggled off ships and onto land.

The Russian Embassy on the Grande Rue became the center for the relief effort organized by the Russians themselves. As power shifted wildly across the old empire—from the tsar, to a provisional government, to the Bolsheviks, to the governments declared in southern Russia by Denikin and Wrangel, and then back to the Bolsheviks—the ambassador and staff had been left to fend for themselves, making up directives and determining loyalties on the fly. Now, at least, there was a Russian government that the embassy could claim to represent, even if it was a government-in-exile. Baroness Wrangel, the army commander's wife, organized a hospital on the embassy grounds to treat the most seriously ill and injured, with her ever-present fox terrier, Jack, providing entertainment. Camps were also set up outside the city, at Tuzla and Gallipoli, to accommodate the refugees, especially the soldiers who remained formally in their military units under Wrangel's command. It was no small irony that perhaps the greatest flowering of civil society in Russian history—the energetic and coordinated beneficence of volunteer groups, professional guilds, and charitable foundations—came only after one version of Russia had ceased to exist.

"I think that one could say, without exaggeration, that nowhere else during the period of immigration, even in the Slavic countries that welcomed us, did the Russians feel more at home than in Constantinople," recalled the Russian lawyer and former senator Nikolai Chebyshev. Soviet propagandists would later cast all these people as ousted aristocrats who had oppressed the peasants, led Russia into a disastrous war, and dined on caviar in the process. But the many refugees who arrived from the Black Sea represented a host of political persuasions, social classes, and ethnicities.

"Some seem to be better off than others," wrote a British soldier to his father, "and occupy their time by parading the Grande Rue de Pera in the exotic finery of Cossack kit complete with diagonally placed breast cartridge pockets, top boots, long black coats and elaborately decorated silver daggers. Others, some evidently sadly descended in the world, eke out a poor livelihood by selling things at the curbs." Some had arrived after Denikin's defeat. Others had come with Wrangel. Still others had struggled across the sea on their own from Crimea or the Caucasus. Noble families shared space on ships with lawyers, circus performers, Cossack cavalrymen, and household servants. The White leadership assiduously avoided discussion of politics and ideology for fear that the many currents within the movement—nationalist, liberal, agrarian, even antisemitic—would strike out on their own or make a separate peace with Lenin's regime. They were united in exile by a desperate effort to get by in an unfamiliar city that was itself still reeling from the privations of war.

Dmitri Shalikashvili was part of the tidal wave of nationalities that descended on Istanbul after the Bolshevik Revolution. He was a Russian subject but not a Russian, born into a princely Georgian family, educated in St. Petersburg, and decorated as an Imperial Guards officer during the First World War. When the Russian Empire collapsed, the mountainous Caucasus region of Georgia declared itself independent and socialist, but not Bolshevik. It was the only remnant of the old empire to be governed by the Bolsheviks' archenemies on the left, the Mensheviks. Although Shalikashvili had little in common with the Mensheviks' ideology of workers' rights and land reform, their commitment to building a national Georgian state appealed to many people in his social class. He turned his experience and military skills to the service of his ancestral country. Yet when the Bolsheviks swooped into Georgia in 1921, ousting the Mensheviks and putting the entire Georgian government to flight, Shalikashvili ended up trapped in Istanbul.

"Thus, on one beautiful springtime day began our sad life of refugees," Shalikashvili recalled. He soon traded his cavalry uniform for civilian clothes and moved out of the small camp that had been created for the Georgian refugees on the outskirts of Istanbul. The streets were full of people of all nationalities wearing all manner of clothes, often some mixture of military uniforms and civilian attire. The refugees—Russians, Georgians, Azerbaijanis, Ukrainians, and others—had blown into Istanbul carrying remnants of past lives and disappeared nations. Massive sheets of paper imprinted with the Russian double-headed eagle could be seen pasted onto walls, laid on tabletops at restaurants, wrapped around parcels, or on offer in stationery shops. The sheets had been used for manufacturing currency in the territories controlled by White Russian troops, but now the money was literally worth only the paper on which it was printed.

For those who had managed to escape with jewels and gold in their luggage, a small amount of capital and moderate ambition could yield a good income. Sometime in 1921, a few months after Shalikashvili arrived, Prince Gigusha Eristavi, Count Petya Zarnekow, and a Colonel Ladyzensky managed to lease a strip of beach near Florya, on the Sea of Marmara not far from central Istanbul. The site was overgrown and rocky, but with some sprucing up, it made a good bathing spot. Using some old tents lent by the British, they opened a ragged but welcoming beachfront resort.

Shalikashvili signed up as manager. He was provided food and lodging on the beach, along with a small salary. He spent his time keeping the beach clear of debris and supervising the building of changing cabins inside the big canvas tents. Muslims had their own bathing areas elsewhere in the city, with rectangles of water curtained off so that women could splash in the sea without offending anyone's sensibilities. Florya was open to both men and women, with no sea curtains to separate the sexes, but it was chastely placed under the sponsorship of the Princess Eristavi and the Countess Zarnekow, the wives of its founders, whose titles lent respectability.

With Europeans providing a ready clientele—former Russian subjects but also members of the Allied occupation forces and their families—Florya was booming. A property dispute with the widow of a Cossack general, who had hoped to open her own beachfront establishment on the same spot, threatened to disrupt the trade, but things were worked out amicably. The Cossacks supplied the food while the Georgians supervised the changing rooms. Music was provided by the silken-voiced Snarsky brothers, late of Georgia's capital, Tiflis.

For the whole summer season, people arrived in droves, enjoying the sea as if it were Yalta or one of the other holiday haunts in the old empire. But as the weather cooled and the skies clouded over, the number of customers dwindled. The tents were soon folded up and returned to the British. Shalikashvili's income likewise dipped, but he heard via a friend about another venture that two Georgian princes had launched in Pera.

Koki Dadiani and Niko Nizharadze—scions of the princely houses of Samegrelo and Imereti, one slender and clad in a well-tailored *cherkeska*, the other stocky and exuding the air of a bon vivant—opened a small wine cellar. Located on a Pera side street, Koki and Niko's, as the place was usually called, served up hearty soups, wine, and dollops of Georgian hospitality, with table service provided by the middle-aged widow of a Russian general and the sister of a storied Russian naval adventurer. Given his experience in Florya, Shalikashvili was offered a bartending job, chatting up customers and managing the cash flow.

Koki and Niko's quickly became something of an unofficial welfare office for a string of imperial down-and-outers. The Gypsy guitarist Sasha Makarov, one of the legends of the St. Petersburg cabaret circuit, was featured as a nightly entertainer. Grizzo, a dashing imperial naval officer, was put to work roasting shish kebabs. A certain Nelidov, a ne'er-do-well with apparently no marketable skills, was given the honorary post of legal counsel, since the princes could not bear to turn him away. Soon, the princes' generosity threatened to bankrupt the establishment. Koki's gambling and Niko's drinking hurt the bottom line as well, and the restaurant was shuttered.

Shalikashvili—who recorded his travails in an unpublished memoir—was at a loss. He moved out of Pera into inexpensive lodgings in a predominantly Muslim section of the city. Food was still cheap and plentiful: mackerel caught fresh and cooked streetside, tinned sardines, olives, and sticky halva on good days or nothing more than Turkish flatbread on bad ones. But steady work was hard to find. Some of his friends found positions with the Allied authorities, serving as warehouse guards or firefighters. Shalikashvili spent most days trading stories with other Georgian men in a neighborhood teahouse. Days that had once been taken up with hunting, cavalry drills, and society masquerades were now passed just waiting for something to happen. Occasionally someone would announce that he was going back to Georgia to join the partisan movement against the Bolsheviks. News would arrive sometime later that he had been killed. Other young men would leave the teahouse to find a drink and, after a night of vodka and wine, lose their way in Istanbul's twisting streets.

Shalikashvili had one skill he could fall back on—his soldiering—and in time he managed to arrange a billet in the Polish army. Poland had fought its own war against the Bolsheviks in 1919 and 1920; in fact, it was the ceasefire in that conflict that had allowed the Red Army to pivot and turn its full attention to defeating Wrangel's Whites. Now, the Poles were eager to entice Georgians, Ukrainians, Azerbaijanis, and others who had been ousted from their homelands into a kind of anti-Bolshevik foreign legion, the spearhead of an emerging alliance against Lenin.

None of the great powers had recognized the new Bolshevik regime, and most were worried that the disease of socialism would spread from Russia to their own class-bound societies. Revolutionaries had already tried to topple governments in Germany and Hungary, and Poland was now on the frontline, coordinating the backlash against the idea of world revolution. In Istanbul, the Poles led the intelligence-gathering effort against the Bolsheviks. They continually fed to the Allied authorities whatever bits of news they could glean from White refugees. They also found plenty of eager fighting men with very personal reasons for hating the Bolsheviks. In the autumn of 1922, Shalikashvili left with his brother, David, who had only recently arrived in Istanbul after being released from Bolshevik internment in Georgia. They sailed for the Romanian port at Constanța. A train took the two brothers on to Poland. Their mother and sister were still in the Caucasus, and neither brother ever saw them—or Georgia, or Istanbul—again.

Desperation and resourcefulness were the two defining qualities of the White Russians in Istanbul. Secondhand shops in Pera were filled with the detritus of past lives being sold on consignment: silver, china, and linen; random family pictures taken in studios in St. Petersburg and Moscow; snuff boxes bearing the Romanov crest; porcelain Easter eggs; military decorations on silk ribbons; Cossack knives and filigreed necklaces; icons in silver covers; embroidery cut from antique gowns; books and parchment manuscripts on all topics; miniature portraits of the favorite courtiers of Catherine the Great.

Like a great migration of souls from one world to the next, talents from former lives were resurrected in new ways. A twelve-piece balalaika band performed on the quarterdeck of a British warship in exchange for dinner in the officers' wardroom. A professor of mathematics might make an ideal restaurant cashier. A voluble society matron might become a gossipy nightclub hostess. Pretty ingénues, who in earlier social seasons would have debuted at balls in St. Petersburg, could end up in a floor show with blonde bobs and bare midriffs.

Window shopping: A woman walking along the Grande Rue,
with both an automobile and a traditional porter,
or *hamal*, in the background.

From Graveyard Street across the Galata Bridge and into the warren of
alleys around the Grand Bazaar, Russian artists turned entire neighborhoods into open-air galleries, displaying their landscapes and portraits
to passersby. Other people relied on more basic skills: washing bodies
at the city morgue, selling peppermint-flavored toothpicks, making rag
dolls painted with the face of Sultan Mehmed VI, even chasing down
dockyard rats and selling the skins to furriers.

The Muslim memoirist Ziya Bey recalled being approached at his
export business by a Russian woman who introduced herself as a princess. He was incredulous, especially once she started naming a string

of business propositions in which she hoped to interest him. Her family had once controlled a tremendous estate in Crimea, she told him, along with the rights to several oil wells in the Caucasus. She would gladly sell those rights for a nominal fee. Ziya Bey explained to her that the offer was worthless. The Bolshevik government had nationalized all the industrial firms and recognized no previous owners or any foreign employers. She tried again: perhaps he would be interested in purchasing some of the jewels that she had hidden away before her quick departure from Crimea? That, too, would be useless, Ziya replied, since it was doubtful they could ever be found; the region had been crisscrossed by armies for years. Even if they could be located, getting them out of the country would be impossible because of Bolshevik restrictions on the export of valuable property. The woman finally settled on one of the few things still in her power to control. Would Ziya know someone interested in French lessons? That, he said, might work, and he put the Russian woman in contact with his American wife, who signed up for occasional conversation practice.

"Constantinople was a completely Russian city," recalled Georgy Fyodorov, a soldier in Wrangel's forces. He remembered the streets of Pera full of people flogging goods and calling out in Russian:

"Fresh full-flavored donuts!"

"Nuts from Lebanon!"

"Wouldn't you like some artificial flowers?"

"*The Evening Press*—latest news in Russian!—get it here!"

"Selling a cheap shirt, completely new! Worn only twice!"

"I'm buying currency—Denikin banknotes, tsarist ones, too!"

Another old soldier remembered an open-air market near the Galata Tower that offered refugees a chance to trade the many different banknotes that had been printed by the White forces. Buyers and sellers, standing with wads of paper in their hands, would call out names of the various types of Russian money, which circulated as informal currencies among the refugees.

"I'm buying and selling. Tsarist notes! Romanov ones! Kerenskys! Dumas! Arkhangelskes! Astrakhans! Tashkents! Kolchaks! And others!"

"I'm selling only Nikolayevs!"

"I'm buying Wrangel and Don notes! I'm paying top price!"

At the Grand Cercle Moscovite, one of the most illustrious restaurants in the city opened by Russian immigrants, an evening of dinner and dancing brought a visitor into contact with a cavalcade of diminished lives. The doorman was a former Cossack of the storied Atamansky Regiment once commanded by the tsar's mother. The manager was a former factory owner from Kiev. The kitchen was run by the former chef at the tsar's Livadia Palace in Crimea. The sous-chef had cooked for the Russian governor-general of the Caucasus. The maître d' had worked at Yar, the most famous restaurant in Moscow. His assistant had been an officer in the light infantry of the Imperial Guards. All the waiters, serving dishes ranging from borscht to *côtelettes à l'Impératrice Catherine IIème*, had been officers in the tsar's forces or the Volunteer Army. The orchestra played Glinka, Borodin, and Tchaikovsky; struck up foxtrots, one-steps, tangoes, and waltzes; or ceded the stage to guitarist Sasha Makarov, eager for work after the closing of Koki and Niko's. When you left, the man retrieving your coat or cape was the former bodyguard of Tsar Nicholas II. "It is the best food I have ever eaten," said Billy Fox-Pitt, the Welsh Guardsman, in a letter to his mother, "but it wouldn't do to make a habit of it, as one would be very ill as well as broke!!"

No one understood this world better than an American then living at the Pera Palace. The French doors in his room opened onto a view of the Golden Horn, but he had little time to appreciate it. Loose papers lay in stacks on a small table. Boxes and valises were piled against a wall or peeked out from under the bed. A typewriter rested on the dresser. He was so busy that he sometimes appeared at meetings with mismatched socks. By midmorning, a long line of Russians snaked up from the Orient Bar to his room on the fourth floor.

Born in 1871 in Cambridgeport, Massachusetts, Thomas Whittemore was named for his grandfather, a prominent Universalist minister and New England publisher. The pastor's theology stressed not only the idea that salvation was a gift eventually available to all people—a basic doctrine of all Universalists—but also the more radical view that the entire idea of hell was incompatible with an all-loving God. A belief in the universal connectedness of humanity was also dear to his namesake. During the First World War, the younger Whittemore had traveled through Bulgaria and the Russian Empire—working for the Red Cross, running supply boats to Crimea, and bringing coats and other clothing to refugee families escaping the Bolsheviks. When the Russian crisis hit Istanbul, he found himself at the center of the relief effort. Next to the Allied administration authorities, he was probably the best-known foreigner in town, at least to the city's neediest. Friends called him "The Flying Mystery." "Whittemore is never in a place," wrote one of his closest confidants, the curator and art historian Matthew Prichard, "he was, he will be; he comes from and is going to; but is never 'here.'"

Whittemore was director of the Committee for the Education of Russian Youth in Exile, which he had founded in 1914 to deal with the brewing problem of refugees displaced by war. The committee had no offices, no personnel except for Whittemore and those he could charm or cajole into helping, and no headquarters other than whichever hotel room he happened to be occupying. Whittemore's experience in Russia before the Bolshevik Revolution had given him a broad familiarity with the range of social organizations that already existed throughout the empire. Many had quickly reproduced themselves in exile, and Whittemore knew that they would be essential to integrating the refugees into new societies. But he also knew one thing that the Russians themselves had not yet come to understand: They were in all likelihood never going back.

On most days, the lobby of the Pera Palace was filled with people waiting to see Whittemore, from artists bringing new paintings for him to consider for purchase to counts and barons hoping to enlist his aid for their own charitable organizations. Like the hierarchical country they had fled, the exiles held fast to the gradations of rank, privilege, and profession that had framed their lives before the revolution. The hotel's lounge was a miniature map of old Russian society, with its many bits and pieces clustered together in conversation around small tables and armchairs. Cavalrymen from the Imperial Guards; officers of the Horse Artillery and the Imperial Navy; veterans of the Russo-Japanese War; recipients of the Order of St. George; bureaucrats from the ministries of justice, interior, and foreign affairs; old parliamentarians; engineers, doctors, lawyers, novelists, and sculptors; Russian Orthodox bishops; Cossacks from the Kuban, Don, Terek, and Astrakhan regions; Caucasus mountaineers; Muslims from the Black Sea coast; Buddhists from Siberia; and councilmen from local administrative bodies, or *zemstvos*—all had regrouped in the months following Wrangel's retreat and were now competing for the limited resources supplied by the Allies and other donors.

Left to their own devices, the leaders of each of these communities would spend much of their time quarreling with one another, much as they had done during the civil war. Part of Whittemore's task was to stitch together the competing factions, especially by mobilizing the energetic countesses who daily streamed into the Pera Palace looking for things to do. Only a few weeks after Wrangel's exodus from Crimea, a registration bureau had been set up to record the names of the refugees, list their particular skills, and reconnect families. Ladies were assigned to go from camp to camp collecting names and filing the information on cheap cards in old cigar boxes.

Training was the key to starting new lives, and Whittemore set about creating a purpose-built education system. Not far from the center of Pera, he located a small plot of land on which several large tents could be erected. Young Russian men were given bunks in the tents, where they could sleep after coming home from their day jobs as *hamals* (porters), salesmen, or deliverymen. Toward evening, the *hamals* would arrive with their special backpacks on which they carried heavy loads. Street hawkers would return carting unsold chocolates and paper flowers. Newsboys came in with papers that they would sell the next day for half price. Water vendors brought in clean Standard Oil cans that could be used in their trade, while fishermen mended nets and street sweepers repaired their brooms.

But then the real work began. Whittemore had organized the tent encampment not just as a refugee home but also as a placement center. Through countless letters to foreign universities, he managed to secure hundreds of places for Russian students who were sufficiently talented to pass the basic entrance examinations. Each night, after a supper of soup and bread, the tents became study halls, with Russian professors providing tutoring in mathematics, engineering, physics, biology, and chemistry. Students who had already had some university coursework assisted those with only secondary education or military training.

In time, an attestation commission was organized among former members of the prestigious Russian Imperial Academy, which certified that the students had reached a level of expertise qualifying them for admission to universities in France, Belgium, Switzerland, Italy, Greece, Germany, Czechoslovakia, and elsewhere. After weeks of waiting to hear about the universities' final decisions, the tents would fall silent when a letter for a student arrived from Paris or Prague. At an annual awards ceremony held in a former Ottoman army barracks, each student would don a makeshift version of Russian national costume—a pair of white pajamas supplied by the Red Cross, cinched at the waist with a belt—and cross the stage to receive a diploma from a professor in a threadbare suit. They were now graduates of an informal finishing school with its administrative offices in the Pera Palace, and their diplomas entitled them to enroll in prestigious institutions ranging from Charles University to the Sorbonne. By the autumn of 1921, hundreds of students had made their way to Europe, some traveling in boxcars, to start new lives. Many more would follow. Whittemore's records, diligently kept by archivists in New York down to the present day, contain more than a thousand individual student files with names that read like the guest list from a Russian imperial ball—Volkonskys, Ostrogorskys, Kuznetsovs, Tolstoys, Ignatievs—the paper trail of an entire world in the process of picking itself up and moving somewhere else.

"[H]aving acquired useful learning while in exile, the young folk, upon their return to Russia, will form the nucleus of educated workers, destined to labour in the task of rebuilding our country," Wrangel wrote to Whittemore, expressing his profound gratitude for the committee's work. Even then, however, in the mid-1920s, this was optimistic boosterism. Shortly before he gave the order to evacuate Crimea, Wrangel had reassured his officers that the retreat would be only a period of rest and re-equipping, to be followed by an "attempt to wrest victory from the hands of the enemy." A little belt-tightening now, and they would be home as soon as the Bolsheviks had exhausted themselves—by the autumn of 1921 at the latest, Dmitri Shalikashvili predicted. But soon the White Russians began to cross the mental borderland between flight and exile. The extraordinary circumstances of losing a war were now giving way to the heartbreaking reality that the loss would be permanent.

Whittemore's students were the last generation of the empire, and it was gradually dawning on them that they might well be the first generation of something else. They had become modern versions of *les ci-devants*, as French revolutionaries had called the washed-up nobility in 1789. The Bolsheviks had a similar name for them: *byvshie*, or "former people." Countess Vera Tolstoy, a cousin of Leo Tolstoy and one of Whittemore's supporters, summarized the situation in an essay for the *Atlantic Monthly*. "If the . . . martyrs of the French Revolution showed their butchers how nobles die," she wrote from her small house on the outskirts of Istanbul, "we, the victims of Bolshevist crime, who have yet escaped with our lives, shall show them how to live."

KONSTANTINOUPOLIS

A man running to catch an electrified Istanbul trolley car.

AFTER THE END OF the Russian civil war, there were perhaps around 860,000 former Russian subjects living abroad as refugees from war and revolution, ethnic Russians as well as representatives of just about every cultural group of the old empire. Many of them were concentrated in Istanbul. The city had shrunk from nearly a million people before the First World War to perhaps seven hundred thousand after the 1918 armistice. Fears of a wartime invasion by Greece, followed by the prospect of Turkish nationalists' exacting revenge in the occupied city, on the model of their reconquest of Smyrna, had pushed civilians—Muslims and non-Muslims alike—to flee. As a result, the Russian invasion represented a staggering increase in the city's overall population. A refugee crisis had become a demographic revolution.

Émigrés is the name societies give to immigrants they happen to like, and it was the smallest of victories that White Russians managed to acquire that label in Paris, New York, and just about everywhere else they landed. In Istanbul, though, Turkish slang referred to them as the "Goodies," the *haraşolar*, from the Russian term for "good" or "fine." The Russian word is a commonplace of everyday speech, but the Turkish variant was a cruel joke. Russians were not doing fine at all. Throughout much of the 1920s, if you encountered a beggar on the street in certain quarters of Istanbul, it was almost certain that he or she would speak Russian.

Letters about individual cases flowed into relief organizations in the city and to charitable groups as far afield as New York and Washington, DC. Aleksei Sterladkin, a blind man who had made his living by playing the harmonium on the Grande Rue, appealed for assistance when the police accused him of illegal begging. A Mr. Tcherniavsky, formerly a singer with the Russian imperial opera, requested that relief workers pass along information about his upcoming concert in Istanbul. Father Michel Vassilieff asked for a small contribution toward organizing an Easter meal for destitute Russian-speaking Christians. A Princess Shakhovskaya wrote to request a visa for getting herself and her husband, a musician with the Tokatlian Hotel orchestra, to the United States.

The problem for the refugees was not simply Istanbul's sluggish postwar economy, which affected Turks and Russians alike, but rather the peculiar way in which their prospects intersected with international politics. On July 24, 1923, Allied and Turkish negotiators finally signed a peace treaty ending the state of hostilities that had existed since 1914. Brokered by the League of Nations, the Treaty of Lausanne allowed the Allies to untangle themselves from the occupation, preserve some degree of dignity in the exit, and legitimize Mustafa Kemal's government as the successor to the deposed sultan. Years had passed since the 1918 armistice, and during that time the political and military situation in Turkey had changed profoundly. The country was no longer ruled by a faltering emperor. It was now headed by an elected parliament and a confident commander in chief who had pushed out foreign invaders and encircled the former capital with loyal troops. Unlike the treaties with Germany, Austria-Hungary, and Bulgaria, Lausanne was the only peace accord negotiated with, rather than simply imposed on, a belligerent power that the Allies had earlier defeated on the battlefield.

The treaty confirmed the state of peace with Turkey, defined its frontiers, and dealt with a range of arcane but vital issues left over from the collapse of the Ottoman Empire, such as how old life insurance policies were to be handled and which creditors could claim their share of the Ottoman public debt. When the signing was announced, Istanbullus fired rifles in the air and beat drums in the streets. Portraits of Mustafa Kemal sprouted in windows and on walls. Allied soldiers found themselves in a weaker position than ever before. "It is a humiliating business for any body out here," wrote Billy Fox-Pitt to his parents in England. "We are not treated with the least respect now by the Turk, the French with still less, and the Italians are ignored of course."

The announcement of the Lausanne accord formally began the countdown to the Allied departure, which took several months to coordinate. There were still nearly 15,000 British soldiers in the city, including Yorkshire infantrymen, Royal Marines, and kilted Scottish highlanders, along with small contingents from other Allied powers. After months of preparation, on October 2, 1923, General Harington and his wife were joined by detachments of Grenadier, Coldstream, and Irish Guards as they made their way to the port. Huge crowds had gathered at the quay to watch the Allied commander inspect honor guards of British, French, Italian, and Turkish troops. Harington saluted each national flag in turn, ending with the Turkish crescent and star, which caused the crowd to surge forward with cheers and hurrahs.

In short order, the general and his military escort boarded the flagship *Arabic* and sailed south out of the Bosphorus, bound for Malta, Gibraltar, and finally England. "It was a wonderful 'send off' from a so-called enemy country," he recalled. The only official reminder of the occupation was his headquarters' Union Jack, which Harington gave to the Anglican church in Galata, where it remains on display today. Four days later, on October 6, Turkish troops marched into the city and assumed full control. Later in the month, on October 23, the Grand National Assembly in Ankara declared the creation of the Turkish Republic, with Mustafa Kemal as president.

For the White Russians, all of this was unsettling, not least because the new republic's closest international partner was the government that had caused them to flee their homeland in the first place. Lenin had been a major supporter of Mustafa Kemal's anti-occupation resistance. The Bolsheviks had supplied arms during the war of independence, and Moscow had been the first world capital to establish diplomatic relations with the Turkish nationalists, sending a mission to Ankara while Istanbul was still being patrolled by British troops.

But Russian loyalties were divided. By one estimate, perhaps ten percent of the exiles were actively supportive of the Bolshevik cause, either as paid agents or as sympathizers who believed it was possible, even desirable, to reconcile with the de facto regime in Moscow. Prominent members of the White Russian emigration decided to make their peace with the Bolsheviks and returned to Russia. Some were promptly shot there, but others became vocal proponents of the transformation that Lenin seemed to be enacting.

In December 1922, the Bolshevik government had declared former Russian subjects living abroad to be outside the protection of the emerging Soviet state. Whites who had not managed to gain citizenship in their new homelands were now officially stateless. A host government could expel them as illegal immigrants, and no other government was obliged to receive them. They were people with no official status in international law. The League of Nations then stepped in, issuing so-called Nansen passports—named for the Norwegian explorer and humanitarian Fridtjof Nansen, the League's high commissioner for refugees—to hundreds of thousands of Russians around the world. That document provided them with a stopgap status that prevented their being automatically deported. But for Russians in Istanbul, the clock seemed to be running out. By 1923, the former Russian Embassy on the Grande Rue had been transferred to Soviet control, and the government in Ankara put increasing pressure on its White Russian guests either to move out of the country or adopt Turkish citizenship. With the arrival of trade delegations and diplomats from the Soviet Union, old enemies were increasingly coming into contact. It was perfectly possible for two people who had faced off across a battlefield during the Russian civil war to be looking at one another across the dance floor of the Grand Cercle Moscovite.

Over the course of the 1920s, Istanbul's Russian community dwindled. Wrangel's Volunteer Army had spent the early part of the decade drilling at Gallipoli with wooden weapons and white tunics made from hospital gowns, their regimental insignia fashioned from velvet piping recycled from ladies' dresses. But arrangements were soon made to pack off the ex-army to Bulgaria and Serbia, where former officers and men were put to work building roads and manning other construction projects. Thomas Whittemore's students likewise left for Prague and other university towns where faculties promised admission and stipends. Other people moved to Hungary, France, Britain, or whatever country would supply a visa. Dmitri Shalikashvili, the memoirist and soldier who had helped create the seaside bathing establishment at Florya, first departed for Poland and then served briefly in the German army. He later moved to the United States, where he spent the remainder of his life. After his death, his body was returned to his ancestral village in Georgia by his son, John Shalikashvili, by that time the chairman of the US Joint Chiefs of Staff.

The old elites departed, too. The Tolstoys ended up in Paris. Wrangel died in Brussels. Denikin—who had passed through Istanbul as he escaped abroad—had a fatal heart attack while vacationing in Ann Arbor, Michigan. He remained buried there for almost fifty years, until Russian president Vladimir Putin had him dug up and reinterred in Moscow, an attempt to appropriate an exiled nationalist for Putin's own regime.

The departure of most of the Russians relieved Istanbul of the burden of caring for them, but the end of the crisis did not transform the city into a model of order. The daily pandemonium of urban life could still be overwhelming. "[A]nything more like a lunatic asylum than Haidar Pasha Station cannot be imagined," recalled Agatha Christie on her first visit in the 1920s. En route to visit her husband, Max Mallowan, an archaeologist digging in Iraq, she bypassed the Pera Palace and stayed at the Tokatlian Hotel on the Grande Rue, which had been recommended to her by a dashing Dutch engineer she had met on the Orient Express. In fact, it was the Tokatlian—not the Pera Palace—where she eventually chose to lodge her Belgian detective, Hercule Poirot, in *Murder on the Orient Express*, which she published in 1934. The front door of the Pera Palace opened onto narrow streets that quickly gave way to slums. The Tokatlian's windows faced the comparative order of nineteenth-century façades and a wide, European-style avenue.

At that point, the city was part of an emerging nation-state, not an empire, but any newsagent would have laughed at the idea that Istanbullus might ever be squeezed into a single national identity. Just before the foundation of the Turkish Republic, Istanbul had eleven newspapers in Ottoman Turkish, seven in Greek, six in French, five in Armenian, four in Ladino and other languages spoken by local Jews, and one in English—the *Orient News*, which became the mouthpiece of the British administration. A short stroll down the Grande Rue led past a Greek Orthodox cathedral, a mosque, and two Roman Catholic churches. If you stepped into a few side streets along the way, you would come across other churches belonging to Armenian Catholics, Armenian Gregorians, Chaldeans, Anglicans, and German Protestants. Four synagogues and several other mosques clung to the slopes leading down through the Galata neighborhood.

A sense of outrage had propelled the Kemalists against Hellenic troops in Anatolia, and it was matched by a sense of relief among Istanbul's Muslims when nationalist forces eventually took control of the city from the Allies. But for local Christians, there was a growing fear that the new Turkish government would exact revenge on those deemed disloyal to the state. During the time of the effective dual Allied–

Kemalist administration of municipal affairs—from the autumn of 1922 through the end of the occupation a year later—Turkish authorities had already begun arresting Greeks who had either worked for the Allies or had actively supported Hellenic territorial claims. Greeks were by no means the only targets; antinationalist Muslims were also arrested and, in some cases, executed. But with so much of the city's commerce visibly in the hands of Greeks, that community naturally came in for the bulk of nationalist ire. Greeks might be accosted in the street or find their property spontaneously seized by a Muslim mob. Many worried about what would happen once the city came under full Turkish control. In response, some 50,000 non-Muslims, including some of the city's wealthiest families, departed at the end of 1922. Another exodus accompanied the 1923 withdrawal of the Allies, the last stratum of protection that Greeks believed lay between them and the new Turkish state.

The war and the occupation also deepened divisions within Istanbul's Greek community. Who properly spoke for the interests of the Greek nation and its diaspora: the Hellenic state, centered in Athens, or the Greek Orthodox patriarch in Istanbul, the clearest direct successor to Greek-speaking Byzantium? Disputes between pro-Hellenic and pro-patriarchal factions sometimes erupted into violence. In the summer of 1923, a band of Hellenic nationalists broke into the patriarchate, interrupted a meeting with other Orthodox leaders, and dragged the patriarch, Meletios IV, down a staircase, leaving him bruised and bloodied, before the melee was stopped by Allied police. After brushing himself off, the patriarch promptly excommunicated the leaders of the invading mob. Fed up with the internal fighting and rattled by the attack, Meletios soon left Istanbul aboard a British ship and retired to a quiet monastery on Mount Athos. A new patriarch was eventually elected from within the Istanbul Greek community, but challenges from Hellenic nationalists and other rivals remained. In 1924, for example, secessionists established their own Turkish Orthodox

Church, an assemblage of Turkish-speaking Orthodox Christians who denied the authority of the Phanar patriarchate to govern them.

An even greater problem for non-Muslim religious leaders such as the Greek Orthodox patriarch, as well as for their communities, lay in the breakdown of the old *millet* system. Muslim and non-Muslim subjects of the sultan had never been fully equal, but inequality and hierarchy were multifaceted. One's station in the complex society of the empire was determined not just by religion but also by one's gender, profession, and many other categories. When Ottoman authorities looked out on their own population, they saw a patchwork of many different kinds of authority, status, and privilege.

The Turkish Republic was a different thing entirely, even if some of its key features had their origins in the Ottoman era. The republic replaced the concept of an imperial subject with modern citizenship, loyalty to the person of the sultan with commitment to the ideals of a secular state, and the crosscutting identities of the old empire with the singular concept of the ethnically defined nation. When the republic adopted its first constitution, in 1924, all citizens were guaranteed equal rights regardless of religion, but in practice the differences were stark, thanks to the introduction of a new legal concept—an ethnic minority—that had largely been absent from the Ottoman imagination.

The new idea was enshrined deep inside the peace accord that had ended the First World War. The Treaty of Lausanne had paved the way for the Allied departure and the entry of Turkish troops into Istanbul, but a major point of contention during the negotiations had been the status of Greeks and other non-Muslims. Turkish negotiators had originally proposed the expulsion of the entire Greek population of Istanbul. If allowed to remain, Greeks would be "the means of importing corruption and disloyalty into our country," insisted the chief Turkish delegate, İsmet Pasha. The Hellenic government, in turn, argued that it had already received massive numbers of Greek refugees from the Ottoman Empire, and adding even more would create a humanitarian disaster. Moreover, formally expelling Greeks and other non-Muslims would reduce Istanbul to a shell—a great center of civilization that would be denuded of its business elite and Christian heritage.

In the end, negotiators reached a compromise. When the Lausanne treaty was signed in July 1923, Article 142 confirmed a separate agreement reached by the governments in Athens and Ankara. A mandatory expulsion of minorities would take place, with the two countries agreeing to "exchange" each other's coreligionists. Certain categories of Greek Orthodox living in Istanbul and on two small Aegean islands, along with Muslims living in the Hellenic territory of western Thrace, would be exempt—an exception that acknowledged the vital role of Greeks in Istanbul's economy and the age-old presence of Muslims in Greece. People caught up in the exchange were compelled to leave their homelands and resettle in the other state. They were legally prohibited from ever returning to their homes without the express permission of their former government. Special intergovernmental commissions were created to determine which families were to be considered "exchangeable" and therefore subject to forced migration—that is, to determine officially who was Greek Orthodox and who Muslim, even if the families practiced no particular religion or were of mixed heritage. The commissions also assessed the value of the property they left behind, the sale of which was to be managed by the Hellenic and Turkish states. Few people received adequate compensation, however. "[T]oday thousands of once-prosperous people are walking the streets of Constantinople and Athens without funds," noted a contemporary report, "and with only a slip of paper bearing an inventory for their property, for which they were to be reimbursed in their new land."

The exchange was meant to true up the lines of religion, ethnicity, and citizenship, and historians sometimes refer to the refugees created by the Lausanne accord with the shorthand labels of "Greeks" and "Turks." But those terms would have seemed bizarre to the refugees themselves. The exchange commissions relied on essentially the same criteria for determining personal identity as the Ottoman Empire had used—religious confession—but pasted onto that old category a new, wholly ethnic label. In this mash-up of imperial and national ways of seeing the world, the mandatory exchange included a great many people whose identities had little in common with the ethnic nationalism at the core of the Hellenic kingdom and the emerging Turkish Republic. In this great unmixing of peoples, individuals were assigned to one and only one identity. A Greek Orthodox family might speak Turkish and have roots in the same Anatolian village extending back many generations. A Greek- or Slavic-speaking Muslim in Greece might similarly have had little in common with the culture of the Turkish Republic. But in the exchange, the former was declared a Greek and the latter a Turk, with both shipped off to a foreign but allegedly co-ethnic home.

The same treaty that ended the First World War also sought to avert future ones. Its method was to remove people from their homes so that no future government could use the desire to liberate them as a reason for war—a prophylactic form of reciprocal exile. "There appeared to be no doubt that this plan would give good results in the future, by creating more homogeneous populations and removing one chief cause of the endless conflicts, often attended by massacres, in the Near East," said one of the plan's originators, Fridtjof Nansen—the same League of Nations official who had worked tirelessly to improve the plight of the exiled Russians.

If one includes the people who had already fled in both directions over the previous year or so, the Lausanne treaty mandated the compulsory exile of around a million Greek Orthodox and five hundred thousand Muslims. In the short term, Lausanne did remove one of the major sources of conflict between two neighbors whose brutal fighting had dragged on long after the end of the First World War. Over the longer term, Lausanne remade the demographic landscape—uprooting ancient communities, creating whole villages of displaced refugees, and making both countries more ethnically homogeneous than they had been in modern history.

Traces of the past survived, however. An inscription on a private building in Istanbul might identify its Greek architect or former proprietor, while one of Greece's premier soccer teams, PAOK, still contains the name *Constantinople* in its title, since it was originally founded in Ottoman-era Istanbul. The passage of time has transformed mutual ethnic cleansing into a version of homeland tourism, with Greeks going to visit the old family apartment building in Pera and Turks seeking to find the destroyed walls of a neighborhood mosque in the old city center of Thessaloniki, the former Salonica. Today bus tours take aging Turks through the towns and villages of northern Greece where their parents or grandparents once lived. Turkish Airlines runs multiple daily flights between Istanbul and Thessaloniki, where tens of thousands of Greeks began their new lives as Hellenes and from where thousands of Muslims began their journey toward becoming Turks. To Turks, the forced migration has come to be called the *Büyük Mübadele*, or the "Great Exchange." To Greeks, it is still known simply as the *Katastrophē*.

Lausanne was a schizophrenic treaty. Parts of it contained a blueprint for uprooting a million and a half people. Other portions seemed a multiculturalist's model for protecting the rights of minorities. Since the treaty allowed for some individuals and groups to remain behind in their old homelands, an entire section was devoted to the reciprocal obligations that Turkey and Greece undertook toward these legal holdouts—principally the Greek Orthodox of Istanbul and the Muslims of western Thrace—such as equality before the law, free exercise of religion, and primary-school education in native languages. The duties of a modern state toward its ethnic minorities replaced the old Ottoman concept of the religiously defined *millet*.

Had history unwound differently, Prodromos Bodosakis-Atha-nasiades—the proprietor of the Pera Palace in the first years of the Allied occupation—would have been among this protected few. But like tens of thousands of others who feared reprisals by the new Turkish government, Bodosakis decided to leave Istanbul at some point in the early 1920s and fled to Athens. The Pera Palace continued to operate, as did many other minority-owned businesses in the city, even with an absent owner. Once the Allies departed the city, however, properties such as these naturally became the principal targets of Turkey's effort to undo the economic power of non-Muslims. At the time, there were perhaps 40,000 "non-exchangeable" Greeks living abroad, people who had voluntarily left Turkey but were not legally subject to mandatory removal. Their absence was now deemed a sign of disloyalty. They had voted with their feet, the Turkish government declared, and had clearly decided to make their lives elsewhere. In the spring of 1923, new legis-lation passed by the parliament in Ankara allowed for the state to seize the properties "abandoned" by these nonresident citizens, even if the owners had made provisions for transferring their assets to a local rela-tive or business partner.

On the eve of the Allied occupation, Istanbul's Chamber of Com-merce and Industry had been cochaired by a Muslim and an Armenian, with eleven of its fourteen core members drawn from Istanbul's Chris-tian and Jewish minorities. By early 1921, the cochairs were both Mus-lim, as were thirteen of its nineteen members. In 1923, the government established the National Turkish Commercial Union to represent the interests of Muslim merchants and coordinate the acquisition of indus-tries, import–export firms, and financial institutions formerly held by non-Muslims. Foreign banks and businesses were pressured to fire their minority employees and hire Muslims instead.

Two-thirds of the Greek barristers in the Istanbul bar were dis-missed. Greek trade unions were shuttered. Greek-owned businesses were threatened with legal action for small infractions or encouraged—

sometimes forced—to take on a Muslim partner. These new associates could then petition the government to have a Greek co-owner designated as "exchangeable" under the Lausanne accord, with that co-owner's share of the business then going to the Muslim partner who remained behind. In 1925 and 1926 meetings of local Greeks, Armenians, and Jews formally renounced any collective rights afforded to these communities under the Lausanne treaty. The renunciations came only after significant pressure from the Turkish government, but they represented the definitive end of any claim to special treatment based on religious confession or ethnic category. When Ankara announced the creation of an alcohol monopoly in 1926, putting the production and sale of intoxicants solely under the control of a state-licensed firm, one of the major fields of non-Muslim commercial activity in Istanbul also became fully nationalized.

In 1923, the Pera Palace—one of the city's foremost properties with an absentee landowner—was declared the property of the state. The move was nominally meant to provide compensation to the national treasury for Bodosakis's unpaid tax bills. However, four years later, in May 1927, a new law declared that all former Ottoman subjects who had not returned to Turkey since the war of independence—including the hotel's old Greek proprietor—were not to be considered Turkish citizens. For Bodosakis, this change meant that his own position was in some ways worse than that of the "exchangeable" Greeks who had lived outside Istanbul. While the latter were able in theory to gain compensation for the property they left behind—in some cases, even being assigned new farmland or housing in Greece—the "non-exchangeable" people who left Istanbul of their own accord had none. Lausanne had removed a million Greeks from the Turkish population on ships and trains. The 1927 law removed tens of thousands more with the stroke of a pen.

These reforms were part of an entire package of legislation, public campaigns, and city ordinances that intentionally reduced the public visibility and economic power of minorities. The new Turkish Republic rejected the confessional, multiethnic, and imperial structures of the Ottomans in favor of those of a nation-state. At best, that vision enabled equal citizenship before the law by doing away with the stove-piping system of religious self-government favored by the Ottomans. At worst, it involved making Muslim Turks the core nation within the new state and relegating everyone else to second-class status. Schools operated by non-Muslim religious institutions or private foundations were required to employ a specific percentage of Muslim teachers and were prevented from including references to religion in their curriculum. Boy Scout troops formed by minority communities were outlawed. Placards in public venues proclaimed *Citizen, Speak Turkish!* For most of the 1920s, non-Muslims living in Istanbul were prevented from traveling outside the city, an attempt to sequester ethnic differences inside the old capital. Armenians in particular were expressly prohibited from settling in eastern Anatolia, the region that had been the ancient center of Armenian culture and the heart of darkness during the genocide. In 1934, a new law required all Turkish citizens to take surnames—something few Turkish Muslims had used before—but expressly forbade people from registering names that had recognizably non-Turkish endings, such as "-poulos" for Greeks, "-ian" for Armenians, and "-off" or "-vich" for Slavs and Jews.

The former Greek patriarch, Meletios, compared Ankara's policies to "Moscow-style Bolshevik Communism," and in some ways he was not far wrong. The Ankara government had taken a lesson from the Bolshevik experience. Just as the new Soviet Union had declared White Russians to be outside the protection of the new state, so too the Turkish Republic cut ties with its old rivals—Greeks and other minorities—now living abroad. Both expropriations stemmed from common sources: the belief that the victors were leading a world-changing political movement, that to the victors belong the spoils, and that the vanquished were little more than spongers and parasites—leftovers from an old and decrepit social order who were now getting their just deserts.

For the Turkish government, and for plenty of average Muslims, the forced expropriations provided a moment of cosmic justice. From their perspective, the rapacious minorities who had bled the Ottomans dry, collaborated with the Allied occupiers, and turned their backs on the war of independence would at last be supplanted by true patriots. To the minorities, it could seem like the end of the world. "I stood on the dusty, rubbish-strewn hillside of Pera . . . and looked down at the harbor, forested with masts and grimy with smoky funnels. . . . It all looked unreal and impossible," Ernest Hemingway wrote in the *Toronto Daily Star*. "But it was very real to the people who were looking back at the city where they were leaving their homes and business, all their associations and their livelihoods. . . ."

Fortunes were lost, and Greeks and other business leaders were ruined. Some were left penniless, wandering the unfamiliar streets of Athens and Thessaloniki. Others, despondent, took their own lives. Turkish newspapers regularly ran sensational stories of desperation and revenge. Just up the street from the Pera Palace, at Hemingway's old haunt, the Hôtel de Londres, the Greek operator, Kofakos, was pushed into bankruptcy in 1928. Some time later, he showed up on the hotel's doorstep, by then a beggar, and was sent away. He returned with a pistol and shot one of the hotel employees dead.

Unlike these cases, however, Bodosakis landed on his feet. The Pera Palace was only one part of his considerable wealth, much of which he had managed to move out of Turkey. In Athens he started new businesses that, in time, would make him one of Greece's most formidable industrialists, with interests in virtually every sector of the economy.

Many of the contacts he had made in the lobby of the Pera Palace—
not least the British soldiers, German businessmen, and French merchants who inevitably stayed there while in Istanbul—may have fueled
his meteoric rise from migrant to magnate. As proprietor of the Greek
Powder and Cartridge Company, Bodosakis became the largest arms
manufacturer in Greece, producing rifle cartridges of all calibers, explo-
sives, antiaircraft grenades, gas masks, and boilers for naval vessels.

In the late 1930s, his business expanded to include silk and wool
production, shipbuilding, and wine and liquor sales. During the Spanish Civil War, he supplied weapons to both the Left and the Right.
In the run-up to the Second World War, he assiduously balanced his
business interests by supplying both British and German war machines.
"He was renowned as a keen-brained businessman who knew how best
to turn a keg of dynamite, a block of foreign exchange or a parcel of real
estate to his economic and political advantage," said an exposé in *Collier's* magazine in 1940. "He is to this war what the goateed late Sir Basil
Zaharoff"—the arms-dealing Istanbul Greek and a generation Bodosakis's
elder—"was to the last World War." When Bodosakis died, in 1979, his
business interests stretched from the munitions industry to wine production, chemicals, and shipbuilding. He was simply "the most powerful man
in Greek industry," according to a historian of the subject, and the charitable foundation established by his family became one of the country's
most illustrious philanthropic organizations, dedicated to rewarding work
in the sciences and medicine and spreading Hellenic culture.

Meanwhile, the Pera Palace languished in a legal netherworld. In
the summer of 1927, at the time when absentee property owners were
being stripped of their Turkish citizenship, the hotel was transferred
from the treasury to the state-controlled Emlak Bank. A few months
later, in December 1927, it seems to have been purchased by a Muslim businessman, Misbah Muhayyeş, who formally registered his
ownership in the municipal property records in 1928. Originally

from Beirut and, like Bodosakis, a relative newcomer to Istanbul, Muhayyeş was an early supporter of the Turkish nationalists, with ties to Mustafa Kemal that stretched back before the First World War. During the war of independence, Muhayyeş had turned his old family business—textiles—toward the Kemalist cause, supplying uniforms to the struggling nationalist army. Those connections allowed Muhayyeş to be granted Turkish citizenship and, with a clear understanding of which way the political winds were blowing, he managed to acquire the nominally abandoned hotel.

He picked up where the Greek family had left off, sprucing up the bar, polishing the brass on the elevator, and restoring something of the hotel's reputation as the obvious place to stay for travelers from Europe or farther afield. The old address, which people had previously known as the corner of Graveyard and Thugs Streets, had undergone a makeover as well. The city authorities had given the road outside the front door the more stately name of Meşrutiyet (Constitution) Avenue. The hotel was now in Muslim hands, and in the alchemy of personal identity and republican politics, Muhayyeş—despite being an Arab— also became a Turk, someone who had demonstrated loyalty to the nation and was now reaping the appropriate rewards. Bespectacled and balding, with a devil-may-care bow tie and pocket square, he was the very image of the new generation of Istanbullus taking over from the Greeks. His family's summer home in the surburb of Yeniköy, an Orientalist fantasy of cupolas and mitered eaves, is still one of the grandest residences on the Bosphorus.

Istanbul's non-Muslim minorities fell from an estimated 56 percent in 1900 to 35 percent by the late 1920s. Other cities had more dramatic decreases. Izmir, the former Smyrna, went from 62 percent non-Muslim to 14 percent. Erzurum, in far eastern Anatolia, a city almost wholly emptied of Armenians by the genocide, fell from 32 percent non-Muslim to 0.1 percent. But the demographic revolution changed virtually everything in the old minority neighborhoods of Istanbul. In the rush to leave, Greeks, Armenians, and Jews dumped the contents of their houses and apartments onto the secondhand market, hoping to gain at least a small amount of cash before boarding a ship or train. The flood of furniture, dishware, phonographs, and pianos was so great that importers of new household items found public demand at a standstill, swamped by the easy availability of cheap used goods.

Turkey as a whole became more Muslim, more Turkish, more homogeneous, and more rural—because of the flight of non-Muslim minorities from the cities—than it had ever been. Some of the families who would go on to become the mainstays of Istanbul's economy emerged in ways not dissimilar to that of Muhayyeş: keeping an eye on changing fortunes and translating political connections into economic advantage once the Greek and other minority businesses went up for sale. There was nothing necessarily dishonest in their dealings, at least at the level of individual transactions, but they rested on a massive transfer of wealth whose origins lay in the republic's preference for national purity over the old cosmopolitanism of the imperial capital. Where a generation earlier the power elite of Istanbul would have stressed magnificence and splendor as their defining traits, clad in brocaded uniforms and luxurious silks, the new Turkish mandarins emphasized the very thing that the old Ottomans had lacked: quiet confidence and a sense of easy superiority. These men and their families now sat for portraits in tailored suits and fashionable Western-style dresses, looking out at the viewer and, like bourgeois everywhere, eager to record themselves at their most attractive and secure.

The seizure of minority properties was an intentional policy, but it was treated by generations of average Istanbullus and their historians as a windfall. If the owners had left during the Allied occupation, they were remembered as having simply abandoned their homes and businesses, quietly locking the door and walking away from the wealth that had taken generations to acquire. In reality, of course, they had been legally prevented from returning to claim their holdings. For visitors today, the entire history of this transformation is on display in the lobby of the Pera Palace itself. Portraits of Bodosakis and Muhayyeş, the two proprietors who took the hotel from empire to republic, hang across from each other outside the Orient Bar—one the target of state policies, the other their roundabout beneficiary, and each clearly confident, in the moment he was captured on canvas or on film, that the city belonged to people like him.

"THE POST-WAR WORLD WAS JAZZING"

The old guard: Former "black eunuchs" of the Ottoman imperial harem, at a meeting in the late 1920s or 1930s.

THE CHOICEST ROOMS IN the Pera Palace were located near the southwestern corner of the building. From there, the windows looked out on the Golden Horn and the thin neighborhoods that had once marked the farthest reaches of the Ottoman city. In the distance, a dark band of parkland had been a favorite picnic spot for Ottoman beys and their families. Veiled ladies had once sat demurely on the grass while children frolicked amid wiry acacia trees or splashed in the twin creeks that emptied into the Golden Horn.

After the end of the empire, ferries still chugged upstream to deposit weekenders. Some were headed to the village of Eyüp and the *türbe*, or mausoleum, of Abu Ayyub al-Ansari, one of the companions of the Prophet Muhammad, which had long been a pilgrimage site for devout Muslims. Others could be seen making for the trees of Kağıthane, which offered picnic spots and seclusion for courting lovers. Over the years, the city had crept into the sparsely wooded areas. Sunset at the Pera Palace made these newer neighborhoods glow. The fading pink and orange sunlight reflected off red tile roofs and plaster façades as lanterns and houselights came up after the late-afternoon call to prayer.

It wasn't only the view that made the southwest side of the Pera Palace the most desirable, however. Since it was the farthest away from the bars and clubs of the old Graveyard Street, it was also the only part of the hotel where a patron could expect a decent night's sleep. At the time of the Allied occupation, Ernest Hemingway had worried about what would happen to Istanbul's nightlife once the Muslims took over the city from the British, French, and Italians. Rumor had it that the Turkish nationalists, bowing to Islamic convention, had outlawed card-playing and upended backgammon tables in the areas already under their control. "The man who raises a thirst somewhere east of Suez is going to be unable to slake it in Constantinople once Kemal enters the city," Hemingway predicted.

But in fact the city seemed to sprout new bars, restaurants, variety theaters, and *cafés chantants* by the week. "Beauty and wit and laughter and song were exalted and worshipped," recalled an American visitor. Small beer halls opened in the tiniest of venues. Even a room that could fit only a few tables featured its own small orchestra. Local entrepreneurs knew an opportunity when they saw it, and the shifts in Istanbul's population could be gauged by the drinking spots that arose to service specific subcategories of newcomers. Tom's Lancashire Bar, run by an immigrant from Salonica, made a play for British clients from the north of England, while St. James's Brasserie sought to attract a more refined English crowd. With the elimination of the sultanate in 1922, even the Yıldız Palace complex—where Abdülhamid II had busily spied on his restive capital—was repurposed. An Italian entrepreneur, Mario Serra, transformed the compound's wood-and-stone chalet, set in a grove of pine, magnolia, and linden trees, into a casino. The facility was able to accommodate three hundred players at its gaming tables and featured restaurants, tearooms, a horse-riding arena, tennis courts, and a shooting range.

The Pera Palace offered dinner with musical accompaniment every evening, plus a *thé concert* on Fridays and Sundays at five o'clock. But just to the north of the hotel stood one of Istanbul's premier nightspots, the Garden Bar, which occupied part of the Petits-Champs park. The bar had been opened by a Jewish immigrant from Bulgaria as a watering hole for artists performing at the nearby Winter Garden Theater. Like many buildings in the city, it went through several iterations, leveled by fire and then rebuilt by a new owner, but by the early 1920s it was drawing crowds of Muslims and foreigners, as well as plenty of visiting patrons from the Pera Palace next door. A musical matinee was available every afternoon and early evening from five to eight o'clock, plus a full variety extravaganza from nine to eleven. Musical touring companies from Vienna, Paris, and other European cities put on revues. A high-wire walker or trapeze artist might even swoop overhead, to the gasps of the crowd. Boxing matches were staged with local and international sportsmen, while drag queens on occasion would entertain the crowd with song and dance.

The Garden Bar's proprietors had their pick of artists because the city was crawling with out-of-work musicians and other performers, most of them part of the bedraggled White Russian invasion of 1920. Boutnikoff's Symphony Orchestra, founded by a Russian émigré, offered concerts twice daily, marking one of the first sustained efforts to bring European classical music to the city. Popular music stars such as the singer Alexander Vertinsky, along with future notables such as the young jazz composer Vladimir Dukelsky—or Vernon Duke—performed at venues throughout the city. Russian circus artists had also made their way south with Wrangel's forces, and Istanbul now saw a boom in knife juggling and acrobatics. When jobs were scarce, the local Red Cross office was inundated with requests for money. A troupe of eight Russian dwarfs applied for assistance with developing a new revue. A man with a menagerie of trained rats, dogs, and a pig requested help in placing his animal show in a suitable nightclub or performance hall. "Artists cannot live in Russia now," the rat trainer said sadly. "The atmosphere is uncongenial to art."

Art was probably not on the minds of most people who ventured north of the Golden Horn, however. At the Garden Bar, the memoirist Ziya Bey reported, "soliciting by both male and female pleasure-seekers is now so aggressively indulged in that not even a self-respecting man dares any more to venture in the place." The whole neighborhood was like the slums of Naples, recalled Alexis Gritchenko, a Russian painter. Misspelled signs in many languages lured customers through dark doorways. The smell of sour wine and rotten fruit wafted up from cellars and taverns. The windows of legal brothels glowed golden. Shouts and laughter continued through the night, broken only by the thunder of a giant hogshead of wine being rolled over paving stones.

Outrageous entertainment and on-demand licentiousness had been part of the city's social order for centuries. The difference now was that it all seemed to be so freely available—on display even—before crowds of strangers packed together inside bars, public gardens, and theaters. As late as 1916, when the first Viennese opera troupes began appearing in the city, concert organizers had to stage special performances for women only, so that the wives and daughters of pashas and beys would not have to interact with other men. Princesses of the imperial household had rushed giggling into the Tokatlian Hotel—the first time they had been allowed to enter a hotel lobby, in fact—surrounded by guardian eunuchs who ushered them through a back exit to the Petits-Champs Theater beyond. Now, in the 1920s, it was hard to imagine that such a chaste and naïve world had ever existed. "At Petit Champs [*sic*] you could watch Cossack dancers, see clean, U.S. tincan sailors piled out of *arabas* [trucks] into the stew of tarts cadging for champagne," recalled Robert Dunn, an American naval official.

The popularity of nightspots rose and fell, victims to changing fortunes, evolving tastes, or a single dull performance that took the life out of the party. That was the fate of one of the earliest sensations in the club life of Istanbul and a major rival of the Garden Bar, a large and hopping dance joint called Maxim.

The club's proprietor was an unlikely impresario. Frederick Bruce Thomas was the son of former Mississippi slaves. He had joined countless other black men from the southern United States who sought jobs and fortunes in Chicago and New York, waiting tables or working as valets. A sense of adventure and a desire to escape the everyday racism

A chorus line: Female dancers at a revue in an Istanbul club.

of Gilded Age America took him to London, Paris, and then, in 1899, to a place very few African Americans had dreamed of visiting: the Russian Empire. Within a few years, he had taken Russian citizenship, found a Russian wife, and—as Fyodor Fyodorovich Tomas—set himself up as one of the premier maître d's in Moscow. The establishment where he worked, Yar, was the city's most elegant eatery and a restaurant known across the continent. He later opened his own Moscow nightspot, which debuted to rave reviews and record crowds.

Thomas had crossed the color line, achieving a status he never could have reached had he remained in the United States, but the tide of politics and revolution was harder to manage. After the autumn of 1917, when Muscovites began taking sides in the emerging civil war, Thomas fled south to the relative safety of areas controlled by the Volunteer Army. Like many Russian subjects, he found a temporary refuge in Odessa, a port city that had passed back and forth between rival armies. In 1919, he moved again, joining thousands of former tsarist loyalists fleeing the Bolsheviks' southward advance. He ended up in

Istanbul, likely the only black White Russian to arrive with the remnants of Denikin's and Wrangel's forces.

In short order, Thomas reestablished himself. He fell in with Bertha Proctor, a Lancashire barkeep and sometime madam whose bar near the Pera Palace was already regarded as one of the most successful in the city. Together they opened a new establishment at the end of a tramline in the Şişli neighborhood. Known by a variety of names—the Anglo-American Villa and Garden, Bertha's, and finally Stella—it became one of the favorite haunts of Allied officers. Within a few years, business was so good that Thomas was able to trade up, and in the autumn of 1921, he inaugurated a new venue nearer the center of Pera on Sıraselviler Avenue. He christened the new dancing and dinner club Maxim, the name of his old business in Moscow and perhaps a clever rhyme with Istanbul's nearby Taksim Square.

In the middle of the 1920s, the *grande salle* of Maxim was "the most frequented locale not only for the Istanbul public but also for foreigners who happened to be passing through," said the memoirist Willy Sperco, who was then living in the city. Even the acerbic Ziya Bey was moved to check out the popular nightspot, visiting with his wife and a Greek friend, Carayanni, who had become rich by jacking up prices on scarce food items during the war. "Never before were Pera and Galata as disreputable as now," he wrote. He found Maxim full of Russian ex-nobles and amateur bohemians, everyone smoking and drinking, with a black jazz band on stage. People had begun to adopt the French habit of kissing women on the hands, but beyond that, few of the more refined habits of Parisian life had taken root in Istanbul. "[T]he only thing which this international crowd has adopted from the Quartier Latin of Paris is free love," he concluded.

Thomas was a talented survivor, and when the times demanded it, he could shift gears. He could transform himself from Western-style clubman to Turkish harem lord with literally the change of a hat. When a group of American tourists wandered in, Thomas would don a fez and order his chorus girls into Turkish pantaloons. The visitors were treated to an evening in a splendid Ottoman harem, with lounging slave girls and obsequious attendants serving a passable beefsteak with horserad-ish sauce. When the evening was finished, the exotic proprietor would bow, press the guests' hands congenially, and then usher them out the door with a warm "Good-bye, effendi."

The good times could not last, however. Thomas had expanded the business too rapidly. The departure of the Russians took away both cli-ents and employees, and rivals were eager to copy what had been a novel and brilliant model of drinking, eating, and dancing, all in one place, with young women serving as the waitstaff. Other clubs were popping up along the Grande Rue—the Rose Noire, the Turquoise, Karpich's, the Kit-Kat. After only five years in the new location, Thomas had racked up a mountain of debt. His creditors forced him to pay up or declare the business bankrupt, much in the way that all non-Muslim businesses were being squeezed at the time. He closed the doors in 1927 and died the following summer. Turkish businessmen later opened a new version of Maxim as a casino, but the life had gone out of the party. "The post-war world was jazzing," noted Thomas's obituary in the *New York Times*, "and [he] saw to it that cosmopolitan Constantinople was not behind." Newspapers labeled him "the sultan of jazz," and a few dozen old friends came out for the funeral, but most of the former clientele had moved on to newer and more exciting venues. It was all a sad affair, remembered Willy Sperco, as depressing as the aftermath of an orgy.

❖

Among Istanbul's local historians, Thomas is often credited with intro-ducing Istanbullus to everything from Western-style dancing to the entire concept of public nightlife. His Maxim probably did feature the first black dance bands in the city, which Thomas brought on tour from France and the United States. A mysterious group that contemporaries remembered as the Palm Beach Seven may have been the first ensemble ever to mute a trumpet or hit a rim shot in Istanbul's history. Maxim's dancing instructors, mainly young Russian women, helped train an entire generation of Istanbullus to do the foxtrot, the shimmy, and other fashionable steps. In 1926, municipal authorities issued orders banning the Charleston—not because it offended Muslim sensibilities but because record numbers of people were being admitted to the hospital for sprains and bruises. The ban was impossible to enforce, of course, and it was mercilessly mocked by the Turkish press, but it did reflect the rapid transformation of the city after the White Russian influx. "They changed the shape of social life," the Turkish memoirist Mîna Urgan, then a young girl, recalled succinctly of the Russians.

Newcomers such as Thomas, however, were actually slotting into a well-worn groove: the habit of eating, drinking, and carousing that Istanbullus themselves had already developed into a high art. European émigrés typically thought of themselves as having pioneered public entertainment in the city, and they probably were responsible for the idea of a restaurant—a place where you could go in the evening, sit at a cloth-covered table, and order from a limited but regularly changing menu, with plated dishes being delivered by a trained server. Nothing quite like that had existed in Istanbul before. But there was no shortage of public eateries and other distractions, even under the Ottomans.

Rough wine and raki could be had at innumerable *meyhanes*, taverns usually owned by Greeks or Armenians. According to the seventeenth-century traveler Evliya Çelebi, the city boasted more than a thousand *meyhanes* in his day—not necessarily an accurate count but still an indication of how easy it was to procure alcohol in the capital of the Islamic world. In fact, the sense that the number of bars and eateries was out of control has been one of the constants in Istanbul's social history. Anyone "who can fry three stinky fish in a pan gets a permit to open a *meyhane*," complained a newspaper in the 1930s. The same sentiment repeated itself just about every time city administrators contemplated how to corral Istanbullus' seemingly boundless desire to offer their neighbors something to eat and drink.

Meyhanes were spread throughout the city, from Eyüp to Üsküdar, and, like neighborhood pubs, each had its regular clientele. Small plates of *meze*—assortments of sardines, fava beans, melon, white cheese, and other dishes—were provided to soak up the Bulgarian and Greek wine, which made slaves of those who drank it, according to Evliya Çelebi. On his own visits to such establishments in the mid-1600s, he regularly came upon drunken men complaining of their plight. "My foot takes no step but to the tavern!" they called out to him. "My ear hears nothing but the bottle's glugging and the drunken cry!" He gave thanks to God that he himself never took anything stronger than sherbet made from Athenian honey, yet he was nevertheless able to recall eight of the most popular *meyhanes* by name, which he listed helpfully in his famous book of travels, the *Seyahatname*.

Despite the theoretical ban on alcohol consumption by Muslims, the Ottoman Empire also developed an extensive alcohol industry, producing everything from anise-flavored raki to wines and beers, again typically the domain of non-Muslim proprietors. Being abstemious was a virtue observed mainly in the breach, which is why Pera was such a useful thing to have in Ottoman and republican Istanbul—an entire neighborhood, across the Golden Horn from the sultan's oldest palace, where just about any kind of debauchery could be had at a price. It was almost as if Las Vegas were always only a bridge away.

Eating and drinking involved being in the public eye. Until well into the twentieth century, a home-cooked meal was a rarity. This mode of dining was almost exclusively the purview of the wealthy, who could afford a permanent kitchen in their villa or mansion, one or more servants to go to the market, and a cook to prepare the food. Average Istanbullus got their food in groups—from street vendors, neighborhood bakers, soup kitchens attached to mosques, canteens associated with some professional class (such as soldiers or the service staff at imperial palaces), or the ubiquitous *esnaf* canteens, or tradesmen's eateries, that serviced specific neighborhoods. People traditionally ate where they worked and worked where they lived, surrounded by other people just like them, such as coreligionists or members of distinct professions, since specialized workshops—coppersmiths, glassblowers, woodworkers—tended to be concentrated in the same parts of the city. In the 1880s, for example, a little over a quarter of Istanbul's population—mainly unmarried men—did not live in private homes but were accommodated in mosque complexes, artisans' shops, and other group lodgings. About eight percent of the people in the city had no fixed abode at all.

Given the need for food that was easily prepared and easily served to large groups, simplicity was key. Minute gradations of quality depended not on doing something new but on doing something familiar particularly well. That is why so many of the memoirists of everyday life in Istanbul are most wistful when they recall a noted baker, the purveyor of an especially good yogurt, or a well-shaded teahouse. A traveler today can today go from a morning *simit*, a pretzel-like bread covered in sesame seeds, to a grilled fish or stew at midday, to a sludge-bottomed coffee in the afternoon and still approximate the foodways—and caloric intake—of average Istanbullus of the past. Classical Ottoman dishes eventually made their way into the city's restaurants, but these concoctions with their whimsical names—such as the lamb and eggplant in *hünkârbeğendi* (The-Sultan-Enjoyed-It), or the eggplant, tomato, and garlic in *imambayıldı* (The-Imam-Fainted)—would have been foreign to the vast majority of the city's population.

Beyond the variety of food and drink available in innumerable public venues, Western visitors have long had a particular fascination with Istanbul's vices. "Narcotic stimulants such as Indian hemp and opium are available," the popular *Meyers Guide* told German travelers as late as 1914.

> The enjoyment of marijuana and hashish enables one to continue working, erases pain, cures various diseases, and creates a pleasant intoxication that stimulates the imagination and increases both appetite and sex drive. . . . Opium smokers (mainly Persians and Arabs rather than Turks) tend to gather only in a few hidden coffeehouses in Yedikule [south of the Golden Horn] and indulge in this vice in secret. For Europeans, joining them is fraught with difficulties since in recent years the government has intervened vigorously against opium smoking.

Illicit drugs remained a part of the city's entertainment after the First World War, and styles and tastes came more in line with European sensibilities. Turkey was not a signatory to conventions on the transport of narcotics, and producers and traffickers flocked to Istanbul as the center of the cross-Mediterranean trade. Newspapers and journals railed against the scourge of one particular new import, cocaine. Because it required none of the complex apparatus involved with smoking hashish or opium, cocaine raced through Istanbul's clubs and bars. New purveyors even set themselves up in the lobbies of major hotels. The white powder was so easily concealable that a vial of it could fit inside a woman's high heel, an Istanbul magazine reported, which meant that no small number of women doing the Charleston or shimmy might also have been acting as well-dressed mules for the drug underworld.

In the past, people interested in Istanbul's seamier side had frequently focused on the one institution they understood the least: the harem. In the sultan's court, the harem was the private and highly regulated world of the sovereigns' wives and concubines. It was guarded by eunuchs and accessible only to a small stratum of men, typically the sultan and his preadult sons. Foreigners imagined a world of supine odalisques, opium pipes, and diaphanous gowns, but the imperial harem in fact was as politically complicated—and often as boring—

as the private household of any other European monarch. Personal intrigues, family disputes, and generational power struggles, not rampant seduction, were its dominant idioms. The word "harem," from the Arabic for "forbidden," was originally more architectural than sexual, referring to the portion of a Muslim home reserved for private family use (the *haremlik*), as opposed to the areas intended for meeting or entertaining guests (the *selâmlık*). Simply substituting the word *household* would probably provide a more accurate and less salacious vision of how sex, power, and private life intersected in Ottoman Istanbul, both at court and in the lesser harems of Muslim high officials and elites. "[D]elete forever that misunderstood word 'harem' . . . and dispel the nasty atmosphere which a wrong meaning of that word has cast over our lives," a prominent Ottoman feminist begged of an American journalist during the First World War.

When Sultan Mehmed VI embarked on a British warship in 1922, he took a small retinue of servants with him, but most of the former guards of the imperial harem—the *kara ağalar*, or black eunuchs—stayed behind. Like the *castrati* of Italian opera, these men, generally of Ethiopian or Sudanese heritage, had exchanged their sex organs for a profession that offered privilege and a certain degree of power—or, more frequently, such a transaction was forced upon them in childhood. They had been brought into slavery by middlemen on the far reaches of the sultan's domains and eventually found themselves at the epicenter of the imperial system. But in a time of changing mores and political revolution, they were out of a job. Many of them drifted into penury. They could sometimes be seen begging on the street, their elongated limbs the visible signs of prepubescent castration. "All that I have known have been big, fine-looking men, very merry and good-natured, and useful mainly to go out with the automobile as a kind of footman. In the same capacity they stood about palace doors, preceded one into drawing-rooms, and served tea," wrote one observer. "Their day is over."

In the late 1920s, as many as fifty of these men established a mutual-assistance society to deal with their plight, setting up a headquarters in Üsküdar and exchanging information on new employment opportunities. Their old skills could be put to new uses. The harem, after all, had made them experts in propriety and politesse, and many of them spent the next several decades as museum guards, receptionists, ushers, and discreet maître-d's at Istanbul's leading restaurants. One of Sultan Abdülhamid II's eunuchs, Nadir Ağa, spent his days with retired imperial officials at the Café Lebon in Pera, speaking a painfully elegant version of Ottoman Turkish full of refined circumlocutions and interminable pleasantries. Even Mustafa Kemal reportedly employed a former imperial eunuch in his household in Ankara.

Where sexual life more closely approximated Western fantasies was in the same place those fantasies were frequently realized in the West—in brothels. As part of the empire's modernizing reforms under Abdülhamid II, an entire system of regulated brothels was introduced in 1884, replacing the informal houses and freelance prostitutes, both female and male, of earlier eras. In the past, prostitution had been seen as mainly a moral problem, one best dealt with via punishments meted out by Muslim *kadıs* (judges) or through raids and banishments organized by individual neighborhoods. Now it became a social issue to be legislated by the state. Brothels were henceforth to be operated only with a government-approved license, with regular inspections by police and health officials, and concentrated in neighborhoods that had been specifically zoned for the sex trade.

This system disintegrated during the First World War. Refugeedom, foreign occupation, and desperate times combined to push women and, in some cases, children into sex work. Some were recruited by established brothel owners, while others were forced to solicit clients on the street, their oversize handbags and ribbon-covered parasols being the accepted trademarks of streetwalkers. One story—apparently true—told of a young Russian refugee who approached such a woman on the backstreets of Pera only to discover that she was both a former baroness as well as his mother.

After 1918, Allied high commissions set about reestablishing a formal system of brothel licensing and inspections, essentially re-creating some of the legal framework that had decayed at the end of Ottoman power. The French, a bit too predictably, were assigned the task of overseeing licensed brothels. They demarcated those reserved for officers and for ordinary soldiers, fixed prices in all the establishments, and arranged weekly medical inspections by French doctors. The British took a different tack. At the YMCA, an Anglican vicar organized Sunday afternoon teas designed to distract the minds of enlisted men, while women from the English community were invited along for conversation and music. (The French system, one suspects, worked rather better.)

Despite these efforts, Allied commanders were very much a product of their era when it came to the organization of sex. Regular sexual encounters for officers and men were seen to be a basic right as well as a useful tool for relieving boredom and maintaining morale. Especially for occupying armies—lodged far from home amid a tense and delicate political situation—providing opportunities for recreational sex was as much a part of a commander's job as ensuring a steady supply of food and adequate equipment. The chief problem, however, was ensuring that Istanbul's well-established industry of available sexuality did not at the same time weaken military units through illnesses acquired in the process.

Venereal disease was "rampant," General Harington reported during the occupation, and he estimated there were perhaps 40,000 prostitutes in Istanbul. A contemporary survey revealed a total of 175 brothels operating throughout the city, most concentrated in Pera and adjacent neighborhoods, with as many as 4,500 women employed there—nearly an order of magnitude smaller than Harington's figure and probably closer to the truth. In another survey, police counted 2,125 registered prostitutes, with another 979 unregistered, although "the number of women whose moral condition has changed for a variety of reasons, can be said to be in the thousands." The majority of both proprietors and prostitutes were Greek and Armenian, but it was estimated that Russians accounted for up to a quarter of the women working there. It was the occupiers, however, who were both the main clients as well as the major vectors of disease, even if plenty of Muslim men probably also availed themselves of the women's services. A two-week snapshot of hospital records in 1919 showed Ottoman soldiers mainly suffering from typhus or smallpox, while British and French troops reported two cases of typhus, one of pneumonia, six of influenza, and eighty-four of gonorrhea and syphilis.

Fortunately, there was a surfeit of doctors available to treat the problem, and their advertisements in the local press were a perfect reflection of the city's multicultural kaleidoscope of Muslim, Christian, and Jewish professionals. From his offices in Kadıköy, Dr. Isaac Samanon promised to "treat all internal and venereal maladies using the newest discoveries of Science." Drs. Mokin and Maxoud, situated in the Tünel Passage, specialized in venereal ailments as well as diseases of the skin. Dr. Ali Riza, a graduate of one of Paris's finest teaching hospitals, received patients at his clinic off the Grande Rue. Dr. A. Schwartzer, late of Petrograd, relieved the distressed "according to the latest methods." Dr. Yervant Tachdjian was available for consultations in Karaköy regarding syphilis, gonorrhea, and other genitourinary infections. Conveniently for many Allied officers, Dr. Djelal Chukri of the Clinique de Péra assisted with the treatment of venereal disease as well as female disorders at his clinic right across the street from the Pera Palace. Since the bar run by the sometime madame Bertha Proctor was just down Graveyard Street from Dr. Chukri's office—a bar that employed women whose names are recorded in history only as Frying Pan, Square Ass, Mother's Ruin, Fornicating Fannie, and Skinny Liz—it was possible for men and women to acquire a disease and be relieved of it on the same city block.

Regardless of the realities of the sex trade in the early 1920s—

relatively small, geographically concentrated, and focused in large measure on servicing Allied soldiers and sailors—the image of Istanbul as a haven for vice and venality only grew. Ernest Hemingway and other correspondents reported on the seediness of Pera, where the mewlings of street prostitutes enticed foreign sailors to their doom. Ziya Bey, who had had some experience in New Orleans, San Francisco, and other notorious port cities, was nevertheless scandalized by what Istanbul had become. "Intoxicated sailors rock from side to side and disappear in little streets," he recalled, "where organs grind their nasal notes of antiquated French, Italian, yes, even American popular songs and where harsh feminine voices greet prospective friends in an international vernacular."

Observers were convinced that prostitution was only one part, although the most scandalous, of the continuing "white slave" trade in Istanbul. Forcible servitude had been common in the Ottoman Empire, even though the last open market for slaves, near the Grand Bazaar, had been closed down even before the abolition of slavery in the United States. In the new language of international law, however, outsiders came to decry the "trafficking" of women, a term invented at the beginning of the twentieth century. In a series of reports published in 1927, the League of Nations identified Istanbul as one of the major centers for the forced movement of women out of Europe and into the Near East. Women were being held against their will, the League said, with a wide network of brothel owners, shippers, and government officials complicit in the sex industry.

The Turkish government repeatedly protested the charges, claiming that much of the recent increase in prostitution could be blamed on the economic plight of the itinerant Russians. The government pointed to the League's own findings that any commerce in women seemed to begin and end in countries such as France and Egypt, with Istanbul serving only as an unfortunate pass-through. Even under the Ottomans, "white slavers" had been regularly deported from the city, and police records showed most of them inhabiting the slippery professional world at the intersection of music-making, saloon-keeping, café-owning, and brothel-running. Officials had listed one deportee's job title, for example, as "pianist/pimp." But the increasing international attention prompted republican officials to act more decisively. In 1930, a government directive prohibited the opening of new brothels and placed the administration of licensed houses under the care of the police. A round of raids and closings followed. The writer Fikret Adil dated the decline of Istanbul's jazz scene to the initial shuttering of the free-form sex trade after the republic's new edict, and he probably had a point—an analytical one if not a moral one.

Three years later, the government backed away from an outright ban and issued a new directive that created a state bureaucracy to oversee the licensing, inspection, and regulation of brothels in the city. "Most of the people in our country are, in terms of culture, still quite primitive," President Mustafa Kemal declared at the time. "The opening of brothels shall be permitted where necessary and according to law, and it is thus necessary that prostitutes be regulated." The venues that were blessed as the new sites of acceptable vice were largely in the same places as during the Allied occupation, a fact that deepened the divisions between the old city south of the Golden Horn and Pera to the north. Travelers from Evliya Çelebi forward had taken for granted that the former was the domain of propriety and Islamic virtue while the latter was the realm of experiment and abandon. Rather than knitting together the former imperial capital, the new republic's drive to modernize social and sexual life actually reinforced the canyon separating the two worlds on both sides of the water. Having a part of the city where anything goes had served the Ottomans well, and in a newly modernizing republic, Pera was beginning to play an even greater role as both the designated red-light district and the avant-garde of popular culture.

That connection certainly continued into the interwar years and beyond. The mutual parasitism of nightlife and vice was in essence little different in Istanbul from that in any large city. To anyone expecting a certain version of Islamic propriety in a country overwhelmingly Muslim by religion and cultural orientation, the enduring affection in Turkish popular culture for Istanbul's drag queens, its famous madames, and its professional roués can come as a shock. Even today, family-friendly eateries share alleyways with transvestite prostitutes who toss down joking hellos from the windows of their second-story aeries.

Pious Turkish Muslims, by contrast, came to see the source of Istanbul's loose behavior and pragmatic ethics as, in one form or another, aliens—at first the occupying Allies, then the refugee Russians, then the local Christians and Jews who, despite the shift in property ownership toward Muslims, still staffed the gin joints and cabarets north of the Golden Horn. Turkish nationalists tended to share that view, seeing Istanbul as a "Byzantine whore"—a common label for the city—that had offered itself up to the occupiers while patriots were dying to save the rest of the country from the Hellenes.

But an underground transformation was happening as well. The very values that many Istanbullus had long taken for granted—a certain cultural openness; an ability to embrace religious conviction and moral license at the same time; and a belief that modernity actually demanded a tolerance for raunchiness—were being written into the informal codes of public behavior then emerging in republican Turkey. In fact, unlike in the past, when the business of public entertainment had been dominated by European performers or down-and-out Russians, a new generation of native Istanbullus was emerging to record the city's darker side in song.

"THE PAST IS A
WOUND IN MY HEART"

Istanbul jazz: A four-piece band, probably in the 1920s, with the female vocalist using a megaphone, a typical amplification device of the period.

THERE IS NO WELL-DEVELOPED field of study called sonic history, but the changes in the audible world would have impressed themselves on anyone living in Istanbul in the interwar years. The first automobile in the city's history had been exhibited in a showroom window on the Grande Rue during the reign of Abdülhamid II and attracted crowds of spectators for months, but now the vroom and sputter of motorcars filled the streets and alleyways. A trolley clanged its way up the Grande Rue. A horn announced the approach of a pilot boat on the Bosphorus. A train screamed as it came around the bend toward Sirkeci station. The low buzz of an airplane's propeller droned overhead.

"At Pera, where I live, a perfect inferno of music is let loose from sunset until two o'clock in the morning," said Marthe Bibesco, a Romanian princess and society maven. She watched weary-faced men and women drag themselves beneath the gaslights from bandstand to bandstand like a flock of sheep. Rival concerts were struck up downhill on the appropriately named Tomtom Kaptan Street, while phonographs wailed from open windows and organ-grinders passed by on the street below. As the night wore on, shouts drifted up from the harbor when sailors were bounced out of bars and made their way back to ship.

Istanbul was, in a way it never had been before, loud. Music spilled from clubs. The sirens of ambulances, military automobiles, and fire engines—a novelty introduced during the Allied occupation—shrieked and howled. "They exasperate and deafen," said an editorial in the *Orient News* in 1919, "but they are probably not so effective in clearing the way as the ordinary horn." Messages and annoyances that had been delivered by the naked human voice—the curses of a frustrated *hamal* or the insistent solicitations from a vendor in the Spice Bazaar—competed with sounds made from afar and conveyed through new technologies. It was now possible for Istanbullus to feel themselves intimately acquainted with people they had never met.

That change was evident in an industry that genuinely took the city by storm in the 1920s. Movies had been screened since the turn of the century, but they were mainly time-fillers between stage acts, one-reel shorts that could be cast on a wall or a makeshift screen while actors were changing costumes or assembling in the wings. Istanbul had its own well-established street theater and an indigenous form of kinetic art, the famous *Karagöz*, in which a puppeteer cast the shadows of flat, semitransparent figures onto a backlit screen. Especially popular during Ramadan and other holidays, *Karagöz* held its own against film until the First World War, when the first permanent movie venue—little more than a converted coffeehouse, in fact—opened opposite the British Embassy off the Grande Rue. In short order, the city's elite politicians, businessmen, and military figures came out to see first-run films, often imported German or French productions. Men and women were kept chastely separate by a partition, but mixed crowds became more common during the occupation years. The venues were still rough coffeehouses that might double as bars and were generally unsuited to the genteel public. "There are a lot of 'movie' shows," reported Billy Fox-Pitt, the Welsh Guardsman, "but they all look pretty bug-ridden!"

Proper cinemas soon sprang up around the city, however. Istanbullus could see French, Italian, and American films, distributed by companies such as Fox, Paramount, and MGM, at any number of often ornate and inviting establishments—the Melek, the Alhambra, the Magic, the Artistique, or the enormous Glorya, seating 1,400 people and opened in November 1930. By the beginning of that decade, the city had thirty-nine cinemas offering both silent films and talkies.

The huge popularity of imported films—and the lucrative job of distributing them—meant that developing a local film industry took time. The first talkie in Turkish, *On the Streets of Istanbul*, appeared in 1931, created by the firm that would become one of the principal film producers in the early republic, the İpekçi brothers. Migrants from Salonica, the five brothers had owned a prominent department store in the Eminönü neighborhood before moving into the cinema business. *On the Streets of Istanbul* was crude, a romp about two men in love with the same woman, and it owed its soundtrack to Paris, where the film was produced, but its popularity did help finance a new Istanbul-based company. Two years later, İpek Film debuted its first locally produced talkie, *A Nation Awakes*. Directed by Muhsin Ertuğrul and with a score by the noted composer Muhlis Sabahattin, the film was a hyperbolic account of the occupation period, with Senegalese infantry-men molesting Muslim girls and Allied soldiers bayoneting Turks in their beds. For the first time, Istanbullus, and Turkish citizens in general, could see a sound-enhanced version of their own recent history flashing before them on the screen. Its impact on popular memory was immense. When later generations of Muslim Istanbullus looked back on the occupation, the uninvited gropings of French African soldiers became a common refrain, even though few people of the era probably ever encountered a Senegalese rifleman at all.

As in other parts of the world, film was emerging as an important medium for communicating exactly the messages that states wanted to get across—the duty of patriotism, the lineaments of civic virtue, the demands of national loyalty—but audiences inevitably voted with their pocketbooks. Tickets were reasonably expensive, as much as a quarter of an ordinary laborer's daily wage, so visits to the cinema had to be worthwhile. Distributors seemed to understand that Istanbullus preferred exactly the same kind of content as their counterparts in western

Europe and the United States. A detailed survey of first-run films in the summer of 1932 revealed the range of Istanbul's viewing preferences: 96 percent of films showed characters using alcohol, 74 percent had a plot concerned with wealth or luxury, 70 percent centered on a love affair, 67 percent had actresses clad in suggestive clothing, 52 percent showed passionate romance, and 37 percent featured sexy dancing. Most of the movies—63 percent—were also determined to have an implausible plot.

Cinemas, like the city overall, were noisy, with people reading the subtitles aloud, standing up, walking out, stamping their feet to the musical score, or arguing with the main character. They were places where all of Istanbul's social classes could, in theory, come together. That was a novel phenomenon that took some adjustments. In the past, most public gathering places in the city had made clear distinctions in terms of rank, with preferred positions or the best seating awarded not just to those who could afford it but also to those whose family ties and government station placed them above the hoi polloi. The Otto-man Turkish language had a multitude of ways of expressing rank, and that hierarchy was made concrete every time two of the sultan's subjects happened to meet in the same place. But in a democratizing, republi-can city, this way of handling things was on the way out.

A widely reported legal case confirmed the transition. In March 1928, three assistant public prosecutors—Baha, Nesuhi, and Midhat—presented themselves at the Opera Cinema and demanded to be admit-ted, presumably free of charge, to the film then playing there. They further demanded to be seated in a box, the only location they believed appropriate to their position as government officials. The proprietor, Cevad, refused. A heated altercation ensued. The police were eventu-ally called, and Cevad was arrested for insulting the prosecutors and obstructing them in the performance of their official duties. The Istan-bul press came to Cevad's defense, pointing out how ludicrous the charges were and objecting to the existing practice of requiring cinema owners to reserve box seats for high officials. The next month, Cevad stood trial. Given that he was going up against three government men, his prospects looked slim. Much to everyone's surprise, however, he was acquitted. One of the pushy assistant prosecutors was removed from his post, and Cevad reported to the press that he intended to sue all three. Cinemas had become one of the republic's great equalizers.

Movie houses were both public spaces and private ones, which is why Cevad believed there was no reason for him to cave to the demands of petty bureaucrats. The element of privacy was also important to people who went there precisely because they wanted to hide. The traditional separation of the sexes had never been an obstacle to determined lovers, even under the Ottomans, but with the rise of dark and comfortable cinemas, there was now a new environment in which the amorous could meet. Depending on their layout and the opportunities for concealment, certain cinemas became well known as rendezvous zones. Those with balconies and closed boxes were the most desirable, especially when tickets were discounted during matinees. After painstaking research in the six leading cinemas, one observer concluded that nearly all the audiences "contained couples who were ostentatiously love making and in many cases kissing and making obvious advances to each other." The average number of amorous couples at each performance was determined to be just over six, while the total number for the twenty-seven surveyed performances was 177. In three cases, "professional women"—that is, prostitutes—were reportedly involved.

The popularity of Western films made Istanbul one of the first destinations outside the major European capitals that came onto the touring agenda of movie stars. Greta Garbo and Betty Blythe (one of the first mainstream actresses to appear on screen in a near-nude scene) made visits to the city, as did Charles Boyer and Marie Bell, both of whom were already famous for their performances with French stage companies. When Josephine Baker made a short personal appearance at the Glorya, the press seemed less worried about the content of her famously risqué performances than thrilled that another celebrity had come to town. Predictably, seeing these stars of stage and screen in the flesh affected the fashion sense and social aspirations of young people. The same report that counted up kissing couples in darkened cinemas also observed that girls in Istanbul could now be neatly divided into three types: sporty, intellectual, and "movie," with the last of these typically appearing on the Grande Rue dressed like their favorite film stars.

Unlike stage acts, however, film had the power not only to bring audiences into a performance venue but also to keep their attention long after they had left. People didn't just watch films. They could imagine themselves inside the screen—having a passionate affair, whistling a signature tune, twirling through the lobby of a grand hotel. "For a city of its size and cosmopolitanism Constantinople is one of the most poorly equipped in the world for satisfying the aesthetic cravings of its population," reported a foreign resident in 1923. But in relatively short order, film, popular songsheets, and recorded music were all within easy reach. Virtually any upper-class Muslim or non-Muslim family had long considered a phonograph to be an essential piece of parlor furniture, and after the arrival of the White Russians, the city was awash in the devices. Victrolas with large metal listening horns were dumped on the market by Russian families who had spirited them out of Crimea as part of their valued belongings. By the early 1920s, they could be had for as little as twenty to thirty lira, easily within reach of many families.

Throughout the decade, importers brought in more and more machines, and at music shops along the Grande Rue—Max Friedman's, the Papadopoulos Brothers, Sigmund Weinberg's—the proprietors found a ready market for mechanical players, recorded disks, and printed music from Europe and the United States. Pirated sheet music became such a large-scale industry that Western embassies increasingly regarded Istanbul as one of the prime offenders in the violation of intellectual property rights. Barely had a dance tune made it onto the market in New York or Paris than a low-priced version could be picked up in Pera.

The advent of international stardom, home entertainment, and recorded sound transformed street life in Istanbul. It also created a new set of careers. In the past, the fame of professional musicians had been limited by geography. Musicians might be highly regarded in a particular neighborhood or sought out for a wedding or other celebration across town, but national or international acclaim was hard to imagine. Now an audience could love someone they had never met and cry at a song they had never heard performed live. Music also came to be divided into clear genres, each with its own artists, fans, and expert critics: a folk song, or *türkü*, from Anatolia; a lyrical air, or *şarkı*, based on Ottoman classical music; a *kanto* that emerged from everyday urban life and mixed in melodies and tonalities from the West.

Turks were eagerly borrowing forms of public entertainment from Europe. New words flowed easily into spoken Turkish, especially from French and English. A young man could spend an evening at a *gardenparti* while being served by a *garson* and imagine himself a member of the *burjuazi* before relieving himself at the *pisuvar*. In the late 1920s, ordinances proscribing signs in foreign languages did little to prevent Turkish businesses from simply altering the spelling without ruining their own reputation. That is why so many of the famous clubs and restaurants of the era had names that seemed utterly nonsensical in Turkish until you pronounced them phonetically: the Türkuvaz (or *Turquoise*), the Rejans (or *Régence*), the Roznuvar (or Rose Noire), the Mulenruj (or *Moulin Rouge*).

Turks also adopted a way of describing a feeling. It was now possible to remember, even pine for, a specific and imagined world at the exact moment when it seemed to be slipping into the irretrievable past. There was little that was Ottoman about these memories, at least not in the sense of thinking wistfully about sultans, harems, and the recumbent life of pashas and beys. Its themes were, rather, a northerly breeze on the Bosphorus, a furtive love, an old wooden house, sheep on a high meadow, or a faraway city to which it was impossible to return.

Turks borrowed yet another French word and called the whole thing *nostalji*—nostalgia. It was the stock-in-trade of three musicians who came to embody the sonic landscape of a changing city.

Roza Eskenazi, Hrant Kenkulian, and Seyyan were all members of the last generation of Istanbullus to call themselves subjects of the sultan. They never shared a stage, and at the time they were born—at some point between about 1895 and 1915; they were coy about, or ignorant of, their actual birth dates—the social dividing lines within Ottoman society would have defined the directions and possibilities available to them. Roza was Jewish, Hrant an Armenian, and Seyyan a Muslim, and had it not been for the collapse of the Ottoman Empire, their lives might have been mapped out mainly within the confines of those religiously defined communities.

But in the early Turkish Republic, their reputations were deeply intertwined. If you knew one, you probably knew all three. What they had in common was an ability to encapsulate loss and longing in a single vocal phrase or pluck of a string. In their own ways, they had a better claim than many artists to capturing the essence of an era—a time when coming to Istanbul, or leaving it, was the defining journey for hundreds of thousands of old Ottoman subjects and new Turkish citizens.

Roza Eskenazi was a native Istanbullu, the daughter of a poor Jewish rag merchant. While still a girl, she found herself caught up in the movement of refugees and opportunity-seekers occasioned by the Young Turk revolution and the Balkan Wars. At roughly the same time that the family of the photographer Selahattin Giz was moving from provincial Salonica to the Ottoman capital, Roza's family set out in the opposite direction, toward a city where Jews were the single largest ethnic and religious group in a mix that included Greeks, Turkish-speaking Muslims, Bulgarians, and others. For a Jewish family looking to move up in the world, resettling in Salonica was a reasonable idea. Roza's father seems to have found work in a textile mill, her mother as a domestic servant, and Roza grew up amid the street life of a city that was in many ways Istanbul in miniature—a cosmopolitan port, Muslim in its political identity, but where mosques shared space with Sephardic synagogues and Greek Orthodox churches in the maze of small streets and avenues winding down to the Aegean Sea.

The family remained there even after the Hellenic kingdom assumed formal control of the city in 1912, but five years later, an enormous fire reduced much of Salonica's docklands and lower city to ashes. Jewish neighborhoods near the port were especially affected, and families had to think hard about whether, and where, to start over. Roza's talent as a singer was noticed while she was still a girl, and through marriage and motherhood, she seems to have nursed the desire to appear on the stage. In the early 1920s, by then a young widow, she moved to Athens and began to work the cabaret circuit. She teamed up with Greek and Armenian musicians, some of them newly arrived "exchangees" from Turkey or migrants from the charred ruins of Salonica. She was already developing her signature style: the rough-hewn and smoky voice, the freewheeling sense of meter, the lyrics that seem to be pronounced with a cigarette hanging from her lips. Plump and almond-eyed, with a shock of curly hair oiled into dark waves, Roza quickly made a name for herself in Athens, but she owed her musical essence to the cities of the Turkish coast, to Istanbul and especially Smyrna, the homeland of the musical genre known as *rebetiko*.

The Greek word *rebetiko* has no clear derivation, but even at the start of Roza's career, anyone in her audience would have known what it meant. It was the torch song of the urban gangster, the lyrical reminiscence of a down-and-out hustler, the soundtrack of a world in which people overspent in poverty and sometimes killed the person they loved the most. It was an Aegean version of the blues, sung in both Greek and Turkish, with hashish dens standing in for American juke joints and the Mediterranean coast taking the place of the Mississippi Delta. *Rebetiko* had been brought to Greece by the people displaced in the great emptying of Smyrna in 1922. Roza had never experienced this world directly; she was an Istanbullu, after all, and was probably only a teenager when she left the Ottoman capital. But she was on the leading edge of westward migration out of the faltering empire. In both Salonica and Athens, she was surrounded by Greeks, Armenians, and Jews who had left everything behind in cities that were now part of a new and foreign republic.

Roza's genius lay not in the quality of her voice. She had the odd habit of speaking in falsetto and singing in a solid alto. Her voice sounds so much like a clarinet, slightly nasal and pinched, that it is easy to forget that the instrument appears in only a few of her recordings. Unlike classically trained singers, her sense of pitch is often approximate, even in an Eastern musical tradition that prizes microtones and unusual modes. But she was unrivaled in her ability to reflect the experience of immigrants still totaling up the lives and fortunes they had lost. It is not too much to say that she had become, by 1930 or so, the truest voice of the Greek diaspora, and as she toured the world—even returning for a string of concerts in Istanbul after the Second World War—her fame only grew. By the time of her death in 1980, she had lived not only through the real birth of *rebetiko* as a concert genre—rather than something to be heard only in dives and *meyhanes*—but also through its second life in the folk revival of the 1960s. She could make people wish they could fly across the sea, leaving behind everything new and settling back into a half-forgotten past. "My soul, that's enough now," she sang, "leave my body / don't make me suffer / give up your hope."

Rebetiko sounds improvised and loose, but it actually owes a great deal to the musical scales and structure of Ottoman classical music. It is intentionally impure, a product of multiethnic cities and mixed urban neighborhoods. The vocal slides and bravura wailing repeat many of the scales and tonalities that would have been familiar to performers and composers who staged command performances for the sultan and other dignitaries in ages past. Musical styles never stay inside their proper lines; they jump over into new and unexpected venues.

The instrument that became the vehicle for these creative transgressions was also the mainstay of the small band that typically backed Roza Eskenazi. It is an eleven-string, fretless instrument called an oud, or *ud* in Turkish. Its closest equivalent is the Western lute. The lute is an eccentricity, a bulbous-backed and short-necked oddity today found mainly in ensembles specializing in Renaissance court music or Shakespearean love ballads. But the oud has a vibrant and widespread, at times even fanatical, following all the way from Morocco to Iran. Children take classes in it. Old men pick it up as a retirement project. Pop stars compete for deals with renowned players who might sit in on a recording session. It is in no sense a folk instrument, nor is it just a curiosity of "world music," a catchall and essentially meaningless category. Its sound is something that hundreds of millions of people across the Muslim world and beyond find instantly familiar.

Among professional as well as amateur oud players, there is no more recognizable name than that of Hrant Kenkulian, or Udi Hrant, as he was generally known. ("Udi" was an honorific title that indicated his position as a master of the instrument.) Blind from birth, Hrant grew up in Istanbul in an Armenian family who had managed to negotiate the multiple transitions from empire to occupation to republic. The massacres and starvation that had emptied parts of Anatolia of its Armenians had been less marked in Istanbul, and the dwindling of the urban community was much like the loss of Greeks—a slow draining of difference, neighborhood by neighborhood, rather than wholesale eradication. The Armenian patriarch, one of several leaders of Armenian Apostolic Christians, remained in place in the neighborhood of Kumkapı, along the Sea of Marmara, and elders within Armenians' other religious communities sought ways of shielding their flocks by demonstrating loyalty to the state. In 1933, when the Austrian writer

Franz Werfel published his famous *Forty Days of Musa Dagh*, a novel depicting the Armenian genocide, Armenian Catholics in Istanbul responded by burning the author in effigy, an attempt to win favor with the Turkish government. Even within a political system that put a premium on Turkishness, living as an Armenian was still possible, especially if one avoided politics, spoke only Turkish in public, and embraced silence as a way of dealing with the past.

Little is known about Hrant's early life, but he emerged in the 1920s as one of the city's most popular oud players, with a surprising set of innovations that expanded the limits of the instrument. He could play double-stops, or two strings at the same time, in the style of a violinist. He could pluck the strings with both his left and his right hands, and, like a guitarist, use both sides of the plectrum, sounding a note on the upstroke as well as the downstroke of his right hand. This might seem like scant reason for renown, but few people had thought of playing the oud in this way, and it was no accident that Hrant developed these techniques at a time when jazz guitarists and violinists, with their free-form styles, could be heard all along the Grande Rue.

Jazz depends on improvisation, which is why it has been described as not just a musical form but an ethical system. It demands that a player really listen to his comrades, with the bravery to step forward when he has something to say and the self-possession to know when he has said enough. It requires virtuosity but also humility. All this was a revelation to musicians such as Hrant, since they had come from a sonic world that by and large kept these virtues separate. A renowned singer might be applauded for his vocal agility or the memorization of a long musical sequence, such as the famed *hafizes* who managed to commit the entire Qur'an to melodic memory. In Turkish classical music, however, ensembles typically played in unison, with multiple instruments carrying the same melodic line and everyone playing all the time.

But Hrant was able to gather the best of these traditions and merge them with the sounds and techniques that would have swirled around him in interwar Istanbul. He was a master of indigenous improvisation, the spiraling and nearly out-of-control music called a *taksim*. Improvisations are musical one-offs, made up on the spot and by nature fleeting and daring. A good *taksim* can never be repeated note for note, because even an accomplished instrumentalist would be hard-pressed to re-create exactly the same bend of a string or precisely the same plectrum stroke. A bad one, though, can wreck a career. It is a species of instrumental music that always threatens to fall flat.

That is why listening to Hrant was both thrilling and nail-biting. He ran up the oud's neck and back down it. He plunked on the lower strings to give himself a steady bass line while laying down a cascade of high notes above. He had rivals among the city's oud players, but no one developed quite the international following that Hrant enjoyed. He toured abroad and, after the Second World War, recorded some of his work in live sessions in New York. Like Roza Eskenazi, he was a multilingual artist, easily moving between Turkish and Armenian and composing his own songs in both languages. He still appeared regularly in Pera nightclubs until his death in the late 1970s.

There was nothing unusual about a world in which a Greek-speaking Jew became the voice of the Greek diaspora or a blind Armenian could revolutionize the playing of an instrument that Turks, Arabs, and Persians all think of as their own. People always somehow manage to lead messier lives than nationalists would like. Artistic genius depends on that fact. What was truly new in this era, however, was not just the emergence of widely known artists but rather the appearance of a very specific type of one: a Muslim woman, her hair and face uncovered, performing before a paying and mixed-gender audience.

Muslim women were studying in theater schools in Istanbul already at the end of the First World War, but a city ordinance in 1921 prevented them from appearing on stage. It was not until eight years later that the first female actress, Afife Jale, took part in a stage play, and even then it was only as a stand-in for an Armenian actress who had fled the country. After that point, however, Turkish Muslim women took to the stage and began to create their own versions of musical styles, from classical to cabaret, which had previously been the purview of minority artists or foreign touring companies. Local singers competed to be the first to indigenize an international musical style, to make a borrowed object into a rooted and Turkish one. The first to do it for the tango was Seyyan.

Like many female performers of the day, she was known only by her given name, with perhaps the title "Hanım," or Madam, suffixed to it. With her flapper bob and kohl-lined eyes, Seyyan was among the earliest singers to reject classical styles in favor of her own interpretation of Western forms. The Turkish Republic was obsessed with trumpeting its modernity by seeking the help of leading practitioners in a variety of fields, especially music. The composer Paul Hindemith arrived in 1935 to set up the first national conservatory; the next year, Béla Bartók was invited to collect Anatolian folk songs and render them into symphonic form, much as he had done in his native Hungary. But while classically trained and an accomplished concert performer herself, Seyyan Hanım developed an interest in tango, which had made its way to Istanbul following the same path that had brought the foxtrot and the shimmy to dance halls over the previous decade. In 1932, she began to debut a tune by Istanbul composer Necip Celal and lyricist Necdet Rüştü that was quickly labeled the first of its genre, a truly original and certifiably Turkish tango.

The song had an over-the-top title—"The Past Is a Wound in My Heart"—and the words were pure melodrama:

> I, too, suffered from love.
> My life was destroyed because of this love.
> I knew that the price of this love
> Was my youth slipping away. . . .
> Finally I fell and drowned

In the green sea of her eyes. . . .
My heart became a ruined land.

But in Seyyan's hands, the song became something more: a simple and heartrending recollection of loss and regret. She ended each of the lines with an upward lilt of her warbly falsetto, hanging there like an outstretched hand, before sliding down to the repeated chorus: "The past is a wound in my heart / My fate is darker than my hair / The thing that makes me cry from time to time / Is this sad memory." A piano provided the backing chords and rhythm, while a violin repeated her vocal line, a nod to the classical tradition of multiple players plodding through a melody in unison.

It was derivative, of course, a style that owed more to Buenos Aires than to Istanbul, but the melody and lyrics were an immediate sensation. "The Past," as it was known, became her signature tune. In a fleeting song, barely three minutes long, she managed to crystallize a set of familiar feelings—that you carried your past with you, that you could change your home without changing your condition, that some journeys never really come to an end. And since "The Past" was also at base a dance tune, Seyyan had pulled off the remarkable feat of helping an audience hear the past while also seeing it enacted before them, a man and woman intertwined, rooted in place for a moment and then propelling themselves somewhere new, a memory floating on the dance floor.

Roza, Hrant, and Seyyan were part of a vibrant and fast-moving world of popular artists in interwar Istanbul and in its urban diaspora. Given changing tastes, demographics, and politics, their fame was sometimes eclipsed by that of other performers. Connoisseurs differed on the ranking of Turkey's greats. The real queen of the stage was perhaps

Safiye Ayla, a Muslim who is usually acknowledged as the first female singer to perform for President Mustafa Kemal. Steeped in both Ottoman classical music and Anatolian folk idioms, she helped create a taste for wistful laments about village love and long caravans, with an essential sweetness and modernity to her voice that is unmatched in Turkish music. The sisters Lale and Nerkis, Muslim immigrants from Salonica, helped revive Ottoman classical music and fuse it with Western-style operatic forms. Yorgos Bacanos, a Greek oud player born near Istanbul, rivaled Hrant as a player and probably surpassed him in technical proficiency on the instrument. Each of these artists is well known to the cognoscenti of Middle Eastern music. They are genuine obsessions to a relatively small band of aficionados, who keep their memory alive, update their Wikipedia entries, and one-up each other in Internet chat rooms. Their tunes can still silence a boisterous bar crowd in Istanbul today. But the fact that their music survived at all is an accident of history and a unique product of Istanbul's age of jazz and exile.

Many of these artists were among the core group of musicians to appear on a record label known in Turkish as *Sahibinin Sesi*, the literal translation of one of the oldest and most storied labels in recording history—HMV, or His Master's Voice. HMV was marketed by the Gramophone Company, the British firm that was one of the first businesses to offer recorded music on flat records, which had gradually replaced cylinder recordings at the beginning of the twentieth century. Its trademark image—a black and white terrier, head cocked in front of the sound cone of a phonograph—is still among the world's most effective and long-lasting corporate symbols. In the early 1930s, after a string of mergers and splits in the recording industry, the company joined with a rival, Columbia Gramophone, to form the British giant EMI. Under a variety of names, the company would continue to be a powerhouse of global popular music up to the present.

HMV had been recording in Istanbul since the late Ottoman

period, part of the label's strategy of scooping up popular artists from around the world. Local singers and instrumentalists were recorded on wax cylinders, which were then translated into 78s that could be played on a variety of different gramophone brands. By the late 1920s, HMV executives realized that, with the growing music scene in Istanbul, a new generation of artists was arising whose fame could easily reach beyond local cafés and cabarets. The result was a recording boom. The company's local affiliate was headed by Aram and Vahram Gesarian, Armenian brothers who signed up virtually all of the major talent of the day.

None of this would have existed, however, had it not been for the experience of migration. The movement of Muslims to Istanbul from Salonica and other Greek and Balkan cities brought a penchant for European musical styles and a long tradition of urban folk singing. The arrival of Muslims from Anatolia brought memories of village life and the folk songs of the countryside. The departure of Greeks from Istanbul and Smyrna made *rebetiko* a genuinely transnational musical form, a style of singing fused with a sense of longing that was itself the product of the Hellenic invasion and the Turkish war of independence. HMV stepped in to record Roza Eskenazi and Seyyan Hanım precisely because there were now people inside and outside Istanbul—exiles, refugees, and migrants—who thought of the work of these artists as the background music of their own lives. They were willing to pay for the chance to hear it all again in the comfort of their living rooms.

The sounds of Istanbul cabarets, nightclubs, and dive bars now had an international influence that previous generations could never have imagined. As more people listened to the recorded music, more also tried to play it, which is why Istanbul also experienced an upsurge in pirated sheet music around the same time that HMV started releasing its new disks. Even instrument manufacturers found an increasing interest in their creations, given that the oud and other regional instruments were being grouped together with pianos and violins in the HMV recordings. Music was not just a profession but also increasingly a hobby, with amateur instrumentalists and record collectors specializing in Istanbul's unique amalgam of classical music, jazz, tango, and other styles. In the case of one family of instrument-makers, the heightened interest in these artistic products helped create Istanbul's first truly global musical brand.

The Zildjians were a family of Armenians whose roots in the city went back centuries. Over time they had developed what can only be called a microniche market. Since the early seventeenth century, they had been the principal supplier of cymbals to Ottoman military bands. (The surname was simply an Armenianized version of the Turkish word for cymbal-maker.) As prominent Armenians, the family was a potential target during the rolling violence of the First World War, and, unlike Udi Hrant's family, whose poverty probably allowed them to avoid deportation, the Zildjians chose to flee rather than wait for the police to knock on the door.

Some members of the Zildjian clan moved to Romania; others went to the United States. During the Allied occupation, it was reasonably safe to return, and by the early 1920s, their business was again in full swing, employing about half a dozen skilled workmen in Istanbul and producing three thousand pairs of cymbals a year. Since Ottoman bands were in decline, the business now focused on the export market, and the Zildjian name rather quickly acquired a stellar reputation among cymbal-fanciers. "The [manufacturing] process is a secret one," noted a diplomatic report on the Turkish music industry, "which is said to impart a peculiar resonant quality." Later in the decade, the family patriarch, Aram Zildjian, decided to move the entire business from Istanbul to Massachusetts, where some members of the family had already settled before the war. There the firm re-created the process of transforming a brass alloy into a cymbal that rang with a clear tone and adequate volume.

The quality of the Zildjian cymbal made an almost immediate impact in the United States. The company began transforming its manufacturing style to meet the needs of jazz orchestras and small ensembles, with cymbals that were lighter and more resonant, to give a muffled stinger slap or a hi-hat shuffle. No longer just a flashy addendum to the beat, saved up and finally spent as a loud crash at the end of an orchestral crescendo or martial fanfare, cymbals became an essential punctuation mark in every phrase of a tune. It was the one piece of equipment that jazz ensembles borrowed whole cloth from military bands and perhaps the only one besides a string bass that it is nearly impossible to imagine a rhythm section without. Over time, the immigrant cymbal-makers acquired a reputation unmatched in the world of percussionists. The Zildjian name, curling over a shiny cymbal in faux-Oriental script, is still one of the most respected brands in the business.

The Zildjians were a direct link between the musical traditions of the Ottoman Empire and Istanbul's emerging jazz era, as well as ambassadors of a cultural scene that was becoming increasingly international. The hushed slap of a closed hi-hat or the zing of a ride cymbal would have been deeply familiar to two other Istanbul migrants, Nesuhi and Ahmet Ertegün. The Ertegün brothers were too young to have experienced some of the great nightspots such as Maxim or the Grand Cercle Moscovite. Both were born in Istanbul in the tumultuous era of war and revolution—in 1917 and 1923, respectively—but they spent most of their lives outside the city. Their father, Münir, was a diplomat in the service of the sultan, but, like many in his profession and social class in the early 1920s, he had to make a difficult choice about whether to continue supporting the flailing Mehmed VI or throw in his lot with Mustafa Kemal's nationalists. He chose the latter and was rewarded with two premier diplomatic posts, first in London and then, by 1935, in Washington, DC, where he served as the Turkish Republic's first accredited ambassador.

His two sons had developed a penchant for jazz while living in Europe, and they jumped eagerly into Washington's raucous music scene, pioneered by the city's foremost performer, Duke Ellington. They spent their weekend evenings along U Street, DC's version of Harlem, and took occasional trips to New York, with its reefer-filled clubs and late-night music sessions. They became avid collectors of obscure 78s, featuring black dance bands from the South or jazz singers who might have cut only one twin-sided disk in their careers. As sons of a diplomat, they had the social standing and resources to indulge their passions, and even though they were far from Istanbul, they were uniquely representative of the world that the political and cultural changes in the city had produced: a new generation of well-traveled and confident Turkish Muslims who were putting ever more distance between themselves and the old empire. At their age, Münir had worn a fez and a frock coat. His sons wore shoulder pads and saddle shoes.

Within a few years, the brothers had decided to turn their musical tastes into a business. With financial support from a family friend, in 1947 they launched their own recording label, which they called Atlantic Records. The rest, of course, is music history. The label would become one of the principal vehicles for everything from Motown to rock, from Ray Charles to the Rolling Stones, Aretha Franklin, and Led Zeppelin. Ahmet in particular was numbered among the greatest impresarios of the recording world, ever present above the mixing table with his trademark goatee and thick-rimmed glasses.

The Ertegüns were products of a moment when Istanbullus were becoming worldly, experimental, and modern in ways that would have shocked their grandparents. The Ottomans had been obsessed with catching up to the rest of Europe, but Istanbullus were now reworking global art forms to reflect their unique circumstances. They bent art to fit their own experience of kaleidoscopic cultures and reveled in the possibilities of self-invention. They were not just envying Western culture. Like Hrant and Seyyan, they were also making it. "[A] younger generation that knew not Thomas, Sultan of Jazz," wrote the *New York Times* about Frederick Bruce Thomas, the American-Russian-Turkish barkeep and clubland impresario, "is dancing steps it never recognized as anything but Turkish republican." All of that was possible only because plenty of people like the Ertegüns and Zildjians were of Istanbul but, for reasons prosaic or tragic, no longer in it.

MODERN TIMES

A group of partygoers in black tie at an Istanbul club, probably Maxim; with
Selahattin Giz second from right.

WHEN REVELERS GATHERED at the Pera Palace on New Year's Eve 1925, they were celebrating something of a first. Never before had all Istanbullus marked exactly the same hour, month, and year. A calendar change in the late empire had introduced Western-style months, at least for dating financial transactions and train schedules, but the republican government still numbered the year from the Prophet Muhammad's flight from Mecca. Greek Orthodox used the Julian calendar, which was thirteen days behind the Western, or Gregorian, one. Observant Jews followed their own lunar reckoning. Pious Muslims counted days according to sunrise, sunset, and the calls to prayer.

Guidebooks included impenetrable tables converting dates and hours from the Ottoman system to the more familiar international style. As the *Guide Bleu* explained in 1920:

Let us suppose that on August 22, for example, we wish to know the Western-style hour that corresponds to 6:45 in the Turkish system. We follow the horizontal line [on the accompanying table] beginning with the number 6 to the column marked August 22 and there we find the number 12:47. Adding 45 minutes to this figure, we have 12:92, that is, 1:32. In other words, 6:45 in the Turkish system corresponds, on August 22, to 1:32 in the Western system.

Because of the changing moment of sunrise, the calculation would be different for any other day of the year, and more than a few travelers probably found that by the time they had figured out the hour, they had to start all over again. Even during the Allied occupation, it was possible for a traveler on the Orient Express to depart Paris, arrive in Istanbul, and find a newspaper declaring that the date was half a millennium earlier than the day he left. But as streamers unfurled and corks popped, marking the start of January 1, 1926, people were stepping into both a new year and a new era. It was the first time that all Istanbullus had technically agreed on a thing called midnight.

Old clock towers erected by the Ottomans had their faces changed to reflect the Western system. New ones soon rose in outlying districts to encourage locals to reorient their days appropriately. When Turks later looked back on the early republic, the transformation of time itself seemed to be a grand metaphor for the changes initiated by Mustafa Kemal's government. The celebrated writer Ahmet Hamdi Tanpınar, for example, parodied the obsession with timekeeping in his sprawling novel *The Time Regulation Institute* (1962), in which an overenthusiastic bureaucracy levies fines for clocks that run too slow or too fast—reprimanding those who fail to keep up with the new world as well as those who get too far ahead of it.

The new clock and calendar were only one part of a long series of reforms. The institution of the caliphate had continued to exist even after the flight of Sultan Mehmed VI in 1922, but the Grand National Assembly voted to abolish the religious office altogether in March 1924. Mehmed's successor as caliph, Abdülmecid, and a few of his family members were delivered to a suburban station, placed on the Orient Express, and packed off to Switzerland. His claim to being the universal leader of Islam came to a sudden end, and with it, Istanbul's place at the center of the Islamic world. The republican government underscored the point by banning Abdülmecid's descendants from ever entering Turkey, a restriction that was kept in place for male heirs for the following half century.

The end of the caliphate resounded across the world. It sparked outrage from pious Muslims, who regarded the caliph's role as a sacred trust that no earthly power could possibly break. In Turkey, however, the steamroller of reforms, both sacred and profane, continued. In a nod toward modernizing the physical appearance of Turkish citizens, beginning in 1925 all men were required to wear brimmed hats, not the red felt fez that had become popular in the late empire. Little boys threw rocks to try to ping the old headgear off recalcitrant fez-wearers. Since the regulation did not affect any other element of clothing, for some time later Muslim men could be seen in the streets wearing a fedora with baggy Ottoman-era trousers.

In 1926 a new civil code, based on Switzerland's, replaced the empire's complex amalgam of Islamic sharia law, several varieties of Christian canon law, rabbinical decisions, royal decrees, and tribal custom. The same year, drinking liquor in public was officially permitted—although the theoretical ban had never before impeded private club owners— and buffalo-drawn carts were prohibited from Istanbul's streets. In 1928, Islam was disestablished as the state religion, and the Arabic alphabet was rejected in favor of the Latin one for writing Turkish. All over Istanbul, street signs came down, with the whirls and swishes of Arabic-style lettering supplanted by labels wholly foreign to most local Muslims. Popular photographs from the period show President Mustafa Kemal in front of chalkboards, instructing the new nation in writing and spelling.

These changes were often collectively referred to as an *inkılâp*—a revolution. Like many revolutionaries, the Kemalists had started out as reformers, seeking to save the sultanate from invaders and occupiers, until it became clear that the old system was beyond repair. But in most other ways, this was a revolution of an unusual type. The

Turks legislated their monarch out of existence without ever marching on a royal palace. They conquered no territory but their own. They embraced the idea of a parliamentary republic but just as quickly enveloped their supreme leader in a cult of personality that exceeded that of the Ottoman sultans. Mustafa Kemal's portrait appeared in every government building, and the press chronicled his every gesture and utterance. He became the father of the nation, the first citizen, and the supreme example of what a good Turk should be. Briefly married and then divorced, he had no "first lady" for most of his long tenure as president and no biological heirs, but he considered as many as seven people his adopted children. The full list of these individuals, as opposed to those merely under his express protection or patronage, is still debated today, but most of them were young women who seem to have impressed the president as especially ambitious, able, and exemplary of the new Turkish woman.

His blue eyes and charismatic personality made him one of the most swooned-over heads of state in the world. He appeared on the covers of major international magazines more often than almost any leader of his time, always dressed with a nattiness bordering on dandyism. His habits of late-night drinking and all-hours conversation gave him a reputation as a seemingly indefatigable transformer—a model for how to wrench an ancient and recondite empire into the twentieth century. Today private businesses no longer feel compelled to keep an image of him on display, but shopowners and restaurateurs might tack up a photograph of Mustafa Kemal in a bathing suit or on the dance floor, a cheeky nod to the maker of a rolling revolution that is nearly a century old and, in a way, still going. Even today, when antigovernment protesters take to Istanbul's streets, they still carry flags with his image and tie on headbands that proclaim "*Atam izindeyiz!*"—"Father, we are following in your footsteps!" It is a supreme testament to his legacy that young, middle-class urbanites can see themselves as conservative and revolutionary at the same time. They oppose the strictures of Islamic

Mustafa Kemal (center) at a New Year's Eve ball in Ankara, 1929.

morality—increasingly promoted by Turkey's religious-leaning governing party after 2003—by looking back to the traditions of the early
secular republic under Mustafa Kemal. Not even the Bolsheviks could
have dreamed of a revolution that would turn out to be so permanent.

During the independence struggle, Mustafa Kemal carried the title
of *gazi*, a kind of Islamic generalissimo, but Kemalism as an ideology
developed in ways less martial than civic and political. It contained
six pillars, symbolized by the six arrows on the flag of the Republican People's Party, the movement he founded: republicanism, nationalism, populism, secularism, statism, and revolutionism. The first five
of these principles owed a great deal to the French republican tradition, the model for the Young Turks after 1908 as well as for Mustafa
Kemal and his associates in the transition from war-making to state-
building. Turkey was not the world's first Islamic republic—that distinction belonged to Azerbaijan, which had been briefly independent
before the Bolsheviks reconquered it during the Russian civil war—

but it was nevertheless committed to building a representative government, if not a fully democratic one. For most of the interwar years, the Republican People's Party was the only legal party, and voters never directly elected their parliamentarians until more than a decade after Mustafa Kemal's death. The government was also given responsibility for guarding against any privileged role for religion, looking out for the true interests of the people, and making state institutions the engine of economic and social development.

Like other revolutionaries, Kemalists wrote their history with an eraser in hand. In the emerging story of their own triumph, their only opponents were held to be the Allies, abetted by treacherous local Greeks and Armenians. The Kemalist revolution was believed to have unfolded naturally and unproblematically across Anatolia, save for minor hiccups produced by the disgruntled and the unenlightened. The army was remembered as traipsing heroically westward from Ankara to the sea, restoring local sovereignty within Turkey's natural frontiers, which happened to coincide, more or less, with those the Ottomans controlled at the time of the Mudros armistice in 1918.

In reality, however, Kemalism was a product of—not the cause of—Mustafa Kemal's hard-won victory over a range of internal opponents. The arrows on his party's flag became principles for building a new state, but they were more importantly weapons aimed at a very specific set of interests. As a diplomatic observer noted in 1923, a partial list of Mustafa Kemal's enemies at the time included:

> All Old Turks and Sultanites.
> All the Generals who have been set aside by Kemal.
> All the deputies of the old who have not been elected to the
>   new Assembly.
> All the old C.U.P. [Committee of Union and Progress]
>   stalwarts . . . .

All those with whom Mustafa [Kemal] has quarreled or of
   whom he is jealous or who are jealous of him. . . .
All those who prefer Constantinople to Angora [Ankara]
   as the capital.
All Ulema, Imams, and Hojas [Muslim clerics]. . . .
All civilians who get no pay, all demobilised soldiers who
   have no other occupation and can find none. . . .

Anyone in Istanbul could have compiled his own similar list. The
brilliance of Mustafa Kemal's strategy lay in his ability to pick the right
opponents to use against the others. He had a knack for bringing into his
own camp some of the most thuggish warlords operating in the political
vacuum created by war and occupation. A host of colorful and ruthless
characters flowed into the ranks of the Turkish nationalists—men such
as Ali the Sword and Osman the Lame, whose guerrilla tactics targeted
political oppositionists, armed clansmen, occupation forces, and civilians alike. The Kemalists generally avoided the show trials and mass
purges that would later engulf the Soviet Union, but a smaller-scale
version of revolutionary courts, known as independence tribunals,
were established under the authority of the Grand National Assembly.
More than seven thousand people were arrested. Close to seven hundred were sentenced to death.

The government allowed occasional experiments with multiple
political parties, even though direct, competitive elections were not
held until 1950. But openness was usually followed by reaction. In the
spring of 1925, a new law on the maintenance of public order provided a reason for closing down newspapers and shuttering opposition
organizations. Small demonstrations or individual acts of dissent were
sometimes exaggerated as "rebellions," which in turn enabled crack-
downs. Communal violence that fell short of threatening the state, such
as the razing of Jewish communities by Turkish nationalists in the city

of Edirne and other parts of Thrace in 1934, was downplayed in press reporting and official discourse. Still, eighteen armed uprisings challenged the Kemalist government before the Second World War, almost all of them in eastern Anatolia. Major revolts by ethnic Kurds in the region, expressing a range of grievances from the loss of the caliphate to the withering of traditional feudal privileges, were harshly repressed. Military planes, one of them piloted by the president's adopted daughter, the aviation pioneer Sabiha Gökçen, were sent to bomb villages. Aerial attacks on Kurdish areas in the Dersim region in 1937–1938 became a kind of Turkish Guernica, a shocking bombardment of civilians under the guise of an antiguerrilla operation. The difference from the famous Spanish case, however, was that the people dropping the bombs and those hiding from them were all citizens of the same country.

One might have expected that the old imperial capital would emerge as the heartland of dissent, given that its streetscape was teeming with ancient reminders of the Islamic values the Kemalists were eagerly putting away. The revolution was, after all, everything that Istanbul wasn't—anti-imperial, forward-looking, and past-negating. But Istanbul's residents found themselves more ignored than feared. With the abolition of the caliphate, the network of local imams and religious scholars centered in Istanbul had begun to fade. The more career-savvy ones moved to Ankara, like their ambitious counterparts in government ministries, where they became part of the growing state apparatus charged not with eliminating religion but with managing it. In 1924 and 1925, the office of *şeyhülislam* was abolished, Muslim religious courts were suppressed, and the wearing of turbans and other religious garb was restricted to a few government-appointed clerics. Even then, the turbaned pious were expected to take off their headgear to salute the flag on Republic Day—October 29—a practice previously unimaginable to the devout.

The Kemalists adopted a French term, *laïcité*, to describe their conception of the new role of religion in the republic. Its Turkish equivalent—*lâiklik*—followed the French model: not separating religion from the state but, instead, actively controlling it. New state institutions were charged with governing mosques, churches, synagogues, and religious foundations. Independent sources of wealth—such as properties belonging to Greek or Armenian church authorities—were either seized or made subject to government oversight.

Although officially secular, the state privileged Sunni Islam as a true marker of Turkish nationality, regardless of an individual's actual level of religious devotion. In the alchemy of religion and identity in Kemalist Turkey, one was judged not so much by which religion one practiced—since piousness was considered a clear sign of backwardness and superstition—but rather by which religious heritage one rejected. Having a devout Sunni grandparent who might quietly complain about how much alcohol you drank was perhaps the truest marker of being both a good republican and a good Turk. "In that case we're purging the past?" asks a character in Ahmet Hamdi Tanpınar's novel of interwar Istanbul, *A Mind at Peace* (1949). "Of course," a friend replies, "but only where needed."

Religious bodies outside the Sunni mainstream, such as Sufi brotherhoods or Alevis, an offshoot of Shi'a Islam, saw their meeting houses closed down or, worse, their beliefs condemned as inimical to the state. The historic Sufi lodge, or *tekke*, just off the Grande Rue had been established even before the Ottoman conquest of Istanbul, when Mevlevi dervishes came into the city bearing the teachings of their founder, the poet and mystic Rumi. Yet it too was closed as a site of worship. Sufi leaders, or sheikhs, were arrested for subversion. Virtually any episode of violence that involved religious men or women was seen as evidence of retrograde fanatics' holding back the forces of progress.

One of Istanbul's signature manmade sounds—the *ezan*, or Islamic call to prayer—was changed, too. The call was traditionally given in each neighborhood by a muezzin, whose powerful voice would summon the faithful to prayer from the minaret of a local mosque. Those with

Men sacrifice rams on the tracks of the Taksim–Tünel trolley line in Pera, perhaps to inaugurate a new trolley car.

pleasing voices or melodic creativity were prized; those with less talent were the object of local gossip and complaints. After 1923, the task was made easier with the introduction of amplified public address systems. The *ezan* was now accompanied by the crackle and hiss of an electric microphone, a descant that floated above the proclamation of faith.

Beginning in early 1932, however, Turkish muezzins no longer chanted the Arabic words "*Allahu akbar*," or "God is great." As part of its reform program, the government mandated that the Turkish version of the phrase, "*Tanrı uludur*," be used instead, with reversions to

Arabic declared a criminal offense. The change was part of the government's broader reform program of purging public space of old imperial influences, including Arabic and Persian elements in the Turkish language. The guttural vowels and the invocation of Tanrı—the sky god of Central Asian nomads—were also nods to a nationalist fantasy: that the truest ancestors of modern Turks were the pony-riding hordes who had once thundered over the Eurasian steppe. Huge crowds gathered to hear the first call to prayer in Turkish at the Sultanahmet mosque. Five of the other largest mosques in the city followed suit. On the Night of Power—the holy evening during Ramadan that commemorates the revelation of the Qur'an—seventy thousand people were packed in and around the Hagia Sophia mosque to hear the full sequence of Islamic prayers delivered for the first time in Turkish. In the new republic, even God had been nationalized, and from morning to night, 1,200 retrained muezzins proclaimed the fact.

Kemalism leapfrogged over Istanbul like it jumped over the Ottomans. Mustafa Kemal assiduously avoided the city until well after the declaration of the republic. He arrived for the first time since the war of independence on July 1, 1927, aboard the sultan's former yacht, *Ertuğrul*. He moored at Dolmabahçe Palace, which had been transformed into a presidential residence. The streets were lined with flags. Balconies were draped with bunting. Each summer thereafter, his comings and goings were attended by invited guests and dignitaries, a secular and republican re-creation of the sultan's weekly procession to the mosque.

The yearly sighting of the president's yacht and a flotilla of smaller vessels was an event as keenly anticipated as the migration of sardines in the Bosphorus. But outside of the president's summer holidays, Istanbul and the old imperial identities it represented were put out of the new national consciousness. The republic was held to be the continuation of the Turks' natural evolution as a nation, despite the half-millennium detour through Islamic imperialism. Turkish schoolbooks taught new generations of students to see their distant ancestors as Turkic tribesmen, even if their grandfathers had actually been Salonican greengrocers or Sarajevan tailors. The "sun language theory," popular among Turkish linguists in the 1930s, posited that all human languages were descended from a Turkic ur-source. The ancient inhabitants of modern-day Turkey, from the Hittites forward, were brought into the family as well, recast as descendants of even more ancient proto-Turkic invaders from the east.

All of this entailed an act of personal and collective imagination. Muslims whose forebears hailed from Anatolia but also from the Caucasus, Albania, Bulgaria, Crimea, Greece, or other far-flung parts of the old empire suddenly transformed themselves from immigrants into indigenes. Under the Ottomans, few of these families would have dreamed of using "Turk" to describe themselves. That label was generally reserved for a country bumpkin more comfortable astride a donkey than in the sophisticated environs of Istanbul. It was a term that represented the very thing that enlightened Ottomans had despised most about their own empire—the benighted, nomadic, and fitfully loyal peasants who inhabited the darkest reaches of Anatolia. One could be a Muslim and a subject of the sultan. No one wanted to be a Turk.

Mustafa Kemal's great innovation—rooted in the theories of the writer Ziya Gökalp, the chief ideologist of Turkish nationalism—was to elevate the derogatory label into a new nationality. Living the ideals of the national revolution was meant to be a personal commitment on the part of each new citizen. "I am a Turk," pupils were eventually instructed to chant at the beginning of each day's classes. "I am honest. I am hardworking. My code is to protect those younger than me, respect my elders, and love my homeland and my nation more than myself. My quest is to rise higher and go farther. May my whole life be a gift to Turkishness." The oath was not so much a pledge of allegiance as a promise of self-improvement. Few countries have gone through revolutions whose aim was to make everything seem so deeply ordinary—making Turkey and the Turks, in other words, a nation just like any other, with their own national liberation movement, national heroes, and national language. But the core of Kemalism was precisely that: a belief that the rump empire and its multilingual, multireligious subjects needed to be dragged, one soul at a time, into modernity.

The nation was hailed as both capacious and aboriginal. Like the simple act of professing belief in one God, a Muslim of Kurdish, Circassian, or Albanian background could participate in the nation-building project with a simple declaration of faith in the new nationalism. "*Ne mutlu Türküm diyene*," said Mustafa Kemal in a speech on the tenth anniversary of the republic in 1933. "How happy is the person who says, 'I am a Turk.'" It became one of his most famous dictums, engraved on stone monuments to the president everywhere. The phrase was at the same time descriptive and cautionary. It was an honor to be a Turkish citizen—the constitution defined all Turkish citizens as Turks, regardless of religion or heritage—but it made life easier if you claimed you were a Turk in an ethnic sense as well. Even a Greek or Armenian Christian, with a bit of inventiveness and a careful silence about who her parents had been before 1923, might manage the same feat.

Turkishness—*Türklük*—became not just an identity but an entire way of being, a disembodied essence of the nation that both infused individuals and floated above them, an aspiration to self-improvement and a totem of the mythical collective will. In the past, insulting the sultan had been a crime, in the same way that most absolutist monarchies deemed *lèse-majesté* a punishable offense. Now, Turkishness took the sultan's place. Writing the wrong kind of newspaper article, making the wrong kind of comment, even wearing the wrong kind of clothes could be an insult to Turkishness, with the transgressor fined or brought up before a judge. The same offense, in altered form, has remained enshrined in Turkish law ever since.

The Ottomans had ruled an empire that was tradition-bound and dynastic, stretching from the Balkans to the border with Iran, but much of its population and wealth had lain squarely in geographic Europe: the fertile plains along the Danube River, the vineyards of upland Bulgaria, the valley pastures of southern Albania, the silver mines of Bosnia and Macedonia. The Turkish Republic, by contrast, was a country that stressed modernity and progress, but given the territorial changes created by the First World War, ninety-seven percent of the country's land area now lay in Anatolia, the heartland that was poorer and more sparsely populated than many of the regions once ruled by the sultan. The Turkish mind may have shifted west, but the Turkish state had shifted east.

For Istanbul the most important evidence of that change came in 1927. Early on the morning of October 28, a leaden calm settled over the city. Galata Bridge, normally black with pedestrians, was bare. Only a few people could be seen staring nervously from their doorways. At the Pera Palace, an American diplomat found himself held captive. "I awoke . . . to an oppressive silence; there was no sound of people on the streets, of automobile horns, or of tramcars," he reported, "and on looking out of the window I saw armed sailors patrolling the streets." For most of that Friday, Istanbul was a city of the dead.

At precisely 10:15 p.m., three cannon shots rang out. People poured from their houses and apartment buildings. Taxis rushed along the avenues. Cinemas and cafés opened, and stores threw up their shutters. Within half an hour, the Grande Rue was thronged. The din of urban life quickly returned, and Istanbullus walked about like liberated prisoners.

The whole day had in fact been meticulously planned. The Turkish government had hired a Belgian statistician, Camille Jacquart, to conduct the first-ever national census. Never before had the inhabitants of the country been systematically counted. On Jacquart's orders, copies of the census questionnaire were published in the press, along with explicit rules governing behavior. Between the zero hour of six o'clock in the morning and the all-clear cannonade in the evening, no one was allowed to leave home, even for Friday prayers. People were prohibited from helping a neighbor put out a fire, visiting shops or restaurants, traveling in cars or trains, or casting off a mooring cable in the port. Thousands of volunteer census-takers swarmed up staircases and down cul-de-sacs, urging people to do their patriotic duty and report honestly and thoroughly on their age, gender, native language, religion, infirmities, profession, nationality, and other traits.

Within a week, the initial results were in, and they were astonishing. Previous estimates had put Turkey's population at seven to nine million, but the census counted many more: some 13,648,270 people. Istanbul was revealed to have a population of a little over 690,000, with around another 300,000 people living in other parts of Thrace, the wedge of Turkish territory west of the Bosphorus. The city was smaller than it had been in the late Ottoman period; the country as a whole had lost about a quarter of its population through war-related death and disease, deportation, and migration since 1914. But Istanbul still dwarfed every other urban center in the republic. Only two cities had more than a hundred thousand people, and Istanbul's closest competitor, Izmir, was less than a quarter of its size. Ankara, already the seat of government for four years, had persuaded only 74,553 people to live there.

Journalists hailed the census as a milestone in Turkey's development. The statistical bureau had demonstrated its ability to carry out a complex feat of modern statecraft. More important, the loss of so much territory in Europe, the Levant, and the Arabian Peninsula had actually increased the Turkish component of the population. As the newspaper *Milliyet* (The Nation) claimed, the census had shown that the vast majority of the republic's citizens—11.7 million people—were "pure Turks"—that is, ethnically Turkish as opposed to Kurdish, Arab, Greek, Armenian, or another identity. That was a dubious conclusion; after centuries of empire and more than a decade of intense war and population movement, Turkey's genetic pool was a swirling mix of ancestries. But the fact that the republic had convinced so many people to claim they were Turks in an ethnic sense was a testament to the power of Kemalist nation-building.

In greater Istanbul, the census counted around 448,000 Muslims living alongside 99,000 Orthodox Christians (mainly Greeks), 53,000 Armenians, and 47,000 Jews, along with nearly 45,000 other non-Muslims. With the exception of Kurdish areas in southeastern Anatolia, Istanbul was now the only place in the entire republic with a sizable minority presence. It contained virtually all of the republic's functioning Greek and Armenian churches, its synagogues, its monasteries, its minority-language schools and presses. Armenian monuments in eastern Anatolia had been dynamited or allowed to fall into ruin, a conscious effort to erase the remnants of communities destroyed in the genocide. Greek properties along the Aegean coast were taken over by Muslim owners. Even the Kurds, with their unique languages and traditions, would eventually be classed by republican ideologues as simply a type of Turk. Less than a decade after the war of independence began, the enormous imperial legacy—the long history of multiple confessions, many languages, origins, and heritages—had been distilled into a single city.

The Kemalist project became the world's largest experiment in squeezing the entirety of modern European history—from the Renaissance to the Industrial Revolution—into a few decades. Life was accelerating, and Turks were urged to run as they built the new fatherland. National life was centered in Ankara, which had been formally announced as the new capital almost two weeks before the Turkish Republic was proclaimed. Radio broadcasting; the opera, ballet, and symphony; the most powerful newspapers; and in time the embassies of foreign governments all decamped there. New government buildings rose on wide avenues and expansive squares.

City planners in Istanbul understood the former capital's core dilemma—not how to build a city from scratch, which was already taking place in Ankara, but how to modernize a place that, as American tourists were fond of saying, just had so much history to it. While new government offices were still rising in Ankara, the Turkish government organized an international design competition to solicit proposals for solving the problem of Istanbul's future development. The French urban engineer Henri Prost was selected as Istanbul's director of urban planning. Many years of pencil sketches, scale models, and bureaucratic infighting followed, but Prost's vision was finally approved by government ministers in 1939.

Prost's plan called for cutting highways around the Grand Bazaar, demolishing most buildings along the Grande Rue, making the shores of the Golden Horn into an industrial park, and building high-rise apartment blocks along the Sea of Marmara. Half the windows in the Pera Palace were to open onto a highway interchange. Prost included green spaces in his designs, but these were by and large orderly promenades created by the bulldozing of things he considered "parasitical"— old structures deemed to be less important than an idealized image of monumental buildings defining the city's silhouette. A level esplanade designed for military processions and centered on a massive new "monument to the republic" was meant to replace the jumble of buildings around the Hagia Sophia and Sultanahmet mosques.

Prost did have the inspired idea of keeping intact the skyline of the old city, the peninsula where most of the Byzantine- and Ottoman-era architecture stands. His insistence on preservation, at least in that part of the city, secured the area against high-rise development and meant that the city's signature profile of domes and minarets, especially when viewed from the sea, would remain undisturbed. But a better place to get some idea of Prost's overall vision is Taksim Square, which was intended to serve as the new heart of the republican city. When John Dos Passos went to a cabaret near Taksim in the early 1920s, he found a Russian lady on stage doing a peasant dance, two English girls crooning in knee socks and sweaters, a troupe of Greek acrobats, and a French woman singing selections from *Lucia di Lammermoor*. In 1928, however, city planners cleaned up part of the square and created a bronze-and-marble monument to the republic's founders. One side showed Mustafa Kemal, İsmet Pasha, and other makers of the new country in astrakhan hats and the military garb of the war of independence. The other side portrayed them as modern statesmen in Western-style suits and ties. Prost's idea was not to continue with the monument-building in Taksim but rather to make way for more automobiles. What resulted was an expansive flatland of asphalt and concrete serving as a subway stop, a major road hub, and an open-air bus terminal. Until radical traffic engineering began to reshape the square in 2013, it took some bravery to cross Taksim on foot.

Prost probably would have cringed at the modern hodgepodge that his planning eventually produced, but his method of leveling and redesigning bits of the city he declared architecturally insignificant was copied by later builders. Taksim was eventually burdened with the Atatürk Cultural Center, which looks rather like the backside of a window air-conditioning unit, and the Marmara Taksim, a slightly more stylish take on a Soviet Intourist hotel. The space is saved only by the area known today as Gezi Park, a swath of green off to one side, which Prost had intended as a formal garden built on the site of an Ottoman-era military barracks that he had deemed parasitical.

The advent of the Second World War halted the full implementation of the Prost plan. Prost himself was let go as chief planner in 1951. The Grande Rue was saved, as was much of the area around the old Petits-Champs Park. After the war, however, urban improvers returned, cutting highways deep into the heart of the old city and pulling down Ottoman-era wooden houses to make way for cheap multistory apartment blocks, especially in poorer districts. Petits-Champs was gone, and the Pera Palace was hemmed in by taller buildings wrapped in reflective glass. Prost's defenders blamed the losses on the piecemeal implementation of his master plan, especially in the 1950s, an era overseen by a bulldozer-friendly prime minister, Adnan Menderes. But had the revolutionary urge to erase and rebuild been visited on Istanbul in the years when Mustafa Kemal himself was around to supervise it, one can only imagine what would have become of the architectural treasures and intimate, messy neighborhoods it still has to offer. It was not until the early 2000s that a Turkish government would turn to remaking Istanbul with something approaching Prostian zeal—and then without Prost's redeeming virtue of preserving the ancient skyline.

Modernity and civilization were the watchwords of the early republic, and the local press took great offense when it learned of representations of the city that failed to remark on its sophistication and seriousness. A large ball organized for tourists in 1929, for example, featured prostitutes doing belly dances around braziers, waterpipes, and divans. The newspaper *Milliyet* condemned the affair and urged the city administration to put a stop to such faux-Ottoman frivolity. "Presenting the Turkish nation, which has made its customs conform to those of the most civilized occidental nations, in such an unfavorable light is an insolent attack," an editorial thundered. "The republican police and republican laws are made to deal with whoever admits having organized such a money-grabbing masquerade." The problem was not sexual license but rather the sense that dredging up the past was an affront to the values of progress and renewal promised by Kemalism. Nowhere were these values more fervently preached than in the campaign to transform the lives of Turkish women.

BEYOND THE VEIL

Two women jump rope in an impromptu session
on an Istanbul street.

For Muslim women, the creation of the secular state was often said to have ushered in liberation from the double yoke of tradition and religion. "The shape of social life changed," recalled Mîna Urgan, a prominent Turkish writer and academic. "Women were no longer kept at home. They could go out with boys, have fun together, eat and drink together."

Unlike the fez for men, Islamic head coverings for women were never fully banned, although official discourse discouraged them as retrograde and uncivilized. Headscarves and veils were not allowed inside state institutions—which included everything from schools to government ministries—and within short order, Istanbul's Muslim elite adopted styles of female dress little different from those in other parts of Europe. Window screens, which had secluded many Muslim women from public view, finally came down in 1930 as part of a national hygiene law to let more light and air into dank interior apartments. That reform alone ended what must once have been a brisk clandestine economy. Travelers' accounts of surreptitious visits behind the screened-off world of feminine Istanbul are so numerous that the Ottoman city must have enjoyed a roaring trade in harem tourism—in reality, probably visits to disguised brothels—for gullible Europeans.

All these practices had already begun to fade by the beginning of the twentieth century, however. The full seclusion of women under the Ottomans was largely a middle- and upper-class Muslim phenomenon, as was the wearing of elaborate veils or other coverings. The types and sizes of veils were matters of adornment and style, not just a marker of religious piety. Women from rural or working-class backgrounds might wear long scarves that could be pulled over their faces in the presence of male strangers, but the full-length *çarşaf*—a large, circular piece of fabric covering the head, face, and clothing—was generally a fashion of the wives and daughters of the elite. The idea of Muslim women being carted through the streets in servant-borne sedan chairs, or gesturing coyly through their window screens at passersby, were likewise already part of the distant—and largely imagined—past.

But the real innovation under Mustafa Kemal was to formalize women's rights in a system of legal equality, in theory making Muslim women genuine partners in building the republic. The new Swiss-inspired civil code abolished polygamy, ended the preferential treatment of men in the inheritance of property, and affirmed a woman's right to divorce her husband. Public harassment was made a criminal offense, and in 1930 women were given the vote in municipal elections. Four years later, the franchise was extended to elections for the Grand National Assembly, and eighteen women were soon elected to the legislature—more than double the number in the US Congress at the time.

Legal rights for women were secured, but the emerging state was traditionalist when it came to their real place in public life. Women were by and large written into the new republic's history as a group but written out of it as individuals. When they did appear, it was usually as cardboard heroines, women who sacrificed themselves for the nationalist cause or took up patriotic professions in service to the republic. Newspapers were filled with stories of female firsts. The first Muslim female lawyer to appear before a court in Istanbul, Beyhan Hanım, approached the bar in 1928 and was later elevated to a judgeship. The first surgeon, Suad Hanım, was accredited in 1931, and the first pharmacist, Belkıs Hanım, accepted her license the same year. The first wrestler, Emine Hanım, stepped forward in 1932 to take on any male competitor who dared accept her standing challenge. The first female tramway conductors did not appear until 1941, but a satisfied public deemed them more polite than their male counterparts.

Like much of Kemalism, however, the world did not change suddenly with the proclamation of the republic, nor did the gains achieved by women erase old social habits. Even in the last days of the sultans, Istanbul women tended to marry later, have fewer children, and divorce more readily than in other Islamic societies. Women were already very much part of social space. They attended public entertainments. They could be seen transacting business in the arcades off the Petits-Champs or dining in the Pera Palace restaurant. By 1920, more than a third of the employees in Pera's department stores were women, and even in the more conservative areas south of the Golden Horn, women accounted for nearly twenty percent of sales clerks. Many of these women were Christians and Jews who led lives little different from those of women in other European cities at the same time, but sizable numbers of Muslim women were clearly in the public eye as well. Tramcars accommodated both genders (even though curtains separated the men's section from the women's), and during the Allied occupation, Muslim men and women appeared together in theaters, cinemas, and other gathering places.

The first women's organizations had been formed soon after the Young Turk revolution, part of the general upsurge in liberal and reform-oriented groups that sprang up in the city in the relative freedom afforded by the restoration of the constitution. Like their counterparts elsewhere in Europe, these associations often sought to liberate women by elevating them. Their leaders—chiefly from prominent Ottoman families—regarded increasing literacy and opening a new range of educational opportunities as essential to preparing women to take a more active role in public life.

Educated Muslim women were involved in the Turkish Hearth

movement, a set of discussion clubs on culture and current affairs that became the nucleus of anti-occupation sentiment after 1918. Their names appeared as bylines in a range of publications on politics, international affairs, education, and other topics, while specialized journals such as *Kadınlar Dünyası* (Women's World) featured work by women essayists and artists. Mass rallies in 1919 and 1920, called to protest the Hellenic occupation of Smyrna and the Allied presence in Istanbul, featured female speakers prominently calling on their Turkish brothers to oppose the dismemberment of their country.

After the First World War, the expansion of women in the workforce probably had as much to do with a fundamental demographic crisis as with the liberal ideas of Turkish nationalists. By the time of the 1927 census, a million women across the country were widows, and in Istanbul a third of all married women had lost their husbands to war, disease, or other causes. More women became the principal breadwinners in their families than at any other time in Turkish history, largely as a result of grueling violence and refugee flight. Women of all classes and religions were taking up public space, confidently and deliberately, long before they were given express permission to do so by the government. Nezihe Muhidin, one of the major organizers of the women's rights movement in Istanbul and founder of the Turkish Women's Union, even attempted to form a women's political party in the summer of 1923. It was technically the first party created in Turkey, founded several months before Mustafa Kemal's own Republican People's Party. The administration refused to register it.

Turkish politicians sometimes claimed that women themselves were the main obstacles to female progress. Burdened by their own narrow horizons, they were simply failing to take up the new opportunities afforded them by changes in the civil code. "The duty of Turkish Women's Societies is primarily to persuade the great majority of Turkish women to accept the rights that have already been granted to them," said *Milliyet* in an editorial in 1927. "These societies, prior to occupy-

Istanbul women walking near the Galata Bridge, with the
Yeni (New) mosque in the background.

ing themselves with the organization of political life and in struggles against men, should interest themselves in other women and should combat the primitive state of mind shown by them."

It was an argument that reappeared with frequency: The advances women had made were the beneficent gift of the state; the deficiencies were of their own making. The republic even had a semiofficial voice dedicated to making precisely that point. Afet İnan, one of Mustafa Kemal's adopted daughters, became the chief female spokesperson for the one-party government. Like so many other republican elites, she was born in Salonica and studied in Istanbul's French schools, later working as a teacher in the city of Bursa. Taken under Mustafa Kemal's wing in the mid-1920s, she studied at the University of Geneva in the 1930s and, as a practicing sociologist, turned her academic training toward crafting the president's personality cult. She remained one of the principal expounders of Kemalism as a coherent political ideology and a major codifier of the official history of the revolution's contribution to women's liberation.

Other women were not so fortunate. Nezihe Muhidin's women's organization was closed down in the 1930s as part of the general retrenchment against independent civic associations. But even then it was still possible to wonder whether the republic might take a different path from the one laid out for it in the ever-narrowing vision of Kemalism. There was no better example of that possibility than one of the women who had stood before the cheering crowds near the Sultanahmet mosque in 1919, railing against the Allied occupation and urging Istanbullus to stand firmly on the side of the nationalists. It was both the first and the last time a woman would have such a prominent political voice at a crucial moment in Turkey's history.

If one were looking for a symbol of late-Ottoman optimism—the hope that Islam, modernity, and imperial revival could be harmoniously combined—Halide Edip would be a good candidate. She represented the best of what the old empire could still produce. She was born into a respected Ottoman family in 1884 and grew up in the green environs of the Bosphorus, first near the forested campus of the sultan's Yıldız Palace and then on the Asian side in the suburb of Üsküdar. The family mansion, covered in wisteria, had a terraced garden surrounded by tall acacias and a low fruit orchard. Pigeons swooped in on gentle breezes, and small fountains featured carved lions spitting water into a burbling pool.

Her father, Edip Bey, was an Ottoman patriot and close adviser to

Abdülhamid II. He kept a household with multiple wives, as was customary in his class and station among Muslims, but in everything from the management of his estate to the education of his children, he was an inveterate Anglophile. Plenty of English travelers fell in love with Turkey, returning to London to eat white cheese with honey and drape their tables with Anatolian carpets. Edip Bey's was probably the only home in Istanbul to return the favor. He ordered his cook to serve only English food at mealtimes.

Edip Bey was convinced that Britain had discovered the path to enlightenment and modernity, and he sought ways of communicating those values to his children. Woods Pasha—or Admiral Henry Woods, as he was originally known—was a distinguished British seaman who donned a fez and came into the sultan's naval service as a senior adviser in the late 1860s. He became a close friend of Edip Bey's family and recalled regularly meeting his young daughter Halide. Flouting Ottoman fashion, she was dressed in English-made dark blue frocks in winter and white linen in summer. She was slight and frail, Woods recalled, but possessed an exceptional intellect. Once she was old enough to begin learning foreign languages, Woods selected stories for her to read in English. It may have been on Woods's recommendation that Edip Bey decided to take Halide in an unorthodox direction. He enrolled her in school.

Private tutors were not uncommon among upper-class Muslim women, much as they were for contemporary women of the same rank in Victorian Britain or elsewhere. But actually sending a girl to school, even a girls' school, was unusual. For Halide's education, Edip Bey chose the American College for Girls, a missionary-run secondary school where instruction was in English. It offered a full complement of subjects from literature to science, and it was one of the mainstays of elite education for religious minorities in the city, including the daughters of English-speaking merchants and diplomats. There she sat amid Jews and Armenians, Bulgarians and Greeks, the only Muslim student in one of the most prestigious institutions in the city. In 1901 she became its first Muslim graduate.

Edip Bey was intent on his daughter's becoming well educated, but he was enough of a traditionalist to believe that the primary purpose of her schooling was to make her a better woman, not to launch her on a career. Almost as soon as she left the college, she was married to a much older man, Salih Zeki, an Istanbul writer and translator who had also served as her mathematics tutor. He was nearly her father's age and quickly positioned himself as a paternal figure to his young wife. "No little Circassian slave bought from the slave-market at the lowest price could have entered upon our common life in such an obedient spirit as I did," Halide later recalled.

She settled into a routine circumscribed by the expectations of her gender, class, and religion: staying secluded at home, serving her husband, and raising their two sons in an apartment overlooking Pera's Grande Rue. The new family's outlook—imperial yet progressive—was evident in their sons' names. The first Halide called Ali Ayetullah, a traditional Muslim name; the second she called Togo, after the Japanese admiral who defeated the tsar in the Russo-Japanese War. With the right mix of tradition and modernization, Muslims like Halide and her husband believed, the Ottoman Empire might repeat Japan's course and outstrip the industrial West. Still, even though she could follow major world events in the international press, her mind was not yet awakened, she said. She was consumed by frequent depression and occasional nervous breakdowns.

Then came 1908. Like many Istanbullus, Halide was caught up in the general enthusiasm for the restoration of the constitution and the parliament. The Ottoman Empire at last seemed to have its own version of a modern European revolution. Political change had come about not through a palace intrigue or the untimely death of a sultan but because of an uprising by liberal-minded military officers who stepped forward to drag the empire away from self-destruction. As a well-read young woman and fluent in English, Halide presented herself to one of the major pro-Unionist newspapers, *Tanin* (The Echo), edited by the well-known poet Tevfik Fikret. She was taken on as a literary columnist. She never visited the newspaper's offices—appearing unaccompanied in public would have been impossible for a high-ranking Muslim woman, even one with an English-language education—but her venture into the world of writing and publishing was a revelation. "I became a writer," she said of her reaction to the Young Turk revolution. Her fame spread, so much so that she regularly received death threats for her columns. In 1909, she traveled briefly to Egypt and Britain, in part to escape the period of reaction against the Unionist government.

Still in her twenties, Halide was a fairly conventional progressive of her era. She prized self-improvement over politics, patriotism over individualism, and the nation as an antidote to disorderly multiculturalism. She was a liberal only in the sense that all the categories of her overlapping identity—as a woman, as a Muslim, and as a Turk—required liberation from various oppressors: men, religious conservatives, and the non-Muslim minorities whom she and her compatriots saw as potentially disloyal neighbors. She was involved in the establishment of some of the first women's organizations in the empire and later became a mainstay of the Turkish Hearth associations, but these efforts were focused mainly on the cultivation of women's minds through edifying lectures in French and English. In 1910, she made her politics personal. When Salih Zeki proposed to take a second wife, Halide requested a divorce, which he granted. She moved out and took the children with her. It was the first time in her life, she said, that she no longer suffered from nerves.

Halide's publishing career erupted. She continued her essay-writing and drifted into fiction as well, publishing novels that sought to open up the world of Muslim Ottoman women, treating them neither as harem slaves nor as revolutionary feminists. She fell into the orbit of the writer Ziya Gökalp, the main ideologue of Turkish nationalism. Originally from Diyarbakır, in southeastern Anatolia, Gökalp had been in Salonica at the time of Unionist agitation and quickly became one of the leading lights among Turkish nationalists. He was short and round, with an old bullet wound in his forehead that made him instantly recognizable, but his odd appearance gave way when he spoke eloquently about the need for Turks to step forward and rescue their identity as a nation from the flames consuming the old empire. Halide eventually broke with Gökalp, whose nationalism, she believed, stepped over the line into ethnic chauvinism. Being in his circle had given her impeccable credentials as a visionary when it came to questions of identity and the Turkish future. In 1918, the Allied occupation illustrated the weakness of the old empire. In 1919 and 1920, the Hellenic seizure of Smyrna and Armenian claims on eastern Anatolia—both of which were eventually supported by the Allies in the Treaty of Sèvres—were its death knell. "I felt stupefied, tired, and utterly sick of all that had happened since 1914," Halide said. "I was conscious that the Ottoman Empire had fallen with a crash, and that it was not only the responsible Unionist leaders who were buried beneath the crushing weight of it. . . . [A]t that moment the absolute finality of the death of the empire was an unavoidable fact."

Halide had no reason to meet Mustafa Kemal, even though both were in Istanbul in 1918 and 1919. In fact, as a public figure, she clearly eclipsed him at this stage. Her ties to the Turkish Hearth movement naturally linked her with the Unionist underground in the city, and her writings had made her one of the most recognizable intellectuals in the empire. During the First World War, she had married for a second time, to Abdülhak Adnan. Small and pale, with prominent round spectacles and a legendary sense of humor, Adnan was a prominent Unionist, medical doctor, and writer. He had served in a senior role with the Red Crescent Society during the First World War and was later put in charge of sanitation in Istanbul—a vital position, given the frequent outbreaks of typhus and other diseases.

Together, Adnan and Halide were a rarity: a husband-and-wife team who were both public personas and both actively engaged in the national movement. They stood at the center of the growing opposition to the Allied occupation. In 1919, Halide later recalled, "I suddenly ceased to exist as an individual: I worked, wrote, and lived as a unit of that magnificent national madness." That summer, she was invited to address the crowds—perhaps two hundred thousand people—gathered outside the Sultanahmet mosque to protest the Hellenic invasion. She felt herself instantly connected to the masses spread out before her. She had finally stepped into a role for which she had been preparing all her life: a public leader of a great cause at a moment of national crisis. "Brethren and sons, listen to me," she said.

> Governments are our enemies, peoples are our friends, and the just revolt of our hearts our strength. The day is not far off when all nations will get their rights. When that day comes, take your banners and come and visit the graves of your brethren who have fought and have fallen for the glorious end. Now swear and repeat with me: "The sublime emotion which we cherish in our hearts will last till the proclamation of the rights of the peoples!"

"We swear!" the crowd thundered in response. It was a watershed moment not only in the history of Turkish nationalism but also for Turkish women. Never before had a woman appeared in such a visible and expressly political role, least of all a Muslim woman. Halide still hid her blonde hair beneath a chaste headscarf.

The next spring, when Mustafa Kemal's military movement began to form in central Anatolia, Halide joined the large numbers of Muslim intellectuals, activists, and politicians making their way east to join the nationalists. Had she and Adnan stayed in Istanbul, they almost certainly would have been arrested by the British authorities and deported to Malta as seditious nationalists. Both also soon had the distinction, with Mustafa Kemal, of being given a death sentence by the Ottoman parliament. It was a badge of honor that nationalists wore with pride. The Ottoman government's reach barely extended beyond the palace and the parliament building in Istanbul, much less eastward into Anatolia. Mustafa Kemal met her and Adnan at the train station when they arrived in Ankara, offering his hand to help Halide down from the carriage.

Ankara was in a state of euphoria, with supporters arriving each day and a sense that a new country was being built from scratch—more egalitarian, more just, more committed to the goal of ridding Turkey of foreign invaders. Given her background as a writer and journalist, Halide became a key figure in the emerging nationalist press. Along with Yunus Nadi, a prominent writer and editor who had also journeyed to Ankara from Istanbul, she set up the Anatolian News Agency, the bureau that quickly became the mouthpiece of the nationalist forces and, later, the official press office of the Turkish government.

When the war against the Hellenes started in earnest, Halide signed on with the nationalist army. She was made a corporal—for all their commitment to women's liberation, the nationalists could not imagine a female officer—and appeared beside Mustafa Kemal in her specially designed tunic, with a long skirt and dark Islamic headscarf. She witnessed the decisive battle of Sakarya and accompanied the commander in chief on his triumphal entry into Smyrna in September 1922. "I feasted my eyes on the sea," she wrote, "and constructed a plan for my life in the future: a rustic house not far away from Angora [Ankara], a fireside where immense logs would constantly burn, a gray goatskin in front of it, where I would lie and dream."

Her fame, however, left little time for dreaming. She wove her experiences into a new series of novels published not long after the Turkish nationalists had taken Smyrna. These and other works became some of the earliest pillars in the emerging literature of the war of independence, the first fruits of a new, republican literary genre, inspired by the anti-occupation movement and informed by firsthand accounts of the glory and gore of war. Later in the 1920s, when Istanbul audiences were packing into cinemas to view some of the first Turkish-made films, one of the sagas they saw unfolding on the screen was an adaptation of her popular novel of the liberation struggle, *Shirt of Flame*, directed by Muhsin Ertuğrul.

Halide and Adnan believed themselves to be at the center of the effort to build the republic. Adnan was vice president of the Grand National Assembly—politically, second only to Mustafa Kemal, the assembly's president—and one of the chief foreign policy figures in the nationalist government. In late 1922, he and Halide returned to Istanbul. It had been two years since they had been in the city, but two centuries' worth of suffering and yearning had been packed into that period, she said. Adnan was given the title of high commissioner, assuming the duties of the initial emissary, Refet Pasha, and serving as a quasi mayor in the transition from Allied to nationalist governance. He was present as representative of the Grand National Assembly at the handover ceremony at Dolmabahçe Palace, when General Harington saluted the Turkish flag and departed the city forever, ending the Allied presence. Halide had a less official role, but as a novelist, publicist, and outspoken feminist, her name was immediately recognizable among the pantheon of figures at the top of the new republican elite. An American diplomatic report was unequivocal in its assessment of the couple: "Dr. Adnan Bey is one of the leaders of the present Nationalist Government, but it is generally felt that his position is due rather to the remarkable personality of his wife than to his own genius."

As she and Adnan set up their new home in Istanbul, they both could sense a change coming. "I have seen, I have gone through, a land full of aching hearts and torturing remembrances, and I have lived in an age when the politicians played with these human hearts as ordinary gamblers play with their cards," she wrote. "I who had dreamed of a nationalism which will create a happy land of beauty, understanding, and love, I have seen nothing but mutual massacre and mutual hatred; I have seen nothing but ideals used as instruments for creating human carnage and misery."

The promise of the republic was that it would put an end to the long period of discord that had defined the entire adult lives of Halide's generation, from the Young Turk revolution through the First World War and the fight for independence. The promise was quickly broken, she felt. Mustafa Kemal's willingness to buy off local warlords, his increasing suspicion of any form of disagreement, and the establishment of independence tribunals to mete out punishment to open rebels as well as quiet dissenters—all seemed the opposite of the world Halide had been trying to create. Mustafa Kemal looked more and more like a dictator and his Republican People's Party like the only approved instrument of governance. The independence war had been a people's struggle, she believed, and no individual could adequately represent the collective desire for freedom. "There will be only the sum total of a people's sacrifice to bear witness to the guarding of their liberties," she wrote in her memoirs.

One after another of their old colleagues was falling away. Some who openly broke with Mustafa Kemal found themselves before a tribunal. Others retired from public life, quietly giving up power to the one-party state. In 1926, Halide and Adnan decided to leave Istanbul, the very year that Turkey's new civil code established legal equality for women. They began a long period of self-imposed exile in France, Britain, India, and the United States. Like their escape from Istanbul under the British, their departure came just in time. The next year, Mustafa Kemal delivered a thirty-six-hour speech known as the "Nutuk," a discourse that rewrote the history of the independence struggle by denouncing his enemies and placing himself at the center of the narrative. Political differences were now raised to the level of truth versus treason. Halide in particular was attacked as someone who had advocated Turkey's becoming a protectorate of a foreign government—perhaps Britain, perhaps the United States—rather than a fully independent country. It was a charge that had little backing, but it was enough to write her out of the republic's founding mythology.

Halide used her time abroad to work on her memoirs, which offered a kind of alternative history of the early republic. The first volume was published in English in the late 1920s, but it had little impact in Turkey. She and Adnan spent time in Paris and New York, living the lives of émigré academics by lecturing, taking up occasional visiting professorships, and recalling old battles that might as well have been ancient history to their students. As Muslim women were taking up new rights in the republic—going about fully unveiled, working as doctors and professors, eventually voting and standing for parliament—one of the principal fighters for their cause was no longer around to witness the changes.

It was not until after Mustafa Kemal's death, in 1938, that Halide and Adnan were able to return to Istanbul. She served briefly in parliament once multiparty democracy was instituted after the Second World War. But the years of exile had made her a political outsider. She had been present at the birth of the republic, yet she had missed its painful adolescence. She ended her career, in a way, by coming back to her childhood in Edip Bey's household on the Bosphorus. She became chair of the English Department at Istanbul University—the institution's first female professor—and translated Shakespeare into Turkish. Her version of *Coriolanus*, about the journey from war hero to tyrant and from exile to revenge, is still admired.

In her earlier years, Halide believed in a salvageable empire, a place where the sultan's many subjects, regardless of confession, could find a place. The experience of war and occupation made her into a nationalist. She believed in the need for a Turkish homeland, but her version of nationalism had a cosmopolitan lining. History and culture, she said, had formed the Turks into the Protestants of the Islamic world—

reformist, pragmatic, and naturally committed to the separation of mosque and state. Being a good nationalist required self-awareness, and embracing one's country demanded that one learn how to criticize it. "It is after I have loved my own people and tried to understand their virtues and their faults with open-minded humility that I begin to have a better understanding of other people's sufferings and joys, and of their personality expressed in their national life," she wrote. Even then, gender still mattered profoundly when it came to the way people actually behaved. For all the claims to equality in an age of republics, nationalism as a political movement was almost always a man's game. "Women," she was fond of saying, "are all one nation."

Rights, Halide believed, were there for the recognizing. They were not granted or bestowed so much as finally accepted and acknowledged, like removing a veil shielding women from public view and clouding their own vision of possible lives. On the battlefield and in front of a mass rally, it was easy to imagine a future Turkey in which Muslim women could develop a feminism that placed them squarely alongside men, powerful and confident, with few of the strictures that religion and tradition had imposed in the past. As it turned out, women's achievements would continue to be celebrated as evidence of the republic's quick progress, but it would be decades before any women would achieve the independent public voice once claimed by Halide Edip.

LIVING LIKE A SQUIRREL

A public rally on Galata Bridge.

AFTER 1927, MUSTAFA KEMAL'S "NUTUK" became the ur-text of republican history and the basic source for interpreting the end of empire and the birth of the Turkish nation-state. Only in recent years have Turkish historians begun to question its one-sided version of events. The sheer scale and complexity of the revolution, however, can best be appreciated not in a political speech or textbook but in a long-form poem titled *Human Landscapes from My Country*, the masterpiece of the writer Nâzım Hikmet. Nâzım began work on *Human Landscapes* in 1941 while interned in a prison in Bursa, a few hours from Istanbul across the Sea of Marmara. At some seventeen thousand lines, it is a vast canvas on which Nâzım gives his own account of the origins of the post-imperial era, told through the eyes of ordinary people caught up in the war of independence and the building of the Turkish Republic.

The poem pans out from Haydarpaşa train station, where Istanbul schoolgirls pass by in black satin uniforms, and plunges into Anatolia, where war and famine rage. There is no glory in the struggle, though. A woman advises:

> "Girl," she said, "you're young—
> grow up,
>   marry,
>   bear sons,

> *then I'll ask you*
> *what war is."*

Its heroes are thieves, peasants, writers, and ordinary soldiers, a stunning array of characters passing across the stage of modern Turkish history—or, rather, caught by the author's camera as it moves slowly across the Anatolian plateau. Earlier in his career, Nâzım had worked as a scenarist for director Muhsin Ertuğrul and the production company run by the İpekçi brothers, whose films played to sold-out audiences along the Grande Rue. He saw *Human Landscapes* as a kind of total art, with techniques drawn from filmmaking as well as poetry and prose. He worked in pans, zooms, and freeze-frames, free verse and narrative, and every literary form from autobiography to fantasy to folk aphorisms. *Human Landscapes* is a chronicle of a human and pluralistic world, one decidedly at odds with the homogenizing ideology that Kemalism seemed to preach. It remains perhaps the most creative and fine-grained assessment of Turkey's transition from empire to republic, a kind of alternative history unspooling alongside the standard story of Mustafa Kemal's necessary triumph and the single-minded modernization he wrought.

By the early years of the republic, Turkish writers had already thrown off the conservative conventions of Ottoman poetry. The republican literary scene was a mixed bag of paeans to the nation, nostalgic celebrations of village culture, and epics of everyday life, many set against the backdrop of national liberation and postwar struggle. But where other Turkish authors were asking how poetry should be written, Nâzım asked what it could do—whether it was possible not just to reflect reality in art but to shape social life at the same time.

Nâzım Hikmet did more than any single individual to introduce Turkish literature to modernity, and today he is widely regarded as Turkey's national poet. The small cultural center that bears his name in the Istanbul district of Kadıköy, with its shaded tea garden and artists' stalls, is an important meeting spot for radical university students and old intellectuals alike. Few national poets have been so unwelcome in their own lifetimes, however. Nâzım spent a good part of his adult life in Turkish prisons. He was eventually stripped of his Turkish citizenship. After his death, his body was buried neither in Istanbul nor even in Turkey.

The reason was that, in a country committed to revolutionism, Nâzım's version of revolutionary zeal was long held to be of the wrong variety. His was a version of modernity that Istanbul, more than any other part of the republic, was well placed to embody: the quiet specter of socialism. Criticism of Turkish nationalism from the Left remained a constant feature of political life, even if much of it stayed, like other forms of opposition, underground. As a diplomatic report noted in 1930, the government's normal stance was to assume that "any malcontent in republican Turkey is at least a communist and probably a spy." The single-party political system meant there was no legal channel for expressing leftist views, and it would not be until several decades later—in the 1970s—that intellectuals could openly advocate socialist causes. Even then, the political establishment perceived activists on that end of the political spectrum as a major internal threat. Like most other rivals to Kemalism, socialism would soon be assiduously written out of the country's history.

Nâzım Hikmet was, like so many other prominent individuals of his day, a native of Salonica. He was born perhaps in 1902—he was never certain about his birth date—into a family of provincial Ottoman officials. On his mother's side, his lineage included several distinguished soldiers and scholars, running back to a Huguenot orphan and a Polish count who converted to Islam and joined the Ottoman army. His mother, Celile Hanım, was an accomplished artist and one of the empire's first female painters. One of his grandfathers was the last Ottoman governor of Salonica, and his father, Hikmet Bey, was a prominent local Unionist working within the Ottoman foreign ministry.

When the Hellenes took over Salonica in 1912, what they got was a provincial Ottoman seaport that nearly burned to the ground only five years later. What Istanbul got, however, was a new soul. Thousands of Muslim families departed Salonica for the capital, carrying with them the European sensibilities and belief in progress that would shape Turkey's first generation of republican elites. Clearly out of a job under the new Hellenic government, Hikmet Bey moved his family to Istanbul as well. He enrolled the young Nâzım in the prestigious Galatasaray Lycée and later pushed him to attend the Ottoman naval college on the island Heybeliada in the Sea of Marmara, where he began to write poetry as a distraction from the interminable lessons in hydraulics and navigation. A persistent lung condition kept him out of military service, and he watched the First World War from the sidelines. He was present in Istanbul when the British warship *Superb* sailed in to announce the beginning of the Allied occupation.

Nâzım was too young to have played a role in the Young Turk revolution and too sickly to be mobilized during the First World War, but when news of Mustafa Kemal's rival government filtered back to Istanbul, he, like many in his age group and social class, made plans to decamp to Ankara. Along with a friend, Vâlâ Nureddin, he made his way to Mustafa Kemal's forces, arriving in early 1921, and presented himself as a foot soldier for the revolution.

With few actual skills and no military real connections—the leaders of the brewing independence war, after all, were already seasoned officers who had fought at Gallipoli and elsewhere—Nâzım was quickly pushed off to a teaching job in a distant village. He could make the revolution from the ground up by educating the populace—a valuable component of the national struggle, if not exactly the role Nâzım had hoped to play in crafting the new world. He wanted to be on the front line of the struggle, not in its rear guard.

After only a few months in Anatolia, he turned his attention northward, to Russia and the transformation that seemed to be happening there. Nâzım had been introduced to socialism on his way to meet Mustafa Kemal's troops, but it was a familiarity that amounted to little more than conversations with someone who had read a few more Marxist tracts than he. To be on the Right was to support the decrepit sultan and the foreign occupation, he believed. To be on the Left was to value liberation and national rebirth. His understanding of Marx was rudimentary, but he didn't need to be a deep theorist to understand the direction that the war of independence was already taking—away from its revolutionary roots and toward the consolidation of power in the hands of Mustafa Kemal and his closest supporters.

❖

To many observers, revolutionary socialism and Turkish nationalism had once seemed to be two strands of a single anti-imperialist uprising on the frontier of Europe and Asia. Relations between Mustafa Kemal's nationalists and the Bolsheviks "probably form today the nucleus of one of the most important movements in the Near East," US High Commissioner Mark Bristol reported in 1921. The tip of the spear would surely be Istanbul. Allied police kept strict watch on alleged underground cells in the city. With so many penniless Russian-speakers on hand, officials believed that it was dangerously easy to turn desperate Whites into Reds. Roundups of suspected agents were common. Allied police even detained Russians who happened to be attending a Berlitz course in Turkish for fear that they were Bolshevik spies underground seeking to brush up on the local language. According to American intelligence sources, the Bolsheviks had even attempted to convince Mustafa Kemal to bring Turkey formally into the Soviet Union, where he would be made the country's federal president. It was an offer that Mustafa Kemal—if it ever reached his desk—quietly passed up.

Bolshevik Russia and Turkey did have certain things in common. Both stressed the role of the state as the engine of social and economic transformation. Both countries had forsaken the multiparty parliaments that the Romanovs and the Ottomans, for all their faults, had managed to create in their final years. They eventually took for granted the view that statism—the government's careful management of the economy and society—worked best when societal transformation was handled by a single political party, the Communist Party in the Soviet Union and the Republican People's Party in Turkey.

Vladimir Lenin and Mustafa Kemal also shared a set of ideological assumptions, not about the details of revolution—Mustafa Kemal looked to nationalism rather than Marxism as his bedrock philosophy—but about how it had to be effected and where their countries fit in the twentieth century's emerging order. Both believed in the idea of a political vanguard and its historical mission of reshaping an entire society. Their strategic vision of the world to come was one in which colonialism would be gone, empires would collapse, and the old powers of the nineteenth century would give way to a set of new, post-revolutionary regimes. Neither man was opposed to the concept of a select group of powerful nations working their will in the international system. They simply believed that their own countries should be admitted to the club.

The Soviet model had demonstrated the transformative power of class war and grassroots revolution. Turkey, however, was a country without a proletariat. Because of the loss of so many urban centers, from Salonica to Damascus, the new republic was even more rural than the Ottoman Empire. In Russia—itself overwhelmingly rural—Lenin and Trotsky had already shown that workers were not essential components of a workers' revolution. All that was required was a small group of conspirators who could form a party, seize the state in the name of the oppressed, defeat the backers of the old regime in a civil war, and then set about building, through industrialization and radical land reform, the very proletariat that they claimed as their base of support. The Kemalist government eventually adopted the five-year plan as an approach to industrial and agricultural development. State-regulated monopolies were allowed to take over major industries, although Turkey did not impose direct government control over the economy. Senior bureaucrats were nevertheless required to be members of the only legal political party.

But the brief courtship between the two revolutionary regimes began to sour even before the nationalists had ousted the Allies. Russia and Turkey had been strategic rivals for centuries, and this long history was difficult to overcome, especially in an era in which Soviets and Turks were both beginning to see themselves as contrasting models of modernity for oppressed peoples everywhere—one based on a proletarian revolution, the other based on a national one. In the contest between rival ideals, the Turks preferred the version that allowed them to build a nation of their own, not one that preached the end of nations altogether.

Still, flirtation with leftist ideas was a consistent feature of early Turkish politics as well as a continuing source of inspiration for people dissatisfied with the authoritarian tendencies of the Kemalists themselves. A Turkish Communist Party was established by Mustafa Kemal's closest military associates in October 1920, but the party seems to have been mainly a vehicle for outflanking other leftists. A rival party, in fact, had been established in Baku, in independent Azerbaijan, the previous month. Its leader, Mustafa Suphi, was a Turkish Bolshevik who had grown up in Paris. He saw himself as the natural conduit through which the tenets of communism would reach Turkey. With the help of Russian Bolsheviks, he and a group of comrades entered Anatolia from the Caucasus at the end of 1920. The following January, they made plans to travel from the port city of Trabzon, following the coast and then going overland to Ankara. By this stage, Mustafa Kemal's power as leader of the national movement was in no sense secure. Mustafa Suphi may have aimed to challenge him.

What happened next is still murky, but Mustafa Suphi and twelve of his associates were last seen on a motorboat heading out of Trabzon. They disappeared on the Black Sea and were presumed dead. Right-wing Unionists were blamed for having organized the disappearance—effectively assassinating a key rival from the other end of the political spectrum—but the Kemalists were the clearest beneficiaries of the Suphi affair. They could now afford to court the favor of Bolshevik Russia without actually allowing Suphi's Bolshevism to infest the ranks of Turkish nationalists. Both Communist parties—the sincere one established by Mustafa Suphi and the faux one launched by the Kemalists—were soon allowed to fade, becoming minor footnotes in the evolution of the national movement.

❈

The death of Mustafa Suphi had a profound effect on Nâzım Hikmet's vision of the emerging regime in his homeland. The Kemalists seemed to have betrayed the revolution before it had even begun. After only a few months in Anatolia, Nâzım decided to cross the border into the Caucasus and join the Bolsheviks. He set off in the autumn of 1921 via the Georgian port of Batumi—just as Dmitri Shalikashvili and other supporters of Georgia's Menshevik government were escaping to Istanbul—and made his way by train to Moscow. He was nineteen years old.

It was the first of what would be a series of stays in Russia and a life lived, by turns, in both Moscow and Istanbul. In Moscow he read Marx beneath the statue of the poet Alexander Pushkin. He studied at the Communist University of the Workers of the East, an institution specifically designed to inculcate revolutionary values in Asian intellectuals who would then return to their homelands and take to the barricades. For the next three years, he was in the middle of a creative churning in Russian art, literature, and performance, from experimental theater to poetry that tossed out all conventions of rhyme and meter. He may have invented the first free-verse lines in Turkish during this period, doing away with the traditions of Ottoman poetry and its complex borrowings from Persian and Arabic verse. When Lenin died in 1924, Nâzım stood guard beside the coffin at the lying-in-state, one of many young representatives of world socialism to pay homage to the deceased leader.

At the end of that year, Nâzım returned to Istanbul. He had left Turkey not long after the probable drowning of Mustafa Suphi, a time when virtually the entire population of real Turkish Communists could have fit in the same boat. Now things were different. Socialist journals were sold openly on the street. Workers' circles met in clubs and private houses. Conferences were staged to consider the world situation and the struggle against capitalism and imperialism. He started to write for a new journal that made its political leanings clear on the masthead— *Orak-Çekiç*, the Turkish for "Hammer and Sickle."

The relative freedom did not last, however. After the first round of Kurdish rebellions in 1925 came a new law on public order. Leftist newspapers were closed. Surveillance of leftists and other activists increased. Socialists were brought before one of the Grand National Assembly's independence tribunals. Nâzım went into hiding but nevertheless was swept up in the wave of accusations and denunciations. He was sentenced in absentia to a fifteen-year prison term.

He soon left Turkey for Moscow, which again became a refuge. Nâzım threw himself into the artistic life of the Soviet capital. But Istanbul was home, and after only two years away he attempted to reenter Turkey through the Caucasus. He was arrested and imprisoned at the border on the odd charge of plotting to rouse ethnic minorities against the Turkish state, an accusation that seems to have had little basis in reality. After months of legal maneuvering, a court at last reversed the original sentence handed down by the independence tribunal, and Nâzım was released and allowed to resettle in Istanbul.

His trial had been eagerly followed by Istanbul intellectuals; when

The poet on trial: Nâzım Hikmet (left) in court.

he was released, he received something of a hero's welcome, at least among the reading public. His poems had already appeared in the Turkish literary press, and in the spring of 1929 he published his first book in Turkey, a selection of poems written earlier in the decade. His work had clearly been influenced by the writings of the Soviet poet Vladimir Mayakovsky, just as his understanding of the rhythms of speech and the possibilities of narrative had been shaped by his acquaintance with the theater director Vsevolod Meyerhold. His two stays in the Soviet Union had been a kind of intellectual apprenticeship, leading him to mimic the disjointed poetic forms of Russian Futurism, its industrial aesthetics and visions of cultural transformation.

In 1929, he also published his first long poem, "La Gioconda and Si-Ya-U," in which Da Vinci's Mona Lisa falls in love with a Chinese Communist and takes flight from the Louvre, only to be burned in Shanghai after joining the revolutionary struggle herself. He became a major writer in the pages of *Resimli Ay* (Illustrated Monthly), a popular journal of Turkish art and culture, and in 1930 record executives in Istanbul approached him to make an audio recording of his poems. Like Udi Hrant and Seyyan Hanım at around the same time, Nâzım could be heard in coffeehouses and private homes by people who had never met him. The record sold out in less than a month.

Nâzım was rarely careful in his writing. More popular than ever, he had little reason to be. The restrictive law on public order had been repealed, and a new wave of liberalism swept over Turkey. But his attacks on capitalism and his unabashed admiration for the Soviet system made him the target of constant surveillance. His increasingly vitriolic dismissal of the Turkish literary establishment, especially former friends who had proclaimed their full adherence to Kemalism, left him with few allies.

He was arrested in 1933, released in 1934, and rearrested in 1938, in part because cadets at his alma mater, the naval college on Heybeliada in the Princes Islands, had apparently been reading his latest work, entitled "The Epic of Sheikh Bedreddin." The poem expanded the boundaries of poetic language, weaving together scholarly prose, magical realism, and multiple voices, much as *Human Landscapes* would later do, but it was the overtly political message of "Sheikh Bedreddin," cloaked in an obscure episode from Ottoman history, that sparked a new round of trouble.

In 1416, a revolt against Sultan Mehmed I broke out in western Anatolia, led by a certain Börklüce, about whom little is known, and the Islamic mystic Bedreddin. Both leaders preached the essential unity of religions and social classes, and their message attracted local Muslims, Christians, and Jews as well as urban merchants and peasants resentful of heavy taxes and feudal landlords. With some difficulty, the Ottomans defeated the rebels. They seized Börklüce and transported him to Ephesus, where he was crucified, strapped to a camel, and led around the countryside as a symbol of the sultan's wrath. Bedreddin escaped for a time, proselytizing in an area along the western Black Sea coast known as the Mad Forest (in present-day Bulgaria), but he, too, was finally captured and hanged.

In "Sheikh Bedreddin," Nâzım clearly overstepped the bounds of political propriety. Given its themes of oppressive rule by a deified leader and the belief in a world where rigid hierarchies and stifling social conventions would melt away, the poem gave the Turkish government a convenient excuse for leveling a charge of inciting mutiny. Nâzım was tried and sentenced to thirty-five years in prison. Unlike his previous sentences, however, this one more or less stuck. He spent the next twelve years incarcerated as a threat to the Turkish state, a rejecter of Kemalism, and a traitorous admirer of the Soviet Union, which had gone from being an early ally of Turkey to a regional rival in the run-up to the Second World War. He was released in 1950 in a general amnesty of political prisoners and only then after a sustained international campaign supported by Pablo Picasso, Jean-Paul Sartre, and other European intellectuals.

Nâzım lived several lives and in several senses. In his personal life, he carried on deeply romantic and sincerely loving relationships with many women, usually young and already married. In his art, he was by turns a naïve patriot, a flirtatious Futurist, a reflective prison poet, a writer of epic verse, and a skillful sentimentalist. His output was enormous. The Turkish edition of his collected works, published from 1988 to 1991, runs to twenty-seven volumes. In his politics, he was genuinely committed to the revolutionary cause, but his encounters with the communism of Joseph Stalin made him long for the Soviet Union he had known during his first visit as a nineteen-year-old, self-exiled from the emerging Kemalist republic. Among the many foreigners who had been seduced by the artistic socialism of a Meyerhold or a Mayakovsky, Nâzım was among the most wistful for that earlier era of Soviet experimentation, before Stalin and the Gulag. His weakness was a common one among his generation: the ability to will himself to look through the awfulness of Stalinism back toward a time when going to Russia could seem, to a teenaged Turk, the ultimate form of liberation.

If there is a theme that runs through all of Nâzım's work, however, it is not a political one at all. It is rather a call for valuing life's casual diversity. *Human Landscapes* is as much a celebration of the randomness of the world—the attractive messiness of meeting an old friend unexpectedly on a crowded Istanbul street, say—as it is a coded call for human liberation and justice. His love poems, addressed to women on two continents, are among the most moving and maturely unsentimental that one can find. "On Living," written during his long prison sentence, is a salute to life beyond the political struggle:

> *Living is no laughing matter:*
> > *you must live with great seriousness*
> > *like a squirrel, for example—*
> > *I mean without looking for something beyond and above living,*
> > *I mean living must be your whole life.*

After his release from prison, Nâzım traveled and lectured widely outside Turkey—the government, in fact, eventually stripped him of his Turkish citizenship—but the Soviet Union became his adopted home. By then, the revolutionary élan of the 1920s was long past. He was a curiosity from the developing world, surrounded by plenty of other leftist dissidents, former spies, and castoffs from capitalism, with no inkling of how popular his work would later become. Toward the end of his life, he was something of a one-man carnival act, lauding the flourishing of the arts under Soviet socialism and denouncing their putrefaction in the bourgeois oligarchies. His literary voice became that of the wizened ex-prisoner, not the firebrand poet of earlier years. Even his love poems began to take on the air of factory oil and ore smelters. "You are a field / I am the tractor. / . . . / You are China, / I am Mao

Zedong's army," he wrote in 1951. When he died, in 1963, he lay in state at the headquarters of the Soviet Writers' Union and was buried, in the company of Chekhov and Gogol, in the Novodevichy Cemetery in Moscow. "Some people know all about plants, some about fish," he had written. "I know separation." He remains there, far from Istanbul, probably the world's most celebrated national poet still in exile from his homeland.

The magnetic pull of the Russian revolution attracted many Turkish intellectuals in the 1920s and 1930s, and Nâzım Hikmet's life and work would continue to inspire Turkish socialists, even to the present day. (His Turkish citizenship was finally restored, posthumously, in 2009.) In one of the many ironic twists in Istanbul's history, however, Nâzım's journey north toward the Soviet Union began around the same time that another revolutionary, a Russian, was heading south. He blew in on a winter gale along with his wife and son—a "cooperative of three," he called them. They were immediately the most famous Russian family in Istanbul, but, unlike Wrangel's flotilla of 1920, they were not Whites. The head of the family, with his round glasses and pointy Vandyke beard, had been one of the supreme leaders of the Reds.

ISLAND LIFE

Bosphorus bounty: A fisherman sorts his catch of mackerel.

LEON TROTSKY WAS PERHAPS the most reluctant visitor ever to arrive in Istanbul. Even before he had stepped ashore, he handed a note to the customs official who boarded his ship. "Dear Sir," he wrote, addressing Mustafa Kemal. "At the gate of Constantinople, I have the honor to inform you that I have arrived at the Turkish frontier not of my own choice, and that I will cross this frontier only by submitting to force. I request you, Mr. President, to accept my appropriate sentiments."

The note was dated February 12, 1929. It was one of the coldest winters ever. Trams had to be dug out from snowdrifts, wolves were spotted in outlying neighborhoods, and for the first time in more than a century, ferries stayed moored to their piers to avoid the chunks of ice that floated down the Bosphorus. The train from Paris spent several days buried in a snowdrift, the incident that would inspire Agatha Christie's *Murder on the Orient Express*. Trotsky and his wife, Natalya Sedova, had spent the previous twenty-two days on trains as well, slowly covering some three thousand miles westward from Kazakhstan to the port of Odessa. For two years, the family had been in internal exile in Central Asia, relegated to the far reaches of the Soviet Union by Joseph Stalin.

Although Trotsky had been one of the makers of the Bolshevik Revolution—a close associate of Vladimir Lenin and leader of the Red Army during the civil war—Lenin's death in 1924 had opened the door to Stalin's ambition. Stalin had chipped away at the edges of the old Bolshevik elite for years, but by the late 1920s he was powerful enough to take on Trotsky, the figure with the widest following outside Stalin's own circle and the clearest claim to succeed Lenin as leader of the Soviet Union. On Stalin's orders, the Soviet secret police, the OGPU, first escorted Trotsky and Natalya to the windy plains of Kazakhstan. Then the police were on hand in Odessa to supervise the family's transfer to the steamer *Ilyich*, with no cargo and no civilian passengers besides the Trotskys and their son Lyova, and the voyage to Istanbul. Turkey had agreed to allow the family to enter the country, but this was not a gesture of sympathy for Trotsky's politics. It was the opposite: evidence of the fact that, by the late 1920s, the Turkish state believed it had adopted the most useful bits of the Soviet model while successfully scotching direct Soviet influence.

In any case, the Soviets intended to keep an eye on their most famous exile. Trotsky was accorded the full courtesy of the Soviet Embassy as he made arrangements for housing. For the next several weeks, a wing of the embassy was reserved for his use. Yakov Minsky, the Istanbul representative of the OGPU, was put in charge of keeping tabs on him as well as helping the family to find longer-term living quarters. It was odd for Trotsky to be treated like a guest by a government that had officially condemned him, in absentia, for counterrevolutionary activity and plotting the overthrow of the state. It was even stranger for the government to allow him to write letters of protest to the *New York Times* and other Western newspapers. But no one, least of all Trotsky himself, believed his predicament would last for long. He had arrived in the city under duress, and he had no intention of staying.

Trotsky had been exiled twice before, to Siberia and the Russian North, during his period as an underground revolutionary in the tsarist era, and he was used to the concept of starting a new life as an émigré. The two earlier periods of exile had given way to triumph: the

1905 Russian revolution that forced the tsar to create a Russian parliament and the October 1917 revolution that elevated the Bolsheviks to power. He had no desire to stay in a country where he could not speak the local language, he told Turkish journalists, and he hoped that soon a visa would come through for Germany, Britain, or France. There, he would be able to continue his political work on behalf of international socialism while also railing against the usurper Stalin.

The Soviets likewise believed his Turkish exile would be a temporary affair. Istanbul had the triple virtue of being an easy sail from the Soviet coast, located in a country willing to take in Trotsky, and full of people who might relish the chance to kill him. After all, with plenty of Whites still hanging around the back alleys of Pera, someone would surely find irresistible the prospect of assassinating an old Bolshevik enemy. Minsky, the Soviet secret police agent, even seems to have kept Trotsky informed about all the White and foreign spies working in Istanbul. That may have been a way of helping Trotsky avoid them. It may equally have been a clever trap: a way of arousing Trotsky's curiosity and laying the groundwork for branding him a foreign spy himself, if he ever happened to have contact with capitalist operatives.

Natalya and Lyova were allowed to leave the embassy to look for housing, and Trotsky himself could occasionally be seen walking along the trolley tracks in Pera, bundled up against the winter cold and flanked by guards. Minsky was nervous about keeping the Trotskys in the embassy for too long, for fear that he would become the de facto landlord of Stalin's nemesis. In the end, Minsky became a reluctant real estate agent. He came forward with multiple options for accommodation, all of which failed to suit Trotsky's specifications, especially in terms of security. Exasperated, Minsky finally booted the family out of the embassy and down the street to the Tokatlian Hotel, from which Natalya could continue the housing search on her own. After another move to an apartment, in late April 1929 she managed to find a place an hour and a half by ferry from the city center. It was a house where

Trotsky could continue his writing and political work in relative safety while making plans for his next move.

Büyükada, or Prinkipo, was the largest of the Princes Islands, a group of nine arid islands popping up like a dinosaur's back from the Sea of Marmara. A convent on Büyükada had once served as the preferred locus of exile for Byzantine nobles who had run afoul of the emperor, and smaller islands in the chain had continued to be dumping grounds as late as the Young Turk era. Stray dogs, for example, had been one of Istanbul's public health hazards for centuries, and beginning around 1910, in a rolling campaign for order and cleanliness, the city government ordered tens of thousands of them rounded up and shipped to the rocky Hayırsızada—Good-for-Nothing Island. Rival packs formed to guard rainwater pools and fight over stray birds. For years afterward, it was said that on quiet evenings, with just the right southerly wind, Istanbullus could still hear their yelps and howls.

In the 1840s, the Ottomans had begun regular ferry service to the habitable islands, and Büyükada in particular became the major summer residence for the city's wealthy merchants, especially Greeks. Wood-frame houses with whitewashed verandas and louvered doors provided relief from the stifling summer heat. Private automobiles were (and still are) prohibited, so horse-drawn phaetons carted locals and visitors around the island's few roads, cushioned by a deep layer of pine needles. At the height of the summer season, white and purple oleander and bougainvillea framed the roadsides and spilled over garden walls. Along the leafy Çankaya Avenue, which wound down to the ferry landing, massive villas and their dependent guesthouses looked out on the turquoise sea and the low hills of the Anatolian coast.

Like Karl Marx in the previous century, Trotsky relied for his well-being on the kindness of capitalists he one day hoped to crush. One after another prominent Turkish businessman came forward to help him begin a new life in exile, perhaps attracted by the thrill of being close to a political celebrity or eager to court an enemy of Stalin. A former Ottoman official offered to rent the guesthouse of his villa. The expansive grounds lay on the downhill side of Çankaya Avenue and ended in a small cliff facing the sea. "The waves of the Sea of Marmara lapped the shore a few steps from our new home," Natalya recalled. "It was a beautiful place, spacious, peaceful, set in the blue sea and bathed in golden sunlight most of the time."

A fire, probably caused by a faulty water heater, raced through the house in March 1931. Trotsky reportedly sued both his landlord and his housekeeper for negligence, but that did not solve the immediate problem of finding new accommodation. The family was once again on the move—first to a hotel on the island, then to a walled house in the Moda neighborhood on the Asian mainland, then back to a red-brick house on Büyükada owned by a Turkish shipping magnate and located a short walk from the original residence. There they settled into life amid plum and fig trees inside what islanders called a *rakı köşkü*—a small house built for sipping anise-flavored liqueur and enjoying the view north toward Istanbul proper. It was now the unlikely home of the prophet of world revolution.

Throughout his stay on the island, Trotsky grew increasingly fearful for his own safety. With both White Russians and Bolshevik agents present in the city, he had reason to be afraid. He routinely carried a small pistol and never appeared outside without a guard. Like a crotchety old man yelling at children to get off his property, he might yank at the beard of a Greek Orthodox priest to make sure he was not an assassin in disguise or pull a gun on a local fisherman who had suspiciously trawled the same spot for too many days in a row.

Islanders were less than enthusiastic about their most famous resident. Trotsky hired local guards, gardeners, and servants, but stories circulated about his peculiar requirements: for deaf cooks, so they would not be able to report on his conversations, or for illiterate cleaning people who would not be able to read his correspondence. His conversation was normally laced with sarcasm. When he happened to find someone in the household taking a rest or reading a book, he would exclaim, "Here is the Russian emigration!" He also had the habit common to people too comfortable with their own power: He would christen those around him with odd nicknames that then became, in his mind, their new identity.

The only friendship he seems to have struck up was with a local Greek fisherman, Haralambos. The two could be seen in a small boat, usually with guards or houseguests, bobbing in the water and dragnetting or line-fishing for red mullet and bonito in season. The fishing party would load up the boat with stones and cast them into the sea to drive the great schools of fish toward the nets. Trotsky and Haralambos would call out to each other in their own private language braided from Turkish, Greek, Russian, and French. In these moments, Trotsky seemed most playful and at ease. "Ah, Comrade Gérard!" he once teased his lawyer, Gérard Rosenthal, "if you strike the bourgeoisie like you attack the fish, they'll have a pretty long life!"

Even then, Trotsky rarely felt truly safe. Once, a small girl—later the distinguished Turkish writer Mîna Urgan—swam toward the boat and grabbed onto the gunwales. An agitated Trotsky yelled at his guard to shoo her away and whack her fingers with his rifle butt. When the fishing was good, though, he would return to the house in excellent spirits and spin off new writings, dictated to a secretary with feverish speed.

Unfettered by the restrictions imposed on his work in the Soviet Union, he could fully speak his mind and communicate with the international socialist community. He began editing—and almost single-handedly writing—a new bulletin that reported on the work of the anti-Stalinist opposition. He started writing his autobiography, *My Life*, based on notes he had already made while in Kazakhstan; he finished a draft within a few months of his arrival in Istanbul. He also made initial notes for a history of the Russian revolution. Book contracts and publishing deals came from Germany and the United States. Editorials and political essays streamed in the opposite direction to major Western newspapers eager to publish Trotsky's thoughts on the world situation—his "ululations from the Bosphorus," as Winston Churchill, one of Trotsky's targets, called them. The revolution was surely over, Churchill said, when "the Communist instead of bombs produces effusions for the capitalist Press, when the refugee War Lord fights his battles over again, and the discharged executioner becomes chatty and garrulous at his fireside."

Lyova was marshaled in to serve as his father's secretary, managing the tide of correspondence and assisting Trotsky with the growing numbers of guests making the pilgrimage from the mainland to see someone who had become Istanbul's—and perhaps the world's—most sought-after has-been. Letters arrived from graphologists requesting handwriting samples. Methodists wrote to explain the advantages of Christianity. Astrologers offered readings of his star chart. Autograph collectors kindly asked to add his signature "to those of two American presidents, three heavyweight champions, Albert Einstein, Colonel Lindbergh, and of course Charlie Chaplin," Trotsky recalled. He later employed a small staff—or chancellery, as he termed it—to deal with the workload of manuscript preparation, letter writing, and monitoring of international affairs.

Trotsky's break with Stalin had been a spectacular development, but it was one part of the larger differentiation among the world's socialists: those who still looked to the Soviet Union as the leader of global revolution, those who were forging their own paths to communism, and those who believed that the Russian experiment was destined to burn itself out, soon to be succeeded by new movements arising in Europe's overseas colonies. Trotsky now came to assume a role he had never held: a pole around which disaffected radicals around the world—especially those most committed to permanent revolution and the spread of revolutionary ideas—could coalesce. Like many famous exiles, he was becoming chiefly a totem, essentially powerless except for the force of his personality and words. "Here on this island of quiet and oblivion echoes from the great world reached us delayed and muffled," he jotted in his diary.

It was one thing to imagine Trotsky as the sage of Büyükada. It was another actually to meet him. Visitors to the island almost always found themselves on a kind of anti-pilgrimage. "He seems too small for the struggle," wrote Max Eastman, the American poet and political radical, who visited in 1932. Eastman expected to engage in deep discussions about the inevitable triumph of the socialist cause, but he found Trotsky obsessing about more mundane concerns, especially his finances.

His writing generated substantial sums of money. A string of newspaper articles brought in fees of ten thousand dollars. The American edition of *My Life* garnered an advance of seven thousand. The *Saturday Evening Post* paid forty-five thousand to serialize his *History of the Russian Revolution*. But Trotsky was spending more than a thousand dollars a month on bodyguards, housing, food, and especially books, since his library and extensive collection of photographs from the revolution had been destroyed in the fire at the first house. To economize, he kept little in the way of furniture, wandering about worriedly in mainly empty rooms. He let the garden go to seed. His dog, Tosca, chased birds through the tall grass and saplings. "We seemed to camp rather than live there," recalled one of his secretaries.

Eastman had signed on as Trotsky's literary agent and was largely responsible for the income flowing into his bank account. But in their conversations, Trotsky tended to talk down to Eastman, complaining about the stinginess of Western capitalists and the tightfistedness of American publishers, even though Eastman was an old friend and one of the leading voices of the American Left. Trotsky squirmed out of contracts and groveled for extensions. He promised to deliver commissioned manuscripts but then insisted he had never done so. During Eastman's visit, Trotsky spent most of their time together trying to convince Eastman to collaborate on a stage play about the American

Civil War. Trotsky believed it would be a hit on Broadway, a work that would combine Eastman's knowledge of American history with his own expertise on troop movements and tactics. Eastman considered the idea ridiculous.

Trotsky had "followers and subalterns," Eastman concluded, but he was incapable of having real friends. Trotsky would not have disagreed. "I do not measure the historical process by the yardstick of one's personal fate," he wrote. "On the contrary, I appraise my fate objectively and live it subjectively, only as it is inextricably bound up with the course of social development." Enemies, he would say routinely, should be shot. He saw this philosophy as a virtue, but most of the people who knew him during his exile seemed to see it as his signature flaw, both as a person and as a politician. He preferred the safety of the podium and the blinding anonymity of the limelight to intimate conversation and real engagement. He was unsuited to exile not because he lost power—his political influence had been waning throughout the period when Stalin's was rising—but because it robbed him of the two things that made it possible for him to live in the world of reality: a platform to inhabit and a program to implement.

Like the Whites, Trotsky believed that both of these things might one day return if he could only move out of Istanbul and find his feet again. When he was not writing essays or corresponding with adherents, he was filling out visa applications. Germany declined to admit him, as did the Netherlands, Italy, Austria, and Spain. Denmark allowed only a short trip to Copenhagen. The British socialists Sidney and Beatrice Webb, founders of the London School of Economics and Political Science, visited Büyükada two months after Trotsky's arrival, but even they could not convince the British government, then under sympathetic Labour Party control, to grant him admission. Trotsky ended *My Life* with a wry chapter he called "The Planet Without a Visa."

Finally, through the intercession of French socialists, he managed to secure asylum in southern France, with the proviso that he never visit Paris and remain under continuous police surveillance. The years in Istanbul had been among the calmest, most creative, and "least unhappy" of his entire exile, according to his preeminent biographer, Isaac Deutscher. Trotsky recorded the final Büyükada days in his diary: "Our house is already almost empty; wooden boxes stand below, and young hands are busy hammering nails. In our old and neglected villa, the floors this spring were decorated with paint of a composition so mysterious that tables, chairs, and even feet stick lightly to the floor even now, four months later." He couldn't pass up the obvious metaphor. He felt that his feet somehow had become stuck to the island. He had aged there. His hair had gone white, and his brow had furrowed. Heart trouble and gout had set in. In July 1933, he and Natalya— Lyova had already managed to move to Berlin—made their way down Çankaya Avenue for the last time and boarded a small ship bound for Marseille.

Trotsky had been delivered from his Turkish exile and was on his way to a new life, first in France, then in Norway, then finally in Coyoacán, a borough of Mexico City. He and Natalya carried newly issued Turkish passports that made their status clear. "The bearer of this passport," declared the first page, "is not under the protection of the Turkish state." But as he sailed along the coast of the island, past the charred upper floor of his first Turkish house and into the open sea, he was now in more danger than ever before. Istanbul, in a way, was going to follow him.

At the beginning of the 1920s, John Dos Passos had come downstairs to find the lobby of the Pera Palace in chaos. In the lounge, Hellenic, Italian, and French gendarmes were trying to converse, each in his own language. A British member of parliament was downing a cocktail while attempting to explain something to a soldier. Bellhops and doormen were carrying out a man in an astrakhan hat and frock coat, leaving behind a pool of blood on the mosaic floor and a stained, plush-red armchair. The hotel manager was walking back and forth with sweat beading up on his brow, trying to learn what had happened. The envoy from Azerbaijan had been assassinated, someone said, and the gunman was a bearded Armenian. Or perhaps it was a clean-shaven Bolshevik, someone else said, who came right up to the doorway and shot him dead. Meanwhile, a waiter implored guests to settle their bills.

It was not an unusual scene, both during and after the Allied occupation. Intrigue of some sort seemed to be the city's common currency. With so many Russians living in Istanbul and its outskirts, the city became both a battleground for intra-Russian disputes and a potential target for Bolshevik agents. In October 1921, the Wrangels' residential yacht, the *Lucullus*, was rammed and sunk by a steamer while at anchor in the Bosphorus, a probable assassination plot that the general and his wife escaped only because they happened not to be on board at the time. A certain Kuznetsov, lodged at the Pera Palace, was known to be the centerpiece of Bolshevik propaganda efforts, with a particular interest in turning Cossacks and other White Russians to the communist cause.

"The Bosphorus was a dumping ground of all Europe's war crooks and spies," recalled Robert Dunn, an American naval official. The Pera Palace and Graveyard Street were natural points of attraction for foreigners and locals caught up in the game of intelligence gathering. The British Embassy stood at one end of the street, with a Turkish policeman permanently stationed outside to direct traffic to and from the Grande Rue. Farther along was the old Petits-Champs Park, with its theater and clubs. Next to the park was the Pera Palace itself and, next to that, the small grounds of the American Embassy. Then came the YMCA, followed by a British police station. During the Allied occupation, the headquarters of British naval intelligence and the officers' mess of the British contingent were located in buildings just across the street. Bertha Proctor's bar and sometime brothel anchored the southern end.

Even by the late 1920s, when the foreign presence in the city was much diminished, it was still advisable to be careful with conversation and to check around corners in that section of Pera. Settling in Istanbul had involved "little deceptions and coercions," Trotsky's wife, Natalya, recalled. Trotsky may have seemed a conspiratorial eccentric to the islanders on Büyükada, but paranoia is a reasonable response if someone really is out to get you. The Soviet Embassy, today the consulate of the Russian Federation, was Trotsky's first home in the city, but it was also the headquarters of the surveillance system that kept constant tabs on him. It lay at the center of a large and growing web of secret agents who hoped to make Istanbul the base for intelligence operations throughout southern Europe and the Near East.

"The network of spies was well-organized at Constantinople," recalled Georgy Agabekov, a senior official in the foreign intelligence branch of the OGPU. Agabekov claimed that virtually all the correspondence of major anti-Soviet émigré groups in Istanbul, such as Ukrainian nationalists and Caucasus highlanders, found its way into Soviet hands. The Soviets were careful to balance the desire to infiltrate enemy organizations with the need for keeping operations low-key enough to avoid offending the Turks. Agabekov claimed that the Soviets had managed to finagle informers inside the Japanese, Austrian, and other foreign embassies; to intercept mail destined for White associations and for Trotsky himself; to sign up an Armenian bishop as a paid agent; and even to place an informant inside Trotsky's house on Büyükada. Much of this was little more than enthusiastic bumbling, however. Agents were proud of their roles as zealous defenders of Bolshevism—too proud, in many instances—and stood out like sore thumbs to counterintelligence operatives in Istanbul, Paris, London, and other cities—"prancing along in [a] blue serge suit made to order by some Russian émigré tailor," noted one disillusioned Soviet official.

Agabekov himself had the dubious honor of being the first defector from Stalin's secret police, and it was his time in Istanbul that caused him to flip sides. In 1929 and 1930, he had been working in the city to set up a string of intelligence operations in Greece, Syria, and Palestine, while leaving Turkish affairs to his OGPU colleagues working out of the embassy. Agabekov always claimed that he had become disenchanted with the Soviet system, but the proximate cause was probably more prosaic. He seems to have fallen in love with a young English woman, Isabel Streater, whom he had hired as a language tutor. He at first offered himself to British diplomats as a defector, but they suspected a trap and treated him coolly. Finally, in January 1930, Agabekov and Streater fled separately to Paris, she via the Orient Express and he by sea, and eventually began a new life together as husband and wife.

Agabekov's defection was a blow to the Soviet effort, but the Istanbul operation was accustomed to the regular turnover of personnel. Less than a year before Agabekov's departure, sometime near the middle of 1929, Yakov Minsky, the OGPU station chief who had originally helped Trotsky settle in the city, fell ill and returned to Moscow. His successor was a dark-haired, round-faced operative with a reputation as a personable comrade. His gray-green eyes and witty demeanor seemed to make him irresistible to a string of female coworkers. Even today it is difficult to establish with clarity to whom he was married and when; he may have been married to several women at the same time. His official cover was that of a diplomat at the Soviet Embassy. His travel documents identified him as someone named Naumov. His superiors gave him the code names "Tom" and "Pierre." His real name was Leonid Eitingon.

In many ways Eitingon had the ideal background for a Soviet agent, especially for someone working in an era long before the clear battle lines of the Cold War had been imagined. For more than a generation his family had cultivated the ability to live in many places at once. Eitingon was part of the extended family of Chaim Eitingon, a prominent Russian-Jewish furrier. The elder Eitingon had built up a fur-trading empire that stretched across the Russian Empire and abroad. When the empire ended, his family remained the principal conduit for the Soviet fur business, a major source of wealth for the new regime.

From Moscow to Leipzig to New York, the family oversaw an import–export firm that weathered the Russian civil war and remained lucrative well into the 1930s, when the Depression and the Stalinist nationalization of key industries shut off the spigot. Chaim's son, Max, had grown up in the midst of a wealthy central European and Jewish world. He was the emblem of a family that had reinvented itself within a single generation, moving from the edges of a Russian shtetl to the European beau monde. Trained as a doctor, Max went on to become one of Sigmund Freud's earliest acolytes and the chief codifier of Freudian training in psychoanalysis.

Max's cousin, Leonid, was from the less-wealthy branch of the Eitingon clan. Born in 1899 in the Mogilev district in what is today Belarus, he was the son of a minor bourgeois factory owner and followed the path of many upwardly mobile Jewish young men in the waning days of the Russian Empire: he joined the communists, at first signing on with the Socialist Revolutionary Party and then, after the Bolshevik coup, enlisting in Trotsky's Red Army. In the civil war, he fought to root out counterrevolutionaries in his native district as a member of the Cheka, Lenin's secret police, a job that he seems to have carried out ruthlessly. He was the first generation of good soldiers fighting for the new socialist motherland and, in those days, for world revolution as well—an outcome that Lenin, Trotsky, and other Bolshevik leaders believed was all but inevitable.

Shortly after the end of the civil war, Leonid Eitingon was assigned to foreign intelligence work in Harbin, a Chinese city that was in many ways the East Asian equivalent of Istanbul at the time. It harbored a large community of former White Russians who had chosen to escape east, rather than south, as Bolshevik armies swept through the old empire. Like Istanbul, it was both cosmopolitan and a hotbed of espionage and intrigue, a small island of old Russian culture in a foreign sea. Eitingon's activities—gathering information, turning Whites to the Bolshevik side, and quite possibly arranging the assassination of key leaders in the White community—eventually raised the ire of the Chinese authorities, who, like the Turks, were reluctant to see their country become a battleground for someone else's disputes. When Chinese police broke into the Soviet Consulate in Harbin and searched its files, Eitingon's true identity as a secret police agent was discovered. He was sent packing to Moscow.

In 1929, when he was transferred to Istanbul, Eitingon was immediately placed in charge of the real prize in Soviet foreign espionage: keeping an eye on the aging exile who had recently taken up residence on Büyükada. It was a sign of Eitingon's fine-tuned political sense that he managed to weather his time in Turkey without acquiring even a hint of Trotskyite leanings. One of the professional hazards of being stationed in Istanbul and monitoring the Soviet regime's archenemy was that the assignment placed an agent in the dangerous position of possibly being turned himself—brought over to the Trotskyite camp and made an informant for the man sitting in isolation on the island. In the 1930s, when Stalin began his purge of the Soviet bureaucracy, at least one former Istanbul agent, Yakov Bliumkin, was dismissed and executed for having gone over to the Trotskyites. There is no evidence that Trotsky's supporters ever managed to engage in such counterespionage on a large scale, but authorities in Moscow clearly feared the magnetic power of Trotsky's personality and ideas.

Eitingon, however, survived the Stalinist purges untainted. After leaving his Istanbul assignment, he was placed in charge of espionage operations in western Europe, serving as one of the most experienced and highest-ranking secret operatives working abroad. He briefly served as case officer for Guy Burgess, the famous British traitor and member of the so-called Cambridge Five spy ring. During the Spanish Civil War, Eitingon served as the Stalinist secret police's deputy head of mission in Spain, training legions of commandos to fight the rightist forces of Francisco Franco and developing a friendship—perhaps even more—with a young Spanish communist named Caridad Mercader. Like Eitingon, Mercader was the product of a bourgeois family and someone whose own political convictions had pushed her into the anticapitalist camp. She had signed up with the anarchists and, after the defeat of the Left by Franco, fled with Eitingon to Moscow. Eitingon's experience in Spain, his reputation for efficient work throughout Europe, and his personal relationship with Caridad all recommended him to head up a new operation that would soon unfold half a world away.

On a late August afternoon in 1940, Eitingon found himself in one of two cars idling on a dusty street on the fringes of Mexico City. He was monitoring an asset, much as he had done many years earlier in Istanbul. The asset was Ramón Mercader, Caridad's handsome son, but things were not going well. Eitingon knew that relying on Ramón was a shaky way to run a mission.

Three years earlier, Eitingon had personally trained him as a commando and dispatched him to the front lines against Franco's army, only to have him return wounded and gun shy. He was indecisive and given to nervous sweats. His only real advantage in the current operation was the fact that he had managed to ingratiate himself with the person who lived in the walled compound down the block, an old man whom Eitingon had personally given the Russian code name of "Utka," the Duck. That personal connection was important, since Ramón's mission was to kill him.

A house alarm was sounding. Dogs were barking. There was a commotion behind the front gate. The backup plan had been for Ramón to use his revolver if the mission went awry, but the absence of gunfire meant that even the fallback plan had gone badly. Eitingon ordered the cars to depart, leaving the assassin to find his own way out of the mess he seemed to have made. It was not until sometime later, once Eitingon was safely back in the Soviet Union, that he learned the details of what had happened.

That day, August 20, Ramón had arrived much as he had done each afternoon, parking his car outside the compound and waving at the armed guards to let him in. He made his way to the study where the old man sat working on a text. Minutes later, he pulled out a short-handled ice ax he had concealed in his raincoat and brought it down on the back of Leon Trotsky's head.

Trotsky let out a piercing cry, so loud that Eitingon might well have heard it down the street. Natalya rushed into the study to find the two men separated, Trotsky leaning against a doorway and Ramón looking on dazed, seemingly surprised that the initial blow had not killed him.

Blood was everywhere. Trotsky's guards burst in and grabbed Ramón, nearly pummeling the young man to death before Trotsky could order them to stop. Ramón's testimony, after all, might be used to uncover who had planned the attack. Trotsky was still able to speak when an ambulance delivered him to a nearby hospital. "I don't want them to undress me. I want you to do it," he told Natalya before slipping into a coma. He died the following evening.

As Eitingon sped away, he could not have known that his career had just reached the high point from which he would begin a very long fall. Eitingon had the distinction of being the only Soviet agent whose own career had bookended Trotsky's exile. He had arrived in Istanbul around the same time as Trotsky and then personally planned the attack that would liquidate him eleven years later. For his service, he and Caridad were awarded the Order of Lenin in a private ceremony in the Kremlin—he as the chief conspirator and she as the mother of the literal hatchet man. Ramón, ever the sap, spent the next twenty years serving a murder sentence in a Mexican prison.

By the early 1950s, however, Eitingon had fallen from grace. He was accused of playing a central role in the Doctors' Plot, an alleged conspiracy by Soviet physicians, many of whom happened to be Jewish, to assassinate key Soviet leaders. In reality, the plot was a fabrication spurred on by Stalin's paranoia over internal enemies, but the effort to unmask the supposed conspirators produced a frenzied anti-semitic campaign that targeted senior Jewish communists. Eitingon was arrested, stripped of his medals, and jailed. He was eventually released but spent the rest of his life, until his death in 1981, as an outcast from the intelligence services, working as an interpreter. "There is one small guaranteed way not to end up in jail under our system," Eitingon once joked to his boss. "Don't be a Jew or a general in the state security service." The old Bolshevik mastermind, who had quietly hounded Trotsky from Istanbul to Mexico City, of course was both, and he died in his own kind of internal exile.

QUEEN

Under scrutiny, early 1930s: A contestant poses for judges in a
Miss Turkey competition.

B Y THE TIME LEON TROTSKY left Büyükada for France and
Mexico, Nâzım Hikmet was serving one of his many jail sentences, Halide Edip was in voluntary exile with her husband, Prodromos Bodosakis-Athanasiades was on his way to becoming Greece's
greatest industrialist, and Mustafa Kemal had fully consolidated his
power as unrivaled leader of the Turkish Republic. Debates over socialism and republicanism, patriotism and feminism, loyalty and leadership had pushed Istanbullus in separate directions. They could even
cause old comrades to part ways. Yunus Nadi, for example, had been
Halide Edip's partner in establishing the Anatolian News Agency, but
from that point forward, their careers diverged. Where Halide became
one of the regime's foremost critics, Yunus Nadi was one of its most
committed spokesmen.

He had worked as a newsman already in the late Ottoman period
and had briefly served in the Ottoman parliament. His credentials as a
reform-oriented publicist and bitingly effective writer were impeccable.
He had been part of the Unionist underground, and, when Mustafa
Kemal's resistance movement emerged, he was one of the early enthusiasts who fled from Istanbul to Ankara to join it. After the proclamation
of the republic, he returned to Istanbul and became the city's leading
newspaper editor and press entrepreneur. He could be fierce in criti-
cizing specific government policies or the inefficiencies of state institu-

tions, but he always did so from inside the circle of power around the president and his core associates.

The newspaper Yunus Nadi established in 1924, *Cumhuriyet*, quickly rose to become one of Turkey's most widely read dailies and a mainstay of ardent Kemalism. Its opinion pages could both reflect and sway public attitudes. Foreign governments carefully scoured its pages for evidence of Turkey's shifting foreign-policy orientations—from early flirtations with the Soviet Union to admiration for Adolf Hitler's growing power in Germany. Turkey was modernizing, and *Cumhuriyet* was there both to record the revolution and to champion it. "For four or five years now, Turkey has been in a period of deep restructuring," Yunus Nadi declared in its pages in 1928. "We want to import all traits of Western civilization to our country. Not long ago . . . our social life rested on Eastern principles. We are turning them upside down."

Round and jowly, he wore his gray hair swept back severely. In broad-lapelled suits and the occasional wing collar, he could seem a cartoon of a press mogul, a Turkish version of Citizen Kane. He could rail on the page and gently persuade in person. Both of those skills came into play when he hit upon an idea for expanding newspaper sales and showcasing the new sense of modernity that Kemalism had brought to the ancient city. In February 1929, Yunus Nadi announced that Istanbul would host the republic's first ever beauty contest.

"Why Wouldn't We Do the Same?" a front-page headline asked. Since all civilized countries held beauty contests, with the winners competing in international pageants across Europe and the United States, a similar competition would mark another milestone in Turkey's march toward social maturity. The newspaper soon announced a search for "the most beautiful Turkish woman," who would be selected to represent Turkey abroad and demonstrate the elevated qualities of the new republican woman to a global audience. It would be no different from a soccer game, Yunus Nadi said, a chance to send the best

Turkish citizens overseas and to measure themselves against the finest products of other civilized nations. Further particulars followed. All Turkish women and girls over the age of fifteen, regardless of religion or ethnicity, were invited to participate. Contestants were asked to send in a photograph, which would be printed in the newspaper, and readers would have a chance to vote on the finalists. There would be no swimsuit element, the newspaper explained, and the jury would consist only of the most respected citizens. Prostitutes were expressly forbidden from taking part.

In a country with one party, one leader, and one acceptable path to the future, being asked to vote freely on anything was a novelty, and Yunus Nadi's idea had its desired effect. Photographs flowed into the newspaper's editorial offices. Readers debated the merits of the various finalists. The Turkish winner should have a good chance of beating out other contestants in an international pageant, one writer declared. The recent winner of a European contest had been a Hungarian woman, and since Turks and Hungarians were genetic cousins—both descended from Central Asian nomads, apparently—odds were in the republic's favor. The discussions were so intense that few people in Istanbul probably noticed the arrival of another celebrity, Leon Trotsky, in the same week the competition was announced.

After readers had selected around thirty finalists, the first competition was held at the newspaper's editorial offices. A jury of fifty notables examined each of the women, who were required to wear a décolleté dress and to produce an identity document certifying their Turkish citizenship. By September 3, the results were in, and *Cumhuriyet* dedicated the entire front page to describing the competition and its winner, one Feriha Tevfik. The young woman rocketed from obscurity to fame in an instant. She went on to an international competition in Belgium, but despite Yunus Nadi's high expectations, she failed to place. Still, moguls of Turkey's emerging film industry came calling. She went on to star in several melodramas and romantic films, a well-known figure if not exactly a household name through much of the 1930s.

Yunus Nadi soon announced that the competition would be an annual event. Beginning in 1930, twenty finalists would be invited to a grand ball at the Turquoise club, where they would parade before judges and paying guests in the style of other foreign pageants. "Beauty Is Not Something to Be Ashamed Of," an editorial headline read. All of this was still shockingly new, however. Yunus Nadi had had to defend the contest from the moment he originally broached the idea, and the negative reaction began to swell. He found himself managing an enormous backlash, not only from conservatives in Istanbul society but also from the Turkish government. When judges selected Naşide Saffet, a Turkish schoolteacher, as Miss Turkey 1931, the Ministry of Education issued a circular threatening dismissal for any teachers and pupils who participated in such contests. Teachers in particular were held up as models of propriety and good sense—and were, to boot, state employees—so having one of their number placed before ogling judges was considered an offense to public morality.

Even worse, Yunus Nadi had failed to deliver the most important thing he had promised: that in bending good taste by staging a beauty contest that included Muslim women, he would at least produce someone who could go on to win an international crown. Three years of entrants fell by the wayside when they stepped onto stages in Belgium and France. The title of Miss Europe 1930 had gone to the entrant from Greece, trouncing her Turkish competitor and delivering a major blow to national prestige. It was at this point that Yunus Nadi seems to have come up with an inspired idea. If beauty contests were seen by conservatives as somehow beneath the dignity of Muslim women—in part because the winners had gone on to film or acting careers, which were still considered a sign of loose morals and déclassé origins—one way to solve that problem would be to put forth a contestant whose background was itself beyond reproach. The person he found was Keriman Halis.

Keriman was only ten years old when the republic was declared, but for families such as hers, the fall of the Ottoman Empire was less the end of an old way of life than a rising wave that, with the right planning and connections, could lift fortunes and redefine opportunities. Her great-grandfather had been *şeyhülislam* of the Islamic community. He was, next to the sultan in his role as caliph, the most powerful religious leader in the entire empire. Her grandfather had been a pasha, a senior general in the imperial land forces. Her father, Halis Bey, was a merchant who built a successful business in the late nineteenth century when Ottoman consumers were hungry for items that marked them as modern and European. He had been among the first importers to introduce fire extinguishers to the empire and, in a way, helped alleviate what had been one of Istanbul's preeminent problems for centuries.

With such a pedigree, Keriman spent her childhood among French nannies, equestrian outings, and the social season of balls and chaperoned excursions. With a round face and sparkling brown eyes, she was regarded as a considerable beauty, and the family home in Fındıklı, on the European shore of the Bosphorus, was a place of quick conversation and optimism about the future. Her father's passion for literature and the arts meant that she was surrounded by a cadre of Muslim writers, artists, and thinkers who were helping to reshape the city in the transition from Allied occupation to national sovereignty. It was an atmosphere similar to the one that Halide Edip, three decades Keriman's senior, had known in her own childhood, but the differences were also stark. Halide had been a member of the first generation of women whose adult lives spanned the turbulent years from empire to republic. Their struggles had been over veiling, seclusion, and civil rights. Keriman's generation, by contrast, took the new public lives and legal status of women for granted. They were the first cohort of young women who, as adults, had known no country but the Turkish Republic.

In the late 1920s, Keriman had little reason to frequent the jazz cafés and ballrooms in Pera, uphill from her family home. Finding someone of her breeding and social standing in such venues—surrounded by Russian singers, Levantine partygoers, and sometime prostitutes—would have been nearly unthinkable. But one of Yunus Nadi's signature talents was bridging these two very different worlds.

Istanbul was in many ways a big village, at least for the thin stratum of Muslims in the highest echelons of business and government. It was easy for one of the city's most respected newspaper editors to fall into the orbit of Halis Bey and his talented and beautiful children. Yunus Nadi reportedly approached Halis Bey on more than one occasion to inquire whether Keriman might be allowed to stand as a contestant in his beauty contest. But in an age when seeing Muslim women on stage in any capacity was still a rarity, it was hard to imagine a father's placing his daughter in a position where she would be intentionally examined by strangers. Keriman was technically old enough to participate in the competition, at least according to Yunus Nadi's own rules, but her father was skeptical. On each approach Halis Bey had demurred. Finally, after several years of gentle cajoling, her father relented, and in 1932 Keriman Halis was put forward as an entrant in *Cumhuriyet*'s Miss Turkey contest. At the competition in Pera that July, she walked away with the prize.

Yunus Nadi had far grander designs than simply ushering Keriman toward national fame, however. He immediately entered her into the competition known as the International Pageant of Pulchritude, more popularly known as the Miss Universe competition. Like Yunus Nadi's contest, the pageant was a public relations stunt. Its origins had lain in Galveston, Texas, a city flattened by a hurricane in 1900 and, even three decades later, still seeking ways of luring visitors. Most of the winners had been Americans—most of the competitions, in fact, had been held in Galveston, even though they were marketed as global talent searches—but pageant organizers soon realized that they had a franchise that could be offered to any city or town seeking to revitalize tourism and develop a brand. That year, the competition moved to Spa, the resort in Belgium. With the worldwide economic depression, hotel and restaurant revenues had dwindled, and the pageant was intended

Miss Universe, 1932: Keriman Halis in a publicity photograph.

to be a source of money as well as good press. In August 1932, contestants, friends, and reporters began arriving in Spa in droves, just as
Istanbul was preparing to send off its own champion.

Twenty thousand Istanbullus reportedly turned up for Keriman
Halis's farewell reception in Taksim Square. She set off by train for Belgium with her father as chaperone. Along the way, crowds gathered at
Turkish stations to see her pass by. Once in Spa, all the competitors
were the object of intense media attention, but Keriman was of particular interest. She was the only contestant from the Muslim world
and a young woman whose family background seemed to give her an
air of respectability and grace—which was precisely why Yunus Nadi
had worked so hard to convince her father to allow her to compete. It
was also perhaps the reason that she took to the stage in Belgium with
the full backing of the Turkish government, in great contrast to Yunus
Nadi's entrants from earlier seasons.

In Spa, she performed much as she had done in Istanbul, walking
regally in a ball gown, conversing with judges, and posing discreetly
for the world's press. By the end of the competition, she was certain
one of the other contestants, a German, had won the grand prize. But
when her name was called, she stepped forward with a tentative smile
and into the flash of cameras. She was declared Miss Universe 1932. In
the ensuing days, nearly thirty thousand telegrams came in with congratulations, and Yunus Nadi devoted an entire issue of *Cumhuriyet* to
covering each minute detail of the story. Mustafa Kemal telegraphed
his warm wishes, as did the Grand National Assembly, the minister of
the interior, and the governor of Istanbul. Yunus Nadi was summoned
to the president's office to receive congratulations from Mustafa Kemal
in person. İsmet Pasha, the old war hero and prime minister, rose in
parliament to proclaim Keriman "a living argument against the numerous voices raised in our disfavor." *Cumhuriyet*, never missing an opportunity for hype, dubbed Keriman "The Turkish Girl Who Conquered
the World."

Public engagements and invitations followed. Keriman was hailed in Belgium, feted in Paris, and celebrated in Cairo. She appeared in Berlin and Chicago, and even stopped over in Athens on a courtesy visit with Eleftherios Venizelos, the old Hellenic enemy who had since patched up relations with Mustafa Kemal. She became an ambassador not only for the pageant but, even more important, for her country. She was never quite what her hosts expected. At one gala dinner, an enthusiastic organizer used small paper fezzes as centerpieces, thinking that the Oriental decorations would please the world's first Muslim beauty queen. Since the hats were a symbol of the old empire and illegal in republican Turkey, she refused to enter the hall until they were removed.

Keriman arrived back in Istanbul to an uproarious welcome. She toured the nation, greeted at each stop with an enthusiasm that rivaled only that shown for President Mustafa Kemal himself. She was invited to appear in a film but refused. Honor demanded otherwise, she said. She eventually married, started a family, and became a celebrated symbol of Kemalist virtue. Pageant participants would pay a ritual visit to her for decades to come. She always rejected the label of beauty maven and insisted that the competition had been an exhibition of female emancipation and Turkish modernity.

Two years after her victory in Belgium, when Turks were required by law to take surnames, Mustafa Kemal announced that Keriman's would be Ece—meaning Queen. It remained the family name thereafter. Halide Edip was still on the lecture circuit abroad, but Turkey's most famous feminist had already been eclipsed by a person who had become both the republic's most recognizable woman and, for an instant, the world's. When Istanbul's commuters drove along the coast road near the Bosphorus, past Keriman's old family home, they found themselves traveling on a street that had been renamed Queen Avenue in her honor.

HOLY WISDOM

A friendly visit, April 1939: Joseph Goebbels (foreground center)
and his entourage touring the Hagia Sophia.

K ERIMAN HALIS WAS CONSIDERED a national treasure not just because she defeated every other contestant in Belgium. More important, she had triumphed over any woman whom Greece had managed to put forward. That was precisely Yunus Nadi's hope. The old Hellenic-Turkish rivalry was a trump card that he had played continually against conservatives who saw the entire concept of a beauty pageant as demeaning to Turkish dignity. The Hellenes had been sending their contestants to pan-European competitions for years, he pointed out, and Turks should not fail to do their part for national greatness by selecting their own native beauty. "If the Hellenes Are Doing It, Why Shouldn't We?" a headline in *Cumhuriyet* asked. Keriman's victory—and, by extension, Turkey's—made his case eloquently.

Just as Keriman was embarking on a world tour, Istanbul was also beginning another great experiment in beauty and modernization. This particular version, though, involved not besting the Greeks but, in a way, embracing them. Across the Golden Horn from the Pera Palace lay the remnants of what had once been some of the greatest churches in eastern Christendom: the Hagia Eirene, dedicated to Christ's attribute of the "holy peace" and later ensconced inside the grounds of the sultan's palace at Topkapı; the diminutive Church of Sts. Sergius and Bacchus, with its unique undulating dome; and the jumble of barrel vaults and arches of the Church of the Holy Savior in Chora, just inside the city's land walls. After the Ottoman conquest, most of these and other churches had been either turned into mosques or allowed to decay. Towering above them all were the four minarets of the grandest mosque in Istanbul, the one the Turks called the Ayasofya, a rendering of the name it had borne as a Greek Orthodox church: the Hagia Sophia.

The grand structure rises at the very heart of the original Greek colony of Byzantium and the political and religious core of Byzantine Constantinople. In the sixth century, Emperor Justinian I ordered a new church to be built on the site of two earlier structures, which he insisted had to be grander and more elaborate than those that had come before. Justinian had expanded the territory of his empire across the Mediterranean and presided over a period of confidence and rebirth in New Rome. The cathedral was meant to showcase that renewed power, and when it was consecrated in 537, its completion was hailed as nothing less than a miracle. "So the church has become a spectacle of marvelous beauty," wrote Procopius, the opinionated chronicler of Justinian's reign, "overwhelming to those who see it, but to those who know it by hearsay altogether incredible." When Justinian entered the building for the first time, he is said to have compared his achievement to that of the biblical builder of the temple in Jerusalem. "Oh, Solomon," he exclaimed, "I have conquered you!"

The church was dedicated to the "holy wisdom"—literally, *hagia sophia* in Greek, one of the attributes of God—but the Byzantines knew it simply as the Great Church. Its shape, structure, and scale created the standard by which every other Byzantine church would be judged for the next millennium. The central area, or nave, is nearly square and surmounted by a central dome more than a hundred feet across. The Byzantines, heirs to ancient Roman architectural techniques, had solved a basic structural problem that would elude Western designers throughout the Middle Ages: how to cover a large space without interior columns. The building is in fact its own support.

The weight of the dome cascades along the periphery of the nave through a series of semidomes, arches, and colonnades, all the way down to the foundation. The same techniques would be adopted by the Ottomans after their conquest of Constantinople, which is why all the great mosques of the Ottoman capital—the Süleymaniye and Selimiye, the Sultanahmet and the Kılıç Ali Pasha, all with airy interiors that can fit row upon row of the kneeling faithful at Friday prayers—in many ways compete to outdo the Hagia Sophia at its own game. Across the world, both Greek Orthodox and Roman Catholic churches often took the Hagia Sophia as their model, from some of the great structures of the Italian Renaissance to the neo-Byzantine revival of the late nineteenth century.

The church's interior decoration consisted originally of patterned mosaics that probably did not depict human forms. In the eighth century, the Iconoclast movement in Eastern Christianity railed against human images, which were viewed as "graven" and therefore prohibited by the Ten Commandments. Enthusiastic monks raced around the empire literally defacing murals and mosaics in churches, monasteries, and public spaces. But shifts in attitude gradually allowed representational art to emerge inside the city's most important sacred space.

From the tenth century forward, the interior of the church was covered with serene angels and devout emperors towering above the nave and peering down from the galleries. A representation of the Virgin seated with the Christ Child on the throne of heaven filled the apse, while the dome sheltered one of the most common yet arresting scenes in Orthodox Christian art: the majestic image of Christ Pantocrator, the all-powerful Jesus with an expression at once kind and stern, his hand raised in benediction and reproach.

The effect, with the eyes of saints seeming to glisten in the candlelight and twirls of incense wafting up into the gloom, must have been mesmerizing. According to tradition, a delegation of Slavs visited in the tenth century and reported back to their prince, Vladimir of Kiev, that "we knew not whether we were in heaven or on earth. . . . We only know that God dwells there among men, and their service is fairer than the ceremonies of other nations." On their recommendation, Vladimir adopted Christianity as the state religion and concluded a marital alliance with the sister of the Byzantine emperor, the beginning of what would later become the Russian Orthodox Church.

Much of the interior decoration was chipped away over the centuries as souvenirs or loot. There was probably no better preservative, however, than Muslim conquest. When Mehmed II marched into Constantinople in 1453, he interrupted a Mass being conducted inside the church for the protection of the city. His forces battered down the imposing bronze doors and killed or captured the embattled worshippers, dragging priests away from the altar in midchant.

But Mehmed quickly realized the architectural—and spiritual—treasure that lay before him. When he stood before the church's gates in the hours after his armies had secured the city, he bent to the ground and scooped a handful of dirt onto his turban, a gesture of ritual purification before a house of God. Inside the vast space, he stood in silence, watching the play of light from thousands of flickering candles. A Muslim imam pronounced that there was no God but God, while Mehmed knelt in prayer before the apse, which pointed roughly southeast, toward both Jerusalem and Mecca. From that day, he ordered, the church would become a mosque. Four mismatched minarets were later added to the exterior. The human figures on the interior walls—in theory, prohibited in Islam—were dealt with as cheaply and efficiently as possible. They were simply covered with plaster and paint.

Christian angels and Greek emperors thus lurked beneath the thin scree only inches away from where the sultan and his retinue came for Friday prayers. Under the Ottomans, they were partially uncovered on only one occasion. In the 1840s, as part of a plan for modernizing the capital, the reformist Sultan Abdülmecid I commissioned two Swiss architects, Gaspare and Giuseppe Fossati, to revitalize the city's most important mosque. The Fossati brothers reworked the exterior decoration, erasing centuries of grime and giving the walls more color and drama, including lateral red candy stripes, a version of European neo-Gothic excess.

The Fossatis had also been the first to remove the interior plaster and reveal the intricate mosaics, which they had discovered by accident while repairing cracks and stabilizing the marble revetment on the walls. Abdülmecid saw himself as an emperor confident in his place in world civilization and able to look with interest on the achievements of the Christian rulers who had come before him. He was delighted by the discovery. For a few months, the mosque was transported back to an earlier time, filled with sparkling light bouncing from the diadem of an empress, the golden halo around the head of Christ, and the dazzling lapis lazuli of the Virgin's cloak.

The Ottoman Empire was given one of its first prolonged gazes at its own Byzantine past, but then, just as quickly, the Islamic state turned away from the representational art that lay beneath the walls of its greatest mosque. The Fossatis catalogued a portion of what they had discovered before the sultan, bowing to pressure from Muslim conservatives, ordered them to seal the images behind fresh plaster and whitewash. Nearly a century later, however, the mosaics would come to light again.

From his suite in the Pera Palace, Thomas Whittemore had been one of the best-connected people in Istanbul in the early 1920s. He had overseen a mini-empire of charitable organizations, fundraising events, refugee assistance centers, orphanages, and student scholarship foundations, all focused on assisting White Russians in escaping their old empire and reinventing themselves in Turkey or elsewhere. He lunched with Allied high commissioners and generals, visited Ottoman dignitaries, and charmed the core activists of what would now be called

Istanbul's civil society, especially the many women who were in large part responsible for philanthropic work in the city.

Whittemore was by nature flamboyant and reclusive, intensely private yet given to searching for the limelight, a depressive self-promoter of the first order, and someone awed by beauty and the thrill of discovery—in other words, the epitome of the public intellectual. In later life, he vamped in his signature trilby for the noted photographer Dmitri Kessel and a spread in *Life* magazine. He posed for noirish studio shots with a serious brow and brim pulled low. Short and thin-framed, he might show up at a meeting swallowed up in a striped North African burnoose, a Balkan shearling coat, or a Kurdish goatskin. He could appear at the oddest of moments—at the coronation of Ethiopia's Haile Selassie, on a transatlantic crossing with W. B. Yeats and Jascha Heifetz, or on the arm of the last king of Italy in the Palazzo del Quirinale. He cultivated in himself what he prized in others: a flair for the unexpected and a love of the "mystic," a word he used with frequency.

As a member of a prominent Boston family, Whittemore had spent his young adulthood, before the First World War, bouncing from one pursuit to another. He took a degree in English from Tufts College and later taught a few literature classes there. He attended graduate lectures at Harvard in art and art history. He dabbled in medieval studies. Through a friend, the renegade curator, art historian, and sometime secretary of Boston's Museum of Fine Arts, Matthew Prichard, Whittemore made his way through the transatlantic society of men usually referred to as aesthetes: fast-talking, witty, less well-read than well-informed, and confirmed bachelors in an age when everyone understood what that meant—Oscar Wildes, of sorts, but with Yankee accents. Traveling together in Paris, Prichard and Whittemore made the rounds of literary events and gallery openings. Prichard may have been the person who introduced Whittemore to his friend Henri Matisse, whom Prichard had met at one of Paris's premier gathering places, Gertrude Stein's salon. The three became close associates. Matisse's sketch portrait of Whittemore remained one of Whittemore's prized possessions.

In 1910, Whittemore visited, perhaps with Prichard, the *Meisterwerke muhammedanischer Kunst*, a Munich exhibition of more than three thousand masterpieces of Islamic art that still counts as the largest single gathering of Islamic miniatures, calligraphy, and decorative arts ever staged. The exhibition was a first. Never before had Europeans displayed items from Muslim lands as autonomous products of the human imagination, not stage props adorning an Orientalist fantasy of a harem or a Bedouin tent. More than a hundred thousand people walked through dozens of halls displaying Islamic objects one piece at a time.

As with many artists, collectors, and critics who saw it, the Munich exhibition transformed Whittemore's understanding of the possibilities and richness of the Near East—its Islamic present as well as its Christian past. Over the next decade, he made a long detour away from art and into the field of refugee relief, but his interest in the region's many-layered heritage never wavered. His mind, he once confided to a friend, was always in Istanbul. On long walks from the Pera Palace, he came to see that his true calling lay almost literally before him—not in the long lines of Russian refugees queueing up in the hotel lobby but rather in the paving stones and plastered walls of the city itself, in the remnants of old Byzantium.

As Whittemore knew, something called the Byzantine Empire was largely a construct of modern historians. The first appearance of the word *Byzantine* in English dates only from 1794, and that in a source relating to botany, not history or culture. The people we now call the Byzantines never used that label, nor did they conceive of their world as politically separate from that of their Roman forebears.

True, they had traded pagan rituals for Christian piety, the coarse Latin of the dying western empire for refined Greek, and the silted and flood-prone Tiber River for the free-flowing, world-connecting Bosphorus. Yet they nevertheless called themselves Romans, or *Romaioi* in Greek, and imagined their civilization as the logical and unbroken continuation of that of Augustus and Marcus Aurelius. The lands under their control expanded and contracted over the centuries, but the Byzantines consistently called anyone living outside their capital city "*hoi exō Romēs*," foreigners from beyond New Rome, that is, Istanbul. They usually referred to their metropolis as simply "the city," much as New Yorkers speak of Manhattan. That habit probably gave us the modern name, since the Greek *eis tēn polin*—"to the city"—is tantalizingly similar to "Istanbul." To this day, ethnic Greeks native to Istanbul are referred to in Turkish as something akin to "Romans," or *Rumlar*, an echo of the name Byzantines gave themselves.

The Byzantine heritage had an obvious richness and resilience, an ability to imagine continuity while adapting to the shifting circumstances of what had become, by the early Middle Ages, a borderland state wedged between rival Christian powers in the Balkans, marauding Crusaders pouring in from the west, and multiple waves of invading Muslims from the south and east. Its influence lived on not only in the civilization of the Ottomans themselves—who actually embraced a fair amount of Byzantine culture, except for the Christian theology—but also in the art, music, spirituality, and architecture of Eastern Christendom, from Greece to Russia to Ethiopia.

But despite these living links, Byzantium was long seen by Western scholars and art collectors as the poor cousin of the material culture of ancient Greece and Rome. At worst, writers echoed the eighteenth-century historian Edward Gibbon, who limped toward the conclusion of his magisterial *Decline and Fall of the Roman Empire* (1776–1789) with a sense of exasperation at the foibles and fractiousness of the Byzantines. "I have reached at length the last reign of the princes of Constantinople," he wrote, "who so feebly sustained the name and majesty of the Caesars." Byzantine art was similarly thought of as essentially in-between: naïve and hemmed in by convention, not so much anti-representational as indifferent to representation, less interesting than the hyperrealism of Greek and Roman sculpture that preceded it and less imaginative than the Renaissance tapestries and paintings that followed—an art purpose-built for a world that was dark and God-bound, smelling of incense and candle wax. The adjective *Byzantine* eventually became a synonym for anything overbureaucratized, recondite, opaque, and ridiculous.

For a small cadre of art historians, however, the Byzantine tradition was a long-forgotten bridge tying together the Greek-speaking Mediterranean, the political legacy of ancient Rome, and the many Eastern influences that would eventually find their highest expression in the architecture of Ottoman Istanbul. The first journal of Byzantine studies emerged in the 1890s, the first international congress (with just thirty participants) was held in the 1920s, and the first international exhibition of Byzantine art was organized in the 1930s. In the interwar years, the entire field of Byzantine studies was given a major boost by the energetic collecting of a single visionary couple, Robert and Mildred Woods Bliss, who stuffed their stately mansion in Washington, DC—Dumbarton Oaks—with artifacts that would prove vital to scholars seeking to understand the lost world of Byzantine emperors, chroniclers, and artisans.

Thomas Whittemore was part of this vanguard of the devoted. He had no degree in art history, and his only real experience with archaeology had been as an assistant on a dig in Egypt before the First World War. What he did have was supreme confidence in his ability to raise enough money to pick up where Gaspare and Giuseppe Fossati had left off—restoring the Hagia Sophia to its former glory and opening its doors to the wider world.

Whittemore had a preternatural ability to sidle up to the great and powerful. During the First World War, he had delivered biscuits and nibbles from the queen of England to her sister, the dowager empress of Russia. His work with Russian refugees had put him in contact with some of the greatest historians and conservators in Europe. The Russian Archaeological Institute, just up the Grande Rue from the Pera Palace, had been the chief institution in Istanbul charged with unearthing the remnants of Byzantium, and with its shuttering after the Bolshevik Revolution, many of its leading lights sought Whittemore's aid. His family connections in Boston gave him access to American philanthropists, while his misspent youth among artists' circles and Parisian salons had sharpened his ability to convert his vague enthusiasms into vital projects. "[H]e had a gift for making himself appear to be a charlatan," recalled Sir Steven Runciman, the distinguished Byzantinist, but "[h]is persuasive powers enabled him also to raise funds . . . from rich American ladies, whom he handled with superb artifice."

In 1930, Whittemore established the Byzantine Institute, with makeshift offices in Paris, Boston, and Istanbul, as a vehicle for fundraising and a letterhead with which he could approach the Turkish government for a concession to work on the Hagia Sophia. Whittemore's version of events was that he simply made an entreaty to Mustafa Kemal, who was so taken with the proposal that he slapped a "Closed for Repairs" sign on the mosque the next day, written in his own hand. But that was a fundraiser's tall tale. Whittemore in fact put to good use the skills he had developed in raising money for Russian refugees: interceding with leading Turkish officials, garnering support from amateur collectors and monied families in the United States, chatting up diplomats in Istanbul and Ankara, and finally approaching a key official named Halil Bey, the former director of the Turkish National Museum and a parliamentarian in the Grand National Assembly. The Harem of Topkapı Palace—the household areas once reserved for women and children—had already been opened to visitors in the spring of 1930. Treating the entire historic area of the old city's promontory as a single zone of historic significance, from the palace to the Sultanahmet mosque, was part of Henri Prost's design for a monumental park in the neighborhood. Things were shaping up in Whittemore's favor.

Politics also played a useful role. Mustafa Kemal's government was still in the midst of realizing two principal goals: unwinding the long tradition that had fused Islam and state power in the Ottoman Empire and transferring wealth out of the hands of ethnic minorities and toward Muslim Turks. The caliphate had been abolished, minorities had been pressed to renounce their collective rights, and Islam had been disestablished as the state religion. Making a museum out of the building that was at once the greatest Greek monument beyond the Parthenon and Istanbul's most important mosque was a brilliant vehicle for realizing the government's core aims. A rapprochement between Turkey and Greece—occasioned by the coming to power of a more conciliatory government in Athens, even though it was headed by the old firebrand Venizelos—also expanded the scope for reassessing the Greek legacy in Istanbul. In October 1930, the two countries signed a treaty of neutrality and cooperation that, against all expectations, would prove to be one of the most longstanding diplomatic agreements in interwar Europe. Two years later, Mustafa Kemal sent Keriman Halis, still wearing her Miss Universe crown, to meet Venizelos as a symbolic recognition that times had changed between the rival nations. The Hagia Sophia was a similar exercise in cultural détente. Ironically, restoring the greatest material expression of Greek Christianity became one of the most powerful levers wielded by the Kemalists in their drive to make the country more Turkish, more secular, and more secure with its neighbors.

In the summer of 1931, the Turkish Council of Ministers authorized Whittemore's Byzantine Institute to lead the expedition to revitalize the church and, in particular, to uncover the old mosaics. By December, wood-and-metal scaffolding rose inside the cavernous interior, giving access to spaces above the doorways and to the elevated galleries on the second story overlooking the nave. Week by week, Whittemore's workmen gently chipped away at the paint and plaster to reveal the glass tesserae, or mosaic pieces, that lay underneath. Tiny bits of surface plaster would cling to the glass, threatening to dislodge the delicate tesserae from their beds, so workmen were instructed to use dental tools to scrape away the vestiges of the Fossatis' work.

Once they were exposed, the tesserae were gently washed with a chamois and a weak ammonia-and-water solution, rubbed with a soft bristle brush, and then buffed with another chamois. The work was achingly slow, and even though Whittemore had never overseen such a project, he managed to hire talented technicians and supervisors. Venetian mosaicists, Russian workmen, French antiquarians, and American architectural historians were all drawn to what was quickly becoming one of the world's most intriguing archaeological feats.

The restoration promised a new way of thinking about the city's Greek heritage. With the old church returned to something of its former glory, the artistic and cultural legacies of the city—the multiple pasts of which the Turks could see themselves as the legitimate and magnanimous custodians—would be revealed as well. If the Acropolis in Athens was one version of what it meant to be Greek—sun-bleached, austere, and pagan—the version being revealed bit by bit in the Hagia Sophia was its natural rival: color-filled, majestic, and a hybrid of East and West in exactly the way that Mustafa Kemal's republic was imagining itself.

But this was also why Whittemore's work courted such controversy at the time. The Turkish president may have given his personal blessing to the project, but newspapers were filled with articles decrying the Americans as destroyers of the city's greatest mosque. Whittemore was denounced as a proselytizer in the guise of an archaeologist, seeking to spread Christianity one chisel cut at a time. Islam prohibited human images, others claimed, and Whittemore was offending religious belief by exposing the mosque's infidel beginnings.

Secular Turks rallied in response. Halil Bey, the parliamentarian and museum curator, rose to Whittemore's defense and stressed the scholarly and artistic nature of the enterprise. Yunus Nadi likewise hailed Whittemore's work as the victory of science over religion. The original decision to plaster over the mosaics under Sultan Abdülmecid I, he wrote in *Cumhuriyet*, had been an expression of brutal religious conservatism. Now, at last, the artistic glories of the city were being freed from their religious veils and revealed to their secular custodians.

In the summer of 1932, Whittemore traveled to Ankara to report directly to Mustafa Kemal. The president dispatched one of his adopted daughters, Zehra, to receive him at the train station and drive him to the presidential farm outside the capital. There, Whittemore and the Turkish leader walked in the gardens and discussed the ongoing restoration, with Zehra serving as translator. When he was shown early photographs of some newly uncovered mosaics, Mustafa Kemal expressed deep interest in the project and satisfaction with the Byzantine Institute's labors. On the crowded train back to Istanbul, Whittemore gleefully noted that the president had made sure to arrange a special sleeping berth for him, while the Japanese chargé d'affaires was left to fend for himself.

Whittemore's earlier digs in Egypt had involved sifting through desert sand or loose rocks, with odds against finding anything but a collapsed wall or a cast-off potsherd. Now, he almost always knew what he was looking for, since the Fossatis had left some record of what they had found nearly a century earlier. Inch by inch, his team retraced the Fossatis' footsteps, discovering the work the Swiss brothers had done to stabilize many of the mosaics and ensure that they remained firmly attached to the interior walls. Whittemore staged films of his team hard at work, his assistants in white lab coats and overalls and he in a dark suit and ever-present trilby.

In early 1933, one of the teams began chipping away at a blank wall in the south gallery, the second-story promenade that looks down into the building's main space. The careful chiseling soon revealed a mosaic covering much of a large, east-facing wall. Its outlines seemed to soar toward the ceiling, dwarfing anything in that portion of the structure. The next season, Whittemore's team turned its full attention to revealing the mosaic tessera by tessera. With each chisel strike or scrape of a dental pick, more and more of a new mosaic revealed itself. Much of it had been lost at some point in the church's history, perhaps destroyed in an earthquake or hacked away in the desperate hours after Ottoman infantry first stormed into the crowd of Christian worshippers in the fifteenth century. Still, within weeks the full dimensions and content of the image had become clear: a huge version of a religious scene that art historians knew as the Deesis, from the Greek word for prayer or supplication. It turned out to be one of the great treasures of Byzantine art.

A Deesis image typically shows a majestic Jesus Christ flanked on his right by the Virgin Mary and on his left by John the Baptist. Mary and John bow their heads toward the savior, their bodies turned partially toward him, while Jesus looks almost squarely at the observer, his head turned slightly to the right and his right hand raised in blessing. The iconic form exemplifies the very thing that worshippers in an Orthodox church are expected to do themselves: adore the savior, approach him in prayer and humility, and seek his forgiveness literally eye to eye. Unlike the iconography of Western churches, Orthodox images are not simply illustrative—telling a story from the Bible, say—or allegorical—revealing an essential truth in the form of a parable or set of meaning-laced symbols. They are meant to *do* something: to serve as a portal, an urgent and direct route to the divine. You don't just admire an Orthodox image; you certainly don't worship it. You interact with it.

The Deesis was a standard form in Byzantine art, but Whittemore's specialists knew that this particular example had managed to exceed the bounds of its form. The entire background was composed of gilded tesserae, which made the huge portraits of Jesus, Mary, and John pop into three dimensions. The folds of their garments are deep and shadowed, with the outer edges picking up the ambient light of Christ in his glory. The savior's lapis-colored cloak shoots out from the flat surface, pushing the duller clothing of the Virgin and John into the background. Jesus's pale and unlined face glows brighter against this golden background, his light-brown beard merging naturally with the flesh-colored skin and pinkish lips, all framed by a massive halo. With the uncanny depth of the folded gowns, and even the subtle indentations defining the line of Jesus's collarbone, it is easy to forget that all this was achieved with tiny pieces of glass all assembled on a flat surface well above the sightline of an observer.

But even though Christ is naturally at the center of the Deesis, in this version it is John who steals the show. He is wrapped in a green-and-brown cloak that is not so much draped as crushed, the lines harsh and angular, suggesting wrinkles more than folds. His hair is a mat of red and brown, furlike and mangled, sweeping back from his head and hanging down his back. His beard ends in rough ringlets, obscuring his mouth and contrasting with the light fuzz on the jawline of Jesus.

The expression on his face is one of the most anguished and moving expressions in the Byzantine tradition. His eyebrows almost touch, angling up to meet his furrowed brow. His eyes are hooded as he strains to gaze on the glorified Christ. It is here that the Deesis has its greatest element of visual depth, an exemplary exception to the general rule that Orthodox images eschewed perspective in favor of flatness. His right eye is slightly smaller than his left, making his face uncannily natural and full of life.

Unlike Christ or the Virgin, unlike the emperors and empresses depicted in other mosaics in the Hagia Sophia, John is neither an object of devotion nor a record of some great personage from the Byzantine past. Almost alone among the scores of sacred images that would have surrounded worshippers at the height of the church's fame, he is meant to be a figure not of veneration but rather of emulation: the very model of piety in sin, rejection of the world, and selfless awe before the holy wisdom.

Literate Greeks would have been able to read the inscription on the far right of the panel. It identifies John not in the way he is normally described in the Western church—as the Baptist, the one who anointed Jesus with water from the Jordan River, a paradoxical act of wiping away the sins of the sinless Son of God. He is here called *Ho Prodromos*, the predecessor, the first on the road, the one who comes before. He literally points the way, his open left hand disappearing into the blankness of missing tesserae as he gestures toward his right, toward the light streaming in from a towering window, casting the viewer's attention away from himself and onto the risen Christ.

Whittemore's team estimated that the Deesis panel had been created in the 1260s, a time when Byzantine art had already begun to incorporate some of the features of early medieval design from the West. The face of John was heart-wrenching in its weighty agony, yet it was also a lost example of what the Byzantine world might have become. The Byzantines had no Renaissance, but there is a quiet hint of it here, a faint glimmer of the sacred art that could in time have produced its own version of a Titian or a Michelangelo. It was also a reminder that, at least in the thirteenth century, the two halves of the church were not that far apart, both of them struggling, like John, to make sense of the incomprehensible Divine. But there was a further secret in the Deesis—a trait that, as it turned out, the mosaic shared with many of the other images adorning the church. It lay not in the subject matter but rather in its tiniest components: the tesserae that the Byzantine mosaicist had used to create the image.

In testing the strength and bonding of each individual tessera, Whittemore's associates discovered that they did not form a smooth surface. Instead, they jutted out at all angles, some of their corners exposed and others pushed deep into the layer of lime and marble dust that formed the base-level adhesive. This was not simply a result of age and the periodic rattle of earthquakes, however. The tesserae had been placed that way for a reason: to turn the golden background of the image, the halos, and even the eyes of the saints into hundreds of individual reflectors, shooting back the candlelight and sunlight. That technique could cause the images to step out of pious myth and into the world of the living. There was even a surprising regularity to the angles. The higher the angle relative to the flat wall, the more light was reflected at the observer: fifteen degrees for the tesserae in the vestibule, which was naturally brighter, and up to thirty degrees in the narthex, where sunlight had a more difficult time penetrating. For an especially vibrant effect, as in the Deesis background, the tesserae were laced with gold leaf and set in a scalloped pattern that made the background glitter and flare.

Whittemore realized that, in the Deesis, his workmen had uncovered not simply an arresting image but also evidence of artists—Greeks, Venetians, or unknown others—who had managed to work within a visual convention while at the same time exceeding and deepening it. Whittemore's team had inadvertently conjured a forgotten moment in time: weeks and months in the thirteenth century when one or more mosaicists, working individually or as part of a small team, stood on creaky wooden scaffolds near the top of what was, at the time, the largest church in the entire world, placing half-inch pieces of cut glass at precisely the right angles so that sunlight, pouring through the church's many windows nearly seven centuries later, would be reflected in dazzling fashion. The Deesis mosaicists had managed to achieve an effect that was both more than and exactly equal to the sum of its parts.

The Deesis and other mosaics that Whittemore unearthed sparked a revival of interest in Byzantine art. Each season's work was covered in the international press, and in time Whittemore devised ambitious plans to copy the mosaics on a grand scale, so that they could be viewed by audiences around the world. His team attached huge rolls of tracing paper to the mosaics and rendered the exact outline of each tessera in pencil. The tracings were then photographed and backed with linen, to create stable platforms that could be painted with egg tempera, re-creating the colors as they appeared on the wall. Plaster casts were also made by running a thin cotton pad across the mosaics, pressing it into the tessera, stabilizing it with shellac, and then using the textured cotton as a mold. The resulting cast could then be painted as a three-dimensional replica of the original. The casts gave the observer the chance to feel the flatness and the crevasses of the glass tesserae. It was almost like being there oneself, teetering on top of Whittemore's scaffolds.

In 1941, the Metropolitan Museum of Art in New York spent $7,500 to purchase one of the copies of the Deesis. Three years later, it became the centerpiece of a grand exhibition dedicated to the restoration of the Hagia Sophia, and it is still there today, featured in the museum's medieval hall. For the first time, thousands of people outside Istanbul were able to see the wonders that Whittemore's ambition had wrought. The visitors no doubt included Greek families who had fled in the 1920s and were making new lives in America, consuming the recordings of Roza Eskenazi and now able to see a restored version of their city's signature landmark. The grandson of a preacher whose core belief had been the oneness of humanity had renewed the public's interest in one of the most religiously mixed-up places on earth—the world's greatest church, then its largest mosque, then a museum housing an iconic wanderer, John, the First on the Road, eyes downcast before his majestic God.

The Hagia Sophia "is the universe of buildings," Whittemore wrote. "It is what the world needs most and has lost." In 1934, the Turkish Council of Ministers formally declared it a museum, and by early the next year it was open to visitors. Edward VIII and Wallis Simpson stopped by, as did John D. Rockefeller Jr., and Matisse, Whittemore's old friend from Paris. The tide of politicians, diplomats, and celebrities became so great that the Byzantine Institute began compiling logs of distinguished guests, the better to promote new projects to future funders. For centuries the most important building in the city had been a place of Islamic worship, accessible to the faithful but generally hidden from non-Muslims. Now it was open to everyone.

The effect of walking into the space is as arresting now as it was then. Sunlight shot through the high windows and made the walls glow, much as they had done on the day Mehmed the Conqueror strode in solemnly in 1453. Whittemore commissioned filmmakers to make studies of light in the interior and to catch the progress of the sun's rays across the floor, a way of understanding the ingenious angling of the tesserae and the optics behind the twinkling and sunbursts that had astounded earlier generations. Watching the films today—kept in the Byzantine Institute's archives at Dumbarton Oaks, now a unit of Harvard University—is like seeing the preserved record of some natural ballet, mesmerizing in its effects, a gentle, almost loving statement of visitors' persistent fascination with the intertwining of light and architectural form in Justinian's Great Church.

In the spring of 1939, a German tourist checked into the Pera Palace and made his way to the Hagia Sophia to see the results of Whittemore's labors. "The dome has a graceful elegance, light and yet monumental," he wrote in his diary on April 14. The sun, still low in the spring sky, illuminated the space and gave the entire scene a fairy-tale quality. He was on his way to lunch at the Teutonia Club with representatives of the local German community. The afternoon was taken up with shopping for carpets and tourist trinkets in the Grand Bazaar. "The folks at home will love these things," he said.

Life seemed wonderful in the old city, but he was struck by the contrast between the resplendent Hagia Sophia and the darkening mood—a kind of "psychosis," he recalled—that seemed to infuse Istanbul. A week before, fascist Italy had suddenly invaded Albania, sparking fears that Benito Mussolini would soon come after Turkey as well. While looking up at the ancient mosaics, hands clasped behind his ecru mackintosh, Hitler's propaganda minister, Joseph Goebbels, knew that change was coming. Even in Istanbul, everyone was expecting war.

SHADOW WARS

Air raid drill, ca. 1944: Istanbul firemen in gas masks stand guard outside the entrance to Galatasaray Lycée on a deserted Grande Rue.

FIVE MONTHS AFTER JOSEPH GOEBBELS checked out of the Pera Palace, Germany and the Soviet Union invaded Poland and the Second World War began. Turkey soon affirmed its neutrality. The country had been an early joiner in the First World War, and Turkish politicians—not to mention the republic's refugee citizenry—could remember the result. Few families had been untouched by the effects of genocide, foreign invasion, ethnic cleansing, and forced migration. At a funeral it doesn't matter where you stand, the Turkish foreign minister told the British ambassador, so long as you're not lying in the coffin.

The commitment to staying on the sidelines was as old as the republic itself. Mustafa Kemal had articulated the principle of "peace at home, peace in the world," and it became the polestar of the country's foreign policy. The concept flowed as much from rational self-interest as from idealism. Turkey had sloughed off its old empire to its own great advantage. Smaller and leaner, the republic had few of the territorial problems that had bedeviled its imperial predecessor. "Where should we be now if, forced to mobilize and put our troops in Thrace, we had at the same time to defend the Yemen?" Prime Minister Şükrü Saracoğlu explained to a colleague. But Turkey was still situated in a complicated neighborhood.

In the Mediterranean, Italy's ambitious rise was seen as a major threat, especially after the Italian occupation of Albania in the spring of 1939. Across the Black Sea, the Soviet Union had become a serious worry. The days of looking to the Soviet model of single-party rule, quick economic development, and breakneck nation-building were gone. Ankara and Moscow were united in a nonaggression pact left over from the early years of the republic, but the concern now was that Stalin would use war as an excuse to grab Turkish territory in eastern Anatolia or to realize the old Russian dream of controlling the Straits. To the south, British and French influence lingered on in those countries' mandate administrations in Palestine, Syria, and Lebanon. Some Turkish politicians saw the old adversaries as prospective allies, but two decades after the occupation of Istanbul and the abortive Treaty of Sèvres, others still looked warily on relations with London and Paris. In the Balkans, Turkey was bound by a treaty with Greece, Romania, and Yugoslavia. The pact committed the signatory states to stable borders and consultations in the event of hostilities, but Bulgaria's refusal to join kept the region tense and Turkey's border unsecured.

Farther afield, Germany was Turkey's most important trading partner and a core market for raw materials such as chromium, used in the German arms industry. Despite the disastrous alliance with Berlin during the First World War, there was considerable sympathy for the confident nationalism and state-dominated economy of Hitler's new order. Some public figures in Istanbul and Ankara shared the Reich's founding ideology as well, declaring Turks and Aryans natural allies in the coming racial struggle. The same month as Goebbels's visit to Istanbul, Berlin deployed one of its most seasoned officials, former chancellor Franz von Papen, as the new ambassador in Ankara. Although a sometime critic of Hitler, von Papen had in fact been one of Nazism's great enablers, assisting in Hitler's rise to the German chancellorship and in winning over Austria to the German cause. His powers of persuasion now seemed to be aimed squarely at Turkey.

All the countries that Turks had once seen as models of civilized behavior—France and Britain in the nineteenth century, Germany in

the early twentieth, the Soviet Union during the war of independence—
were hurtling toward mutual destruction. Turkish foreign policy thus
involved careful balancing. The strategy was to build a protective web
of alliances, counteralliances, and nonaggression agreements, all the
while trying to convince each major power that Turkish neutrality was
in everyone's best interest. In 1936, Turkey had signed the Montreux
Convention governing shipping on the Bosphorus and the Dardanelles. The government was required to keep the Straits open to civilian
traffic in peacetime and to restrict the deployment of naval vessels not
belonging to states bordering the Black Sea. When at war, Turkey was
authorized to place its own limits on the passage of both military and
civilian craft of belligerent countries. Those provisions gave the Turkish
government a convenient out: They provided a legally binding reason
for dealing evenhandedly with all countries, whether Allies, Axis, or neither. But as Europe raced toward war, old treaties and commitments
were falling by the wayside. Few people could predict how Turkey's foreign policy might evolve in the immediate future. The reason was that
the country was itself in the middle of the most profound period of
political uncertainty since the foundation of the republic.

When the law requiring surnames was passed in 1934, the Grand
National Assembly voted to award Mustafa Kemal the name Atatürk,
often translated as "Father of the Turks." Atatürk was certainly perceived that way at the time: as the military liberator, first president,
and visionary modernizer of his country—the true founding father
and model citizen for the earliest generation of republicans. But a better translation would be something like "Papa Turk." Not only was he
the driving force behind the country's sweeping cultural, political, and
economic changes; he was also regarded as an avuncular figure whose

every utterance gave rise to reverent and—so far as these things can be discerned—genuine adoration.

Atatürk was very much in the mold of other twentieth-century dictators. He ground down political opposition and held firm to the belief that state planning could realize the true interests of the nation, without ever feeling the need to ask the nation what its interests happened to be. Yet, unlike a Mussolini or a Franco, he knew where to draw the line. He was one of the few supreme leaders of the era to develop a cult of personality that staved off its own inevitable decay. The reason was a matter of timing.

Atatürk had the good fortune, in a way, to exit the stage while his reputation was still near its height. He spent the summer of 1938 in Istanbul, much as he had done each of the previous ten years, visiting Florya beach and lodging at Dolmabahçe Palace and aboard the *Savarona*, a yacht the Turkish government had purchased for his use. Much of his youthful vigor was gone, however. His stocky physique and upright bearing had given way to a stoop. His skin had gone sallow and green. Cirrhosis of the liver had sapped his strength, and nosebleeds, rashes, and pneumonia had caused him to withdraw from daily tasks. At a frail fifty-seven years old, he had become more a venerable head of state than the energetic head of government who had pushed through the last batch of monumental reforms—the surname law, women's suffrage, a constitutional guarantee on secularism—only a few years earlier. In mid-October, he fell into a coma, recovered briefly, and then slipped back into unconsciousness. He died on the morning of November 10 at Dolmabahçe, the site of so many other defining moments in Istanbul's modern history, from the exile of the last sultan to the departure of the Allied occupation force. To this day, the clock in his palace bedchamber is set permanently to 9:05, the moment of the president's death.

The city, like the country as a whole, went into a frenzy of grief. Children poured from schools weeping, to be picked up by worried parents who themselves had tears streaming down their faces. Newspapers appeared in midday editions with their pages framed by black borders. Atatürk's last words had been a Muslim salutation—"Peace be upon you"—but his funeral arrangements were decidedly secular. His body was embalmed, rather than buried immediately as required by Islamic law, and lay in state at the palace for an entire week. The crowds were vast and inconsolable. Nearly a dozen people were trampled to death in the crush. A few days later, his coffin was taken in solemn procession to a battleship. As the cortege departed the city, hundreds of thousands of people watched from the shore, lined up like seabirds on piers and breakwaters. The ship continued across the Sea of Marmara and transferred its cargo to a train for the onward journey to Ankara, where the president was interred. He was later moved to an august mausoleum overlooking the capital.

Atatürk's final gift to his country was his failure to name a preferred successor. That act of silence meant that the regular process for selecting a new president was allowed to work. The constitution specified that the head of state was to be elected by parliament, as Atatürk himself

A farewell salute, November 1938: Wailing crowds and police officers at the funeral procession of Atatürk.

had been, term after term. The Grand National Assembly soon selected İsmet İnönü—the field commander from the war of independence and sometime prime minister—as the republic's second president.

İnönü had been one of Turkey's great political survivors. He had managed to outlast most of the other early allies of Atatürk and had become a dutiful second-in-command to the president, although by no means always within his good graces. His invented surname harked back to 1921, when, as İsmet Pasha, he had led nationalist forces at the dual battles of İnönü, engagements that marked early milestones in the nationalists' strike against the Hellenic army. In addition to the presidency, the parliament awarded him the honorific title of "National Leader," but it was an uncomfortable fit. Thin and mustachioed, İnönü was a manager and a strategist, with none of the charisma or drive of an Atatürk—a figure who, even in death, was given the even grander title of "Eternal Leader."

All of that turned out to be a good thing, however. İnönü had done a great deal of backroom maneuvering to ensure his succession as president, but outwardly the transition was smoother than anyone had expected. According to the British ambassador, Hughe Knatchbull-Hugessen, "The only change noticeable was the introduction of a quieter and more orthodox life in political circles." İnönü flirted with a Turkish version of blood-and-soil nationalism and remained suspicious of ethnic minorities, but his approach to foreign policy was to embed Turkey in a set of treaties and explicit undertakings with rival governments. As Hitler and Stalin jointly occupied Poland, İnönü first turned to the West, signing a mutual assistance pact with Britain and France. Once German troops marched into Paris and German planes began targeting London, that lifeline came to look more like a sea anchor threatening to drag Turkey into the conflict. In June 1941, Turkey pivoted and signed a nonaggression treaty with Germany. The same month, Hitler launched his sudden attack on the Soviet Union, opening a new front in the war and seemingly confirming the bet that Ankara had made on Germany's ascendancy.

As both a neutral country and one with a geographical position at the intersection of Europe, the Soviet Union, and the Middle East, Turkey was never short of strategic suitors. Trying to figure out which direction Turkish public opinion was moving and seeking to use it to the advantage of either the Axis or the Allies became one of the great parlor games of the war. It was also a project pursued by countless free-lance agents, paid operatives, and professional intelligence services, all energetically spying on one another and hoping to turn Turkey toward their cause.

"You could almost throw a stone out of the window of any leading hotel and hit an agent," recalled an American official about wartime Istanbul. "In fact, we should have." Foreign embassies had left behind their ornate Ottoman-era buildings in Pera and their summertime res-idences on the Bosphorus for more utilitarian quarters in Ankara. But the easy accessibility of Istanbul and its status as the largest urban cen-ter in the republic still made it a vital arena for gathering information on Turks as well as enemies.

That task was aided by the city's large number of foreigners, a population that had grown over the course of the 1930s. Virtually every European language was represented in Istanbul, and among each of these communities it was not difficult to find someone—a business leader, a banker, a shopkeeper, a professor, a bar attendant—dissatisfied enough with his old homeland to provide information to a rival power. German politics in particular had produced a tide of refugees eager to work against Nazi rule. Just as Istanbul had been the way station for White Russians pushed out of Bolshevik Russia, it now served as a lifeline for academics, especially Jews, dismissed from their posts by the Nazis.

Through Swiss intercessors, German and Austrian scholars made contact with the Turkish Ministry of Education and managed to secure posts as lecturers in Istanbul. The desire to rid German universities of the racially impure and politically suspect was to Turkey's immediate benefit. The republic had recently established its first real Western-style institution of higher education, Istanbul University. German-speaking professors became its principal teaching cadre, delivering lectures with the assistance of local translators and helping to structure the new institution's departments along European lines. When the first German professor stepped into a lecture hall, in November 1933, Yunus Nadi ran a front-page headline in his newspaper to announce the fact. Turkish higher education, he claimed, had finally joined the Western world.

University students suddenly had access to some of the continent's leading lights in virtually every field of study. Philosophy and geography were taught by Alexander Rustow from Nuremberg, the noted socialist activist (and the father of political scientist Dankwart Rustow). Leo Spitzer, the comparative philologist, moved from Cologne to head up the faculty of foreign languages. Walter Gottschalk, one of Berlin's greatest Orientalists, organized the university library and catalogued the substantial scholarly collection that Sultan Abdülhamid II had amassed at Yıldız Palace. Erich Auerbach, the literary theorist, moved from Marburg to teach philology. He began one of his masterpieces, *Mimesis*—a study of the fluidity of representation and reality in Western literature—while teaching on the Bosphorus. Albert Einstein might have been part of the cohort as well, if an invitation from the Institute for Advanced Study in Princeton, New Jersey, had not come through before he was able to move to Istanbul.

These scholars were not just out of work in their home countries. They were also without home countries. Many would eventually have their citizenship revoked by the Nazi regime. They were known as *Heimatlose*—legally homeless—much as the White Russians had been after the advent of Bolshevism. But they were also living in a city that, as in the 1920s, placed victors and victims in close quarters. In addition to the refugee professors, there were perhaps a thousand German citizens in Turkey, most in Istanbul. Many of these expatriates were organized into *Landesgruppen*, or regional organizations, of the Nazi Party. The party organization was headquartered in Moda, a fashionable neighborhood on the Asian side of the Bosphorus. On Sundays, local Germans and their sympathizers working for the party would gather there at the local affiliate of *Kraft durch Freude*—or Strength through Joy, the Nazi tourist agency—to receive instructions for the coming week. Many of the senior officers had their lodgings at the Deutsche Schule, the prestigious German-language high school just off the Grande Rue, which was also a short stroll from the Teutonia Club, the principal meeting place for the party elite.

Nazi race laws tended to reproduce themselves abroad, and German citizens were instructed to conduct business only with firms that had been vetted as both politically and racially pure by the German Consulate—that is, no commerce with anti-Nazi sympathizers among the German-speaking diaspora, or with businesses thought to be in the pocket of the Allies, or of course with Istanbul's Jews. The Tokatlian Hotel, run by an Austrian, Nicolaus Medović, was on the approved list, as were the bookstores on the Grande Rue run by Erich Kalis and Andres Kapps, the rug shop owned by Josef Krauss in the Grand Bazaar, and the travel bureau in Galata run by Hans Walter Feustel. Local Jews, in turn, responded with their own boycott. In 1938, when Medović began to fly the Nazi flag outside his establishment—a nod to the Anschluss between Germany and his native Austria—Jewish Istanbullus organized a campaign to convince fellow citizens to avoid the hotel and its restaurant. The Tokatlian had been one of the premier establishments in the city, a favorite venue for everything from society weddings to receptions for Yunus Nadi's Miss Turkey competition. With the boycott, however, the Tokatlian's fortunes plummeted, much to the advantage of other locales such as the Pera Palace.

The presence of such a large, vocal, and politically committed German community also made Istanbul the ideal site for clandestine intelligence-gathering by all sides. It was the natural route of communication between Europe and the Middle East. A long history of German ties to the Turkish military, going back to the late Ottoman period, meant that many educated and successful Turks had sympathies for the German cause. Moreover, the presence of White Russians who were reliably anti-Soviet, Armenians who were potentially anti-Turkish (and could therefore be enlisted to provide information on Turkish affairs), and a Turkish policy establishment with long experience in spying on its own population meant that Istanbul was fertile ground for both Axis and Allied spycraft.

By one count, seventeen separate foreign intelligence agencies were active in Istanbul during the war. The problem was not that operatives from many countries were conducting work inside Turkey. That was to be expected in a neutral state, and Istanbul had been prime ground for collecting information since the days when the sultan's own agents had been politely asked to vacate their tables to paying customers at the Pera Palace. As long as a foreign country kept its activities discreet and at a level that did not inconvenience the host, Turkish officials were generally content to allow the clandestine derring-do to flourish. On occasion, however, the shadow war moved into the light, and when that happened, it became evident to many Istanbullus just how vulnerable their city had become.

In the crush of passengers and station touts that accompanied the arrival of the Sunday evening train from the Balkans, diplomats scrambled to find their luggage and hail a fleet of taxis. It was March 11, 1941, and the entire British mission to Bulgaria had been expelled. Bulgaria was a German ally now—just as it had been in 1914—and no longer welcoming to officials whose country was being targeted by German bombers. Sixty British diplomats were being evacuated to the safety of Istanbul. The last time so many Allied officials had arrived in the city at once had been aboard the *Superb* and other British vessels during the occupation. Now they were arriving as guests of the Turkish government.

It was not the way they had expected to leave their posting. On March 1, German advance troops had entered Sofia. Soon afterward, the British ambassador, George Rendel, visited the Bulgarian prime minister, Bogdan Filov, and in a sharp exchange delivered his country's note severing diplomatic ties. Rendel's daughter, Anne, made a point of driving around town with a Union Jack fluttering behind her car.

Rendel returned to the embassy and ordered all the documents burned. A huge pile of trunks, suitcases, and parcels accumulated in the embassy's drawing room. American diplomats, still nonbelligerents in the war, were on hand to take the building keys and receive the ambassador's thanks for looking after the property in the Britons' absence. The luggage at last sorted, the diplomats formed a long convoy of cars and lorries toward a suburban station. Two German security officers were on hand to watch the departure from the sidelines. To keep up the evacuees' spirits, the American ambassador and a few pro-British Bulgarians accompanied the group on board the train as far as the Bulgarian border. Farewells were toasted with champagne, and then the extra passengers disembarked just before the train crossed the Maritsa River and continued toward Turkey.

Looking out the train windows at the undulating countryside of Thrace, Rendel fell into a gray mood. In Sofia, he had seen the disciplined German soldiers, the mechanized transports, the crisp uniforms. Now he could see Turkish soldiers being sent to reinforce the border: an army of oxcarts and ponies, and men armed with what looked like antique muskets. "My impression was strengthened that, if the Germans decided to attack and occupy Turkey, there would certainly be nothing to oppose them until they got to the Bosphorus, if then," Rendel recalled.

The British diplomats arrived in Istanbul around six o'clock in the evening. Sirkeci station was humming. Friends from the British Consulate were there to welcome the group, along with representatives of the governments-in-exile of Nazi-occupied Poland, Belgium, and the Netherlands. As they made their way down the quay and out through the brick-and-granite façade, they had their first glimpse of the heights of Pera, with house lights just coming on around the Galata Tower and fishing boats bobbing on the Golden Horn.

The taxis left the station and crossed Galata Bridge, heading out of the forest of minarets in the city center and toward Tepebaşı and then onto Meşrutiyet Avenue, the former Graveyard Street. After a few blocks, the cars swung around a corner and pulled up at the Pera Palace. Porters unloaded the steamer trunks and leather suitcases into the marble foyer. Clerks rushed to take down passport details. Once the formalities were completed, Rendel accompanied his daughter to their room and began to unpack. Other members of the mission took the short flight of steps toward a nightcap in the velvety darkness of the Orient Bar.

A flash of light, then a deafening boom suddenly shook the hotel. The elevator creaked on its cables and plummeted to the bottom of its shaft. The glass canopy collapsed, showering shards on the reception hall. Inlaid cabinets and mahogany chairs slid in pieces across the parquet. Blood spattered the marble stairs and plaster walls, and small fires erupted from the wood paneling.

An eerie silence followed, soon broken by the moans of the injured emerging from the smoke and plaster dust. A jagged canyon had been cut through the ground floor into the cellar; in the darkness, dazed guests tumbled into it unaware. Two British Embassy employees lay in agony and would soon succumb to their wounds. Several Turkish hotel workers and bystanders were also either dead or dying, while others were missing limbs or covered with excruciating burns. Two local

Jewish doormen, the hotel's Greek general manager, Mr. Karantinos, a Muslim chauffeur, two Turkish policemen, the Greek head clerk, a Muslim night watchman, and a range of other workers and guests all sustained injuries. In all, six adults and the unborn child of an embassy staffer would be listed as fatalities. Outside, people lay unconscious or wandered up the avenue in shock. Windows and storefronts were blown out in the surrounding streets, and upstairs, guests rushed from their rooms, certain that German planes had launched an air raid.

Some of the survivors knew immediately that the cause lay else-

An explosion's aftermath, March 1941: The lounge of the
Pera Palace after the detonation of a suitcase bomb.

where. Their thoughts raced back to the busy train station in Sofia. The owners of two pieces of stray luggage had not been identified before the train left Bulgaria, but in the rush to depart, officers with the legation had decided simply to load the suitcases with the others and sort out the ownership once everyone arrived in Istanbul. As soon as the explosion rocked the Pera Palace, one of the diplomats raced to a nearby hotel where other members of the party were checking in. He identified the second stray suitcase, ran with it outside, and flung it onto a patch of open ground. There was no explosion, but when the police arrived soon afterward, they realized there well could have been. The bag contained a fuse and a powerful charge of TNT.

Only sometime later was the entire chain of events put together. Bulgarian agents, working in league with the Germans, had placed the explosive luggage in the British pile. It was a shoddy and fruitless piece of sabotage, aimed at little more than creating a sensational mass assassination of enemy diplomats. The Turkish government remained diffident, worried about escalating a crisis whose target was apparently not Turkey itself. The public prosecutor, who issued a report the next month, was officiously clear: "Having come to the conclusion that the event . . . is an attempt against the staff of the British Legation and prepared at Sofia by a German or Bulgarian organization or an organization dependent on them, and as no proof whatever has been found to the effect that this attempt has been organized and prepared within the frontiers and by a person or an organization residing in Turkey, our Office has decided that there was no room to undertake any legal proceedings against anybody."

That was the end of the affair, at least as far as diplomacy was concerned. The Pera Palace had not been intentionally targeted by the bombers. Its fate was a function of its reputation. Neither of the two bombs had exploded in the way they were apparently intended, on the train; the devices only arrived at the hotels because the British legation had selected them as comfortable places to stay. The British government eventually paid out benefits to the families of the two embassy personnel killed in the Pera Palace blast—typists Gertrude Ellis and Therese Armstrong—along with several other British subjects who were injured. London also compensated the Turkish government for the death benefits and medical expenses of a substantial group of local individuals killed or injured by the fire and flying debris.

As Misbah Muhayyeş, the hotel's unlucky proprietor, began making plans for rebuilding, the bombed-out Pera Palace stood as a reminder of just how close the war was coming. German troops were already in Bulgaria, and in April and May 1941, the Wehrmacht began its campaign in the Balkans, quickly occupying Yugoslavia, Greece, and Crete. Istanbul was on the front line, and more than ever before, Turkey would have to be prepared to defend its borders, noted Yunus Nadi in *Cumhuriyet*. Istanbullus had already been practicing air-raid drills and blackouts since the previous November. Trees, sidewalks, and electric poles had been painted white so people could navigate them more easily in the moonlight. During the drills, firemen lined the Grande Rue in gas masks that made them look like creatures from another world, as three hundred sirens blared throughout the city. To conserve fuel, private automobiles were banned from the streets, and half of the nearly two thousand taxis were pulled out of commission.

For foreign governments, the expansion of the war meant that Istanbul was more important than ever, not just as a venue for gathering intelligence but also as a station for organizing multiple underground campaigns: to shift Turkish public opinion toward one side or the other, to organize operations against Germany and its allies in southeastern Europe, and to funnel money and arms to resistance fighters holding out in the rugged uplands of Greece and Yugoslavia. Once Hitler invaded the Soviet Union in June 1941, Turks were surrounded by active military campaigns on virtually every side. For the Turkish government, being neutral was no longer just about refusing to enter the fray. It entailed buying friends and understanding potential enemies—in other words, playing the spy game as actively as the belligerents themselves.

Mahmut Ardıç and Reşat Mutlugün were two of the six people killed by the blast at the Pera Palace. Both men were Turkish Muslims, judging by their first names, and they probably were the first people in a long line of ancestors to have family names that could be passed down from father to children. Ardıç and Mutlugün were variously identified as detectives or gendarmes, but a grand hotel would have been an unusual place to find a beat cop or a gumshoe investigator, especially since there is no record of any significant crime having been committed there in the days leading up to the explosion. What is more likely is that the two men—whose surnames made them the unlikely duo of Officers Juniper and Happy Day—were members of the Turkish secret police, the Emniyet. Their untimely deaths, a result of nothing more than the ill fortune of being at the Pera Palace when the rigged suitcase exploded, were emblematic of the intertwined worlds of foreign intelligence, diplomacy, and business in the wartime city.

Emniyet officers would have been expected to be on hand to supervise the arrival of a large foreign delegation, especially one that was being evacuated from an enemy country aboard a special train. Keeping tabs on visitors was part of the organization's job, along with surveilling political dissidents, poets, journalists, religious zealots, subversives, terrorists, militants, revolutionaries, communists, socialists, and virtually any other category that the Emniyet perceived to be a present or possible threat to the state.

The Emniyet had only been around since 1926, but it was part of an entire system of surveillance and repression that had grown up alongside the single-party government created during Atatürk's presidency. It also rested on a longstanding Turkish obsession with public order and the machinations of unseen forces. Half a century earlier, Abdülhamid II had spent much of his day reviewing the written reports of his network of spies, who noted everything from foreign arrivals to antigovernment jokes overheard in the street. The sexual peccadilloes of diplomats were of particular interest to the sultan, who would casually drop hints to red-faced ambassadors to let them know that their most intimate moments in a Pera bordello had been watched. In those days, Muslims seen conversing with Europeans could be threatened with exile, tramcar passengers remained studiously silent, and public conversations in the Pera Palace were usually conducted in whispers.

Now, the Emniyet became the central body tasked with both protecting the Kemalist revolution and uncovering its internal enemies. It specialized in unveiling conspiracies, and, as in the case of enemies of the state such as Nâzım Hikmet or rambunctious exiles such as Halide Edip, it developed a particular sideline in observing the supposed links between opposition currents in the Turkish Republic and their external backers. As with all clandestine services, however, the line between neutralizing a real danger and manufacturing one precisely so that it could be neutralized was always somewhat hazy. Intelligence work could be a closed circle. Sometimes the evidence that a threat existed was no more than the fact that some security operative had decided to report that it did. It was a way of thinking about security, politics, and foreign intrigue that was built into the basic structure of the republic and its police apparatus.

An information-hungry city naturally produced a surfeit of information suppliers, which is probably why officers such as Ardıç and Mutlugün had found themselves at the Pera Palace on the day of their death. Hotels were at the center of an intricate economy of information gathering and sharing. "Istanbul has many people who try to make a living by selling information to anyone who will buy it," noted a secret US intelligence dispatch. The more foreigners, the more work, and the more work, the more lucrative intelligence became. The Emniyet regularly supplied written reports, photographs, arrival and departure lists, hotel registration information, and even passport photographs of any person whose likeness a foreign intelligence agency might wish to track down—and pay for. When a newcomer arrived at a hotel and delivered his passport to the concierge, he could be certain that it would soon be shown to the Turks, the Soviets, the Americans, the Germans, the British, the Italians, "and probably the bartender in his favorite café."

Many efforts to elicit information or to buy Turkish sympathies were not surreptitious but, rather, public and invariably creative. In February 1943, Germany returned the decayed corpse of Talât, the Unionist leader and mastermind of the Armenian genocide, who had been shot more than two decades earlier by an Armenian assassin in Berlin. It was a goodwill effort built on the macabre return of an old exile—a controversial figure whose historical role had been down-played during Atatürk's lifetime but who was now ceremonially resurrected and elevated to the pantheon of Turkish nationalists. In a grand procession attended by President İsmet İnönü, Prime Minister Şükrü Saracoğlu, Ambassador Franz von Papen, and Turkish and German officers in full dress, the old pasha's remains were reinterred on a small hilltop in Istanbul. He would eventually be joined by other Young Turks, including his associate Enver, whose remains were brought from Tajikistan in the 1990s. In a twist that no one seems to have noted at the time, the hill happened to look across to one of the city's main Armenian cemeteries.

The Allies, too, worked assiduously to move Turkish public opinion and lure the republic out of its neutral stance. Their relative success depended mainly on the course of the war, however, rather than on intelligence coups. Turkey's nonaggression pact with Germany looked like a reasonable move in the summer of 1941, as the Wehrmacht swept quickly eastward. By the next fall, however, the Axis advance into the Soviet Union had stalled at Stalingrad, German strength in North Africa was withering, and the Allies were beginning to press Turkey

War's lighthearted moments, ca. 1944: An office worker demonstrates his gas mask to a female colleague.

to enter the war on the Allied side. The long history of ducking and weaving, tactical reassessments, and elaborately orchestrated dissimulation was coming up against the dawning reality that Hitler could well lose the war. Once Mussolini fell from power in Italy, in July 1943, the Axis was effectively split, and Turkey's position of calculated neutrality appeared increasingly untenable.

British intelligence services, including the renowned Special Operations Executive, or SOE, were operating in the city already at the time of the Pera Palace blast. Istanbul had become the center of SOE activities in the Balkans, which meant that British officers were not only acquiring information but also planning specific acts of sabotage or assistance to underground fighters in other countries, especially in Bulgaria, Yugoslavia, and Greece. As the war wound on, the SOE put in place a plan for coordinating resistance operations in the event of a German invasion of Turkey, including cultivating agents who posed as loyal Nazis and would therefore presumably form part of the post-invasion occupation force, effectively serving as double agents inside German institutions.

Once the United States joined the war, the American Office of Strategic Services, or OSS, eventually set up shop in the city as well. Lanning "Packy" Macfarland, a Chicago banker, arrived in the summer of 1943. He had been recruited into the service in the United States and initially worked out of the US Consulate in Istanbul before renting an apartment not far from the Pera Palace. The Americans intended to use the city's substantial émigré communities—Germans, but also Czechs, Hungarians, and others from Nazi-occupied or Axis lands—as sources of information, much as the British had been doing for some time.

A detailed history of this silent war comes from the most boring and inadvertently revealing of sources: the reimbursement forms that intelligence handlers filled out after making contact with a secret informant. Agents received between 50 and 500 Turkish lira per month as retainers; Turkish police were given up to 400 lira per month for supplying hotel arrivals and departures lists. Handlers' reimbursement forms included a printed line item for "Bribery," where OSS employees could claim expenses for everything from paying telephone operators not to report long-distance calls to the all-encompassing "purchase of strategic information" from a Turkish or other source. Handlers expensed the purchase of musical instruments, tennis rackets, and men's suits. The underground economy of tattling and whispering was operating in a warren of streets where people on opposite sides of a worldwide war could literally bump into one another as they went about their work. It was all a bizarrely intimate business. If an agent needed a hernia belt, for example, it might be an American handler who supplied it.

Running agents in Istanbul was like fishing in a trout pond. There was never any trouble getting a strike on the line; the real issue was making sure that it was the fish you really wanted. "Espionage directed against other countries from Turkey is regarded as a kind of lucrative game at which anyone can play with relative impunity," said an OSS report. In a city teeming with willing agents, the most important job was to vet them for reliability. It was a field that American operatives called X-2, or counterespionage. In July 1943, an American operative named Joseph Curtiss arrived in Istanbul with $25,000 in private donations allegedly to cover the purchase of antiquarian books for libraries at three East Coast universities. For the next several months, he established his credentials by consulting with book and manuscript dealers in the Grand Bazaar and spreading the word that he was looking for exceptional texts for scholarly collections. The money he carried, however, was for paying agents, not buying rare books. By October—long enough for Curtiss to develop his cover story—it was safe enough for him to have direct contact with Macfarland, the OSS station chief, in order to lay out a plan of action. He was given an office in the OSS headquarters and set up shop before the arrival of another X-2 operative and eventually the branch's overall director, John Maxson, the following January.

Curtiss and Maxson were running a shoestring operation, but they quickly realized that they had at their fingertips a network that no one had yet put fully to use: the sizable American community working in the city. Business leaders had been some of the earliest OSS recruits. Archibald Walker, the director of the Socony-Vacuum Oil Company, had in fact run the spy operation before the arrival of Macfarland. But X-2 soon set about systematically contacting Americans, many of them working at Robert College, the brother institution to the American College for Girls and a Protestant missionary school that had become one of the country's best educational centers. Professors, receptionists, and the registrar were all signed up as providers of information. Betty Carp, the matronly administrative officer at the US Consulate and—despite her American-sounding name—a native Istanbullu of Austro-Hungarian background, became one of the major suppliers and vetters of information. Her quiet tradecraft and sharp judgment were so renowned that she had earlier been deployed to Washington. There she had regularly invited the wife of Soviet ambassador Maxim Litvinov to the movies and then reported their conversations back to the OSS. Her fluency in multiple languages, including German and Turkish, and her low-key ability to ingratiate herself with virtually anyone in Istanbul, gave her unprecedented access. Few Germans probably realized that the short, middle-aged figure standing nonchalantly outside the Teutonia Club was actually making detailed mental notes on who was coming and going.

One of the few Americans not working in some capacity as an agent was the redoubtable Thomas Whittemore. His ability to spin fantasy into reality was invaluable in fundraising for the Hagia Sophia, but in the world of spycraft, it was a detriment. "Mr. Thomas Whittemore is a very well known Byzantine scholar . . . [and] he is well informed and has contacts with the various Cabinet Ministers," noted Betty Carp in a secret report. "He is however the type who never condescends to give his information to anyone lower than Churchill or Roosevelt."

In a city where information was at a premium, any agent was under enormous pressure to sell it to the highest bidder as well as to attract multiple buyers for the same product—that is, to become a double agent. "They are everywhere in Istanbul," reported the Istanbul office to the OSS director in Washington, General William "Wild Bill" Donovan. Part of the work involved keeping tabs on the movement of "enemy nationals" in Istanbul, and the results were substantial. Within only a few months after its establishment, the OSS's X-2 branch had assembled some three thousand notecards, each providing background and intelligence on a distinct person. The problem was that German handlers were even better, at least when it came to soliciting informants with truly interesting things to say. In particular, the Abwehr—the German military intelligence wing—had a remarkable ability to recruit the kind of agent that Allied personnel seemed to find irresistible, the community that a secret American X-2 report called "bar girls, artistes, and the like." German handlers spent lavish sums on bribing and covering the expenses of agents working in hotels, restaurants, and nightclubs. Americans seemed especially willing to believe that "any attractive girl who shed a few tears and told him how much she hated the Germans was genuinely anti-Nazi." Employees of American intelligence services had reportedly thrown "large and rather drunken parties" where women known to be German agents were present. Tongues loosened by alcohol were the stock-in-trade of this particular brand of Istanbul spy.

By 1944, the security breaches had reached such a level of absurdity that American handlers developed their own theme song, written by a US government employee and given a rousing premiere at a local dance-bar. Its words were mimeographed and distributed to the audience, and it became such a fashionable tune that orchestras throughout the city would strike it up whenever a group of Americans came through the door. The title and refrain—"Boo Boo Baby I'm a Spy"—were the last thing an undercover operative wanted to hear as he walked into a lounge.

"I'm involved in a dangerous game," the song went:

> *Every other day I change my name,*
> *My face is different but the body's the same,*
> *Boo Boo Baby I'm a spy.*

> *Of course you've heard of Mata Hari,*
> *We did business cash and carry,*
> *But Pappy caught us and we had to marry,*
> *Boo Boo Baby I'm a spy.*

> *I'm a lad not altogether bad,*
> *In fact I'm a damn good lover,*
> *But listen, sweet, let's be discreet*
> *And do this under cover. . . .*

A government employee's openly touting his position as a spy in a cabaret tune was, at the very least, poor tradecraft, and American officials reported the lyrics to Washington as a security threat. But the song was mainly an exercise in bravado. "I'm so cocky I could swagger," went the chorus. "I'm ten percent cloak and ninety percent dagger." In fact, American spies rarely had the inside dope at all.

Much of their information came from an extensive array of eastern European émigrés then resident in the city, a group of individuals known as the Dogwood chain, after the code name of its principal liaison with the OSS, a Czech engineer named Alfred Schwarz. Recruited by Macfarland, Schwarz developed what may have been the largest information network in occupied Europe, funneling information on troop movements, airfields, munitions dumps, and fuel terminals back to the OSS station in Istanbul. The problem was that many of the subordinate agents in the chain were actually double agents for German intelligence. Dogwood was deemed to be so unreliable that Macfarland ordered it terminated in the summer of 1944.

Most of the Dogwood reports had been, at best, mediocre. That was par for the course in Istanbul, and perhaps the inevitable result of too much money chasing too many willing spies. Few espionage efforts produced spectacular results, and those that did were predictably located in Ankara. In early 1944, the British secured the defection of Erich Vermehren, the secretary to the local Abwehr chief. That success proved to be a considerable blow to German morale in Turkey, but the Abwehr had in fact already gone one better.

The British ambassador, Hughe Knatchbull-Hugessen, was an irreproachable member of the diplomatic corps. The product of Kentish village life, Victorian rectitude, and the scholarly trail leading from Eton to Oxford, Knatchbull-Hugessen was the image of a British Foreign Office official, with a trim mustache and three-piece suit. The ambassador was supremely well respected within the diplomatic corps, even by his archrival von Papen. The Turks' only complaint about him, it seems, was his unpronounceable name. But his exalted position may have lured him into complacency. In one of the greatest insider jobs of the war, the Germans in the autumn of 1943 had recruited a person they code-named Cicero. He turned out to be the ambassador's valet.

Cicero had in fact fallen into the Germans' lap. He had presented himself to the first secretary at the German Embassy in Ankara, speaking poor French, using the name "Pierre," and promising an unbelievable array of secret documents, which he was happy to turn over to Berlin for a fee. "You see, I hate the British," he explained simply, and he threatened to offer his services to the Soviets if the Germans were not willing to pay the asking price. The diplomats were skeptical, but the valet soon delivered the goods. He was able to access the safe in Knatchbull-Hugessen's office and photograph secret dispatches between the ambassador and London, including details of wartime conferences and hints of Operation Overlord, the plan for the Allied invasion of Normandy. Some of these documents made it all the way to Hitler, but the Abwehr was never able to capitalize fully on Cicero's access, largely because of persistent fears that he was too good to be true. In a country where double agents were common, German handlers repeatedly worried that Cicero himself was one. In fact, Cicero seems to have been a sincere purveyor of reliable information, which might have changed the course of the war had Germany heeded it. Instead, the real double cross worked the other way around. The considerable sums of money that Cicero—an Albanian named Elyesa Bazna—received for his services as a spy, the equivalent of several hundred thousand British pounds sterling, turned out to be counterfeit.

The bombing of the Pera Palace was a rare exception to the general rule that governed espionage in a neutral country: Don't bother the hosts. By and large, the war in Istanbul was carried out in private apartments and secret meeting places, with handlers and agents mainly interested in avoiding one another in public whenever possible. Even at Turkey's Republic Day celebrations on October 29, when diplomats were invited to a grand reception at the foreign ministry in Ankara, Turkish officials provided two separate rooms so that enemy powers would not have to share the same hors d'oeuvres and champagne. The foreign community was so small that bumping into a rival operative was reasonably common, however. Teddy Kollek, an Austrian citizen by birth, recalled being approached by a Nazi agent at the Abdullah Efendi restaurant in Istanbul, a popular dinner spot for both Allied and Axis officials. The agent began eagerly speaking to him in German, which Kollek spoke fluently. The conversation abruptly came to a halt when the agent realized he had made a terrible mistake. Kollek was actually working for the Zionist underground in league with British and American intelligence agencies.

Kollek's work was only the beginning of a long and storied career. Among other things, after the war he went on to become mayor of Jerusalem. But during his time in Istanbul, he participated in the one operation that could claim to be an unqualified success. By 1944, just as OSS operatives were beginning to wrap up their work in the city, clearing financial accounts and thinking about the next stages in their own careers, a new kind of intelligence effort was kicking into overdrive. Its organizers knew that their work depended not on placating the Turkish authorities but rather on bothering them a great deal. It was a form of undercover work that, more than any other, bumped up against the Turkish Republic's most hallowed precepts—its claim to ethnic purity, its slow-burning war on its own minorities, and its desire to deal evenhandedly with both Axis and Allies. Rather than gathering information, however, it involved a desperate and risky effort to gather exiled people.

PAPER TRAILS

Fascists on parade: Young Italians—probably members of Istanbul's own small Italian community—give the Roman salute as they march past the Republic Monument in Taksim Square.

M ISBAH MUHAYYEŞ'S ACQUISITION OF the Pera Palace had been a stellar business deal in the 1920s, but after the bomb explosion in 1941, he had reason to rue his decision. The repairs were extensive, and the headline-grabbing blast was the last kind of notoriety that a hotelier wanted for his establishment. Muhayyeş tried to recoup his losses in whatever way his imagination could conjure. He cabled Winston Churchill demanding compensation. He sued Ambassador George Rendel for negligence in allowing the booby-trapped luggage to be brought into the hotel. He was eventually awarded hundreds of thousands of Turkish lira in compensation, but since an Istanbul court had no jurisdiction outside the country, the entire issue was largely moot.

Even before the explosion, the hotel's fortunes had been declining. The brief boost provided by the Jewish boycott of its rival, the Tokatlian, couldn't make up for the fading velvet, a certain griminess to the marble, a sense that the establishment as a whole, like talkative regulars at the Orient Bar, was making a living from past exploits and a few good stories. When the Pera Palace made headlines, the news was mainly about seediness and scandal. In 1935, a prominent Turkish diplomat, Aziz Bey, took out a room, placed some money on a table, which he instructed was to be used for his funeral, and then slit his throat with a razor blade. In 1939, a Yemeni man checked into the hotel, along with three Mexican female companions, and opened a tab by claiming to be a well-heeled Indian prince. It took the administration three months to realize he was penniless.

Social life in Pera had begun to shift northward, away from the Pera Palace's immediate environs. At the southern end of the neighborhood, the Grande Rue frayed into narrow alleyways and stair-step streets that twisted past stationers, music shops, and glass dealers. Farther north in Taksim, the creation of the Republic Monument in 1928, followed by Henri Prost's energetic reengineering in the 1930s, made the square into a focal point for the modern city. When schoolchildren gathered to honor the memory of Atatürk or local fascists goose-stepped down the Grande Rue, they invariably headed toward Taksim. Each footfall was one more step away from the Islamic empire and toward the republic.

The Park Hotel took advantage of this northward slide. Located not far from Taksim Square, on an avenue that wound down toward the coast road, it stood on the site of the old family home of the last Ottoman grand vizier, Ahmed Tevfik Pasha. With the German Consulate situated next door, the hotel's dining room came to serve as an unofficial canteen for the growing consular staff, much as the Pera Palace had done for its own diplomatic neighbors: the American Consulate, housed in an old Ottoman mansion next door, and the British Consulate, just up Meşrutiyet Avenue near the fish market. The oscillations in Turkey's foreign policy could once be gauged by whether there were more Turkish officials drinking at one end or the other of the Grande Rue—at either the Pera Palace or the Park. With the former temporarily out of commission, while its ground floor was being pieced back together and the elevator rehung after the fatal bombing, the latter seemed to have won the contest.

In the Park Hotel's narrow lobby, American and British businessmen walked past Japanese, Bulgarian, and German officials. Diplomats arrived with their families, and the foyer often doubled as a playground for rambunctious children who had spent too many days on trains or ships. In the restaurant, the Japanese held court early in the evening before surrendering tables to the Germans, who would carry on with postprandials until midnight. Rumor had it that all the rooms were bugged, and everyone knew that the waiters had a habit of lingering too long after taking an order or lifting the plate cover from the main course. Anything they overheard would find its way to one consulate or another. But this mutual uncertainty created a balance of power in the hotel's dining room. It kept the conversation light and the politics discreet. Just knowing your enemies was a certain kind of security.

That was why, in blustery February 1944, the place seemed so appealing to a raven-haired, round-faced Bloomingdale's executive with a penchant for natty bow ties and unkempt pocket squares. Ira Hirschmann was new to Istanbul, and if circumstances had been different, he might have passed his time negotiating a deal for cloth shipments to New York's Garment District or buying up intricate Ottoman inlay work. In another life, he might have been a music impresario. Wherever he went, he spent his free time organizing impromptu concerts with a promising local violinist or piano maestro. He had no qualms about correcting the tempo or tuning of any hotel-lobby orchestra he encountered. He was a born organizer, a big thinker, and supremely confident in his ability to make things happen.

But Hirschmann spent most days in Istanbul as a detail man: leasing rust-bucket cargo ships, reoutfitting them as passenger vessels, and interceding with frontier officers, local police, and harbormasters over the minutiae of shipping regulations and manifests. Before he retired to dinner at the Park, he finished each day at the office by burning his working papers. What few of the other guests would have known was that Hirschmann was at the leading edge of yet another wave of exile. It would end in one of the single largest efforts to get Jews out of occupied Europe. His engagement with Istanbul had started in a roundabout way a few months after the Pera Palace bombing, but it involved a tragedy of a much grander scale.

Pushed along by the south-flowing top current in the Bosphorus, the *Struma* quietly dropped anchor in Istanbul on December 15, 1941. The journey from the Romanian port of Constanța, nearly two hundred nautical miles away, had been horrific. A repurposed sailing vessel, the ship had been used most recently as a ferry for livestock. Its engine was a refurbished castoff that had been hauled from a sunken tugboat. The old wooden hull, covered with thin metal plating, was ill equipped to weather the winter storms on the Black Sea.

On board, the only thing that kept the passengers from being tossed around like dolls was the fact that they were packed tightly, filling the decks and passageways, women and men with leather suitcases and fur-trimmed overcoats, children with a favorite toy or storybook. Nearly eight hundred people were squeezed below decks.

They had passed through minefields and avoided surface ships and submarines patrolling in deep water. Most had been stripped of their citizenship by Nazi-allied governments. Germany had prohibited Jews from leaving German-controlled areas and was putting pressure on Romania, its Axis partner, to do the same. As they sat anchored off Sarayburnu, they were finally inside a neutral country, and from there they hoped to arrange passage to Palestine. The Bosphorus was no longer just a strait that defined the eastern edge of Europe. For the Jewish families pressed inside the *Struma*, it was an escape tunnel.

Week after week, the ship waited in Istanbul, not far from where Wrangel's flotilla of refugee Russians had anchored two decades earlier. Snow fell. Gray ice ringed the Golden Horn. Port authorities ferried food and water in small boats. The Turkish government refused to let the refugees step ashore, for fear of upsetting its neutral balancing act in the war and setting a precedent that would flood Istanbul with destitute immigrants. The British Mandate authorities in Palestine, who had placed strict limits on Jewish migration, denied clearance to set course for the Palestinian port of Haifa. The passengers were thus both formally stateless and lacking an approved destination—from nowhere, belonging nowhere, and going nowhere.

The yellow quarantine flag was posted on the *Struma*'s mast, and communication with land was strictly monitored by Turkish police. Sympathetic humanitarians could occasionally pass messages back and forth to passengers, but this required waiting until a police officer who could be bribed was placed on watch. Simon Brod, a local textile magnate and Jewish humanitarian, worked to provide blankets and other small necessities. Other members of Istanbul's Jewish community tried to intercede with the port authorities on the passengers' behalf.

On January 2, 1942, six men on board the *Struma*—Emanuel and Edouard Ludovic, Israel and David Frenc, Teodor Brettschneider, and Emanuel Geffner—managed to pass a letter to the port police describing their circumstances. Most had Romanian passports and entry and transit visas for Palestine, Syria, and Turkey, but the period between receiving the visas and actually boarding a ship in Romania had been so long that the papers had expired. They asked the port police to allow them to make contact with the respective consulates in order simply to extend their travel papers.

The Ludovics were deemed not to have proper paperwork and were required to remain on board, but Brettschneider, Geffner, and the Frencs were allowed to leave the ship. They passed into the city and began making arrangements to travel by land to Palestine. The Jewish Agency for Palestine—a group of Palestinian Jews active in organizing transports such as the *Struma*—used this small opening to appeal to the British authorities. If the entire ship could not pass on to Haifa, perhaps the authorities would at least issue Palestine visas for the ship's fifty-two children between the ages of eleven and sixteen—passengers who were old enough to travel on their own but not too old to represent a threat to any country. The suggestion neatly plumbed the thin line between humanitarianism and the rational interests of the two governments in control of the refugees' fate, the Turkish and the British.

In a flurry of telegrams and telephone calls, Jewish Agency officials at last managed to secure an agreement allowing passage for the children. The British Embassy in Ankara dispatched a letter to the Istanbul city authorities confirming the children's entry visas. The Turks were then to pass the order to the port police, requesting that the children's passports be forwarded to the British consular official for stamping. However, the port police—wary of acting independently on such an important matter—insisted that the arrangements be confirmed by a direct order from their superiors in Ankara.

While they were waiting for the instructions to arrive, a countermanding order came through. The *Struma* was to be towed back out to sea, where the captain would be instructed to restart the engine and make for another port, either in Bulgaria or back to the point of origin, Romania. In the struggle between multiple bureaucratic directives—disembark the children or expel the ship from Istanbul—the easier and clearer order won the day. After ten weeks in diplomatic limbo, the Turkish government had decided to solve the problem simply by removing the ship from Turkish waters.

A Turkish tugboat secured a towline, and on February 23, the tandem vessels began fighting the current northward beyond the rocky headlands where the narrow Bosphorus widens into the open sea. As the *Struma* was pulled silently out of the harbor, Istanbullus could see a sign that passengers had painted on sheets and hung over the railings: "Save us!"

Once well into the Black Sea, the tugboat cut the line and turned back toward the Bosphorus, leaving the ship adrift. The crew struggled to restart the engine, which had failed numerous times during the outbound journey. The *Struma* bobbed quietly for a few hours, and then, around dawn on February 24, 1942, a massive explosion ripped through the hull. The ice-cold seawater flooded compartments and swept across the deck. In minutes, the *Struma* broke in half.

The next day, Joseph Goldin, one of the Jewish Agency's representatives, telegraphed the news to his superiors in Jerusalem. "Struma wrecked blacksea four miles from bosphorus," the operator tapped, "missing details disaster and number survivors stop fearing great number victims."

In the hours that followed, Goldin worked desperately to compile a list of survivors. He first included the names of the Ludovics, who had tried to disembark with the other visa-holders, then penciled a question mark beside their names, then crossed them out. Over the days that followed, he drew a line through nearly every other name on the ship's manifest. The Ludovics, whose visas had expired, and dozens of children whose papers had been preapproved by the British, had all perished. Only nine passengers had been allowed to exit the *Struma* before the tugboat reattached its line to the ship and pulled it toward the Black Sea. Of the roughly 785 Jews and six Bulgarian crew who remained on board—the exact numbers remain uncertain even today—only one survivor, David Stoliar, was found alive by a Turkish rescue boat and brought ashore.

Over time, the reason for the explosion emerged. The ship had been targeted by a Soviet submarine acting on orders to hit any ship on the Black Sea as a means of blocking aid to Germany and its allies. Few people in Istanbul, however, spent much time thinking about the *Struma*. The local reaction to the carnage was muted. Refugees had come and gone for a very long time, and headlines in local papers were taken up with what was perceived to be a much bigger story: a botched assassination attempt in Ankara against Franz von Papen, the German ambassador, which occurred the day after the *Struma* sinking. It turned out to be the handiwork of Leonid Eitingon, the same operative who had successfully managed Trotsky's assassination eighteen months earlier.

A few weeks later, Istanbul's German-language newspaper, the *Türkische Post*, carried an official statement by Prime Minister Refik Saydam. The authorities had done everything possible to prevent the regrettable *Struma* affair, he said, but in the end Turkey could not serve as someone's surrogate homeland or "a refuge for the unwanted." Saydam followed up by dismissing the Jewish employees of the Turkish state press agency, on the grounds that they had spread Jewish propaganda by reporting the sinking.

Newspapers around the world carried the story of the *Struma*. It was by far the largest refugee disaster up to that time, but it was also part of a long line of tragedies, quixotic voyages, and missed opportunities associated with what Jewish activists called the *aliyah bet*—the project of getting Jews out of Europe and into Palestine.

Fifteen months earlier, the *Patria* had lain at anchor in the harbor at Haifa. The Jewish passengers on board were classed by the British as illegals, since they did not have the proper immigration papers. The plan was to send the ship to Mauritius, where the British hoped to make provisions for resettling the refugees. Before the ship could set sail, however, Jewish operatives planted a bomb on board, hoping to disable the engine and force the British hand. But a miscalculation led to a much larger explosion, which killed some 267 people. A month later, another refugee ship, the *Salvador*, ran aground in a storm in the Sea of Marmara south of Istanbul. More than two hundred people died.

Ira Hirschmann read about all these events in the New York press. He had seen other stories of ships being turned away from European ports or sent on long, fruitless voyages seeking permission to dock in Britain, the United States, Palestine, or elsewhere. But the *Struma* disaster affected him most profoundly. The sheer scale of the tragedy, along with the fact that bureaucratic paperwork had blocked an easy solution for at least the older children, seemed outrageous. As the months went by, Hirschmann paid more and more attention to reports of refugees attempting to flee via the Balkans and Turkey, the last routes that seemed to be open to Jews escaping from Nazi occupation or from roundups conducted by Axis governments. "It was an avalanche of sad statistics," he recalled.

Hirschmann had made his career by getting things done in fields that he had little experience in managing. His father had immigrated to Baltimore from Latvia as a teenager and made his fortune as a men's clothier and banker. The Hirschmann household was fueled by ambition and filled with the easy optimism of an upper-middle-class Jewish family, with a piano and music lessons, good schools, and taken-for-granted success. But Hirschmann himself was on the road to a solid career as a ne'er-do-well. He studied briefly at Johns Hopkins University but dropped out before choosing a major. He joined a Baltimore advertising agency but found the work tedious.

His real talent lay in what would now be called networking. He left Baltimore rather abruptly to seek more excitement in New York, and, as an outgoing young man of some standing, he fell into the circle of Jewish philanthropic and business organizations in New York and New Jersey. One of them was the American Jewish Joint Distribution Committee, or the Joint, the country's largest philanthropic association for American Jewry. Through social gatherings and activities sponsored by the Joint, he happened to meet the owner of one of Newark's most successful department stores, Bamberger's. Hirschmann parlayed the contact into a job as a low-level copywriter in the store's advertising department. From there, his career skyrocketed. Identified as an up-and-comer in the retail world, he moved to Lord and Taylor and then to Macy's, which had acquired the declining Bamberger's, and eventually to Bloomingdale's.

As one of the new lords of advertising, Hirschmann's primary job was to know people: to solicit the wealthy and famous and to divine the hearts and minds of everyone else. He sought the advice of Louis Brandeis and Felix Frankfurter. He stumped for Fiorello La Guardia. He lunched with Toscanini. It was the *Struma* affair that made him pay attention to international affairs, however. After reading about the disaster, his "pent-up feelings erupted," he later wrote.

At the time, millions of people were fleeing persecution, pogroms, and advancing armies. Entire communities had been destroyed by war and occupation in Poland and Soviet Ukraine. In Hungary, Romania, and Bulgaria, large-scale deportations of Jews had not yet taken place, but these Axis allies were under increasing pressure to fall in line with the Final Solution and surrender their Jewish residents.

Geographically, Turkey was the obvious exit route for Jews seeking to escape. Its neutrality offered relative freedom of movement, provided that any rescue effort did not push activities too far into the open and create a public relations problem for the Turkish government. In two nights, a ship could sail from Romania to Istanbul; an overnight train ran from Sofia, Bulgaria. With new stories emerging from Europe about planned killing centers and mass expulsions of Jews to labor camps, the hope was that Allied governments would at last start paying attention. The Emergency Committee to Save the Jewish People of Europe—a group formed in New York in the summer of 1943 to pressure the US government to deal with the Jewish refugee problem—had floated the idea of sending someone to Turkey to investigate the possibility of emigration via Istanbul. Hirschmann volunteered.

Some weeks later, Hirschmann and the president of the Emergency Committee, Peter Bergson, met with Breckinridge Long, the assistant secretary of state in charge of overseeing US responses to the refugee crisis in Europe. Long insisted that the government was doing everything possible to provide relief for European civilians caught up in the war. Bergson mentioned that the Emergency Committee wanted to send a special representative to Europe and that Hirschmann had stepped forward to take on that task. Long was skeptical, but he agreed to send a telegram to Laurence A. Steinhardt, the US ambassador to Turkey, to seek his advice and his agreement to work with Hirschmann. Steinhardt cabled back that he had no objection, and in January 1944 Hirschmann prepared to make the rounds in Washington, arranging meetings with agency heads and getting up to speed on the business of refugee assistance.

In the middle of his preparations, he was awakened by an early morning telephone call. On the line was Oscar S. Cox, a confidant of President Franklin Roosevelt. "The president has just signed the order," he said. Hirschmann knew instantly what he meant. Cox had recently shown Hirschmann the text of Roosevelt's order creating a body called the War Refugee Board, composed of the secretaries of state, war, and the treasury. The board's task would be to take immediate action to rescue from the Nazis as many members of persecuted minorities— ethnic, religious, or political—as possible. At last there would be a US government body whose sole mission was to relieve the plight of civilian victims of war—in other words, to try to ensure that there would be no more *Struma* affairs. Hirschmann's role was to be the State Department's special attaché for Turkey and the Middle East, Cox continued. His task would be to carry out the board's work in that region.

Hirschmann was elated. He would now be an official representative of the US government, rather than just a private citizen on a humanitarian mission to aid displaced families. The next day, he boarded a plane for Miami. After a week cooling his heels waiting for a US Army transport plane for Turkey, he found a berth. At the end of January, the C-54 took off with a group of young officers bound for India and one middle-aged civilian hitching a ride. After five days en route, via air hops to Puerto Rico, Brazil, Ghana, and Egypt, several days in Jerusalem, and a twenty-eight-hour train ride across the Taurus Mountains and half of Anatolia, Hirschmann at last arrived in Ankara on Valentine's Day, 1944.

"An old world seems slipping away from me," he wrote in his diary, "and I seem to be racing into a new." The Turkish capital had been willed into existence, and it still took an act of imagination to see it as a real city. The wide streets and purpose-built government buildings seemed soulless and merely functional. Hirschmann was happy to have a social invitation shortly after he arrived, to attend a diplomatic luncheon at the residence of Ambassador Steinhardt. Guests milled around the spacious residence, but as they made their way to their next appointments, Hirschmann lingered behind for a chance to speak with Steinhardt privately.

Besides their Jewish heritage, the two men had little in common. Steinhardt had had the kind of career that Hirschmann might once have dreamed of: a life of diplomatic adventure at missions in Sweden, Peru, the Soviet Union, and now Turkey. Hirschmann was flattered by the ambassador's eagerness to talk.

Hirschmann was to remain indefinitely in Ankara, Steinhardt informed him, and to have the status of special attaché to the US Embassy. His orders from Washington included an almost-unprecedented power. Unlike other diplomats, who were prevented by law from conversing with agents of enemy countries, Hirschmann would be expected to engage with enemy powers for the purpose of spiriting refugees out of harm's way. Support was to be provided by the embassy staff, but Hirschmann was to have main responsibility for the "transportation, rescue, relief, and maintenance of refugees" under his care. Americans were a people with a conscience, Hirschmann recalled thinking on hearing his orders for the first time, but now they "had a government with a conscience, as well as policy."

As he made his inquiries around Ankara, Hirschmann found the buck being passed from one office to the next, from an embassy to a Turkish government agency, and from government officials back to embassies. He began to feel like a wandering refugee himself. The British had agreed to allow a precise quota of immigrants to come to Palestine, but the number had been persistently under-filled for a simple bureaucratic reason: Being legally admitted to Mandate Palestine required papers—an exit permit from a Nazi-allied country, for example, plus a transit visa via a neutral state, plus an immigration certificate from British Mandate authorities. Even if transport could be arranged—in secret or at great risk, as in the *Struma* case—papers were still the one thing that only governments could supply.

In the middle of February, as the icy winter winds roared down Ankara's avenues, it gradually dawned on Hirschmann that the person who would be key to his efforts was not in a governmental role at all. He was technically a private citizen living in Istanbul who had a penchant for making lists. Unlike Hirschmann, he could only afford rooms in the Pera Palace, which at this point had become somewhat desperate for customers. That fact gave him a telegraph code—the equivalent of an e-mail address today—that would become one of the most widely known of the entire war: "*barlas perapalas beyoglu.*"

Chaim Barlas was an old Istanbul hand, at least compared to the novice Hirschmann. He was easy to miss in a crowd: slight of stature, swallowed up in an ill-fitting overcoat, with hooded eyes that marked him as an inveterate insomniac. But he knew everyone who was anyone in the city and most people of rank in the country as a whole. His correspondence files included regular letters and notes from the American, French, and British ambassadors; the Swedish military attaché; the consuls of Greece, Yugoslavia, Romania, Czechoslovakia, France, Afghanistan, Switzerland, Spain, and Italy; and folders brimming with memoranda, telegrams, contracts, and reports from Turkish shipping magnates, business leaders, and political luminaries. He was probably the best-connected man in Istanbul, polite to a fault as a letter writer, solicitous in conversation, and obsessive about getting names, birth dates, and places of birth exactly right. It was a rare combination of gifts, and the lives of many people depended on how well he wielded them.

Barlas's official title was Representative of the Immigration Department of the Jewish Agency for Palestine. Both his title and his organization's name gave little hint of the enormous role that both would soon play. By agreement of the League of Nations, the former Ottoman territory of Palestine had been placed under British administrative authority as part of the settlements governing the breakup of the sultan's empire at the end of the First World War. Part of that mandate provided for the establishment of a Jewish Agency for Palestine to act as the official voice of the local Jewish community, or *yishuv*, and to liaise with the British authorities on any matters connected with the community's affairs. Headed by David Ben-Gurion, the agency created its own self-defense unit, the Haganah, and oversaw the social and economic development of the Jewish community. As time went on, it became the body that facilitated migration by arranging entry permits for Jews seeking to move to Mandate Palestine. It was the organization that would eventually morph into the government of independent Israel.

Immigration lay at the root of the Zionist cause. It was a way of changing the demographic realities in Arab-majority Palestine and creating, literally one person at a time, a Jewish homeland in the land of Israel. But with the advent of the Final Solution in Europe, migration also became a pathway to survival. The United States, Britain, and other European countries had begun to impose strict quotas on Jewish immigration after 1938, precisely at the time that anti-Jewish laws and attacks ramped up in central Europe. Like Turkey, these governments feared that Jewish refugees, pushed out of Germany and the Nazi-occupied regions of Europe, would seek to immigrate permanently, a fear stoked by widespread antisemitism in the receiving states. The Palestine option was thus a route to safety that more and more Jews were eager to take.

Sometime after arriving in August 1940, Barlas took up residence at the Pera Palace. The location was ideal. Not only were the Americans and British close by, but the hotel was also safely away from the Park and the Tokatlian, whose Axis leanings were well known. And since the Pera Palace had its own telegraph station, Barlas could almost treat the lobby as his personal office. Even after he managed to locate a larger, permanent office on the Grande Rue, runners were constantly going back and forth to send wires at the hotel.

Barlas and his associate Joseph Goldin were the only two individuals working openly as representatives of the Jewish Agency, but behind them lay a larger network of Jewish activists living in Istanbul as journalists and businessmen while secretly providing assistance to the rescue effort. Turkish authorities generally assumed that any foreigner was up to some kind of spy game, and they kept close tabs on the Barlas group. Surveillance could lead in bizarrely amusing directions. One of Barlas's associates, Teddy Kollek, recalled being approached on the street by a passerby who overheard him speaking Hebrew. The man was a Jewish importer of dried fruits who had come to Istanbul to arrange a shipment of produce to Palestine. When his visa expired, he applied to the Turkish police to have it extended, but the police saw his real job as an unbelievable cover story. They insisted that he reveal which foreign agency he was working for, and when he protested that he wasn't working for any of them, his visa was denied. Kollek managed to convince one of his contacts in British intelligence to claim the distraught businessman—falsely— as one of their own. That satisfied the police, and the fruit merchant was sent away with visa in hand.

While Jewish Agency representatives were in some ways dependent on the help of British officials, the same government also provided their greatest roadblock. At the beginning of their work, Barlas and his associates realized they were caught in a double bind. To begin with, the Jewish Agency had to work to convince the British authorities to allow Jews into Palestine. While the British had delegated to the agency the right to vet Jews for entry, full approval still depended on British consular authorities' making the final call. Since 1939, however, the British had placed strict limits on Jewish entry. An earlier migration campaign organized by the *yishuv* had led to a massive influx of Jews in the 1930s while also sparking resistance from local Arabs. The British response was a famous white paper issued by the government of Prime Minister Neville Chamberlain. The policy paper committed Britain to supporting the transition toward a Palestinian state jointly governed by Jews and Arabs, but in order to maintain demographic balance, it capped new Jewish immigration at 75,000 people over the five years from 1940 to 1944.

The other problem for Barlas was gaining Turkish assent for Jews to transit via Istanbul, either by rail or by ship. Jews quickly found themselves trapped, as Hirschmann once quipped, between a white paper and the Black Sea. Since the beginning of the war, the Turks had been playing a delicate balancing game—not only with all the major powers that were courting them to join the war but also with their own past. Turkish immigration law had been crafted less as a way of forestalling a flood of refugees during war—although that was how Turkish officials explained their behavior—and more as a way of preventing the return of minorities who had fled the country in the 1920s and 1930s. The regulations were so strictly enforced that American sailors with Greek names were sometimes refused permission to step ashore in Istanbul, for fear that they were secretly ex-Istanbullus returning to reclaim the family estates.

Old habits were reinforced by wartime fear and the persistent belief that local minorities were a potential fifth column that could be put to use by enemies. Everyday antisemitism and racialized nationalism were becoming commonplace. Antisemitic cartoons, a mainstay of the Turkish press, portrayed local Jews as parasites eager to profit from the war-ravaged economy and immigrant Jews as unscrupulous wealth-mongers who would strip Turkey bare in their race to get out of

Europe. In France and elsewhere, individual Turkish diplomats made attempts to prevent Jews with Turkish citizenship from being deported to Nazi camps and death facilities. But while these examples were later highlighted as evidence of Turkey's collective heroism, only one unambiguous case of genuine rescue seems plausible: the effort by Selahattin Ülkümen, the Turkish consul on the island of Rhodes, to prevent the Nazis from deporting forty-six Jews, most of whom were Turkish citizens. Many more might have been saved had the Turkish government intervened more energetically on behalf of people trapped in Nazi-occupied Europe who also happened to be Turkish citizens.

The treatment of Jews in Turkey was part of a broader pattern of squeezing minorities, nationalizing the economy, and encouraging non-Muslims to leave. In November 1942, the government enacted a one-off levy on "wealth and extraordinary profits," an intentionally vague wording. This new "wealth tax" was intended in part to raise funds in case Turkey were forced to enter the war and in part to crush war profiteers who had supposedly benefited from inflation and scarcity. Some 114,368 individuals and businesses were assessed by specially appointed commissions, with no right of appeal except directly to the parliament. The bulk of the tax burden fell on Istanbul, but none of the major Turkish-owned hotels, including the Pera Palace, seems to have been much affected. The reason is that the largest tax assessments were handed out to Greeks, Armenians, and Jews. "This law is also a law of revolution," said Prime Minister Saracoğlu at the time. "We will in this way eliminate the foreigners who control our market and give the Turkish market to the Turks."

Families and minority businesses found it impossible to meet the requirements. According to a secret report by the OSS, the tax assessments for Armenian property owners amounted to 232 percent of their property's real value, 179 percent for Jews, and 156 percent for Greeks, while Muslims were assessed at just under 5 percent. Many of the most successful businesses in the city—including the Gesarian brothers' gramophone company, which had recorded Seyyan, Udi Hrant, and other leading artists of the day—became targets. Faik Ökte, the Turkish official responsible for administering the tax in Istanbul, later wrote a tell-all memoir denouncing the affair and blaming the prime minister, Saracoğlu, for coming up with the idea. It was all a shameful episode, Ökte concluded, the "misbegotten offspring of German racialism and Ottoman fanaticism."

Betty Carp, the American consular administrator and OSS agent, recalled the effects of the tax on friends and acquaintances, few of whom were rich or propertied. One Greek friend, Irini, witnessed the police arrive at her house and cart away everything except a bed and mattress, a few items of china and dishware, and, in exchange for a bribe, her clothes. The men of the household were herded into an open garbage truck and, in a raging snowstorm, taken away. In the end, more than a thousand Istanbullus—including prominent industrialists and commercial leaders—were assembled at Sirkeci station and deported from the city to pay off their debts through forced labor, many of them at a special camp in Aşkale, in eastern Anatolia. Their personal belongings were sold in public auctions at the Grand Bazaar.

The wealth tax was repealed in March 1944 and prisoners were allowed to return home, but their properties were never restored. In fact, the effort to pay the exorbitant tax rates had produced another massive wealth transfer among Istanbul's ethnic communities on the model of the 1920s. Greeks, Armenians, and Jews owned nearly eighty percent of the property sold off during the era when the wealth tax was in force. Ninety-eight percent of the buyers were Turkish Muslims or the Turkish government. "According to the best-informed sober judgments," a diplomat reported at the time, "this represents the first step of a bloodless massacre."

The bureaucratic obstacles that faced Jews were thus part of the Turkish state's deeper nervousness about minorities and movement in general. Chaim Barlas was juggling a host of diplomatic conundrums.

As soon as one door opened, another closed. The Turkish government agreed to facilitate the dispatch of food packages of raisins, nuts, figs, and margarine to Jewish communities via the Red Cross, a kind of stopgap while Jews were awaiting permission to emigrate. But because of rationing, the Turkish authorities mandated that packages containing meat could only include pork—a product in low demand among Muslims but, of course, prohibited for observant Jews as well. Similar problems affected transportation. Turkey had eased its restrictions on group transit of refugees in February 1943, but two months later Bulgaria closed its frontiers to people traveling in large groups—effectively stopping any substantial flow across the crucial land border between the two countries. Barlas next approached the Ministry of Foreign Affairs in Ankara, requesting that Turkey reverse its policy and instead allow individuals to transit the country rather than requiring that they be part of a preestablished group.

It was a bold request. This was precisely the problem that Turkish authorities had feared: an influx of individual families—difficult to monitor and impossible to control once they had entered the country—making their way to Turkey and getting effectively stuck there, with the government having no way of knowing whether they had in fact exited and continued toward Palestine. The response was to accede to Barlas's request but to place a nearly impossible restriction on movement: Only nine Jewish families were permitted to transit the country per week. Moreover, the Turkish government required that everyone admitted as part of this quota exit the country before another quota could be admitted. At that rate, Ira Hirschmann later reckoned, it would have taken two hundred years to ease the bottleneck of displaced people seeking to flee Hungary, Romania, and Bulgaria.

The plan went into effect that September, but in the following two months only 215 people—some from Romania, others from Poland who had escaped to Hungary—made their way to Istanbul. By December 1943, Barlas had already compiled a list of more than a thousand other names. Small numbers of refugees had also arrived on the Turkish coast from Greece, and arrangements were being made for acquiring immigration papers for Palestine.

In December, Barlas wrote to Ambassador Steinhardt that only 1,126 people had made their way out of Nazi-dominated Europe via Turkey. In fact, nearly twice as many Turkish Jews—2,138 people—had left for Palestine as the number of rescued Jews escaping the Nazis. If that balance continued, the Jewish Agency would be emptying Istanbul of its Jews far faster than it was able to aid Jews trapped inside Axis Europe.

Hirschmann's arrival in February 1944 gave a new impetus to the effort. Hirschmann set about pulling together the many organizations that were working, sometimes at cross purposes, to facilitate rescue. He now had the full authority of the American government, and the personal endorsement of President Roosevelt and key members of the cabinet. What he also brought to the table was money.

Workmen clear the tracks of ice and snow for a trolley car.

From his years in New York and New Jersey, Hirschmann had a long association with the American Jewish Joint Distribution Committee; in his new role at the War Refugee Board, he helped transform the board into a conduit for Joint funds. The Joint had been active since the First World War in channeling assistance from the American Jewish community to needy people abroad. It now became the principal financier for the Turkish relief effort, as well as for many other programs around the world. The War Refugee Board persuaded the US Treasury Department to waive restrictions on trading with enemy countries to allow the Joint to carry on financial transactions in Axis-dominated zones: to exchange currency, distribute resources, and where necessary buy tickets and arrange for travel for individual Jewish families. Other funds—nearly $700,000—indirectly financed operations in Turkey and transport to Palestine, in addition to hundreds of thousands of dollars spent on transit from Hungary and other countries and distribution of food via Turkey. Further Joint-funded programs delivered food to concentration-camp internees and Jewish refugees hiding in the Russian Far East; sent burlap-wrapped food packages to Jews languishing in Romanian ghettos (with the burlap to be used for clothing and blankets); supplied physicians and public health workers to Balkan refugee centers; and provided direct financing for the ongoing work of Jewish schools, hospitals, and other community organizations in Istanbul, Ankara, Izmir, and other Turkish cities.

In relatively short order, Hirschmann, Barlas, Steinhardt, and other major players managed to work out an informal arrangement involving the US government, the Jewish Agency, and private American philanthropists, all focused on getting as many Jews as possible into and out of Turkey. Hirschmann was also in regular contact with Lanning Macfarland and the OSS station in Istanbul, using the resources of the US intelligence mission while passing along any information he had been able to glean from his own sources about conditions in Axis Europe.

Since the day the war began, Barlas told Hirschmann, he had

devoted himself to the task of rescue. Now, at last, he felt "confident that nothing can further disturb our cooperation which has only one aim in view: the rescue and bringing into safety of our brethren." But as the winter of 1943–1944 faded into a bright Istanbul spring, a singular problem remained: If the Nazis were increasingly killing Jews in groups—and now on a scale that even skeptical Allied observers could no longer deny—the only way to save them was in groups as well.

As long as a private citizen had the requisite papers, there was no problem in theory with being able to enter a neutral state such as Turkey. But theory and reality were often far apart. In the summer of 1938, the Turkish government had officially barred the door to Jews coming from countries with antisemitic laws. Ankara may have believed that these people, even though the neediest, were also the most likely to stay in Turkey. Once Germans began transporting large groups of Jews to established killing sites in Poland, a possible route of rescue was to transport Jewish refugees to Turkey en masse in specially outfitted ships or trains. But the devil lay in the bureaucratic details.

The process began with Barlas. As representative of the Jewish Agency, he was empowered by the British Mandate authorities in Palestine to draw up lists of candidates for immigration, based on information provided by his own agents or directly from people with family members still in Axis-dominated lands. The information required was substantial, and war made it hard to obtain. It could take two to three weeks to gather a complete list of names, dates of birth, places of birth, and current addresses for a group of people large enough to fill a ship or train.

Once the list was assembled, Barlas would forward the information to Palestine. The authorities there would go down the list name by name, either endorsing or denying a person's candidacy. The finalized list would then be forwarded to London for approval. That entire process took another two to three weeks. After that, the British passport control officer in Istanbul would be instructed to draw up his own prioritized list—again over a period of two to three weeks. From there, the officer would communicate directly with the British Embassy in Ankara with details of which families were approved for immigration.

The final list would then go from the embassy to the Turkish Ministry of Foreign Affairs, where it would eventually—over three or four days—find its way to the Turkish consular affairs department. That department would in turn transmit the list of approved candidates to Turkish consuls in Bucharest, Budapest, Sofia, or other cities where officers were empowered to release transit visas. In the end, a Jewish family could expect to wait at least two and a half months, if everything went smoothly, to receive permission both to transit Turkey and to enter Palestine. The wait was often considerably longer. After that, it was Hirschmann's job to sort out the even more complex issue of arranging ships and trains to get people with the appropriate paperwork out of harm's way.

For the applicants, the entire process was excruciating. You wrote a letter or filled out a form, waited, then perhaps wrote it all again. Abraham Slowes had immigrated to Palestine from Poland in 1930 and made a successful career in Haifa as a power-station engineer. His parents, Moshe and Malka, were respected dental surgeons who were still living in the family home in Vilna. The city—eventually renamed Vilnius—had undergone immense changes: It was part of the Russian Empire when the Slowes family first moved there; it had been made part of Poland after the First World War; it was captured by the Red Army in September 1939 and incorporated into Soviet Lithuania. As Hitler and Stalin jointly moved through eastern Europe, Vilnius was at the center of the vise. In early March 1941, Abraham received a simple telegram from his father. "Send certificates," Moshe Slowes wrote, requesting that his son get travel documents for himself, his wife, and another family, the Fiksmans.

Abraham wrote back quickly to say that he was doing everything possible to arrange the certificates of immigration to Palestine via Turkey. In fact, he had already made an application on his parents' behalf, but that request had been denied in February 1940. In the months that followed, his family's predicament worsened. Germany and the Soviet Union were allies when Moshe sent the first telegram to his son. Three and a half months later, the two countries were enemies. The German invasion of the Soviet Union placed the family squarely on the front line of a new war. Abraham now ramped up his efforts, sending a steady stream of letters and telegrams to virtually anyone he thought might be able to help. Finally, in March 1942, more than two years after his first request, the Department of Migration in Jerusalem wrote with superb news. The British passport control officer in Istanbul had been instructed to release immigration certificates for Moshe and Malka. They would simply need to apply in person in Istanbul.

The first problem for Abraham was getting this news to his parents; the second was getting his parents to Istanbul. He must have known at the time that things were desperate in Vilnius. The Wehrmacht had captured the city from the Soviets in the first days of the invasion in the summer of 1941, and Jews in the city had been rounded up and confined to a ghetto. But the uncertainty of war and the bureaucracy of the process created new obstacles. When Abraham asked the Red Cross to contact whoever was living at his parents' last known address, the receiving officer wrote back instructing him to fill out the required form. Abraham quickly returned the form—listing eight family members who were believed to reside in the occupied zone—and included a postage stamp to pay for the cost of forwarding. He wrote to the Swedish consul in Jerusalem and even to the Vatican. "I venture to hope that assistance will not be denied to aged people who have during all their lives helped the sick as physicians, in these hard times," he told the

Swedish official, enclosing his parents' photographs as identification. The consul in Jerusalem wrote back, asking him to address his request to the Swedish consul in Haifa. Similar replies came from his other correspondents. Regrettably, they all said, contact with the German-occupied territories had ceased.

Finally, Abraham reckoned that going closer to the source might yield better results, and in early August 1944 he wrote to the British Embassy in Moscow requesting that news of the immigration certificates be forwarded to his parents' address. Only weeks earlier, the Red Army had retaken Vilnius, so Abraham hoped that the lines of communication would once again be open. In November, an attaché at the embassy wrote back with the first clear news. "With reference to your letter of 8th August enquiring about the whereabouts of your father," the letter said, "I regret to inform you that a letter sent to the address you gave has been returned marked 'Addressee has died.'"

A follow-up note from the embassy the next spring contained more information: The family apparently had been killed at the beginning of the German occupation four years earlier. The people to whom the Palestine authorities had issued immigration certificates, to whom the passport control officer in Istanbul was prepared to issue a validation, and to whom Turkish officials were asked to issue a transit visa were already dead by the time the first stamp had been placed on any of their documents. For individual families, as well as for Barlas and Hirschmann—all of them busy creating long lists of people waiting to be saved—filling up a passenger manifest was sometimes like assembling a ship of ghosts.

AT THE GATE OF FELICITY

A safe haven, August 1944: Jewish refugees, probably survivors of the doomed *Mefkûre* convoy, arrive at Sirkeci station from the Black Sea coast.

THERE WAS A MUNDANE everydayness to acts of heroism. The telegraph operator tapping away Barlas's messages from the Pera Palace was just one piece of an intricate bureaucratic puzzle. Filling out forms, collating official papers, negotiating with a transport company, arranging for the repair of a ship's engine, and doggedly pursuing Turkish officials more interested in having a problem go away than in resolving it were all critical elements of rescue and escape.

Survival required planning, and before planning came paper, lots of it. War, occupation, and atrocity blocked the Slowes family's paper chase. For many Jews, however, the core problem was not just getting the permits to enter Turkey and then Palestine. Rather, outside the areas of German occupation, there was still a set of officious and maddening technicalities involved in convincing a government—even a reasonably cooperative one—to let people leave. "It would appear from the telegrams received by Hirschmann and myself that the War Refugee Board is under the impression that the principal difficulty with which we have been confronted has been a reluctance on the part of the Turk Government to cooperate," Ambassador Steinhardt wrote to Washington in March 1944. "Thus far this has not been the case. Up to the present time our principal difficulty has been the refusal of the Axis authorities in the Balkans to permit Jewish refugees to depart."

Romania was the intended point of exodus for growing numbers of Jews, just as it had been for the ill-fated *Struma* passengers. Some were native to Romania and had spent the war living openly in the capital, Bucharest, or in other cities. Others had been interned or deported to Transnistria, the stretch of occupied Soviet Ukrainian territory where the Romanian government herded hundreds of thousands of Jews into camps and ghettos. Still others had fled to Romania from farther north, from Poland or other areas under direct German rule.

Even though Romania was a Nazi ally, it was still possible to live relatively safely inside the country's prewar borders, despite the growing pressure that Berlin was exerting on Bucharest to round up local Jews and send them to German-run camps. What united the many Jewish communities thrown together by war inside Romania was the government's requirement that a Romanian official formally approve any request to emigrate by issuing an exit visa and, when necessary, a passport. This was a common practice in many countries at the time; it was simply a way of keeping tabs on citizens' comings and goings across international frontiers. But in the context of persecution and flight, it created enormous obstacles for Jews in particular.

Even after the Turks had ceased requiring transit visas for Jews holding valid immigration certificates, the Romanian government insisted that migrants present special exit documents before departure. Since many Jews had been stripped of their citizenship by the Romanian government in 1938, as part of a string of antisemitic laws, getting out of the country required that Romanian Jews apply to have their citizenship reinstated or verified. Bureaucrats dutifully kept all these records, much like an immigration officer today would be able to provide a full accounting of which airport one departed at precisely what hour.

At a minimum, getting out of Romania required that a Jewish applicant present the following documents:

a current photograph

a statement of the applicant's birth date, place of birth, height, hair color, eye color, nose shape, forehead shape, mouth shape, chin shape, and facial hair

a certificate confirming that the applicant had no pending legal cases against him

a notarized affidavit from two witnesses confirming the identity of the applicant, his parents, birth date, residence, and identity as a Jew

a notarized affidavit confirming the identity of the two witnesses above

a certificate from the Ministry of Finance stating that the applicant was not in arrears on taxes in the past five years

a special form, signed by the applicant, expressly requesting permission to leave the country

It was the last requirement on this list that was the most insulting. The form required that the applicant sign a simple statement swearing to the following:

> By these presents, I, the undersigned, _____, living at _____, declare that, in obtaining a passport and leaving the country, I understand that I will be permanently settling abroad with my entire family.

The bureaucratic language masked the perverse reality: The Jewish applicant was in effect restored to a version of Romanian citizenship only on the condition that he and his immediate relatives never set foot in the country again.

In addition to restrictions on the Romanian side, the Turkish government continually threw up roadblocks as well. Officials in Ankara were wary about using Turkish-flagged vessels in any rescue efforts, even if the full costs were borne by private organizations or foreign governments, for fear that this would tip Turkey too far to the Allied cause and bring down Hitler's wrath. The *Struma* affair had made the government even more cautious. In the event of another catastrophe at sea, Ankara believed, the blame would land squarely on Turkish heads, repaying any assistance in the rescue effort with international condemnation. Even as seemingly simple a matter as allowing relief organizations to trade Turkish lira at the same preferential exchange rate allowed for diplomatic missions was treated carefully. Delaying tactics and a retreat into the arcana of diplomatic consultations and official inquiries were the normal responses to Ambassador Steinhardt's requests for assistance.

By the middle of 1944, however, things were working better than ever before. So many foreign organizations were seeking to aid Jews via Istanbul—some Jewish, some American, some international, such as the Red Cross—that the entire process threatened to collapse under its own weight. Given the fact that it was in a refugee's interest to be in contact with as many aid groups as possible—hedging bets in the hope that at least one of them would be able to help—multiple agencies sometimes devoted incredible energy to a particular case only to find that a matter had already been resolved by another.

As Ambassador Steinhardt wrote to Barlas in June, many of these groups sent their representatives to Turkey for only a few days and had little understanding of the complexities of the local environment. There were even instances when multiple rescue groups were bidding on the same ship, driving up the price that an owner could ask. And since some of them were expressly involved in illegal migration—flouting Turkish immigration law in the hope of getting more people out of central Europe—their activities threatened to bring a halt to the hard work of the Jewish Agency and others in securing legal permission to transit to Palestine. Earlier that spring, Foreign Minister Numan Menemencioğlu had told Steinhardt explicitly that the Turkish authorities were well aware of the illegal activity being carried out in Istanbul and that the government could easily activate plans for stopping it. For that reason, Barlas had always been wary of mixing *aliyah bet* with his own above-board campaign to get official transit visas and Palestine certificates for as many Jews as possible.

In all of these efforts, both legal and illegal, information was the crucial component of survival. If you knew where family members or friends were located and how to get to them, and if you had the wherewithal to assemble official papers that could easily have been mislaid or destroyed, the chances of making it to safety were immeasurably greater. That is why Barlas and Hirschmann frequently made the short trip from the Pera Palace and the Park Hotel, across Taksim Square, and toward the neighborhood of Harbiye. Their destination was the Cathedral of the Holy Spirit.

Harbiye's name was derived from the root word for "war," but there was probably no more peaceful or secure place in the city. It had been the site of the old Ottoman military training academy—hence the name—and had graduated the elite of the sultan's imperial land forces, including Mustafa Kemal. It had also been selected by the British occupation troops for their headquarters after the First World War. Like most of the suburban highlands north of the Golden Horn, where many non-Muslims had resided during the Ottoman era, the district was a hodgepodge of Christian churches, cemeteries, shops, and lodgings for foreigners, all lying uneasily alongside barracks and parade grounds. When he set up his offices during the Allied occupation, General Charles Harington found an overgrown Armenian cemetery nearby. He ordered it transformed into a sports field. The old tombstones were rearranged into makeshift bleachers from which members of the British colony could enjoy refreshments and watch amateur cricket matches.

The neighborhood was far away from the old city, both geographically and culturally. A major Turkish novelist of the era, Peyami Safa, entitled one of his most famous works *Fatih–Harbiye* (1931), contrasting the traditionally Muslim district of Fatih south of the Golden Horn with its upwardly mobile opposite to the north. Secular Muslims were increasingly moving into multistory houses and new apartment buildings in Harbiye, but the district had long been known for its Christian businesses, schools, and places of worship. In 1846, the Ottoman authorities had allotted land in the neighborhood for what would become Istanbul's most important Catholic church. It was the seat of the spiritual leader of the group still referred to today as the city's Latins or, more commonly, Levantines.

Istanbul's Levantines were comfortable in many cultures but perhaps never truly at home in any. The church's parishioners included Arab merchants, Maltese bankers, and Italian financiers—usually French- or Italian-speaking but also inherently multilingual—who were products of the long period of interaction between the Ottomans and Catholics in the eastern Mediterranean. Among them were some of the city's wealthiest families, who lived clustered in villas and apartment buildings in Pera. They were "a strange community," said the writer Harold Nicolson, "isolated, important, polyglot and yet united by a common function" as economic go-betweens linking Ottoman producers with European markets. The memoirist Ziya Bey was more pointed and probably reflected a view common among Muslims. The Levantines were, he said, "a nondescript people . . . whose one purpose is to make and spend money and who are ready to sell anything for the purpose." Ziya Bey's disdain was directed at a tiny portion of the city's population, however. There were fewer than 23,000 Levantines in the city at the time of the first republican census in 1927, two-thirds of them foreign citizens, and that number declined steadily thereafter.

Catholic communities in the Middle East always retained the flavor of an earlier time in the church's history. In Christendom's great schism of 1054, the churches now labeled Orthodox—Greek, Russian, Romanian, and others—decided to hew to the concept of church hierarchies being tied to distinct national or cultural communities. They parted ways with the idea that one leader among them—the bishop in Rome—could lay claim to universal authority. But Rome realized that touting its universality too loudly in the East would harden the position of its Orthodox rivals; worse, it might alienate loyal congregations that had developed their own traditions. That is why Istanbul, like Damascus or Beirut, developed an enormous variety of churches that, in the West, would all simply be called Catholic, from Armenian Catholics to Syrian Catholics to Latin (that is, Roman) Catholics. The result was the broad mosaic of Catholicism in its many Eastern forms, each with its own liturgy, vestments, hierarchy, and even, for some, married priests. In that sense, the Levantines—although purely Roman Catholic—might be seen as the easternmost Westerners or the westernmost Easterners, depending on one's point of view, within the Catholic communion.

Among these Catholics, the pope always tended to tread rather lightly. That may have been why the apostolic delegate—the pope's personal representative in Turkey—ended up in a rather out-of-the-way location, in Harbiye, rather than establishing himself in the middle of the old Christian district of Pera. The Cathedral of the Holy Spirit is by no means the most appealing Catholic church in Istanbul. Its plaster façade frames a mildly interesting mosaic of a dove descending and tongues of fire sprouting from the heads of the faithful. Wisteria and English ivy spill into the courtyard. What the cathedral lacked in architectural appeal, however, it made up for in temporal power, which is why Chaim Barlas had been trying so hard to get there through the early winter of 1943.

Even though Barlas's telegraph station in the Pera Palace was less than a half-hour walk from the cathedral, protocol demanded that he go through the proper channels. He corresponded with the apostolic delegate's chief secretary, Vittore Righi, in hopes of arranging a meeting. He may have already gained access in January, but it is more likely that the process dragged on for several weeks, as pleasantries were exchanged and requests forwarded.

On February 12, 1943, Barlas found a telegram waiting for him in the lobby of the Pera Palace. It was from Isaac Herzog, the chief rabbi in Jerusalem, and warned of the "extreme danger" that Jews in Italy were facing. He urged Barlas to make contact as quickly as possible with the pope's representative to see whether something could be done. There was no plan to bring Italian Jews to Istanbul; Barlas already had his hands full trying to arrange passage for the much larger communities besieged in eastern Europe. But the hope was that a respected senior church leader might be able to intercede with papal officials in Rome. In any case, Barlas now had yet another talking point on which to engage the Vatican's representative.

Pope Pius XII had chosen to observe a calculated neutrality in the war, even when it became clear that Jewish communities were being destroyed en masse throughout Europe. His staunch opposition to communism pushed him away from an open endorsement of the Allied cause, which would have placed him effectively in the same camp as the Soviets. His concern for protecting Rome and Vatican City from Hitler's armies also pushed him to speak cautiously when addressing the issue of German atrocities, even though Vatican diplomats were fully aware of the horrors being perpetrated in occupied Poland and the Axis-occupied parts of the Soviet Union. However, equal treatment of both sides became the polestar guiding Pius XII's diplomacy. "He explained that when talking of atrocities he could not name the Nazis without at the same time mentioning the Bolsheviks . . . ," said Harold H. Tittmann Jr., the American chargé d'affaires at the Holy See. "He stated that he 'feared' there was foundation for the atrocity reports of the Allies but led me to believe that he felt there had been some exaggeration for purpose of propaganda."

Barlas knew the church's position, which is why he was so careful in his approach to the papal representative living near him in Istanbul. Finally, in the spring of 1943, Barlas walked through a small doorway off Cumhuriyet Avenue and into the presence of someone with the weighty title of Titular Archbishop of Mesembria and Apostolic Delegate to Turkey and Greece.

Monsignor Angelo Giuseppe Roncalli had been in Istanbul much longer than Barlas. He had served as apostolic delegate since 1934 and, before that, had enjoyed a promising ecclesiastical career. But he was also imbued with the core quality that was of most interest to Barlas: a commitment to social activism and the church's role in the world.

Roncalli was born in 1881—making him an exact contemporary of Mustafa Kemal—near Bergamo, the son of sharecropping farmers who produced a hearty Italian household of thirteen children. It was not unusual for a large family to have at least one son destined for the priesthood, but Roncalli seemed to take to theology with unusual fervor. He completed studies as a local seminarian, then as a scholarship student in Rome, and finally as a doctoral candidate. In 1904, he was ordained as a priest. He eventually returned to Bergamo to serve as secretary to the local bishop, a position that gave him his first real access to the church hierarchy. Bergamo was one of the centers of progressive social thought, the view that the great wealth and power of the church should be used both to improve the lot of individual parishioners and to nudge political institutions into directions that were more equitable and just.

The job of chief confidant and adviser in the bishopric placed Roncalli squarely within the major currents of progressive teaching. His organizational experience also recommended him to higher authorities. By 1920, he had been elevated by Pope Benedict XV to become director of the Society for the Propagation of the Faith, a position that gave him added experience as administrator of the church's missions in Italy and abroad. That international experience placed him in line for an appointment outside Italy, and in 1925 he was named archbishop and papal representative in Bulgaria, a position that, in 1931, Roncalli convinced both the church and the Bulgarian government to raise to the level of apostolic delegate. Three years later, he was transferred to the same position in Istanbul.

Roncalli quickly grew fond of Turkey and the Turks. His decade of service in Bulgaria had already made him an expert in negotiating the societies and cultures of southeastern Europe, and he threw himself into his new job with enthusiasm. He began learning Turkish, although the intricacies of the language made him think of the project mainly as a form of mortification and penance. His real challenges were less cultural than political. "My work in Turkey is not easy," Roncalli wrote candidly in his journal. "The political situation does not allow me to do much."

In the world of ecclesiastical diplomacy, an apostolic delegate's role was delicate. He had no legal diplomatic standing and, unlike the higher office of papal nuncio, could not speak on behalf of the Vatican. His bishopric was based in Istanbul, where most of Turkey's Roman Catholic community resided, but that location also kept him at some remove from the foreign policy intrigues—and political power—in Ankara. The Turkish government had extended its commitment to secularism into the international realm; any communication between Roncalli and Foreign Minister Menemencioğlu was treated as strictly personal, not as a form of diplomatic correspondence. In 1939, when Roncalli contacted the Ministry of Foreign Affairs with the official announcement of the death of Pope Pius XI and the accession of Pius XII, the foreign ministry's response was that the event was a purely religious matter and had no bearing on interstate relations. Like other priests, Roncalli often had to leave his ecclesiastical collar in his closet, since the Turkish government generally prohibited the wearing of religious garb in public. Nor did Roncalli have a claim to any particular administrative power over the bishops in the territory where he happened to be located. His only real tools were moral suasion and a direct line of communication with Rome. In Roncalli's case, any hindrances were lessened by a wealth of local experience, contacts, and "a great deal of tact and ability," in the words of the French ambassador.

There is no transcript of Barlas's first encounter with Roncalli, but he presumably made the points to the delegate that he had earlier made in correspondence with Righi: that the Jewish Agency was ramping up its efforts to get Jews out of occupied Europe; that the church could do more to condemn the atrocities being committed across the continent; and that the church could play a very particular role in mobilizing its contacts to make sure that Jews were able to access the immigration papers they would need to exit their home countries, transit Turkey, and finally arrive in Palestine. In any case, the channels of communication were now open. Throughout the spring and summer of 1943, Barlas either met personally with Roncalli or passed documents to him through Righi. In June, Barlas wired a quick update to Jerusalem: "Have seen today his eminence the pappal [*sic*] nuncio [*sic*] who is doing utmost render help."

Barlas's requests were becoming ever more pointed and concrete. Barlas was asking Roncalli not only to use his resources to press Rome on taking a stronger stance against the persecution of Jews but also to use the Vatican network for the express purpose of assisting individual families in escaping. The relationship was mutual, in fact. Given his past experience in Bulgaria, Roncalli knew of families who were seeking to flee. On multiple occasions, he asked Barlas to follow up on whether a specific person in Sofia or elsewhere had received immigration papers. In November the chief rabbi in Jerusalem wrote to thank Roncalli for the "precious assistance that you have continually rendered in [Barlas's] efforts to come to the aid of our poor brothers and sisters."

Another crisis was yet to come, however. Axis-aligned countries such as Hungary and Romania had already enacted harshly discriminatory anti-Jewish laws and shuttered Jewish businesses. They had no qualms about murdering Jews in territories that they had occupied during the war. In Hitler's carve-up of eastern Europe, Hungary was awarded slices of Czechoslovakia and Soviet Ukraine; Romania took an even larger portion of Soviet Ukraine, including the strategic city of Odessa; and Bulgaria received part of Macedonia and western Thrace. All three countries rounded up and deported foreign Jews from these occupied territories; some participated in the large-scale murder of Jewish civilians who were blamed for opposing the occupation or aiding the Allied enemy.

But these governments were also surprisingly patriotic about their own Jews. They resisted German pressure to load local Jews onto trains for deportation to Nazi-run killing centers abroad. Jews living inside Hungary, Romania, and Bulgaria proper were by and large spared the worst ravages of the early stages of the Holocaust.

In Hungary, that situation began to change in the spring of 1944. As the likelihood of an Allied victory became more and more apparent, Hungary's government began putting out secret feelers in Istanbul and other neutral capitals. If the Allies would agree to certain conditions—such as avoiding a Soviet occupation of Hungary and forgoing any punitive border changes in a peace settlement—Hungary might switch its allegiance from the Axis to the Allied cause. German intelligence was intimately aware of these conversations, and as German troops retreated from the Soviet Union after the defeat at Stalingrad, plans were drawn up for the full-scale invasion of Hungary—a way of scotching Hungary's exit from the Axis and creating a buffer against an Allied advance through southeastern Europe. In the process, the Nazis would be able to realize a goal that the uncooperative Hungarian government had blocked since the beginning of the war: the large-scale deportation and murder of Hungary's substantial Jewish community, which numbered some 725,000 people before the war. In March 1944, Wehrmacht troops crossed the border, accompanied by SS and Gestapo units. The attack on Jews began later that summer, a phased campaign personally overseen by Adolf Eichmann, the senior SS commander in Budapest.

Jewish property was confiscated, Jewish families were forced into a string of ghettos, and then, beginning in May, trainloads of Jewish citizens were assembled for transport to Auschwitz-Birkenau. Many were gassed soon after their arrival.

By this stage, Barlas had an ally in Hirschmann, who was committed to using his funding and contacts to secure ships for rescue operations on the Black Sea. The Hungarian situation presented a particular kind of challenge. Much of the Jewish community had remained persecuted but reasonably safe. Now the Nazi eradication effort was kicked into overdrive. Nazi authorities were also aware of the particular concern that Allied governments had developed for the fate of Jews, and officials in Budapest sought to exploit this concern for reasons of propaganda and economics.

With Eichmann's consent, in mid-May 1944 two emissaries, Joel Brand and Andrea György, were sent to Istanbul to open secret negotiations with the Allies. Brand, well known to Barlas and other Jewish agents there, was a young Jewish industrialist in Hungary who had been active in attempts to get Jews out of his native country. His traveling companion, György, was a Hungarian Jew who had converted to Catholicism and a man equally well known by a range of different names. He was sometimes called Grosz, sometimes Gross or Grenier, sometimes Trillium, the code name that he had been given by his American handlers: He was part of the OSS's Dogwood network and as such an invaluable informant for Allied intelligence.

Brand and György carried a grotesque offer: The German authorities would agree to release Jews in exchange for needed goods. "We are in the fifth year of the war," Eichmann had told Brand in Budapest. "We lack supplies. Well, you want to save Jews, especially the young and the women of childbearing age. I'm a German idealist, and I respect you as a Jewish idealist. You've got 1,200,000 Jews in Hungary, Poland, and so forth. I am selling you the goods." Eichmann's terms were startlingly specific. A limited number of Jews would be allowed to exit Hungary if the Allies would provide the Germans with two million bars of soap, two hundred tons of cocoa, eight hundred tons of coffee, two hundred tons of tea, and ten thousand trucks.

The emissaries were detained by Allied operatives for further questioning in Istanbul and Cairo, and the offer was roundly rejected. No Allied government could bear the thought of paying blood money to the Nazis, and the Soviets in particular feared that additional war matériel or supplies might embolden the Germans to launch a new offensive on the eastern front. Similar ransom plans had been proffered before; the *yishuv* leadership was eager to explore any option for getting Jews out of Europe, even if it meant making pacts with the devil. The Brand mission, however, illustrated the desperation of the Germans— now clearly in retreat in the east and focusing their attention on eliminating as many Jews as possible before the war ended.

The Brand mission also showed that the window for action had not fully closed. Escape routes might still be available, even as the deportations accelerated. Through his channels of communication with church officials in Budapest, Roncalli learned that Jews who had not yet been deported might be allowed to exit the country. What they required was immigration certificates for Palestine, certificates that could be obtained only in Istanbul. But if the threatened Jews could not come to Turkey to receive the certificates, the only possible solution was to take the certificates to them—inside a Nazi-occupied country that had, by midsummer of 1944, already deported more than 400,000 Jews to labor and death camps.

That was where Barlas and Hirschmann came to rely on the apostolic delegate. In a series of exchanges that summer, the Jewish Agency and the War Refugee Board made arrangements to transfer packets of immigration certificates to Roncalli, for onward transmission via church networks to Jewish communities in Hungary. Barlas authorized his team to identify as many Hungarian Jews as possible. His associates scoured Istanbul for people who might supply the names and addresses of friends or family members. Others took to copying down any recognizably Jewish name from the Budapest phone directory.

On June 5, Roncalli wrote to Barlas: "I am pleased to inform you that the certificates for the Jews of Hungary which you passed to me are being sent to Budapest by a reliable courier." "Thanks to these documents," Barlas replied the next day, Hungarian refugees "could be saved." In doing this, Roncalli was circumventing his superiors in Rome. Before the Hungarian deportations began, the War Refugee Board had informed him of the plans for the mass murder of Hungarian Jews. Roncalli forwarded the report to the Vatican—an eyewitness account by two Slovak Jews who had managed to escape from Auschwitz—but with little public result. Later, the papal nuncio in Budapest personally informed Rome of the round-up of Hungarian Jews. Yet Pope Pius XII continued to refuse to name Jews as Hitler's principal victims or to condemn Nazi policies directed against them.

At the very least, Roncalli was overstepping his role as a religious leader with no diplomatic standing in a neutral country. He must also have realized that he was actively participating in a plan that the church had previously refused to endorse: the large-scale immigration of Jews to Palestine. In the context of the Final Solution, the lines between rescue and resettlement—effectively between immigration and Zionism—quickly faded. In late July, Hirschmann called on Roncalli at his summer residence on Büyükada. "He has helped the Jews in Hungary and I beseech his further help," Hirschmann wrote in his diary. Thousands of immigration certificates had already been dispatched to Hungary, but further ships were now being prepared to bring Jewish refugees across the Black Sea.

On Pentecost Sunday, Roncalli stepped into the pulpit of the Cathedral of the Holy Spirit to give one of his most poignant and pointed

sermons of the war. "We are called to live in a painful epoch of destruction and hate," he said, "in which individuals are sacrificed to national
egoism with a brutality that is a disgrace to the human race." Even as
he spoke, Jews were on their way to Palestine, many of them carrying
papers that had been delivered by Roncalli's network.

Few of the escapees saw much of Istanbul en route, however. For
those arriving by train, the Turkish authorities carefully guarded the
groups during their transfer from Sirkeci station and across the Bosphorus to Haydarpaşa station. New arrivals had little time to take in
their surroundings. They were quickly moved along to the next stage
of what must have seemed a never-ending succession of trains, check-
points, and formalities. Similar strictures governed the transfer from
sea to land.

At every step, the small group of activists from the Jewish Agency,
the War Refugee Board, and the Joint were responsible for organization and provisioning. While Barlas and his associates took care of the
paperwork and Hirschmann handled the politics, the everyday details
fell to Simon Brod, a local philanthropist who had weathered the
Turkish wealth tax and was well regarded by both Allied and Jewish
agents throughout the city. His perpetual trail of cigarette smoke and
tuft of white hair were often the first thing that Jewish refugees saw in
Istanbul.

The entire effort could seem abstract—a matter of lists, timetables,
and telegrams—until a ship or train that Hirschmann and Barlas had
organized actually arrived in Istanbul. In early July 1944, the *Kazbek*
sailed into the Bosphorus from the Black Sea with 758 people on board.
The ship was rated for only three hundred passengers, and Hirschmann
recalled seeing people sprawled over the deck as the ship pulled into
port. The manifest included 256 children rescued from Transnistria,
the Romanian-occupied area of Soviet Ukraine.

The city authorities allowed Hirschmann and a few other activists
to observe the arrival and departure from a bobbing launch that drew

up alongside. The refugees were disembarked, carrying bundles and small packages of belongings, and escorted by Turkish police to second- and third-class carriages waiting at Haydarpaşa. As with all transports, the Joint had provided food and water—typically hundreds of loaves of bread, thousands of cucumbers and tomatoes, and plenty of packages of cigarettes, even when many of these items were strictly rationed in Istanbul. Passengers settled into their carriages quietly and stoically.

Suddenly, one of the refugees, a woman, ran down the quay, breaking windows and shouting, before being restrained. She had been this way the entire journey, someone told Hirschmann, ever since her mother and three children were shot before her eyes. Other Jews resident in Istanbul crowded into the station, seeking to make contact with someone who might know the whereabouts of relatives. In some instances, Jewish Agency officials were allowed to enter the carriages and bring back news about a specific family. "As expected, it was very bad," one of the inquirers later wrote in a thank-you note to the agency.

The train finally pulled out after sundown, and on the cool ferry ride back to the European side, Hirschmann watched as the early evening lights came up across the city. He could look across to Sarayburnu and the spires and domes of Topkapı Palace, its interior courtyards hidden behind stone walls and cypress groves. The palace's innermost areas—the sultan's old private quarters and the Harem—were accessed through an ornate portico that the Ottomans called the Gate of Felicity. In the Ottomans' diplomatic correspondence, Istanbul itself was frequently known by a variant of the same name, *Dersaadet*. Hirschmann realized that his work in Istanbul was only one segment of a much longer chain, a line of the stateless and homeless, passing through to somewhere else. The world, he said, seemed very tired.

Ships and trains were now arriving with greater ease and regularity than ever before. But the route was still treacherous. Later that summer, on August 3, 1944, a convoy of three ships—the *Morina*, the *Bülbül*, and the *Mefkûre*—left the Romanian port of Constanța, each crammed beyond capacity with refugees bound for Istanbul. By the second day at sea, the *Bülbül* and the *Mefkûre* had fallen out of sight of the faster *Morina*, with the *Mefkûre* then falling even farther behind because of engine trouble.

Around 12:30 a.m. on August 5, the *Mefkûre* came under strafing fire, probably from a Soviet submarine repeating the scenario that had doomed the *Struma* more than two years earlier. Large-caliber bullets ripped into the ship's wooden hull. Fire quickly spread on deck. The Turkish captain and four crew members escaped in the only available lifeboat.

A few dozen passengers jumped into the sea. The rest, asleep in the hold when the attack started, went down with the burning ship, which sank about a half hour after the gunfire began. Five passengers managed to survive by clinging to a piece of debris and, four hours later, drifted on the sea's currents to within sight of the *Bülbül*. The rest of the 320 refugees were shot or drowned.

The two remaining ships anchored off İgneada, a Turkish town near the Bulgarian border, and their passengers were taken to Istanbul by train. Exhausted but smiling with relief, they pushed expectantly against the barriers at Sirkeci station and were offered lotus glasses of tea from a silver tray. They soon made the transfer to Haydarpaşa station and the route to Palestine.

By the time the *Mefkûre* sank, Allied powers had landed in Normandy and, on the eastern front, the Soviet Union was continuing its largest offensive of the war. The Red Army had already liberated the first in a string of Nazi death camps. Romania had evacuated Transnistria and, hoping to stave off a full-scale Soviet invasion, announced later in the summer that it would switch sides and join the Allied cause. Bulgaria, after a leftist coup, would follow suit.

Rumors were rife that Turkey was planning to declare war on Germany. The Bosphorus and the Sea of Marmara were empty, with only a few boats bobbing in the current. Turkish authorities had ordered naval and civilian vessels removed offshore, for fear that the Germans would launch a preemptive attack. Air-raid drills were stepped up, and blackout curtains replaced drapes in businesses and apartments.

At the Park Hotel, the Germans ate in silence, and newspapermen hovered in the lobby to cover Germany's shifting fortunes. Rooms were going for half price as Germans crowded the checkout desk with their children and suitcases in tow, seeking to leave as soon as possible before Turkey's neutrality ran out. Franz von Papen, the German ambassador, arrived from Ankara and quickly departed for Berlin from Sirkeci station, waving his hat to a cheering crowd of local Germans, Japanese, and Turks. In mid-August, the Turkish Ministry of Foreign Affairs declared that the country was severing relations with Germany. Turkey formally joined the Allied cause in February 1945.

After the war, people continued to filter through Istanbul toward Palestine, but the flotillas, special trains, and desperate paper chase began to slow as the immediate danger to the surviving refugees lessened. The vessels that had carried them became part of the epic of forced exodus from wartime Europe. Family histories now contained not only the names of a long string of ancestors, running back to lost villages and emptied neighborhoods in Poland, Hungary, or Romania. They also wove together the exotic names of overcrowded ships that had ferried the survivors to safety: the *Milka* and the *Maritza*; the *Bellacita*, *Kazbek*, and *Morina*; the *Bülbül*, *Salahattin*, and *Toros*; along with the doomed *Mefkûre* and *Struma*. These ships carried 4,127 refugees, and many more arrived in Istanbul by train or in smaller groups aboard coasting vessels and small launches. In all, from 1942 to 1945, a total of 13,101 Jews went via Turkey to Palestine and other destinations. In the end, more than a quarter of all the Jews who made it to Palestine during the Second World War passed through Istanbul to get there.

"The results of the immigration in numbers are in no comparison with the tragic situation of Jewry in the enemy-occupied countries," Barlas reported, "but . . . I may say that it is a miracle that even this small number has escaped from . . . hell."

Chaim Barlas checked out of the Pera Palace and returned to Palestine, where he became head of the immigration department for the entire Jewish Agency, soon to form the new government of Israel. Ira Hirschmann left the Park Hotel, returned to New York, and took up a vice president's title at Bloomingdale's. He had only been in Turkey for about six months—coming and going to keep up his networks and report on his efforts—but the experience shaped the rest of his life in public service. When the United Nations was created, he became one of its key administrators dealing with the plight of refugees.

Angelo Roncalli left Istanbul as well. He was transferred to France in 1944 as papal nuncio. It was a post that called for a combination of tact and decisiveness, since one of his most difficult tasks was to deal with the fate of French priests who had collaborated with the German occupation during the war. Pius XII eventually elevated him to the rank of cardinal, but this was more a recognition of his piety and long experience in the field than a statement of his power within the ecclesiastical hierarchy. He had been abroad for a very long time, with little inside knowledge of the workings of Rome and the networks that would allow him to become a major voice among the princes of the church. It was therefore a stunning surprise when, upon the death of the pope in 1958, his fellow cardinals raised him even higher. He soon took the name John XXIII.

Of the people who departed from Istanbul as part of the rescue effort, at least 3,994 of them—close to a third of Barlas's total—had not experienced the Holocaust at all. They were Istanbullus, either Sephardic Jews whose families had lived in the city for generations or eastern European immigrants who had already put down roots there.

The wealth tax, the antisemitic propaganda, and a secure lifeline to Palestine now prompted many to leave, much as Armenians had done after the First World War and Greeks after the end of the Allied occupation.

One evening in the late summer of 1944, as Istanbullus watched this new wave of émigrés pass out of the city, most of the musicians of the Park Hotel's orchestra took the night off. The first violinist, Fritz Guth, stepped onto the stage to give a solo concert. He put aside his jazz charts and instead played Schubert and Mozart for the small number of paying guests in the dining room. It was his last performance in Istanbul. The son of a Viennese Jew, he had managed to get his name on one of Barlas's lists, and he soon left with his wife and baby for Palestine.

EPILOGUE

Two women share a bicycle on an Istanbul street.

E VER SINCE HE TOOK OVER ownership of the Pera Palace in
1927, Misbah Muhayyeş had come to know more about departures than arrivals. The tensions of the war years and the wealth tax
had driven away business. The 1941 bomb explosion had scared away
entire seasons of paying customers. By the time Allied operatives and
Jewish rescuers checked out at the end of the Second World War, the
Pera Palace's reputation had come to rest on the signatures in its old
registry books. The most famous guest in recent memory—Joseph
Goebbels—was quietly left out of the marketing materials.

Muhayyeş was in his late fifties at the close of the war. His adult life
had paralleled the rise of the Turkish Republic and the rapid expansion
of Istanbul's culturally Muslim but deeply Kemalist bourgeoisie. He
was extraordinarily wealthy by any standard. A long string of invest-
ments, running from Beirut to Istanbul, had paid dividends. He could
afford the annual write-off that the Pera Palace had become. Although
he had no children of his own, his summers were spent among nieces
and nephews at his Yeniköy *yalı*.

Through the 1940s and early 1950s, he visited the hotel regularly
to supervise its operation. The life had gone out of the party, however.
Worldly and adventurous Turks were looking for clean lines and modern furnishings, not velvet curtains and imperial excess. The hotel was
now surrounded by tumbledown tenements. The front door opened
onto dark, narrow streets. The back side, still with one of the best sun-

set views in the city, towered over gritty neighborhoods where Turkish migrants from the Black Sea coast and central Anatolia hung laundry from the windows of their apartments.

One day in October 1954, at the age of sixty-eight, Muhayyeş went up to a room on the second floor and ordered a bottle of whiskey. Early the next morning, the night porter heard a loud noise from inside the room and opened the door to find his boss bleeding on the bathroom floor. Theories swirled about a fatal mishap—a drunken fall on wet marble, maybe—or a possible murder, but the hint of an explanation came from a comment he had made to friends a few days earlier. "Now that my cat is dead," he reportedly said, "I can't go on living." When his will was later unsealed, no one expected the news. He had turned over the hotel to three charities for children, for the elderly, and for the fight against tuberculosis.

The hotel remained open, since the philanthropies wisely leased it out to a private company for management, but the country was changing quickly and, with it, the tastes and expectations of Istanbullus and travelers alike. In 1950, a few years before Muhayyeş's death, Turkish citizens had been given their first chance to choose a parliament in free and direct elections. They voted to sweep out the party that Atatürk had founded. Celebrations erupted in the streets, an outpouring of popular enthusiasm for change not seen since the revolution of 1908. President İsmet İnönü stepped aside, opting to head up the new parliamentary opposition rather than remain head of state. Members of the rival Democratic Party filled senior government posts.

The old Republican People's Party had claimed to have the wind of history at its back. Atatürk had dragged Turks out of their imperial stupor and had shaken them into modernity, the party maintained, and even after death, Kemalist ideals would best be realized through the party that Mustafa Kemal himself had founded. The new Democratic Party leadership, by contrast, saw popular will, not national destiny, as its mandate. The Democrats' landslide victory at the polls seemed to confirm it. These dual claims to authority would become one of the mainstays of Turkish politics, regardless of the specific parties in power and in opposition. One group wore the mantle of breakneck modernizer; the other promised to speak on behalf of the previously silent masses.

The Democrats' prime minister, Adnan Menderes, moved to dismantle the old one-party system, even though he accepted the basic tenets of Kemalism as a political ideology. Property belonging to the Republican People's Party was taken away and given to the national treasury. Landholdings that party leaders had acquired under Atatürk were placed under state control. Privatization enriched a new class of landowners and industrialists. In foreign policy, the new government moved away from the balancing act that had defined the Atatürk and İnönü eras. Turkey had been one of the founding members of the United Nations—a position facilitated by its decision to join the Allies in the closing months of the Second World War—and in 1952 the Menderes government secured Turkey's role in NATO, locking it in as a member of what was already called the free world. Turkish troops shipped out to Korea, the first major time they had stood alongside Western soldiers, rather than across from them, since the Crimean War. All these policies were repaid at the next election two years later, when the Democratic Party came away with even more seats in the Grand National Assembly.

These were substantial achievements, but the economy soon turned sluggish. Debt grew and inflation spiked. The Republican People's Party saw an opportunity and began to hammer at Menderes, the first real show of parliamentary defiance. The prime minister was outraged. The Democrats were as unaccustomed to the idea of a loyal opposition as their predecessors had been. Criticism looked like ingratitude and sniping, not constructive assistance. Menderes retreated into suspicion and pique, convinced that the people, regardless of the views of the nattering politicians in Ankara, were really on his side. When a foreign policy crisis loomed—another round of controversy with Greece, this time over the vexed issue of Cyprus—he appealed to the nation directly. His plan was to call for public rallies where the people would speak with one voice in support of the government. The result was a new pogrom.

In the early autumn of 1955, a rumor was circulating that Hellenic radicals had torched the Turkish Consulate in Thessaloniki. The consulate happened to be located in the childhood home of Atatürk, which the government had purchased during one of the periods of good relations between the two countries. The rumor raced through the back streets of Istanbul. Crowds soon converged along the old Grande Rue, which had long ago been renamed İstiklâl, or Independence, Avenue. On September 6–7, looters stormed into shops and homes owned by Greeks, Armenians, Jews, and other non-Muslims, seeking revenge for the supposed desecration of a spot sacred to Kemalism. At least eleven people were killed, and more than 5,600 shops, homes, restaurants, churches, and schools were damaged. İstiklâl and the side streets leading toward the Pera Palace were littered with debris and overturned vehicles. Crowds crunched through broken glass as they surveyed the destruction.

The "September events," as they are still called in Turkey, were the last straw for many of Istanbul's minorities. Each year marked a retreat. Armenian churches sealed themselves behind metal gates. Greek congregations disappeared, turning over the keys to a Turkish doorman to keep watch on a sacred spring and pay the electric bill. The government built guardhouses outside synagogues to discourage vandals and terrorists, but the smoked-glass boxes made the places of worship look more like foreign embassies than longtime neighbors. Menderes—after leveling portions of Istanbul in grand public-works projects—was ousted in a military coup in 1960 and, along with two of his ministers, hanged. Two more military coups, for different reasons and involving different sets of players, followed in 1971 and 1980. The threat of another brought down a government as late as 1997.

After the turmoil of the 1950s, shops reopened under new owners, and Muslim immigrants from Anatolian towns and villages moved in to take over abandoned apartments. But the heart seemed to have been dragged out of old neighborhoods. Grand plans for urban renewal were proposed by the city government and then only partially implemented. A new building might pop up in Pera, too big for its plot but not big enough to hide the peeling plaster and sagging rooflines around it. Tourists preferred the bed-and-breakfasts in Sultanahmet, with its carpet shops and Byzantine antiquities. In 1979, a California psychic, Tamara Rand, revealed her vision that Agatha Christie had left some deep secret hidden in Room 411 of the Pera Palace. The story made good copy and boosted business for a while, as people looked for what the secret might be, but it was in the end a confused fabrication. Nothing turned up but an old key, and the lore that Christie wrote *Murder on the Orient Express* while staying in the hotel has remained one of its most delicious myths.

Since the Pera Palace was one of the few historic hotels left in Istanbul, it began vacuuming up famous people, regardless of whether they had in fact ever signed the registry books. One who actually did was the poet Joseph Brodsky, but by the time he checked in, in the 1980s, most business travelers and wedding parties had decamped to the Hilton, the Swissôtel, and other chains. The neighborhood streets, observed Brodsky, were "crooked, filthy, dreadfully cobbled, and piled up with refuse." He reported having a nightmare in which three stray cats tore apart a giant rat at the base of the Pera Palace's marble staircase.

The American Consulate next door had hidden itself behind a rough cinder-block wall. The British Consulate up the street was a gated greensward with little connection to the rough streets around it. Few outsiders came to Pera and its outskirts—the small plateau of Tepebaşı, the steep inclines of Şişhane and Tarlabaşı, the dark canyons of Galata leading down from the former Grande Rue. You were best to stay on the ridges in that part of Istanbul, especially at night, and the Pera Palace was on the downhill slope.

Modern European history has two dominant modes, the national and the elegiac. Both are, in their way, fictions. National history asks that we take the impossibly large variety of human experience, stacked up like a deck of playing cards, and pull out only the national one—the rare moments in time when people raise a flag and misremember a collective past—as the most worthy of our attention. The elegiac asks that we end every story by fading to black, leaving off at a point when an old world is lost, with a set of ellipses pointing back toward what once had been.

Neither is an adequate way of thinking about the rest of the story: the blindingly familiar moments when the nation matters less than families and neighborhoods, or the arc of a single lifetime when, on the lee side of awfulness, someone wills into existence an instant of starting over. People live the present as a grand improvisation—misunderstanding their predicaments, laughing when they ought to mourn, staying when they should leave, and packing up their belongings when it would be better to stay at home. They rarely experience life as rushing toward something. More often, it seems like a ship jerkily pulling away from a pier. You see the docklands slide out of view, then the trees and buildings, until home is a gray thread between water and sky.

Ottoman bourgeois became ardent Turkish republicans. Muslim villagers remade themselves as apartment-dwelling Istanbullus. White Russians became Parisians. Greeks started new lives in Athens and Thessaloniki. Some of their grandchildren no doubt rolled their eyes at old stories about a shop on a long-forgotten foreign avenue. Armenians went to America or, in their tens of thousands, stayed put in their old homeland, living quietly as Turkish citizens and, sometimes, as self-declared ethnic Turks. Scrub trees grew in old Jewish graveyards, but the small remaining community built new ones, with head-stones that memorialized a recent death in Turkish rather than in the once-familiar Ladino.

Possibility is sometimes tragedy's unexpected gift. The Park Hotel was eventually torn down to make way for urban renewal. The Tokat-lian Hotel became an unrecognizable box destined for bad redevelop-ment. The Grand Cercle Moscovite, the Garden Bar, and the Turquoise are gone. The old community of Muslim émigrés from cosmopolitan Salonica—the builders of modern Turkey from Nâzım Hikmet to Atatürk—has been replaced by new waves of hopeful migrants from the cities of eastern Anatolia and the Black Sea coast. Where Halide Edip and Keriman Halis took off their head coverings in a demon-stration of modernity, some Istanbullu women today wear theirs as a declaration of Islamic feminism—a freedom of choice enabled by the secular reformers of the early republic. Russians still walk up and down the boulevards, but they are more likely to be curious tourists than needy refugees. Istanbul's Greek, Armenian, Jewish, and Levan-tine societies are all diminished from the days when questions were asked on the Grande Rue in one language and answered in another. In old Christian neighborhoods, gatekeepers still ring the church bells at eight in the morning and five in the afternoon, not to call so much as to remind.

But in the city's dawning moment as a global hub and polished metropolis, the last of the grand old establishments that defined Istan-bul's era of jazz and exile is still there. The Pera Palace is now a rein-vented version of its old self. The dazzling white ballroom has been refreshed, the cast-iron elevator has been rehung, and the faux marble has been repainted, all under the stewardship of a luxury firm from Dubai. It is a stunning reminder of the fact that all of us—the natives who become immigrants and the newcomers who become natives—are, in the end, only custodians.

On most days, Istanbul can be a city of harsh and dazzling light. Even at dusk the fading sun glints painfully off the water. Millions of lamps flick on in houses and apartments on both sides of the Bosphorus. Illuminated billboards flash their messages in the major squares. With medieval towers floodlit and prominent, and the minarets of imperial mosques strung with light bulbs during Ramadan, it is easy to retrace the entire history of the city's skyline, from Byzantine churches to the Ottoman royal residences to the skyscrapers of Turkish megafirms, even after dark. From Eminönü at the foot of the old city to Kadıköy on the Asian side, up the Bosphorus past the milky marble palaces at Çırağan and Dolmabahçe to the crenellated castle at Rumelihisarı, across the bridges and highways with their red brake lights and soul-killing traffic jams, to the green bulb of an oil tanker's starboard sidelight reflecting off the black water, Istanbul always shines.

Even in the gray and quiet winter, tired ferry commuters clamber for an outside seat near the railings, taking in the dappled light on a ship's hull or the black arrow of a cormorant skimming beak-high off the water. When the sky is bruise-blue and cold, crowds of gulls and pigeons still bounce along the shoreline. Sparkle-headed grackles and magpies strut deliberately beneath the dormant oleander. Snow-covered Judas trees share the coastal hills with evergreen cypresses. On blustery mornings, the Sea of Marmara is a dull sapphire, with leaden domes and gilded spires muted on the shore, everything radiating a cool blue light once the early mist burns away.

Over the last two decades, Istanbul has again become one of the world's great cities, both in terms of its sheer size and because of the vibrancy and ambition of its businesses and creative classes. No place can ever again become the capital of the world, but at least today—unlike in the years of the Pera Palace's decline—you can see how someone might once have thought of Istanbul in that role. Yet in the race toward a bright future full of hypermarts and earnest entrepreneurs, it is easy to skip over the city's earliest experiments with modernity and renewal—an era when the old cosmopolitanism of empire began to drift away just as new immigrants were finding in the city a permanent home or temporary haven. The hidden origins of modern Istanbul are there in one grand hotel standing on a single plot of land: the Muslim foundation that first owned it, the Armenians who marked it out for development, the Belgian multinational firm that made it famous, the Greek businessman who bought and lost it, and the Arab-born Turkish Muslim who guided it, somewhat the worse for wear, through the Second World War.

It does not take too much effort to imagine people like these on an ordinary Istanbul day, at an hour when new arrivals are checking in, for example, in the spring of 1941, a Tuesday—the moment just before the flash comes through the wood-frame doors and the gilded windows, before the boom calls people out onto the Grande Rue and the Pera Palace's glass canopy falls, before the floor opens up and the six deaths, before the shock wave throws shards and fire across the former Graveyard Street. From the correspondence and casualty lists of those caught up in the Pera Palace bombing, we know their names.

Here are the hotel's two Jewish doormen, Muiz and Avram, standing not far from two Greek drivers, both named Constantine. Three English women are at the reception desk—Miss Ellis and Miss Armstrong, who have just arrived on the train from the Balkans, and Mrs. McDermott, visibly pregnant, whose baby will not survive the night. Mahmut and Reşat, the two Emniyet officers, are near the stack of luggage, and a Muslim chauffeur, Şükrü, is sorting valises from trunks. Mr. Karantinos, the hotel's general manager, is watching Costas, the head clerk from Greece, who is supervising Mehmet, the Turkish passport officer, who is rushing to take down everyone's details. Süleyman, a Muslim night watchman, has to pitch in, too.

Down the hill, Madame de Téhige, whose brother was once the chief procurator of the Holy Synod of Russia and is now, she will write to the British consul in a few weeks, a "begar," worries that her land-lady will soon "poot me in the street." Talât, a Muslim villager, broke and unmarried and just arrived that day from Giresun, his hometown on the Black Sea, has come up from the docklands, perhaps looking for work. In an apartment nearby, a Muslim musician, the son of Balkan immigrants, is practicing his contrabass. And around the corner, on the street named for the little vine-covered mosque, someone the neighbors call Shalom, Mordecai's son, has come out for an evening walk.

ACKNOWLEDGMENTS

"They are all writing their Turkey books," says Aunt Dot in Rose Macaulay's novel *The Towers of Trebizond*. This one is mine.

Depending on how you count, it has taken three years or twenty-seven. I have been enchanted by Istanbul since I first arrived there—with a backpack and my college roommate, now Kevin Crumpton, MD—in the summer of 1987. It is one place, perhaps the only place, that has seemed entirely fresh and surprising to me on every visit. Across more than a quarter century, I have had many people to thank for acquainting me with it.

Through the kindness of Hakan Altınay, Tony Greenwood, and Kağan Önal, I have had the pleasure of staying in three of Istanbul's most intriguing neighborhoods: Rumelihisarı, Kuzguncuk, and Arnavutköy. Tony, as director of the indispensable American Research Institute in Turkey, always provided an excuse to return to Arnavutköy for insightful conversation and good fish. Michael Thumann and Susanne Landwehr were fonts of wisdom about contemporary politics and society. I have learned a great deal from two former students of mine, Dr. Lerna Yanık and Dr. Nora Fisher Onar, who have made Turkey their passion. A string of Turkish language instructors, most recently Zeynep Gür, have tried to twist my brain around subordinate clauses. Present and former colleagues Gábor Ágoston, Mustafa Aksakal, Sylvia Önder, Scott Redford, Sabri Sayarı, and the late Faruk Tabak were unfailingly kind to a novice in their field.

This book relies in part on the work of specialists from a variety of different domains that are not normally put together, such as Turkey, Trotsky, and tango. I am grateful to the many historians and others whose writings are acknowledged in the notes and bibliography, in particular Rıfat Bali, who has made available to the public so many primary sources from a forgotten era. I have also benefited from conversations with Gökhan Akçura, Ozan Arslan, Savaş Arslan, Murat Belge, Elif Batuman, Andrew Finkel, Caroline Finkel, Corry Guttstadt, Hope Harrison, Brian Johnson, Tuna Aksoy Köprülü, Steve Lagerfeld, Ansel Mullins, Cullen Nutt, Yigal Schleifer, Douglas Smith, Gerald Steinacher, Ronald Grigor Suny, Leon Taranto, Frances Trix, Thomas de Waal, Sufian Zhemukhov, and my dear companion, Margaret Paxson, who has always steered me true—*bay mir bist du sheyn*. Lawrence and Amy Tal, Anatol and Sasha Lieven, and Leslie Vinjamuri and Oliver Wright were welcoming hosts during research trips to London. (Thanks also to Matthew, Luke, Phoebe, Misha, Katya, Alex, Henry, Olivia, and Scrubby, whose space I occasionally borrowed.)

I am especially grateful to Abdullah Gül and Ayhan Uçar of the Yapı Kredi archive in Istanbul, who facilitated access to the Selahattin Giz photograph collection. Fra Lorenzo Piretto, OP, educated me about the Latin community and showed me the wonders of the Church of St. Peter and St. Paul. Fıstık Ahmet Tanrıverdi shared childhood memories of Trotsky's bodyguards and helped me find both of Trotsky's houses on Büyükada. In his Manhattan violin shop, Harold Hagopian re-created the Istanbul music scene of the 1920s and 1930s. I sadly missed speaking with Keriman Halis Ece, who died only a few months before I began this book, but her daughter and granddaughter, Ece Sarpyener and Ayşe Torfilli, graciously shared recollections of her. Meral Muhayyeş took Margaret and me on a magical Bosphorus boat ride and told family stories of her great-uncle Misbah. Pınar Kartal Timer, general manager of the Pera Palace Jumeirah, and Suzan Toma of the marketing department, enlightened me about the hotel's restoration and its recent history.

Fırat Kaya offered his extensive knowledge of Istanbul's architecture and urban landscape; our walks through the city—sometimes with a 1934 guidebook in hand—were the closest I will ever come to experiencing a time machine. Ekin Özbakkaloğlu carefully read through more than two decades of Turkish newspapers and uncovered some gems. Fatima Abushanab tracked down references and taught me about women and Islam. Ronen Plechnin helped with a valuable source in Hebrew, as did M. Fatih Çalışır with one in Ottoman Turkish. This is the fifth book of mine for which Chris Robinson has drawn the excellent maps.

Archivists and librarians at the institutions listed in the bibliography guided me through their collections. Special thanks to Shalimar White and Rona Razon of the Dumbarton Oaks Image Collections and Fieldwork Archives, who helped me understand the life and career of Thomas Whittemore. I am lucky enough to live within walking distance of two of the world's treasures: the Library of Congress and the US Holocaust Memorial Museum. At the latter, Ronald Coleman, Rebecca Erbelding, Krista Hegburg, and Vincent Slatt provided superb guidance.

All or part of the manuscript came under the careful eyes of Mustafa Aksakal, Julia Phillips Cohen, Rebecca Erbelding, Ryan Gingeras, Corry Guttstadt, Andrea Orzoff, Mogens Pelt, Michael Reynolds, and Shalimar White. I am very thankful indeed for their criticisms and corrections, although I alone am responsible for any shortcomings that remain.

In 1998, a Fulbright senior fellowship in Turkey and Romania sparked some of the ideas that eventually led to this book. A fellowship from the Wilson Center enabled me to spend the academic year 2012–2013 focusing on Turkey's past and present. The center's library staff—Janet Spikes, Michelle Kamalich, and Dagne Gizaw—were models of energy and friendly responsiveness. Research funds provided by

Georgetown University's Edmund A. Walsh School of Foreign Service and the Department of Government allowed repeated visits to Istanbul. Thanks to Dean Carol Lancaster, Senior Associate Dean James Reardon-Anderson, faculty chairs David Edelstein and Jeffrey Anderson, and department chairs George Shambaugh and Michael Bailey for their leadership.

This is the second book I have completed with William Lippincott of Lippincott Massie McQuilkin. I would be adrift without his enthusiasm and counsel. I have twice been privileged to work with Alane Salierno Mason at W. W. Norton, a dream of an editor who has taught me so much about writing with a reader in mind. Anna Mageras, Eleen Cheung, Nancy Palmquist, and Kathleen Brandes were essential partners in the journey from typescript to book.

Cătălin Partenie is acknowledged on the dedication page. More than twenty years ago, a chance encounter with him via an Oxford bulletin board started me on a career in the other half of Europe.

CHRONOLOGY

7th century BC	According to tradition, area of modern Istanbul settled by Greeks from the Aegean coast, who name the colony "Byzantium" after their leader, Byzas
330 AD	Roman emperor Constantine moves capital to Byzantium, soon renamed "New Rome"
537	Church of the Holy Wisdom (Hagia Sophia) consecrated during reign of Justinian I
1204	Constantinople sacked by Venetians and their allies in the Fourth Crusade, who wrest power from the Byzantines
1261	Restoration of Byzantine control
1453	Ottoman conquest of city under Mehmed II (the Conqueror)
1520–1566	Reign of Süleyman the Magnificent: height of Ottoman power
1839–1876	Tanzimat period: Ottomans begin range of modernizing reforms
1853–1856	Crimean War
1870	Great Pera fire
1876–1909	Reign of Sultan Abdülhamid II
1883	Inaugural journey of the Orient Express

1892	Pera Palace Hotel established
1908	Young Turk revolution
1909	Exile of Abdülhamid II
1909–1918	Reign of Sultan Mehmed V
Oct. 1914	Ottomans enter First World War on side of Central Powers
Dec. 1914–Jan. 1915	Battle of Sarikamish: Russian imperial forces inflict major defeat on Ottoman army in eastern Anatolia
Apr. 1915–Jan. 1916	Gallipoli campaign: Ottomans repel British, Australian, and New Zealand forces from peninsula southwest of Istanbul
Apr. 24–25, 1915	Armenian community leaders deported from Istanbul, with many later killed
1918–1922	Reign of Sultan Mehmed VI
Oct. 1918	Mudros armistice ends hostilities between Ottomans and Allied powers
Nov. 1918	Armistice ends hostilities between Germany and Allied powers; Allied naval detachment sails into Bosphorus and takes up positions in Istanbul
May 1919	Hellenic troops occupy Smyrna (Izmir); Mustafa Kemal arrives in Black Sea port of Samsun; beginning of nationalist resistance to the Allies and the Turkish war of independence
Mar. 1920	Allies announce formal military occupation of Istanbul
Aug. 1920	Treaty of Sèvres
Nov. 1920	Flotilla of White Russian army and civilians arrives in Istanbul
Jan.–Sept. 1921	Battles of İnönü and Sakarya: turning points in favor of Turkish nationalists against Hellenic troops

Sept. 1922	Retreat of Hellenic army and flight of civilians from Smyrna
Nov. 1922	Sultanate abolished; flight of Mehmed VI
1922–1924	Caliphate (but not sultanate) of Abdülmecid
Oct. 1922	Mudanya agreement paves way for transition to Turkish nationalist control
July 1923	Treaty of Lausanne
Oct. 1923	Last Allied troops leave Istanbul; Ankara named capital of Turkey; declaration of Turkey as a republic (Oct. 29), with Mustafa Kemal as president
1924	Caliphate abolished
1925	Fez banned; calendar reform; "Sheikh Said rebellion" among Kurds in eastern Anatolia; law on the maintenance of public order allows shutting down of newspapers and banning of opposition groups.
1926	Adoption of new civil code and abolition of religious law; ban on public consumption of alcohol lifted
Oct. 1927	Mustafa Kemal's lengthy "Nutuk" (Speech) sets out narrative of the war of independence and the victory of Turkish nationalists
1928	Disestablishment of Islam as state religion; adoption of Latin alphabet for Turkish; unveiling of Republic Monument in Taksim Square
1929	Leon Trotsky arrives in Istanbul
1930	Women allowed to vote in municipal elections
1931	Thomas Whittemore begins restoration of Hagia Sophia
1932	Keriman Halis wins Miss Universe competition

1933	Leon Trotsky departs Istanbul
1934	Law requires Turkish citizens to adopt family names; women gain full suffrage; Mustafa Kemal becomes "Atatürk"; pogrom against Jews in eastern Thrace
1937–1938	Military campaign against Kurds in eastern Anatolia
Nov. 10, 1938	Death of Atatürk; İsmet İnönü elevated to presidency
Sept. 1, 1939	Beginning of Second World War
Mar. 11, 1941	Suitcase bomb explodes at Pera Palace
June 22, 1941	German invasion of Soviet Union
Feb. 1942	Sinking of the *Struma*
Nov. 1942	Wealth tax aimed at Istanbul's ethnic minorities
June 6, 1944	Allied landings in Normandy
Aug. 1944	Turkey breaks off diplomatic relations with Germany
Feb. 1945	Turkey declares war on Germany, becoming an Allied power
May 8, 1945	End of Second World War in Europe
1950	First free and direct parliamentary elections in Turkey
Sept. 6–7, 1955	"September events": mobs attack Greek and other minority homes and businesses in Istanbul

NOTES

Abbreviations used in notes

CERYE   Committee for the Education of Russian Youth in Exile Records, Bakhmeteff Archive, Rare Book and Manuscript Library, Columbia University

DBIA   *Dünden Bugüne İstanbul Ansiklopedisi*

DO-ICFA   Dumbarton Oaks Image Collections and Fieldwork Archives

FDR   Franklin Delano Roosevelt Presidential Library

GUL   Georgetown University Library, Special Collections Research Center

HIA   Hoover Institution Archives

IWM   Imperial War Museum Archives

JAP-IDI   Jewish Agency for Palestine Records, Immigration Department Office in Istanbul, USHMM

JOINT   Selected Records from the American Jewish Joint Distribution Committee, 1937–1966, USHMM

LC   Library of Congress

LTEP   Leon Trotsky Exile Papers, Houghton Library, Harvard University

NARA   National Archives and Records Administration

NAUK   National Archives of the United Kingdom

USHMM   United States Holocaust Memorial Museum Archives

WRB   Papers of the War Refugee Board, USHMM

Note: Archival citations use p./pp. to refer to running page numbers of a printed text or manuscript and f./ff. to refer to sheet numbers, if given, within a particular file. Citations to WRB sources refer to the digitized collection compiled by Rebecca Erbelding of the USHMM.

PAGE   PROLOGUE

4   *"From all I had seen"*: "Constantinople, Dirty White, Not Glistening and Sinister," *Toronto Daily Star*, Oct. 18, 1922; idem, "Waiting for an Orgy," *Toronto Daily Star*, Oct. 19, 1922; and idem, "A Silent, Ghastly Procession," *Toronto Daily Star*, Oct. 20, 1922, all reprinted in Hemingway, *Dateline: Toronto*, 227–32.

6   "[W]e civilised people": Toynbee, *Western Questions*, 1.

                          GRAND HOTEL

13   *"As for the site"*: Busbecq, *Turkish Letters*, 34.

14   *One way to preserve*: Price, *Extra-Special Correspondent*, 38. *"I am willing to run"*: Quoted in Dalal, "At the Crossroads of Modernity," 135. See also Gül, *Emergence of Modern Istanbul*, 54. *Trains slowed to a crawl*: Christie, *Come, Tell Me How You Live*, 12. *"Is it? No, yes, it must be"*: Dos Passos, *Orient Express*, in *Travel Books and Other Writings*, 133.

15   *Only a blind man*: Herodotus, *The Histories*, 4.144.

16   *But according to the contemporary chronicler*: Procopius, *Secret History*, in *Procopius*, 25.2–6. *When Sultan Mehmed II took the city*: George Makris, "Ships," in Laiou, ed., *Economic History of Byzantium*, 99. *The number of oars*: White, *Three Years in Constantinople*, 1:38–41.

17   *"[T]he limpid freshness"*: White, *Three Years in Constantinople*, 1:51. *By his day*: White, *Three Years in Constantinople*, 1:51–52. *But foreign sailors could still watch*: Private Papers of G. Calverley Papers, p. 36, IWM.

18   *"Do not suppose"*: Pirî Reis, *Kitab-ı bahriye*, 1:59. *Massive earthquakes*: DBIA, 3:33–35.

19   *It was all so familiar*: DBIA, 7:425–26. *"As soon as it gets dark"*: Bibesco, *Eight Paradises*, 229. *Huge fires occurred*: DBIA, 7:426–38. *"I have walked over"*: Pears, *Forty Years in Constantinople*, 314.

20   *On his first visit*: Herbert, *Ben Kendim*, 26–27. *Even the Divanyolu*: Çelik, *Remaking of Istanbul*, 4.

21   *Photographs from the time*: DBIA, 7:426–38. *The airy, open vistas*: Gül, *Emergence of Modern Istanbul*, 49–51.

23   *It could also be*: Barsley, *Orient Express*, 20. *Nagelmackers had visited*: Behrend, *History of the Wagons-Lits*, 3.

24   *At the frontier*: Behrend, *History of the Wagons-Lits*, 7. *The entire journey*: Cookridge, *Orient Express*, 86. *By 1850, the Ottoman Empire*: İnalcık with Quataert, eds., *Economic and Social History of the Ottoman Empire*, 2:804.

25   *It was, said an observer*: A. Van Milligen, *Constantinople* (1906), 205, quoted in Çelik, *Remaking of Istanbul*, 102. *"I am going by it!"*: Christie, *Come, Tell Me How You Live*, 12.

26   *The property had once belonged*: Çelik, *Tepebaşı*, 172–74. *Its sister establishments*: Behrend, *History of the Wagons-Lits*, 12. *Like the Four Seasons*: Sperco, *Istanbul indiscret*, 80. *As the Guide Bleu later noted*: De Paris à Constantinople, 178. *Insurance maps from the period*: See *Jacques Pervititch Sigorta Haritalarında İstanbul* and Dağdalen, ed., *Charles Edouard Goad'ın İstanbul Sigorta Haritaları*.

27   *When Le Corbusier visited*: Quoted in Mansel, *Constantinople*, 354.

THE GRAY FLEET

32   *More than half a million Muslim migrants*: Zürcher, *Young Turk Legacy*, 287. *The number of informants*: Price, *Extra-Special Correspondent*, 40.

33   *"The motley rabble"*: Edib, *Memoirs*, 259. *Young boys threw rocks*: Pears, *Forty Years in Constantinople*, 249.

36   *"Ayesha, angel of beauty"*: Letter from a Turkish Officer, IWM.

38   *By March, Unionist leaders*: Akçam, *From Empire to Republic*, 166. *The Unionist sons of Muslim refugees*: See Zürcher, *Young Turk Legacy*, 285–95. *On the night of April 24–25*: Akçam, *Young Turks' Crimes*, 183–93. *He was among the fortunate*: Balakian, *Armenian Golgotha*, 77. *Tripod scaffolds*: See C. J. Brunell Photograph Collection, IWM.

39   *However, over the course of the war*: Reynolds, *Shattering Empires*, 155. For a detailed discussion of evidence regarding the Istanbul deportations, see Akçam, *Young Turks' Crimes*, 399–406; and Kévorkian,

Armenian Genocide, 251–54, 533–43. This description comes from Charles and Louisa Vinicombe to Hélène Philippe, Oct. 25, 1920, C. Vinicombe Papers, IWM.

40   *"The grand sight"*: Charles and Louisa Vinicombe to Hélène Philippe, Oct. 25, 1920, pp. 20–21, C. Vinicombe Papers, IWM.

41   *"It was a sight"*: Entry for Nov. 12, 1918, F. W. Turpin Papers, IWM. Turpin carried over his description into the next day, Nov. 13. *Local Greek Orthodox*: Musbah Haidar, *Arabesque*, 165. *Families had flattened*: Mufty-zada, *Speaking of the Turks*, 150, 153, 229. *"Effendi, what bad times"*: Balakian, *Armenian Golgotha*, 414.

42   *Senegalese infantrymen*: Sperco, *L'Orient qui s'éteint*, 46. *Later, the French commander*: Bridges, *Alarms and Excursions*, 257. *"It was . . . like having"*: Bridges, *Alarms and Excursions*, 258.

43   *Istanbul had long been*: *Constantinople*, 9. *The Spanish flu*: Musbah Haidar, *Arabesque*, 169, 187.

44   *"Greedy or inviting"*: Mufty-zada, *Speaking of the Turks*, 153. *"Prostitution, dishonesty, misery"*: Mufty-zada, *Speaking of the Turks*, 153. *Ottoman police officers*: Mufty-zada, *Speaking of the Turks*, 151.

45   *By Ziya's estimate*: Mufty-zada, *Speaking of the Turks*, 150. *"[W]hat will happen"*: Mufty-zada, *Speaking of the Turks*, 136–37.

OCCUPATION

49   *"Pera has three things"*: İnalcık with Quataert, eds., *Economic and Social History of the Ottoman Empire*, 2:651.

50   *"To catalogue completely"*: Carus Wilson to father, July 19, 1920, Carus Wilson Papers, IWM.

51   *Each Friday the* selâmlık: Harington, *Tim Harington Looks Back*, 106. *Among the city's non-Muslim residents*: Hissar Players program for "Nathan the Wise," Jan. 28, 1920, GUL, Engert Papers, Box 2, Folder 13. *The Annual Yuletide recital*: Yuletide Recital Program, Dec. 21, 1919, GUL, Engert Papers, Box 2, Folder 13. *Its sister institution*: Program from commencement exercises at Constantinople College, June 1920, GUL, Engert Papers, Box 2, Folder 13.

52   *On the same day the Allies*: Mango, *Atatürk*, 195–96.

54   *Members of foreign delegations*: Musbah Haidar, *Arabesque*, 166. "*The rich, having made money*": Balakian, *Armenian Golgotha*, 415–16. *General Milne was staying*: Price, *Extra-Special Correspondent*, 103. *A host should not be*: Mansel, *Constantinople*, 388.

55   *When they met*: Price, *Extra-Special Correspondent*, 104. "*What I want to know*": Price, *Extra-Special Correspondent*, 104. "*There will be a lot*": Price, *Extra-Special Correspondent*, 104. *The British kept crucial information*: Criss, *Istanbul Under Allied Occupation*, 71. It was not until November 1920 that Allied authorities could agree on who among them was in overall charge, with the command shared on a rotating basis, beginning with the British.

57   *By early 1919*: Mango, *Atatürk*, 204. *Just before the First World War*: Toprak, "La population," 64–65.

60   *Jews had lived in Istanbul*: Rozen, *History of the Jewish Community of Istanbul*, 10–11. *Over the next century*: Rozen, *History of the Jewish Community in Istanbul*, 51, 87.

61   *Down a winding street*: See Shaul, *From Balat to Bat Yam*, 37–50. *In the modern era*: Eldem, "Istanbul: From Imperial to Peripheralized Capital," in Eldem, Goffman, and Masters, *The Ottoman City between East and West*, 151–52. In 1934, the municipal administration's official guidebook to the city listed 192 distinct *mahalles* west of the Bosphorus, plus many others sited to the east. *İstanbul Şehri Rehberi*, 206–8. "*Ni a fuego*": Shaul, *From Balat to Bat Yam*, 46.

62   *As late as 1922*: Johnson, ed., *Constantinople To-Day*, 263. *That social position*: Shaul, *From Balat to Bat Yam*, 59. *A popular joke*: Shaul, *From Balat to Bat Yam*, 59.

63   *Jews were likewise divided*: For example, the greatest of the city's expatriate Jewish banking families—the Camondos—oversaw a financial empire that stretched across the breadth of Europe, with its epicenter in the narrow passageways of Galata. Istanbullus walked past the stately Camondo mansion, mounted the steep streets by walking up the art nouveau Camondo steps, or went to schools and hospitals financed by Camondo philanthropy. Over the course of the nineteenth century, the family left the cosmopolitan world that had allowed them to flourish under the Ottomans and decamped to Paris. It was in France that their

Jewishness came to matter most, and in the most tragic of ways. During the Second World War, the last of the family line—the aging matriarch Béatrice de Camondo and her two children, Fanny and Bertrand—were packed onto trains by the Nazis and deported from France. They perished at Auschwitz-Birkenau. Had the family stayed in Istanbul, the Camondo line almost certainly would have survived the war.

64 *He spent his youth*: Sperco, *Turcs d'hier et d'aujourd'hui*, 146. *Allied officials had a clear preference*: Toynbee, *Western Question*, 32.

65 *"The Hellenic and Christian character"*: Telegram, Jan. 16/29, 1920, NARA, RG59, M353, Reel 21. *"The best Turkish homes"*: Furlong to Woodrow Wilson, Mar. 23, 1920, p. 1, NARA, RG59, M353, Reel 21.

66 *British soldiers would scream*: Edib, *Turkish Ordeal*, 5.

RESISTANCE

69 *He had taken over the Pera Palace*: Çelik, *Tepebaşı*, 174. *According to the memoirist*: Mufty-zada, *Speaking of the Turks*, 152.

70 *He was married*: Pelt, *Tobacco, Arms, and Politics*, 178. I thank Mogens Pelt for additional biographical details. *The Hellenic presence*: Mango, *Atatürk*, 198.

71 *But as a brother-in-law*: Finefrock, "Ataturk, Lloyd George and the Megali Idea," D1049.

72 *When news of Smyrna's capture*: Alexandris, *Greek Minority of Istanbul*, 59. *In February 1920*: Mango, *Atatürk*, 266; Criss, *Istanbul Under Allied Occupation*, 9.

74 *Crucially, it was the first*: Mango, *Atatürk*, 269. *They were prepared*: Letter of Mar. 24, 1920, Wethered Papers, IWM. See also Garner Papers, IWM. *Local police and military*: Edmonds, *Occupation of Constantinople*, 12. *Rumors of it had circulated*: Dunn, *World Alive*, 285–86.

75 *The Ankara assembly prescribed*: Mango, *Atatürk*, 279.

76 *"The United States entered"*: Bristol to Secretary of State, May 7, 1920, pp. 1–2, NARA, RG59, M353, Reel 21.

77 *"It is perhaps no exaggeration"*: Winston S. Churchill, *The Aftermath*, quoted in Fromkin, *A Peace to End All Peace*, 432.

78 *Newspapers in Athens*: Finefrock, "Ataturk, Lloyd George and the

Megali Idea," D1049, D1053. Greek nationalists had earlier urged Constantine, upon his coronation, to take the name Constantine XII, thus linking his own dynasty with that of the Byzantines, even though the two had no familial links at all.

79   *"The retreat that started"*: Quoted in Hasan Kayalı, "The Struggle for Independence," in Kasaba, ed., *Cambridge History of Turkey*, 138. *The two forces were roughly equal*: Mango, *Atatürk*, 338.

80   *"The atrocities perpetrated by the Greeks"*: Second Section of the General Staff, *Greek Atrocities in Asia Minor, First Part*, 1. *Mobs ruled the streets*: Mango, *Atatürk*, 345. *A fire broke out*: Price, *Extra-Special Correspondent*, 128. *Some 213,000 people*: Mango, *Atatürk*, 346. *Three quarters of the city*: Mango, *Atatürk*, 345. *"Foreigners are nervous"*: Hemingway, "British Can Save Constantinople," *Toronto Daily Star*, Sept. 30, 1922, reproduced in Hemingway, *Dateline: Toronto*, 211. *Processions of Turkish Muslims*: Fox-Pitt to mother, Oct. 7, 1922, Fox-Pitt Papers, IWM, Box 2, File 10. "

81   *A fear of the future"*: Carus Wilson to father, Oct. 17, 1922, Carus Wilson Papers, IWM. *A special commission*: Criss, *Istanbul Under Allied Occupation*, 76. *Possible death sentences*: "To the Civilian Population of Constantinople," Greco-Turkish War Intelligence Reports, 1922–1923, IWM. *Before the Smyrna offensive*: "Comparative Table of Dispositions of Ottoman Forces During the Main Phases of the Nationalist Movement," Greco-Turkish War Intelligence Reports, 1922–1923, IWM.

82   *"I know somebody"*: Fox-Pitt to mother, Oct. 7, 1922, Fox-Pitt Papers, IWM, Box 2, File 10. *"No humbler setting"*: Price, *Extra-Special Correspondent*, 132–33.

83   *"Life went on gaily"*: Harington, *Tim Harington Looks Back*, 106.

84   *"There was something for everyone"*: Harington, *Tim Harington Looks Back*, 106. *The hounds ran at Maslak*: Bridges, *Alarms and Excursions*, 274. *A small bear*: Bridges, *Alarms and Excursions*, 274. *"[T]he main preoccupation"*: Price, *Extra-Special Correspondent*, 136. *On November 4*: Memo from British Delegation, Istanbul, Nov. 22, 1922, NAUK, FO 839/2.

85   *"Measures now being taken"*: Henderson to Foreign Office, Nov. 24, 1922, p. 1, NAUK, FO 839/2. *"It certainly came as a surprise"*: Harington to

Secretary of State for War, Oct. 1923, p. 4, NAUK, CAB 44/38. *"Considering my life in danger"*: Quoted in Harington, *Tim Harington Looks Back*, 125, 129. My account of the sultan's departure from the palace is based on Harington, *Tim Harington Looks Back*, 130–31; and Fox-Pitt to mother, Nov. 10, 1922, Fox-Pitt Papers, IWM, Box 2, File 10.

87 *They were eventually reunited*: Harington, *Tim Harington Looks Back*, 131.

MOSCOW ON THE BOSPHORUS

91 *Despite the Unionists' deportation*: Ekmekçioğlu, "Improvising Turkishness," 10. *They now shared space*: Yıldırım, *Diplomacy and Displacement*, 90.

92 *The US Navy set up*: "Russian Refugees in Constantinople," p. 2, Bristol Papers, LC, Box 74, File "Russian Refugees." *Members of Britain's Hampshire Regiment*: Harington, *Tim Harington Looks Back*, 101. *Within weeks of his arrival*: Harington to High Commissariat for Refugees, League of Nations, July 14, 1923, p. 1, NAUK, FO 286/800. *Colored chits were issued*: Harington, *Tim Harington Looks Back*, 100. *By the end of 1920*: Harington, *Tim Harington Looks Back*, 101.

93 *It was all "a salad"*: Bridges, *Alarms and Excursions*, 279. *They formed the so-called Volunteer Army*: Robinson, *White Russian Army in Exile*, 3.

94 *From the railings, people watched*: Strafford to mother, Mar. 31, 1920, Strafford Papers, IWM, Box 2, Folder "Transcriptions of Original Letters." Exceptions were made on board the transports for two horses—Minoru and Aboyeur—that were famous as winners of the Derby in 1909 and 1913. They had been sold to Russian owners and were only discovered by British soldiers during the evacuation. They ended up safely in Serbia. Bridges, *Alarms and Excursions*, 292. *"The things in Russia"*: Tenner to Strafford, Nov. 14, 1920, Strafford Papers, IWM, Box 2, Folder "Transcriptions of Original Letters." *Twenty-year-old Vladimir Nabokov*: Nabokov, *Speak Memory*, 176–77.

95 *His nickname referenced*: Robinson, *White Russian Army in Exile*, 13. *On Wrangel's estimate*: Wrangel, *Memoirs*, 307. *It was soon joined*: Kenez, *Civil War in South Russia*, 307. *As seagulls wheeled*: Wrangel, *Memoirs*, 320–26.

96 *"The plight of those poor people"*: Harington, *Tim Harington Looks Back*,

101. *Some of the larger ships*: "Refugees from the Crimea," Dec. 18, 1920, p. 1, NAUK, WO 32/5726. *[The vessels were] "like cattle ships"*: Bristol to Secretary of State, Nov. 19, 1920, Bristol Papers, LC, Box 73, File "Russia—Denikin and Wrangel Campaigns, January–December, 1920." *When a small group of caiques*: Harington, *Tim Harington Looks Back*, 101. *Harrington boarded*: "Refugees from the Crimea," p. 1. *Counting Wrangel's flotilla*: "Russian Refugees in Constantinople," p. 1. Peter Kenez gives the figure of 145,693 people evacuated in the Wrangel exodus. Kenez, *Civil War in South Russia*, 307. *The harsh winter*: Bristol to Secretary of State, Nov. 15, 1920, Bristol Papers, LC, Box 73, File "Russia—Denikin and Wrangel Campaigns, January–December, 1920." *Representatives from the Pera Palace*: *Konstantinopol'-Gallipoli*, 34. *The hotel owners seemed more than willing*: Stone and Glenny, *Other Russia*, 152. *Istanbul was probably outfitted*: Hobson to Rumbold, Mar. 26, 1923, p. 1, NAUK, FO 286/880.

97   *Dead bodies*: Hobson to Rumbold, Mar. 26, 1923, p. 2. *Baroness Wrangel*: "Refugees from the Crimea," p. 2. *fox terrier, Jack*: Bumgardner, *Undaunted Exiles*, 79. *Camps were also set up*: Harington to High Commissariat, July 14, 1923, p. 1, NAUK, FO 286/800. *"I think that one could say"*: Chebyshev, *Blizkaia dal'* in *Konstantinopol'-Gallipoli*, 127.

98   *"Some seem to be better off"*: Carus Wilson to father, July 19, 1922, Carus Wilson Papers, IWM.

99   *"Thus, on one beautiful springtime day"*: "Constantinople," p. 2, HIA, Shalikaskhvili Papers, HIA. *Massive sheets of paper*: "Constantinople," p. 4.

100 *Music was provided*: "Constantinople," pp. 7–13. *Koki Dadiani and Niko Nizharadze*: "Constantinople," p. 17. *Located in a Pera side street*: "Constantinople," p. 20. *The Gypsy guitarist Sasha Makaraov*: "Constantinople," p. 22–24.

101 *Food was still cheap*: "Constantinople," p. 29. *Other young men*: "Constantinople," p. 35.

102 *They continually fed*: Bristol to Secretary of State, Aug. 22, 1921, NARA, RG59, M340, Reel 7. *Their mother and sister*: "Constantinople," pp. 42–43. *Secondhand shops*: Bumgardner, *Undaunted Exiles*, 56. *A twelve-piece balalaika band*: Memoir of George Calverley, p. 36,

Calverley Papers, IWM. *A professor of mathematics*: Stone and Glenny, *Russia Abroad*, 231.

103   *From Graveyard Street*: Bumgardner, *Undaunted Exiles*, 142. *Other people relied*: Bumgardner, *Undaunted Exiles*, 148–58. *The Muslim memoirist Ziya Bey recalled*: Mufty-zada, *Speaking of the Turks*, 124.

104   *"Constantinople was a completely Russian city"*: Giorgii Fedorov, "Puteshestvie bez sentimentov," in *Konstantinopol'-Gallipoli*, 273.

105   *"I'm buying and selling"*: A. Slobodskoi, "Sredi emigratsii," in *Konstantinopol'-Gallipoli*, 80. *At the Grand Cercle Moscovite*: Bumgardner, *Undaunted Exiles*, 117–29. *"It is the best food"*: Fox-Pitt to mother, Oct. 19, 1922, Fox-Pitt Papers, IWM, Box 2, File 10. *Loose papers lay in stacks*: Bumgardner, *Undaunted Exiles*, 42–44, 53.

106   *Friends called him*: Bumgardner, *Undaunted Exiles*, 29. *"Whittemore is never in a place"*: Prichard to Gardner, July 5, 1924, Thomas Whittemore Papers, DO-ICFA, Box 11, Folder 161: "Materials from Isabella Stewart-Gardner Related to T.W." (copy of letter from the Isabella Stewart Gardner Museum, Boston, via Archives of American Art, Smithsonian Institution).

107   *Cavalrymen from the Imperial Guards*: Bumgardner, *Undaunted Exiles*, 172–73. *Ladies were assigned*: Bumgardner, *Undaunted Exiles*, 189–202.

108   *Young Russian men were given bunks*: Bumgardner, *Undaunted Exiles*, 54–55. *After weeks of waiting*: Bumgardner, *Undaunted Exiles*, 55–56.

109   *By the autumn of 1921*: Bumgardner, *Undaunted Exiles*, 20–25. *"[H]aving acquired useful learning"*: Wrangel to Whittemore, Nov. 24, 1923, CERYE, Box 1, File 32. *Shortly before he gave the order*: Wrangel, *Memoirs*, 311. *A little belt-tightening*: "Constantinople," pp. 4–5.

110   *"If the . . . martyrs"*: Tolstoy, "Compensations of Poverty," 308.

KONSTANTINOUPOLIS

113   *After the end of the Russian civil war*: Gatrell, *Whole Empire Walking*, 193. No accurate figures exist for the total number of Russian refugees, with estimates ranging from 500,000 to 3 million. See Smith, *Former People*, 208. *The city had shrunk*: Toprak, "La population," 70. *Letters*

about individual cases: See Bristol Papers, LC, Box 74, File "Russian Refugees."

115 *Portraits of Mustafa Kemal*: Fox-Pitt to mother, June 25, 1923, Fox-Pitt Papers, IWM, Box 2, File 10. *"It is a humiliating business"*: Fox-Pitt to father, June 7, 1923, Fox-Pitt Papers, IWM, Box 2, File 10. *There were still nearly 15,000*: Printed Shipping Programme for the Withdrawal of British Troops from Turkey, Aug. 1923, IWM. *"It was a wonderful 'send off'"*: Harington, *Tim Harington Looks Back*, 139.

116 *By one estimate*: Bumgardner, *Undaunted Exiles*, 197.

117 *Wrangel's Volunteer Army had spent*: Bumgardner, *Undaunted Exiles*, 96–97.

118 *"[A]nything more like a lunatic asylum"*: Christie, *Autobiography*, 354. *Just before the foundation*: Criss, *Istanbul Under Allied Occupation*, 46–48.

119 *In response, some 50,000 non-Muslims*: Alexandris, *Greek Minority of Istanbul*, 82, 96. *Fed up with the internal fighting*: Alexandris, *Greek Minority of Istanbul*, 146–49. *In 1924, for example, secessionists*: Alexandris, *Greek Minority of Istanbul*, 151–57.

120 *If allowed to remain, Greeks would be "the means"*: Quoted in Alexandris, *Greek Minority of Istanbul*, 85.

121 *"[T]oday thousands of once-prosperous people"*: "Exchange of Population Between Greece and Turkey," *Advocate of Peace Through Justice* 88, no. 5 (May 1926): 276.

122 *"There appeared to be no doubt"*: Nansen, *Armenia and the Near East*, 25.

124 *At the time, there were perhaps 40,000*: Alexandris, *Greek Minority of Istanbul*, 117. On the legal structure enabling the seizure of minority-owned assets, see Akçam and Kurt, *Kanunların Ruhu*. *On the eve of the Allied occupation, Istanbul's Chamber of Commerce and Industry*: See *Journal de la Chambre de commerce et d'industrie de Constantinople*, June 1918 and Feb. 1921. *Two thirds of the Greek barristers*: On the shifting presence of Greeks in the economy, see Alexandris, *Greek Minority of Istanbul*, 107–12.

125 *The renunciations came only after*: For a detailed treatment of these renunciations, see Bristol to Secretary of State, Nov. 3, 1926, and Nov. 24, 1926, NARA, RG59, M353, Reel 21. *In 1923, the Pera Palace*:

Çelik, *Tepebaşı*, 174–75. *However, four years later*: Alexandris, *Greek Minority of Istanbul*, 120.

126   *For most of the 1920s*: See NARA, RG59, M353, Reel 76. *In 1934, a new law*: Ekmekçioğlu, "Improvising Turkishness," 166–69. *The former Greek patriarch, Meletios*: Quoted in Alexandris, *Greek Minority of Istanbul*, 118, in the original French as "Bolchevico-Communisme de Moscou."

127   *"I stood on the dusty"*: Hemingway, "Constantinople, Dirty White, Not Glistening and Sinister," *Toronto Daily Star*, Oct. 18, 1922, in Hemingway, *Dateline: Toronto*, 229. *He returned with a pistol*: "Londra Oteli Cinayeti," *Cumhuriyet*, Sept. 9, 1929.

128   *As proprietor*: Pelt, *Tobacco, Arms, and Politics*, 78–79. *"He was renowned"*: Frank Gervasi, "Devil Man," *Collier's*, June 8, 1940: 17. *He was simply "the most powerful man"*: Pelt, *Tobacco, Arms, and Politics*, 81. *In the summer of 1927*: For property records, see Çelik, *Tepebaşı*, 174–75. I am grateful to Meral Muhayyeş for sharing family stories and memories of Misbah Muhayyeş in an interview in Istanbul, July 18, 2013.

129   *Izmir, the former Smyrna*: Finkel, *Osman's Dream*, 547.

130   *The flood of furniture*: Ravndal to State, Nov. 26, 1923, pp. 4, 6, NARA, RG59, M353, Reel 49. *Turkey as a whole*: Finkel, *Osman's Dream*, 547.

"THE POST-WAR WORLD WAS JAZZING"

136   *"The man who raises a thirst"*: Hemingway, "Hamid Bey," *Toronto Daily Star*, Oct. 9, 1922, in Hemingway, *Dateline: Toronto*, 220. *"Beauty and wit"*: Bumgardner, *Undaunted Exiles*, 132. *Small beer halls*: Carus Wilson to father, July 19, 1922, Carus Wilson Papers, IWM. *Tom's Lancashire Bar*: See the advertisements in *Orient News*, July 12, 1919. *The facility was able to accommodate*: Greer, *Glories of Greece*, 319–20. *The Pera Palace offered dinner*: See the advertisement in *Le Courier de Turquie*, Apr. 1, 1919. *The bar had been opened*: Adil, *Gardenbar Geceleri*, 7–8.

137   *A musical matinee was available*: See the advertisement in *Le Courier de Turquie*, Apr. 1, 1919. *Boxing matches were staged*: Adil, *Garden-*

bar Geceleri, 25–27. *Boutnikoff's Symphony Orchestra:* Bumgardner, *Undaunted Exiles,* 141. *"Artists cannot live in Russia":* Quoted in Bumgardner, *Undaunted Exiles,* 143. *At the Garden Bar, the memoirist Ziya Bey reported:* Mufty-zada, *Speaking of the Turks,* 152.

138   *The whole neighborhood was like the slums:* Gritchenko, *Deux ans à Constantinople,* 278–79. *Princesses of the imperial household:* Musbah Haidar, *Arabesque,* 98–100. *"At Petit Champs [sic] you could watch":* Dunn, *World Alive,* 287.

140   *Known by a variety of names:* See Sperco, *Turcs d'hier et d'aujourd'hui,* 143; Mufty-zada, *Speaking of the Turks,* 159; *Orient News,* July 13, July 18, and July 29, 1919. For biographical details on Thomas, I am indebted to Vladimir Alexandrov's painstaking research in his biography *The Black Russian. In the middle of the 1920s:* Sperco, *Turcs d'hier et d'aujourd'hui,* 143. *"Never before were Pera and Galata":* Mufty-zada, *Speaking of the Turks,* 154. *"[T]he only thing which this international crowd":* Mufty-zada, *Speaking of the Turks,* 154. *When a group of American tourists:* Farson, *Way of a Transgressor,* 470.

141   *Other clubs were popping up:* Sperco, *Turcs d'hier et d'aujourd'hui,* 140. *"The post-war world was jazzing":* W. G. Tinckom-Fernandez, "Life is Less Hectic in Constantinople," *New York Times,* July 8. 1928. *It was all a sad affair:* Sperco, *Turcs d'hier et d'aujourd'hui,* 144. *A mysterious group:* Adil, *Gardenbar Geceleri,* 20–23.

142   *Maxim's dancing instructors:* Sperco, *Turcs d'hier et d'aujourd'hui,* 143–44. *In 1926, municipal authorities issued:* "Review of the Turkish Press," Nov. 7–20, 1926, p. 9, NARA, RG59, M353, Reel 75. On the "Charleston debate" in Istanbul, see Woodall, "Sensing the City," chapter 4. *"They changed the shape":* Urgan, *Bir Dinozorun Anıları,* 155. *According to the seventeenth-century traveler:* DBIA, 5:434. *Anyone "who can fry three stinky fish":* "Meyhaneler Çoğalıyor," *Cumhuriyet,* Jan. 12, 1939.

143   *"My foot takes no step":* Evliya Çelebi, *An Ottoman Traveller,* 20–21.

144   *About eight percent:* Shaw, "Population of Istanbul," 269. *Given the need for food:* For two examples of memoirs that discuss local foodways, in this case in the Beşiktaş and Balat neighborhoods, see Mintzuri, *İstanbul Anıları,* and Shaul, *From Balat to Bat Yam. "Narcotic stimulants such as Indian hemp":* *Balkanstaaten und Konstantinopel,* 222.

145 *Turkey was not a signatory*: Russell, *Egyptian Service*, 239–40. *The white powder was so easily concealable*: Woodall, "Sensing the City," 67–79.

146 *"[D]elete forever that misunderstood word"*: Ellison, *An Englishwoman in a Turkish Harem*, 17. *"All that I have known"*: Goodrich-Freer, *Things Seen in Constantinople*, 19.

147 *In the late 1920s, as many as fifty*: "Review of the Turkish Press," June 28–July 11, 1928, p. 17, NARA, RG59, M353, Reel 76. *One of Sultan Abdülhamid II's eunuchs*: Sperco, *Turcs d'hier et d'aujourd'hui*, 122. *Even Mustafa Kemal*: Mango, *Atatürk*, 441. *As part of the empire's modernizing reforms*: See Wyers, *"Wicked" Istanbul*. I thank Wyers for my understanding of changes to Istanbul's sex trade from the Ottoman era through the early republican period. *One story— apparently true*: Duke, *Passport to Paris*, 71.

148 *At the YMCA*: Commanding Officer to Senior US Naval Officer, Turkey, Feb. 9, 1919, Bristol Papers, LC, Box 1, File "February 1919." *Venereal disease was "rampant"*: "British Forces in Turkey, Commander-in-Chief's Despatch, Period 1920–1923," p. 8, NAUK, CAB 44/38; and Harington to High Commissariat for Refugees, League of Nations, July 14, 1923, p. 2, NAUK, FO 286/800. *A contemporary survey revealed*: Johnson, ed., *Constantinople To-Day*, 356–57. *In another survey, police counted*: Quoted in Bali, *Jews and Prostitution*, 27.

149 *The majority of both proprietors and prostitutes*: Johnson, ed., *Constantinople To-Day*, 356–57. *A two-week snapshot*: Medical Officer to Senior US Naval Officer Present in Turkey, Feb. 25, 1919, Bristol Papers, LC, Box 1, File "February 1919." *Fortunately, there was a surfeit*: See the advertisements in *Le Journal d'Orient*, May 24, May 25, June 1, June 7, 1919. *Since the bar run by the sometime madame*: Dunn, *World Alive*, 288, 420.

150 *"Intoxicated sailors rock from side to side"*: Mufty-zada, *Speaking of the Turks*, 151–52. *Even under the Ottomans, "white slavers"*: Bali, *Jews and Prostitution*, 58–62.

151 *The writer Fikret Adil dated the decline*: Adil, *Gardenbar Geceleri*, 31–32. *"Most of the people in our country"*: Quoted in Wyers, *"Wicked" Istanbul*, 137.

"THE PAST IS A WOUND IN MY HEART"

155   *The first automobile*: Çelik, *Remaking of Istanbul*, 103. *"At Pera, where I live"*: Bibesco, *Eight Paradises*, 225–27.

156   *"They exasperate and deafen"*: "The Street Hogs," *Orient News*, June 19, 1919. *Especially popular during Ramadan*: Bali, *Turkish Cinema*, 28. *"There are a lot of 'movie' shows"*: Fox-Pitt to mother, Oct. 14, 1922, Fox-Pitt Papers, IWM, Box 2, File 10. *Istanbullus could see French*: "'Glorya' Açıldı," *Cumhuriyet*, Nov. 7, 1930.

157   *By the beginning of that decade*: Bali, *Turkish Cinema*, 34–43. *For the first time, Istanbullus*: Bali, *Turkish Cinema*, 21. *Tickets were reasonably expensive*: Bali, *Turkish Cinema*, 44.

158   *A detailed survey of first-run films*: The report, by Eugene M. Hinkle, is reproduced in Bali, *Turkish Cinema*. The percentages are on p. 76. *A widely reported legal case*: Grew to Secretary of State, Mar. 28 and Apr. 19, 1928, NARA, RG59, M353, Reel 50.

159   *After painstaking research*: Bali, *Turkish Cinema*, 81. *Greta Garbo and Betty Blythe*: Bali, *Turkish Cinema*, 66. *When Josephine Baker made a short personal appearance*: "Jozefin Beyker," *Cumhuriyet*, Jan. 20, 1934; and "Jozefin Beykerle Mülakat," *Cumhuriyet*, Jan. 20, 1934.

160   *The same report*: Bali, *Turkish Cinema*, 81. *"For a city of its size"*: Ravndal to State, Nov. 26, 1923, p. 2, NARA, RG59, M353, Reel 49. *By the early 1920s, they could be had*: Ravndal to State, Nov. 26, 1923. *Throughout the decade, importers brought*: Ravndal to State, Nov. 26, 1923, p. 8. *Barely had a dance tune*: Ravndal to State, Nov. 26, 1923, p. 3.

162   *But in the early Turkish Republic*: I am grateful to Harold Hagopian for his insights into the music of the period, as well as the liner notes to his rereleases of the music of these performers on his Traditional Crossroads label.

164   *"My soul, that's enough now"*: Eskenazi's version of "Gazel Nihavent" is available on the album *Rembetika: Aşk, Gurbet, Hapis, ve Tekke Şarkıları* (Kalan Müzik, 2007).

166   *In 1933, when the Austrian writer Franz Werfel*: "İstanbul Ermenilerinin F. Werfele mukabelesi," *Cumhuriyet*, Dec. 16, 1935.

171   *The company's local affiliate*: Akçura, *Gramofon Çağı*, 29–30.

172 *During the Allied occupation, it was reasonably safe*: Ravndal to State, Nov. 26, 1923, p. 4. *"The [manufacturing] process is a secret one"*: Ravndal to State, Nov. 26, 1923, p. 4. *There the firm re-created*: See the family's historical timeline at www.zildjian.com.

173 *The Erlegün brothers were too young*: On the life and career of Ahmet Ertegün, see Greenfield, *The Last Sultan*.

175 *"[A] younger generation that knew not Thomas"*: Tinckom-Fernandez, "Life is Less Hectic."

MODERN TIMES

179 *Never before had all Istanbullus*: Sperco, *L'Orient qui s'éteint*, 131–32. *As the* Guide Bleu *explained*: *De Paris à Constantinople*, 185.

181 *Little boys threw rocks*: Orga, *Portrait of a Turkish Family*, 223. *Since the regulation did not affect*: "Review of the Turkish Press," Dec. 19, 1926– Jan. 1, 1927, p. 17, NARA, RG59, M353, Reel 75. *The same year, drinking liquor*: "Review of the Turkish Press," Aug. 15–28, 1926, p. 24, and Dec. 19, 1926–Jan. 1, 1927, p. 15, NARA, RG59, M353, Reel 75.

184 *As a diplomatic observer noted*: Henderson to Vansittart, Oct. 31, 1923, NAUK, FO 794/10, ff. 5–6.

185 *Close to seven hundred*: Findley, *Turkey, Islam, Nationalism, and Modernity*, 253. The reevaluation of the early Kemalist period is now a major theme among historians of Turkey. The leading figure in this reassessment has been Erik J. Zürcher, whose works are cited in the bibliography. *Small demonstrations or individual acts*: On the elevation of small affairs into major events, see the corrective in Brockett, "Collective Action." *Communal violence that fell short*: Guttstadt, *Turkey, the Jews, and the Holocaust*, 61–70; see also Bali, *1934 Trakya Olayları*.

186 *Still, eighteen armed uprisings*: Findley, *Turkey, Islam, Nationalism, and Modernity*, 251. *Even then, the turbaned pious*: Ostrorog, *Angora Reform*, 74.

189 *Five of the other largest mosques*: "6 Camide Türkçe Kur'an," *Cumhuriyet*, Jan. 29, 1932; and "Türkçe Kur'anla Mukabele," *Cumhuriyet*, Jan. 30, 1932. *On the Night of Power*: "70 Bin Kişinin İştirak Ettiği Dini Merasim," *Cumhuriyet*, Feb. 4, 1932. *In the new republic, even God*:

The ban on the Arabic-language call to prayer, although irregularly enforced, continued until 1950. See Azak, "Secularism in Turkey." *He arrived for the first time*: Mango, *Atatürk*, 460–61.

192 *The Turkish Republic, by contrast*: Pallis, "Population of Turkey," 441. *"I awoke . . . to an oppressive silence"*: Richardson to Grew, Oct. 29, 1927, p. 1, NARA, RG59, M353, Reel 57. *At precisely 10:15 p.m.*: Grew to Secretary of State, Nov. 8, 1927, pp. 1–2, with the attached "Communiqué of the Stamboul Vilayet Indicating the Manner in which the Census Shall Take Place on Friday, October 28, 1927;" and Richardson to Grew, Oct. 29, 1927, all at NARA, RG59, M353, Reel 57.

193 *Previous estimates had put Turkey's population*: Pallis, "Population of Turkey," 440–41. *The city was smaller than it had been*: Şevket Pamuk, "Economic Change in Twentieth-Century Turkey: Is the Glass More than Half Full?" in Kasaba, ed., *Cambridge History of Turkey*, 275. *Only two cities had more than a hundred thousand*: *Türkiye İstatistik Yıllığı: 1950*, 41. *As the newspaper* Milliyet: Grew to Secretary of State, Nov. 8, 1927, p. 5.

194 *In greater Istanbul, the census counted*: Shaw, *Jews of the Ottoman Empire and the Turkish Republic*, 287.

195 *Prost's plan called for cutting highways*: For details, see Gül, *Emergence of Modern Istanbul*, 98–106; F. Cânâ Bilsel, "Henri Prost's Planning Works in Istanbul (1936–1951): Transforming the Structure of a City through Master Plans and Urban Operations," and idem, "European Side of Istanbul Master Plan, 1937," both in *İmparatorluk Başkentinden*, 101–65, 245–76.

196 *When John Dos Passos went to a cabaret*: Dos Passos, *Orient Express*, in *Travel Books and Other Writings*, 136. *Prost probably would have cringed*: It was no small irony that the salvation of Gezi Park, which was slated to be replaced by a reconstruction of the old barracks, became the inspiration for widespread antigovernment demonstrations in the summer of 2013. The Turkish government insisted its plan to remodel the park was in fact about historic restoration, reaching back beyond Prost to an authentic Ottoman past. The public saw it as rampant destruction.

197 *"Presenting the Turkish nation"*: Quoted in "Review of the Turkish Press," Mar. 7–20, 1929, p. 23, NARA, RG59, M353, Reel 77.

BEYOND THE VEIL

201 *"The shape of social life changed"*: Urgan, *Bir Dinozorun Anıları*, 155. *Unlike the fez for men*: Mango, *Atatürk*, 434–35. *Window screens*: "Kafesler Kaldırılacak," *Cumhuriyet*, Nov. 5, 1930.

202 *The types and sizes of veils*: Ekrem, *Everyday Life in Istanbul*, 98. *Public harassment was made*: "Kadınlara Laf Atanlar Derhal Tevkif Edilecek," *Cumhuriyet*, Sept. 10, 1929. *Four years later, the franchise*: Ayten Sezer, "Türkiye'deki İlk Kadın Milletvekilleri ve Meclis'teki Çalışmaları," unpublished paper, Hacettepe University, available at www.ait.hacettepe. edu.tr/akademik/arsiv/kadin.htm#_ftn21. *The first Muslim female lawyer*: "Review of the Turkish Press," Nov. 29–Dec. 12, 1928, p. 23, NARA, RG59, M353, Reel 77. *The first surgeon . . . first pharmacist*: "Review of the Turkish Press," Mar. 5–18, 1931, p. 9, NARA, RG59, M1224, Reel 20; and "Review of the Turkish Press," Apr. 16–29, 1931, p. 9, NARA, RG59, M1224, Reel 20. *The first wrestler*: "Digest of the Turkish Press," Aug. 21–Sept. 24, 1932, p. 20, NARA, RG59, M1224, Reel 21.

203 *The first female tramway conductors*: "Tramvaylarda Kadın Biletçiler İşe Başladı," *Cumhuriyet*, Apr. 16, 1941. *Even in the last days of the sultans*: See Duben and Behar, *Istanbul Households*, chapters 5 and 6. *By 1920, more than a third*: Yavuz Köse, "Vertical Bazaars of Modernity: Western Department Stores and Their Staff in Istanbul (1889–1921)," in Atabaki and Brockett, eds., *Ottoman and Republican Turkish Labour History*, 102. *Tramcars accommodated both genders*: "Constantinople," p. 37, Shalikashvili Papers, HIA.

204 *Mass rallies in 1919 and 1920*: Yeşim Arat, "Contestation and Collaboration: Women's Struggles for Empowerment in Turkey," in Kasaba, ed., *Cambridge History of Turkey*, 391. *By the time of the 1927 census*: Shorter, "Population of Turkey," 431, 433fn. *"The duty of Turkish Women's Societies"*: Quoted in Crosby to Secretary of State, July 18, 1927, p. 4, NARA, RG59, M353, Reel 22.

206 *She remained one of the principle expounders*: On Afet İnan, see Yeşim Arat, "Nation Building and Feminism in Early Republican Turkey," in Kerslake, Öktem, and Robins, eds., *Turkey's Engagement with Modernity*, 38–51. *The family mansion, covered in wisteria*: Edib, *Memoirs*, 3.

207   *Flouting Ottoman fashion:* Edib, *Memoirs,* 23. *She was slight and frail:* Woods, *Spunyarn,* 2:66. *Once she was old enough to begin:* Edib, *Memoirs,* 149.

208   *"No little Circassian slave":* Edib, *Memoirs,* 206.

209   *"I became a writer":* Edib, *Memoirs,* 260. *It was the first time in her life:* Edib, *Memoirs,* 275.

210   *He was short and round:* Edib, *Memoirs,* 217. *"I felt stupefied":* Edib, *Turkish Ordeal,* 3. *Small and pale:* Biographical sketch of Adnan Bey in Dolbeare to Secretary of State, Jan. 3, 1923, p. 1, NARA, RG59, M353, Reel 21.

211   *In 1919, Halide later recalled:* Edib, *Turkish Ordeal,* 23. *That summer, she was invited:* Edib, *Turkish Ordeal,* 31. *"Brethren and sons, listen to me":* Edib, *Turkish Ordeal,* 33fn.

212   *Mustafa Kemal met her:* Edib, *Turkish Ordeal,* 127. *"I feasted my eyes on the sea":* Edib, *Turkish Ordeal,* 381.

213   *It had been two years:* Edib, *Turkish Ordeal,* 404. *"Dr. Adnan Bey is one of the leaders":* Dolbeare to Secretary of State, Jan. 3, 1923, p. 1. *"I have seen, I have gone through":* Edib, *Memoirs,* 275–76.

214   *"There will be only the sum total":* Edib, *Turkish Ordeal,* 407.

215   *History and culture, she said, had formed the Turks:* Edib, *Turkey Faces West,* 209–10.

216   *"It is after I have loved my own people":* Edib, *Memoirs,* 326. *"Women," she was fond of saying:* Edib, *Conflict of East and West in Turkey,* 235.

LIVING LIKE A SQUIRREL

219   *"Girl," she said:* Hikmet, *Human Landscapes,* 72.

221   *As a diplomatic report noted in 1930:* "Review of the Turkish Press," Mar. 19–Apr. 16, 1930, p. 16, NARA, RG59, M1224, Reel 20. *He was born perhaps in 1902:* I have relied on two important studies—Blasing, *Nâzım Hikmet,* and Göksu and Timms, *Romantic Communist*—for biographical details.

223   *Relations between Mustafa Kemal's nationalists and the Bolsheviks:* Bristol to Secretary of State, Aug. 22, 1921, NARA, RG59, M340, Reel 7. *With so many penniless Russian-speakers:* Dunn, *World Alive,* 288.

Allied police even detained Russians: N. N. Chebyshev, "Blizkaia Dal'," in *Konstantinopol'-Gallipoli*, 142–43. *According to American intelligence sources*: Bristol to Secretary of State, July 21, 1926, p. 3, NARA, RG59, M340, Reel 8.

224   *They eventually took for granted*: See Hirst, "Anti-Westernism," for a discussion of the interactions between the two systems in this period.

225   *A Turkish Communist Party was established*: Mango, *Atatürk*, 293.

226   *Right-wing Unionists were blamed*: Mango, *Atatürk*, 303–4. *In Moscow he read Marx*: Blasing, *Nâzım Hikmet*, 18.

227   *He may have invented*: Blasing, *Nâzım Hikmet*, 52. *He was arrested and imprisoned at the border*: Blasing, *Nâzım Hikmet*, 78.

229   *The record sold out*: Blasing, *Nâzım Hikmet*, 93.

231   *"Living is no laughing matter"*: "On Living," in Hikmet, *Poems of Nâzim Hikmet*, 132. *"You are a field"*: "You," in Hikmet, *Poems of Nazim Hikmet*, 155.

232   *"Some people know all about plants"*: "Autobiography," in Hikmet, *Poems of Nazim Hikmet*, 259. *He blew in on a winter gale*: Trotsky, *My Life*, 547.

ISLAND LIFE

235   *"Dear Sir"*: Trotsky, *My Life*, 565–66. *It was one of the coldest winters*: "Review of the Turkish Press," Feb. 21–Mar. 6, 1929, p. 21, NARA, RG59, M353, Reel 77; "Dün Kar Tipisi Şehrin Umumi Hayatını Durdurdu," *Cumhuriyet*, Feb. 3, 1929; "Fırtına İstanbulu Kastı Kavurdu!" *Cumhuriyet*, Feb. 4, 1929; "Kar Afeti Bugün De Devam Edecek," *Cumhuriyet*, Feb. 5, 1929. *Trotsky and his wife*: Trotsky, *My Life*, 566.

236   *On Stalin's orders*: The main Soviet security service was known by a succession of names, from the Cheka, or Emergency Commission, to the KGB, or State Security Committee. The service carried the name OGPU, or Unified State Political Administration, throughout much of the 1920s and early 1930s. *Yakov Minsky*: Agabekov, *OGPU*, 225–26.

237   *He had no desire to stay*: "Troçki Anlatıyor," *Cumhuriyet*, Mar. 20, 1929. *Minsky, the Soviet secret police agent*: Van Heijenoort, *With Trotsky in*

Exile, 45. *Exasperated, Minsky finally booted*: Agabekov, *OGPU*, 226. *After another move*: Van Heijenoort, *With Trotsky in Exile*, 6.

238 *For years afterward*: Neave, *Twenty-Six Years on the Bosphorus*, 271.

239 *"The waves of the Sea of Marmara"*: Serge and Trotsky, *Life and Death of Leon Trotsky*, 164. *A fire, probably caused*: Van Heijenoort, *With Trotsky in Exile*, 25. *Trotsky reportedly sued*: "Troçki'nin Ziyanı," *Cumhuriyet*, Mar. 22, 1931. *The family was once again*: Van Heijenoort, *With Trotsky in Exile*, 6–7. *He routinely carried*: Van Heijenoort, *With Trotsky in Exile*, 18. *Like a crotchety old man*: Author's interview with Fıstık Ahmet Tanrıverdi, Büyükada, Aug. 16, 2012. *Trotsky hired local guards*: Tanrıverdi interview. *When he happened to find*: Van Heijenoort, *With Trotsky in Exile*, 20.

240 *He also had the habit*: Van Heijenoort, *With Trotsky in Exile*, 17. *The two could be seen*: Van Heijenoort, *With Trotsky in Exile*, 12. *Trotsky and Haralambos would call out*: "Farewell to Prinkipo," in Trotsky, *Leon Trotsky Speaks*, 273. *"Ah, Comrade Gérard!"*: Quoted in Rosenthal, *Avocat de Trotsky*, 96. *Once, a small girl*: Urgan, *Bir Dinozorun Anıları*, 155–56. *He started writing his autobiography*: Serge and Trotsky, *Life and Death of Leon Trotsky*, 165. *Editorials and political essays*: Churchill, *Great Contemporaries*, 198.

241 *Autograph collectors kindly asked*: "Farewell to Prinkipo," in Trotsky, *Leon Trotsky Speaks*, 271. *"Here on this island"*: Quoted in Deutscher, *Prophet Outcast*, 216.

242 *"He seems too small"*: Eastman, *Great Companions*, 154. *The American edition*: Deutscher, *Prophet Outcast*, 27. *But Trotsky was spending*: Eastman, *Great Companions*, 158–59; Serge and Trotsky, *Life and Death of Leon Trotsky*, 189. *To economize, he kept little*: Rosenthal, *Avocat de Trotsky*, 72. *"We seemed to camp"*: Van Heijenoort, *With Trotsky in Exile*, 11. *During Eastman's visit*: Eastman, *Great Companions*, 158–59.

243 *Trotsky had "followers"*: Eastman, *Heroes I Have Known*, 248. *"I do not measure"*: Trotsky, *My Life*, 581–82. *Enemies, he would say routinely*: Van Heijenoort, *With Trotsky in Exile*, 42. *The British socialists*: Trotsky, *My Life*, 577.

244 *The years in Istanbul had been*: Deutscher, *Prophet Outcast*, 217. *"Our house is already almost empty"*: "Farewell to Prinkipo," in Trotsky, *Leon*

Trotsky Speaks, 272. *His hair had gone white*: Van Heijenoort, *With Trotsky in Exile*, 41. *Heart trouble and gout*: Memorandum, Mar. 19, 1930, LTEP, Item 15742. *"The bearer of this passport"*: Passports of Lev Sedof and Latalya Sedov, LTEP, Item 15784. *At the beginning of the 1920s*: Dos Passos, *Orient Express*, in *Travel Books and Other Writings*, 135.

245   *A certain Kuznetsov*: Robert Imbrie, "Memorandum of Bolshevik Activities at Constantinople," Feb. 1921, p. 1, NARA, RG59, M353, Reel 20. *"The Bosphorus was a dumping ground"*: Dunn, *World Alive*, 282. *Then came the YMCA*: Dunn, *World Alive*, 282.

246   *Settling in Istanbul*: Trotsky, *My Life*, 567. *"The network of spies"*: Agabekov, *OGPU*, 208. *Agabekov claimed that virtually all*: Agabekov, *OGPU*, 208. *The Soviets were careful to balance*: Agabekov, *OGPU*, 211–13. *Agents were proud of their roles*: Nikolai Khokhlov, *In the Name of Conscience: The Testament of a Soviet Secret Agent*, quoted in Wilmers, *The Eitingons*, 149.

247   *Agabekov himself had the dubious honor*: Agabekov, *OGPU*, 247–48; Sudoplatov, *Special Tasks*, 47–48; Brook-Shepherd, *Storm Petrels*, 107–51. Agabekov was reportedly assassinated by Soviet agents in 1937 or 1938, either on the border between France and Spain or in Paris. His body was never found. Streater died in 1971 in New York, where she had worked as a secretary at the United Nations. *Less than a year before*: Agabekov, *OGPU*, 207. *Even today it is difficult to establish*: Sudoplatov, *Special Tasks*, 33–36. *His travel documents identified him*: Agabekov, *OGPU*, 207. *His superiors gave him*: Sudoplatov, *Special Tasks*, 31. *In many ways Eitingon had*: I have taken family details about Leonid Eitingon and his relatives from Sudoplatov, *Special Tasks*, especially chapter 2, and Wilmers, *The Eitingons*.

249   *In 1929, when he was transferred*: Agabekov, *OGPU*, 208. As chief "legal" OGPU officer in Istanbul, Eitingon would have had ultimate operational command over the Trotsky case, even if day-to-day operations might have been handled by the considerable "illegal" OGPU presence in the city. "Legals" were officers who came with legitimate diplomatic cover and were generally well known to the Turkish authorities. "Illegals" were those who operated in secret as

businessmen, journalists, or other unofficial roles. *He briefly served as case officer*: Sudoplatov, *Special Tasks*, 34. *During the Spanish Civil War*: Patenaude, *Trotsky*, 206. I have taken Caridad Mercader's biographical details from Sudoplatov, *Special Tasks*, 70. On the relationship with Eitingon, see Andrew and Mitrokhin, *Sword and the Shield*.

250   *His only real advantage*: On the code name as Eitingon's idea, see Sudoplatov, *Special Tasks*, 69. *A house alarm was sounding*: Trotsky's final hours have been narrated by a variety of sources, but for overviews see Serge and Trotsky, *Life and Death of Leon Trotsky*, 266–70; Deutscher, *Prophet Outcast*, 483–509; and Patenaude, *Trotsky*, 279–92.

251   *For his service*: Patenaude, *Trotsky*, 294.

252   *"There is one small guaranteed way"*: Quoted in Sudoplatov, *Special Tasks*, 36.

QUEEN

256   *"For four or five years now"*: "Baş Muharririmiz Yunus Nadi Bey'in Bir Belçika Gazetesinde İntişar Eden Beyanatı," *Cumhuriyet*, Oct. 7, 1928. *"Why Wouldn't We Do"*: "Aynı şeyi biz niçin yapmayalım?" *Cumhuriyet*, Feb. 4, 1929. *The newspaper soon announced*: "En Güzel Türk Kadını," *Cumhuriyet*, Feb. 5, 1929. *It would be no different*: "Güzellik Müsabakamız," *Cumhuriyet*, Feb. 14, 1929.

257   *There would be no swimsuit element*: "En Güzel Türk Kızı Kimdir Acaba?" *Cumhuriyet*, Feb. 15, 1929. *Prostitutes were expressly forbidden*: "Her Genç Kız Müsabakamıza İştirak Edebilir," *Cumhuriyet*, Feb. 10, 1929. *The recent winner of a European contest*: "Türkiye'nin En Güzel Kızı Olmak İstemez Misiniz?" *Cumhuriyet*, Feb. 17, 1929. *A jury of fifty notables*: "Türkiye Güzellik Kraliçesi," *Cumhuriyet*, Sept. 2, 1929. *By September 3, the results were in*: "1929 Türkiye Güzellik Kraliçesi İntihap Edildi," *Cumhuriyet*, Sept. 3, 1929.

258   *Beginning in 1930, twenty finalists*: "Güzellik Balosu," *Cumhuriyet*, Jan. 8, 1930. *"Beauty Is Not Something"*: "Güzellik Ayıp Bir Şey Değildir," *Cumhuriyet*, Jan. 13, 1930. *When judges selected*: "Review of the Turk-

ish Press," Feb. 5–18, 1931, p. 11, NARA, RG59, M1224, Reel 20. *The title of Miss Europe*: "Mis Avrupa!" *Cumhuriyet*, Feb. 7, 1930.

259 *Keriman was only ten*: I am grateful to Ece Sarpyener and Ayşe Torfilli, the daughter and granddaughter of Keriman Halis, for sharing details of her biography and ancestry, along with a home movie, in an interview in Istanbul, Oct. 9, 2012.

262 *Twenty thousand Istanbullus*: "20 Bin Kişi Dün Gece Kraliçeyi Alkışladı," *Cumhuriyet*, July 8, 1932. *Along the way, crowds gathered*: "Kraliçe Geçerken," *Cumhuriyet*, July 14, 1932. *In the ensuing days, nearly thirty thousand*: "Dünya Güzeli 30,000'e Yakın Telgraf Aldı," *Cumhuriyet*, Aug. 2, 1932. *Yunus Nadi was summoned*: "Gazi Hz. Başmuharririmize Dedi Ki: 'Türk Milleti Bu Güzel Çocuğunu, Şüphesiz, Samimiyetle Tebrik Eder,'" *Cumhuriyet*, Aug. 3, 1932. *İsmet Pasha, the old war hero*: "Digest of the Turkish Press," July 24–Aug. 6, 1932, pp. 6–7, NARA, RG59, M1224, Reel 21. Cumhuriyet, *never missing an opportunity*: "Dünyayı Fetheden Türk Kızı!" *Cumhuriyet*, Aug. 4, 1932.

263 *She appeared in Berlin and Chicago*: "Digest of the Turkish Press," Feb. 5–18, 1933, p. 17, NARA, RG59, M1224, Reel 21. *At one gala dinner*: "Digest of the Turkish Press," Aug. 7–20, 1932, p. 6, NARA, RG59, M1224, Reel 21. *When Istanbul's commuters drove along*: "Digest of the Turkish Press," Aug. 7–20, 1932, p. 4.

HOLY WISDOM

267 *"If the Hellenes Are Doing It"*: "Yunanlılar Yapıyor, Biz Neden Yapmıyalım?" *Cumhuriyet*, Feb. 19, 1929.

268 *"So the church has become"*: Procopius, *Buildings*, in *Procopius*, 1.1.27. *"Oh, Solomon"*: Quoted in Kinross, *Europa Minor*, 141.

269 *According to tradition, a delegation of Slavs*: Quoted in Nelson, *Hagia Sophia*, 14.

270 *From that day, he ordered*: Runciman, *Fall of Constantinople*, 147–49.

271 *The Fossatis had also been the first to remove*: Teteriatnikov, *Mosaics of Hagia Sophia*, 3.

272 *He posed for noirish studio shots*: Whittemore Papers, DO-ICFA, Box

9, Folder 144. *Short and thin-framed*: Whittemore Papers, DO-ICFA, Box 9, Folder 151; Downes, *Scarlet Thread*, 39. *He could appear at the oddest of moments*: "Yeats and Heifetz Sailing on Europa," *New York Times*, Dec. 27, 1932; Downes, *Scarlet Thread*, 39. *Prichard may have been*: Whittemore probably also knew Gertrude Stein from her time as a student at Radcliffe in the late 1890s. See Klein, "The Elusive Mr. Whittemore: The Early Years, 1871–1916," in Klein, Ousterhout, and Pitarakis, eds., *Kariye Camii, Yeniden/The Kariye Camii Reconsidered*, 473fn31.

273   *In 1910, Whittemore visited*: Klein, "The Elusive Mr. Whittemore," 475. *His mind, he once confided to a friend*: Whittemore to Isabella Stewart-Gardner, Aug. 24, 1921, Whittemore Papers, DO-ICFA, Box 11, Folder 161 (copy from Isabella Stewart Gardner Museum, Boston, via Archives of American Art, Smithsonian Institution).

274   *The lands under their control*: Hélène Ahrweiler, "Byzantine Concepts of the Foreigner: The Case of the Nomads," in Ahrweiler and Laiou, eds., *Studies on the Internal Diaspora*, 2. *"I have reached at length"*: Gibbon, *Decline and Fall*, 6:413.

275   *The first journal of Byzantine studies*: Elizabeth Jeffreys, John Haldon, and Robin Cormack, "Byzantine Studies as an Academic Discipline," in Jeffreys with Haldon and Cormack, eds., *Oxford Handbook of Byzantine Studies*, 5. *During the First World War, he had delivered*: Equerry of Queen Alexandra to "All Military, Civil, and Customs Authorities concerned," Mar. 11, 1919, CERYE, Box 99, Folder 2.

276   *"[H]e had a gift"*: Runciman, *Traveller's Alphabet*, 56–57. *Whittemore's version of events*: "Rose Petal Flavored Ice Cream in Company of a Harvard Scholar," *Boston Globe*, Aug. 19, 1948. *The Harem of Topkapı Palace*: "Topkapı Sarayının Harem Dairesi Açılıyor," *Cumhuriyet*, Apr. 8, 1930.

277   *In October 1930, the two countries*: Alexandris, *Greek Minority of Istanbul*, 179. *In the summer of 1931, the Turkish Council of Ministers*: Nelson, *Hagia Sophia*, 176.

278   *Once they were exposed*: Teteriatnikov, *Mosaics of Hagia Sophia*, 44. *Islam prohibited human images*: "Mosaics Uncovered in Famous Mosque," *New York Times*, Dec. 25, 1932.

279   *Now, at last, the artistic glories*: "Ayasofya'nın Mozayıkları: İlme Hürmet
       Lazımdır," *Cumhuriyet*, Nov. 14, 1932. *On the crowded train back to
       Istanbul*: Whittemore to Gano, July 19, 1932, Byzantine Institute
       Records, DO-ICFA, Subgroup I: Records, Series I: Correspondence,
       Box 1, Folder 5. *Whittemore staged films of his team*: See Byzantine
       Institute Records, DO-ICFA, Subgroup II: Fieldwork Papers, Series
       IV, Subseries D: Moving Images (16mm films).

280   *It turned out to be*: The Fossati brothers had made sketches of the mosaic
       and took steps to stabilize it, but it had never been fully described or
       restored, a fact that led the great Byzantinist Cyril Mango to describe
       Whittemore's work as a "rediscovery" of the Deesis. Mango, *Materials*, 29.

282   *Whittemore's team estimated*: Teteriatnikov, *Mosaics of Hagia Sophia*, 47.

283   *The higher the angle*: Teteriatnikov, *Mosaics of Hagia Sophia*, 52. *For an
       especially vibrant effect*: Teteriatnikov, *Mosaics of Hagia Sophia*, 56.

284   *Plaster casts were also made*: Teteriatnikov, *Mosaics of Hagia Sophia*, 61.

285   *The Hagia Sophia "is the universe of buildings"*: Quoted in Nelson,
       Hagia Sophia, 170. *In 1934, the Turkish Council of Ministers*: "Ayasofya
       Müzesi," *Cumhuriyet*, Jan. 26, 1935. *Edward VIII and Wallis Simpson*:
       See Byzantine Institute Records, DO-ICFA, Subgroup II: Fieldwork
       Papers, Series IV, Box 45: "Photographs: Hagia Sophia and Kariye
       Camii, ca. 1930s–1940s," Folder 482: "Photographs of Thomas Whit-
       temore with Edward VIII of England"; and Natalia Teteriatnikov, "The
       Byzantine Institute and Its Role in the Conservation of the Kariye
       Camii," in Klein, ed., *Restoring Byzantium*, 51. *In the spring of 1939, a
       German tourist*: "Dr. Göbbels Şehrimize Geldi," *Cumhuriyet*, Apr. 13,
       1939. *"The dome has a graceful elegance"*: Goebbels, *Die Tagebücher von
       Joseph Goebbels*, Apr. 14, 1939.

286   *Life seemed wonderful*: Goebbels, *Die Tagebücher von Joseph Goebbels*,
       Apr. 14, 1939.

SHADOW WARS

289   *At a funeral it doesn't matter*: Deringil, *Turkish Foreign Policy*, 184.
       "Where should we be now": Quoted in Knatchbull-Hugessen, *Diplomat
       in Peace and War*, 138.

290   *The same month as Goebbels's visit*: von Papen, *Memoirs*, 446.

292   *Yet, unlike a Mussolini*: Knatchbull-Hugessen, *Diplomat in Peace and War*, 135. *His skin had gone sallow*: Runciman, *A Traveller's Alphabet*, 57. *Cirrhosis of the liver had sapped*: Mango, *Atatürk*, 518–19. *Children poured from schools*: Sperco, *Istanbul indiscret*, 69.

293   *Atatürk's last words*: Mango, *Atatürk*, 525. *Nearly a dozen people*: Mango, *Atatürk*, 525.

294   *According to the British ambassador*: Knatchbull-Hugessen, *Diplomat in Peace and War*, 144.

295   *"You could almost throw a stone"*: Transcript of Ira Hirschmann speech, Oct. 22, 1944, p. 2, Hirschmann Papers, FDR, Box 3, File "'Saving Refugees Through Turkey,' Address by Ira Hirschmann Over CBS, 10/22/44."

296   *When the first German professor*: "Bir Ecnebi Profesör İlk Defa Türkçe Ders Verdi," *Cumhuriyet*, Nov. 23, 1933. *Albert Einstein might have been part*: Shaw, *Turkey and the Holocaust*, 5–8. For an exhaustive study of German academics and refugees, see Reisman, *Turkey's Modernization*.

297   *Many of these expatriates*: "The German N.S.D.A.P. Organization in Turkey," Feb. 5, 1943, p. 1, NARA, RG226, Entry 106, Box 36. *On Sundays, local Germans*: Memorandum from Betty Carp, Mar. 3, 1942, p. 1, NARA, RG226, Entry 106, Box 35. *Many of the senior officers*: "The German N.S.D.A.P. Organization in Turkey," Feb. 5, 1943, pp. 1–3. *The Tokatlian Hotel*: "List of German and Pro-German Firms in Istanbul, Turkey," Feb. 15, 1943, p. 1, NARA, RG226, Entry 106, Box 36. *With the boycott*: Bali, *Bir Türkleştirme Serüveni*, 316–20.

298   *Moreover, the presence of White Russians*: "A History of X-2 in Turkey from Its Inception to 31 August 1944," p. 1, NARA, RG226, Entry 210, Box 58, File 5. *By one count, seventeen*: Rubin, *Istanbul Intrigues*, 5.

299   *Rendel's daughter, Anne*: Rendel, *The Sword and the Olive*, 181. *Two German security officers*: Rendel, *The Sword and the Olive*, 186. *Farewells were toasted*: Rendel, *The Sword and the Olive*, 187. *"My impression was strengthened"*: Rendel, *The Sword and the Olive*, 188.

300   *A flash of light*: My account of the Pera Palace explosion is based on

memoranda, photographs, witness reports, and letters in NAUK, FO 198/106, 198/107, 371/29748, 371/29749, 371/29751, 371/37529, 371/48154, 781/57, 950/10, 960/139, and 950/631; and Rendel, *The Sword and the Olive*, chapter 16.

302   *The bag contained a fuse*: Knatchbull-Hugessen to London, Mar. 12, 1941, NAUK, FO 371/29748, ff. 143–44. *Bulgarian agents*: "Background Paper on the 'Pera Palace' Explosion of March 11, 1941, and Claims Arising Therefrom," n.d., NAUK, FO 950/631. *"Having come to the conclusion"*: Istanbul Assistant Public Prosecutor, "Copy of Decision," Apr. 10, 1941, p. 4, NAUK, FO 371/37529. *The British government eventually paid*: "Pera Palace Claimants," n.d., NAUK, FO 950/10; and Knatchbull-Hugessen to Foreign Office, Mar. 13, 1941, NAUK, FO 371/29749, f. 17.

303   *Istanbul was on the front line*: "Tehlike Kapımızı Çalarsa," *Cumhuriyet*, Mar. 31, 1941. *Trees, sidewalks, and electric poles*: "Seyrüsefer Tedbirleri," *Cumhuriyet*, Nov. 28, 1940. *During the drills*: "Bugün Dikkatli Olunuz!" *Cumhuriyet*, Jan. 20, 1941. *To conserve fuel*: "Balkan Intelligence Center Report," Nov. 1940, NAUK, WO 208/72B.

305   *The sexual peccadilloes of diplomats*: Woods, *Spunyarn*, 2:111. *In those days, Muslims seen conversing*: Herbert, *Ben Kendim*, 37. *"Istanbul has many people"*: Boyd to Donovan, Sept. 25, 1944, p. 3, NARA, RG226, Entry 210, Box 58, File 4. *The Emniyet regularly supplied*: "A History of X-2 in Turkey," p. 10, and Lt. Col. John H. Maxson, "Report on Organization and Operation of X-2, Turkey, 1944," p. 16, NARA, RG226, Entry 210, Box 58, File 5.

306   *When a newcomer arrived*: Kollek, *For Jerusalem*, 42–43. *In February 1943*: On the details surrounding the return, see Olson, "Remains of Talat."

307   *British intelligence services*: See "Istanbul Office—History," Mar. 15, 1945, NAUK, HS 7/86.

308   *He had been recruited into the service*: Boyd to Donovan, Sept. 15, 1944, p. 2, NARA, RG226, Entry 210, Box 58, File 4. *A detailed history of this silent war*: See expense vouchers in NARA, RG226, Entry 199, File 1193. *If an agent needed a hernia belt*: Receipt from Ucuz Çanta Pazarı, Dec. 31, 1943, NARA, RG226, Entry 109, Box 187,

File 1208. *"Espionage directed against other countries"*: "A History of X-2 in Turkey," p. 2.

309 *The money he carried*: Maxson, "Report on Organization and Operation of X-2," p. 4. *He was given an office*: "A History of X-2 in Turkey," p. 3. *Professors, receptionists, and the registrar*: "A History of X-2 in Turkey," p. 3.

310 *There she had regularly invited*: Carp to Dulles, Mar. 13, 1942, NARA, RG226, Entry 106, Location 190/6/4/03. Carp and Allen Dulles had known one another since Dulles's brief period at the American Embassy in Istanbul during the Allied occupation. He remained one of her principal contacts in the OSS during the war and eventually became the first civilian head of the OSS's successor, the CIA. *"Mr. Thomas Whittemore"*: Carp to Gurfein, Jan. 12, 1943, NARA, RG226, Entry 106, Location 190/6/4/03. *"They are everywhere"*: Wickham to Donovan, Aug. 11, 1944, p. 11, NARA, RG226, Entry 210, Box 194, File 9. *Within only a few months*: "A History of X-2 in Turkey," p. 3. *In particular, the Abwehr*: "A History of X-2 in Turkey," p. 11.

311 *Americans seemed especially willing*: "A History of X-2 in Turkey," p. 11. *Tongues loosened by alcohol*: Maxson, "Report on Organization and Operation of X-2," p. 22. *Its words were mimeographed . . . it became such a fashionable tune*: "Addenda, History—Security Branch—OSS Istanbul," May 1943–Sept. 1, 1944, p. 1, NARA, RG226, Entry 210, Box 185, File 9; and "History—Security Branch—OSS Istanbul," May 1943–Sept. 1, 1944, p. 3, NARA, RG226, Entry 210, Box 185, File 12. *"I'm involved in a dangerous game"*: "History—Security Branch—OSS Istanbul," May 1943–Sept. 1, 1944, Appendix C, p. 2, NARA, RG226, Entry 210, Box 185, File 12.

312 *Most of the Dogwood reports had been*: Wickham to Donovan, Aug. 11, 1944, p. 4. *The Turks' only complaint about him*: Massigli, *La Turquie devant la guerre*, 133.

313 *"You see, I hate the British"*: Quoted in Moysich, *Operation Cicero*, 31. *The considerable sums of money*: Rubin, *Istanbul Intrigues*, 247.

314 *Even at Turkey's Republic Day celebrations*: Rubin, *Istanbul Intrigues*, 4. *Teddy Kollek, an Austrian citizen by birth*: Kollek, *For Jerusalem*, 43.

PAPER TRAILS

317   *He cabled Winston Churchill*: Muhayyeş to Churchill, n.d., NAUK,
       FO 371/29751, f. 18. *He was eventually awarded*: "Bombed British
       Officials Must Pay, Turks Decide," *New York Times*, Apr. 24, 1947. *In
       1935, a prominent Turkish diplomat*: "Col. Aziz Bey a Suicide," *New
       York Times*, Oct. 1, 1935. *In 1939, a Yemeni man*: "50 Kuruşla Perapa-
       las'ta Üç Ay Yaşayan Adam!" *Cumhuriyet*, Oct. 13, 1939.

318   *Located not far from Taksim Square*: Mansel, *Constantinople*, 419. *In the
       restaurant, the Japanese held court*: Hirschmann, *Life Line to a Promised
       Land*, 136.

319   *Before he retired to dinner*: Hirschmann, *Life Line to a Promised Land*, 136.

320   *Pushed along by the south-flowing*: The most thorough account of the
       Struma affair is Frantz and Collins, *Death on the Black Sea*, on which I
       have based some of the details in my own retelling. The book contains
       a very fine essay by Samuel Aroni that tries to reconstruct the passen-
       ger manifest, a much more difficult task than it might seem.

321   *Sympathetic humanitarians could occasionally pass*: Goldin to Jewish
       Agency, Feb. 26, 1942, JAP-IDI, Reel 72. *On January 2, 1942, six
       men*: Ludovic, et al., to Director of the Port Police, Istanbul, Jan. 2,
       1942, JAP-IDI, Reel 72.

322   *The* Struma *was to be towed*: Goldin to Jewish Agency, Feb. 26, 1942.
       There is some debate about whether the *Struma* even had an engine at
       this point, since the motor had earlier been removed for repair and may
       never have been returned to the ship before the towing order was put
       into effect. *"Save us!"*: Hirschmann, *Life Line to a Promised Land*, 5.

323   *"Struma wrecked blacksea"*: Goldin to Jewish Agency, Feb. 25, 1942,
       JAP-IDI, Reel 72. *He first included the names*: "Survivors," Mar. 8,
       1942, JAP-IDI, Reel 72. *Only nine passengers*: Frantz and Collins,
       Death on the Black Sea, 335. *It turned out to be the handiwork*: Sudo-
       platov, *Special Tasks*, 35; Rubin, *Istanbul Intrigues*, 13–14.

324   *The authorities had done everything possible*: "Die Juden der 'Struma,'
       die England nicht nach Palästina liess," *Türkische Post*, Apr. 21, 1942.
       Saydam followed up by dismissing: Guttstadt, *Turkey, the Jews, and the
       Holocaust*, 117. In fact, the Turkish agency reported not on the sinking

but on the day of mourning held in Palestine for the *Struma* victims. I thank Corry Guttstadt for pointing out the difference.

325 *"It was an avalanche"*: Hirschmann, *Life Line to a Promised Land*, 17. *Identified as an up-and-comer*: See Hirschmann, *Caution to the Winds*.

326 *After reading about the disaster*: Hirschmann, *Caution to the Winds*, 127.

327 *"The president has just signed"*: Quoted in Hirschmann, *Life Line to a Promised Land*, 19. *After five days en route*: Hirschmann, *Life Line to a Promised Land*, 22. *"An old world seems slipping away"*: Hirschmann diary entry, n.d. [Feb. 1944], p. 2, Hirschmann Papers, FDR, Box 1, Folder "Portions of Ira Hirschmann's Diary, Feb.–Oct. 1944," Part 1.

328 *Support was to be provided*: Hirschmann, *Life Line to a Promised Land*, 23–24. *Americans were a people with a conscience*: Hirschmann, *Life Line to a Promised Land*, 26. *He began to feel*: Hirschmann, *Life Line to a Promised Land*, 33.

331 *That satisfied the police*: Kollek, *For Jerusalem*, 43–44.

332 *Jews quickly found themselves trapped*: Hirschmann, "Palestine as a Refuge from Fascism," *Survey Graphic* (May 1945): 195. *The regulations were so strictly enforced*: Memorandum from G. V. Allen, Division of Near Eastern Affairs, US Department of State, Dec. 1, 1941, Shaw Collection, USHMM, File 2, pp. 1–3. Since my research was conducted, the Shaw Collection files have been rearranged, with a new finding aid available from USHMM.

333 *But while these examples*: Guttstadt, *Turkey, the Jews, and the Holocaust*, 296–98. *In November 1942, the government enacted*: Translation of "Law Concerning the Tax on Wealth," p. 1, Nov. 11, 1942, RG59, M1242, Reel 31. *Some 114,368 individuals and businesses*: "The Capital Levy: A Key to the Understanding of Current Trends in Turkey," p. 6, May 3, 1944, NARA, RG59, M1242, Reel 31. *"This law is also a law of revolution"*: Quoted in Bali, *"Varlık Vergisi" Affair*, 55. *According to a secret report*: "The Capital Levy," p. 3. Muslims believed to have Jewish ancestry—the so-called *dönme*, descendants of a Jewish sect whose members converted to Islam in the seventeenth century—were given impossibly high assessments as well. *Many of the most successful businesses*: Akçura, *Gramofon Çağı*, 30.

334   *It was all a shameful episode*: Ökte, *Tragedy of the Turkish Capital Tax*,
      14. *The men of the household*: Murray to Welles, Mar. 13, 1943, pp.
      1–2, NARA, RG59, M1224, Reel 31. *In the end, more than a thou-
      sand*: Ökte, *Tragedy of the Turkish Capital Tax*, 73–74. *Their personal
      belongings were sold*: Guttstadt, *Turkey, the Jews, and the Holocaust*,
      72–81. *Greeks, Armenians, and Jews owned*: Ayhan Aktar, "'Tax Me
      to the End of My Life!': Anatomy of an Anti-Minority Tax Legis-
      lation (1942–3)," in Fortna et al., eds., *State-Nationalisms in the
      Ottoman Empire, Germany, and Turkey*, 211–12. *"According to the
      best-informed"*: Istanbul to State, Dec. 8, 1942, p. 1, NARA, RG59,
      M1224, Reel 31.

335   *But because of rationing*: Goldin to Jewish Agency, Nov. 17, 1943, JAP-
      IDI, Reel 48. *The response was to accede*: See Chaim Barlas, "Report on
      Immigration," Dec. 15, 1943, JAP-IDI, Reel 1. *Moreover, the Turkish
      government*: "History of the War Refugee Board," Vol. 1, p. 14, WRB,
      Folder 17. *At that rate, Ira Hirschmann later reckoned*: Hirschmann, *Life
      Line to a Promised Land*, 32. *The plan went into effect*: Barlas, "Report
      on Immigration," p.1. *By December 1943, Barlas had already compiled*:
      Barlas, "Report on Immigration," p. 1.

336   *Small numbers of refugees had also arrived*: Barlas, "Report on Immi-
      gration," p. 1. *In December, Barlas wrote to Ambassador Steinhardt*: Bar-
      las, "Report on Immigration," p. 2. *In fact, nearly twice as many*: Barlas,
      "Report on Immigration," p. 2. See also Resnik to Hirschmann, July 3,
      1944, JOINT, Reel 108.

337   *The War Refugee Board persuaded*: "History of the War Refugee Board,"
      Vol. 1, p. 15. *Other funds*: "History of the War Refugee Board," Vol.
      1, p. 15. *Further Joint-funded programs*: Resnik to Hirschmann, July
      7, 1944, JOINT, Reel 108; and "Report on Activities from February
      1944 to March 21, 1944," JOINT, Reel 111. *Hirschmann was also in
      regular contact*: Macfarland to Donovan, Aug. 11, 1944, p. 3, NARA,
      RG226, Entry 210, Box 194, File 9.

338   *Now, at last, he felt*: Barlas to Hirschmann, Mar. 23, 1944, JAP-IDI,
      Reel 1. *In the summer of 1938*: Guttstadt, *Turkey, the Jews, and the
      Holocaust*, 132–33. *But the devil*: Hirschmann, *Life Line to a Promised
      Land*, 40–45.

339   *"Send certificates"*: Moshe Slowes to Abraham Slowes, Mar. 12, 1941, Slowes Collection, USHMM.

340   *"I venture to hope"*: Abraham Slowes to Swedish Consul, Jerusalem, Aug. 18, 1943, Slowes Collection, USHMM.

341   *"With reference to your letter"*: British Embassy, Moscow, to Abraham Slowes, Nov. 10, 1944, Slowes Collection, USHMM. *A follow-up note*: T. C. Sharman to Abraham Slowes, Apr. 5, 1945, Slowes Collection, USHMM. Slowes's mother and six other family members are believed to have been killed at Ponary, an infamous mass-execution site in the suburbs of Vilnius, Lithuania, in late 1941 or 1942. His father probably perished in a Nazi labor camp in Estonia. The only immediate family member to survive was an older brother, Salomon, who had the perverse good fortune of having been taken prisoner by the Soviets in 1939, which meant that he escaped almost certain death when Germany invaded in 1941. Salomon later joined Polish volunteers fighting alongside Allied forces in Iraq, Palestine, North Africa, and Italy, and settled after the war in Tel Aviv.

AT THE GATE OF FELICITY

345   *"It would appear from the telegrams"*: Steinhardt to Secretary of State, Mar. 3, 1944, p. 4, Hirschmann Papers, FDR, Box 1, Folder "Dispatches from U.S. Embassy, Ankara, to War Refugee Board, 2/8/44–6/2/44."

346   *At a minimum, getting out of Romania required*: Application materials of Marcel Leibovici, Romanian General Directorate of Passports Office Records, 1939–1944, USHMM, Reel 3.

347   *The form required that the applicant*: Application materials of Linder Maier, Romanian General Directorate of Passports Office Records, 1939–1944, USHMM, Reel 3. *The* Struma *affair had made the government*: Steinhardt to Resnik, June 15, 1944, JOINT, Reel 104.

348   *Even as seemingly simple a matter*: Steinhardt to Resnik, June 8, 1944, JOINT, Reel 104. *And since some of them were expressly involved*: Steinhardt to Barlas, June 5, 1944, JAP-IDI, Reel 1. See also Steinhardt to Pehle, May 18, 1944, and Steinhardt to War Refugee Board, June 1,

1944, Hirschmann Papers, FDR, Box 1, Folder "Dispatches from U.S. Embassy, Ankara, to War Refugee Board, 2/8/44–6/2/44." *Earlier that spring, Foreign Minister*: Steinhardt to Barlas, Apr. 3, 1944, Shaw Collection, USHMM, File 3.

349   *For that reason, Barlas*: Kollek, *For Jerusalem*, 44. *The old tombstones were rearranged*: Harington, *Tim Harington Looks Back*, 137.

350   *They were "a strange community"*: Nicolson, *Sweet Waters*, 23. *The Levantines were*: Mufty-zada, *Speaking of the Turks*, 146–47. *There were fewer than 23,000*: Ives to Secretary of State, Nov. 14, 1928, pp. 7, 10, NARA, RG59, M353, Reel 57. "Levantine" was not a category used on Turkish censuses, so the figure presumably comes from an American diplomat's use of the term to describe local Catholics in general.

352   *On February 12, 1943*: Peter Hoffmann puts the first meeting on January 20, 1943, but this is an inference based on materials that Barlas passed along to the apostolic delegate, rather than on a record of the meeting itself. Given the telegram from Jerusalem on February 12, it seems more likely that Barlas had not yet visited the cathedral when the telegram was received. But at least by May, Barlas and Roncalli had established a regular series of meetings. Hoffmann, "Roncalli in the Second World War," 83; Barlas to Roncalli, May 22, 1943, JAP-IDI, Reel 1. *"He explained that when talking"*: Tittmann, *Inside the Vatican of Pius XII*, 124.

354   *He began learning Turkish*: John XXIII, *Journal of a Soul*, 233. *"My work in Turkey is not easy"*: John XXIII, *Journal of a Soul*, 234–35. *The Turkish government had extended*: Massigli, *La Turquie devant la guerre*, 98. *In 1939, when Roncalli contacted*: Righi, *Papa Giovanni XXIII sulle rive del Bosforo*, 194.

355   *In Roncalli's case*: Massigli, *La Turquie devant la guerre*, 98. *"Have seen today his eminence"*: Barlas to Herzog, June 12, 1943, JAP-IDI, Reel 1. *On multiple occasions, he asked Barlas*: Roncalli to Weltmann, July 31, 1943; Weltmann to Roncalli, July 31, 1943; Barlas to Goldin, Aug. 10, 1943; Barlas to Roncalli, Aug. 10, 1943; Barlas to Roncalli, Aug. 12, 1943; Barlas to Roncalli, Mar. 27, 1944; Barlas to Roncalli, June 6, 1944, JAP-IDI, Reel 1. *In November the chief rabbi*: Herzog to Roncalli, Nov. 22, 1943, JAP-IDI, Reel 1.

357 *He was sometimes called*: Friling, "Nazi-Jewish Negotiations," 405. *"We are in the fifth year"*: Quoted in Barlas, *Hatsalah*, 114. *A limited number of Jews*: Steinhardt to War Refugee Board, May 25, 1944, Hirschmann Papers, FDR, Box 1, Folder "Dispatches from U.S. Embassy, Ankara, to War Refugee Board, 2/8/44–6/2/44."

358 *Through his channels of communication*: Schwartz to War Refugee Board, July 20, 1944, JOINT, Reel 108.

359 *Others took to copying down*: Guttstadt, *Turkey, the Jews, and the Holocaust*, 127. *On June 5, Roncalli wrote to Barlas*: Roncalli to Barlas, June 5, 1944, JAP-IDI, Reel 1. *"Thanks to these documents"*: Barlas to Roncalli, June 6, 1944, JAP-IDI, Reel 1. *Roncalli forwarded the report*: Cornwell, *Hitler's Pope*, 324–26. *Later, the papal nuncio*: Phayer, *Catholic Church and the Holocaust*, 50. *"He has helped the Jews"*: Quoted in Hoffmann, "Roncalli in the Second World War," 90.

360 *"We are called to live"*: Quoted in Righi, *Papa Giovanni XXIII sulle rive del Bosforo*, 261. *The ship was rated for only three hundred*: Hirschmann, *Life Line to a Promised Land*, 87.

361 *As with all transports, the Joint had provided*: Barlas to Hirschmann, Aug. 24, 1944, JAP-IDI, Reel 1. *She had been this way*: Hirschmann, *Life Line to a Promised Land*, 88. *"As expected, it was very bad"*: Frankfort to Goldin, July 10, 1944, JAP-IDI, Reel 1. *The world, he said*: Hirschmann, *Life Line to a Promised Land*, 87–89.

362 *Around 12:30 a.m.*: On the matter of Soviet responsibility, see Ofer, *Escaping the Holocaust*, 195–98. *A few dozen passengers*: "Report on the Sinking of the m/v 'Mefkure,'" Sept. 9, 1944, JAP-IDI, Reel 173.

363 *Turkish authorities had ordered*: Hirschmann, *Life Line to a Promised Land*, 142. *At the Park Hotel, the Germans ate*: Hirschmann, *Life Line to a Promised Land*, 142. *Rooms were going for half price*: Hirschmann, *Life Line to a Promised Land*, 144. *Franz von Papen, the German ambassador*: Hirschmann, *Life Line to a Promised Land*, 145. *These ships carried*: "Boats," JAP-IDI, Reel 122. *In all, from 1942 to 1945*: "Summary of Immigrants from 1942 to the End of 1945," JAP-IDI, Reel 122. *In the end, more than a quarter*: Ofer, *Escaping the Holocaust*, 318.

364 *"The results of the immigration in numbers"*: Chaim Barlas, "Report on

Immigration," Dec. 15, 1943, p. 2, JAP-IDI, Reel 1. *Of the people who departed*: "Summary of Immigrants."

365 *The first violinist*: Hirschmann, *Life Line to a Promised Land*, 147. I thank Corry Guttstadt for discovering the violinist's name.

EPILOGUE

370 *Early the next morning*: "Perapalas Otelinin Sahibi Odasında Ölü Bulundu," *Milliyet*, Oct. 13, 1954. *"Now that my cat is dead"*: Quoted in "Millionaire, Broken Over Dead Cat, Dies," *Baltimore Sun*, Oct. 14, 1954. *He had turned over the hotel*: "Misbah Muhayyeşin Mirası Tesbit Ediliyor," *Milliyet*, Oct. 15, 1954; "Misbah Muhayyeşin Vârisleri Çoğalıyor," *Milliyet*, Oct. 19, 1954.

371 *Landholdings that party leaders had acquired*: Zürcher, *Turkey: A Modern History*, 233.

372 *At least eleven people*: Güven, *6–7 Eylül Olayları*, 40, 181. The number of deaths and level of property damage remain controversial. For higher figures, see Vryonis, *Mechanism of Catastrophe*, 549.

373 *One who actually did was the poet Joseph Brodsky*: "Flight from Byzantium," in Brodsky, *Less Than One*, 396–97.

377 *It does not take too much effort*: My reconstruction of the last moments before the explosion relies on: "Pera Palace Claimants," NAUK, FO 950/10; De Téhige to Ambassador, Apr. 21, 1941, NAUK, FO 198/106; "Pera Palas Bomb Outrage," Apr. 2, 1941, NAUK, FO 198/106; Vardarsu to British Embassy, Apr. 20, 1941, NAUK, FO 198/106; and a list of victims and compensation from the Turkish Ministry of Foreign Affairs, Nov. 13, 1941, in NAUK, FO 198/107.

GLOSSARY

Alevis	community of Muslims whose beliefs combine elements of Shi'a Islam and Sufi traditions
aliyah bet	illegal Jewish immigration to Mandate-era Palestine
bey	gentleman; man of rank
caique	narrow, oared boat used on the Bosphorus and Golden Horn
caliph	supreme spiritual leader in Islam; title claimed by Ottoman sultans until the caliphate's abolition in 1924
çarşaf	Islamic female covering, typically black and draping the entire body
cherkeska	long tunic with small ammunition-holders on the chest worn by men from the Caucasus
Circassians	cultural group with ties to the historic region of Circassia in the northwest Caucasus in modern-day Russia
dervish	adherent of a Sufi religious order
Emniyet	Turkish secret police
esnaf	guild of tradesmen or artisans
ezan	Islamic call to prayer
gazi	conqueror or hero in Islamic warfare

hamal	porter
han	hostel or boardinghouse, typically for traveling traders
hanım	lady; woman of rank
harem	household; wives and concubines of the sultan or other Ottoman men of rank
haremlik; Harem	private portion of a traditional household reserved for family use
imam	leader in Islamic worship
inkılâp	revolution
janissaries	elite infantry of the Ottoman Empire before the 1820s
lâiklik	secularism; state management of religious institutions
Karagöz	traditional entertainment featuring semitransparent puppets on a backlit screen
Kemalism	political ideology of modernity and secularism associated with Mustafa Kemal Atatürk
Ladino	language of Sephardic Jews, based on Spanish and written in either Hebrew or Latin script; also called Judeo-Spanish
mahalle	neighborhood
meyhane	restaurant typically serving wine, raki, and small plates of food
millet	Ottoman legal category defined by membership in a religious community (e.g., Muslims, Orthodox Christians, Armenian Apostolic Christians, Jews)
millet system	religious self-government in the Ottoman Empire, based on quasi autonomy of *millets*
muezzin	cantor who delivers the Islamic call to prayer

muhacirs	Muslim refugees, especially from the Balkans and the Caucasus
OGPU	Stalinist secret police and predecessor of KGB
OSS	Office of Strategic Services; American intelligence organization and predecessor of CIA
oud	musical instrument resembling a Western lute
pasha	military general or high-ranking official
patriarch	supreme leader of an independent Orthodox Christian church
raki	anise-flavored liqueur
rebetiko	urban folk music associated with Greeks originally from Smyrna and Istanbul (also spelled *rembetiko*)
selâmlık	public portion of a traditional household used for business or receiving guests; also, the sultan's public procession to Friday prayers
Sephardim	Jews from the Iberian Peninsula who immigrated to the Ottoman Empire in the fifteenth century
şeyhülislam	chief Islamic cleric
sharia	Islamic canon law
sheikh	Islamic religious leader or saint, especially in Sufi orders
Shi'a	community of Muslims who recognize the spiritual successors to the Prophet Muhammad through Ali, his son-in-law
SOE	Special Operations Executive; British intelligence service
Sufi	general term for a number of ecstatic or mystical religious orders in Islam, typically associated with a founding sage

sultan	ruler of the Ottoman Empire
Sunni	community of Muslims who recognize the spiritual successors to the Prophet Muhammad through a line of caliphs
sürgün	forced resettlement
Tanzimat	period of centralization, reform, and modernization in the Ottoman Empire, 1839–1876
tekke	Sufi lodge or meeting house
tulumbacı	foot-borne fireman
türbe	mausoleum, especially of an Islamic sage or holy person
Unionists	members of the Committee of Union and Progress, the makers of the 1908 revolution; also known as Young Turks
wagon-lit	sleeping carriage on a train
yalı	house near the water on the Bosphorus, typically made from ornately mitered wood
yishuv	Jewish community in Mandate-era Palestine
Young Turks	*see* Unionists

BIBLIOGRAPHY

ARCHIVES AND SPECIAL COLLECTIONS

Bakhmeteff Archive, Rare Book and Manuscript Library, Columbia University, New York
  Adam P. and Feofaniia V. Benningsen Papers
  Mitrofan Ivanovich Boiarintsev Papers
  Committee for the Education of Russian Youth in Exile Records
  Aleksandr Pavlovich Kutepov Papers
  Georgii Aleksandrovich Orlov Papers
  Russkii Obshche-Voinskii Soiuz (Russian Universal Military Union) Papers
Dumbarton Oaks Research Library and Collection, Image Collections and Fieldwork Archives, Washington, DC
  Byzantine Institute and Dumbarton Oaks Fieldwork Records and Papers
  Thomas Whittemore Papers
  Robert L. Van Nice Records and Fieldwork Papers
Georgetown University Library, Special Collections Research Center, Washington, DC
  Cornelius Van H. Engert Papers
Hoover Institution Archives, Palo Alto, California
  Dmitri Shalikashvili Papers
Houghton Library, Harvard University, Cambridge, Massacussetts
  Leon Trotsky Exile Papers
Imperial War Museum Archives, London

Wing Commander D. L. Allen Papers

Charles Bambury Photograph Collection

Major T. B. Bardo Papers

C. J. Brunell Photograph Collection

G. Calverley Papers

Lieutenant M. M. Carus Wilson Papers

Letters of Brigadier General W. B. Emery

Major General W. A. F. L. Fox-Pitt Papers

Lieutenant C. H. Garner Papers

J. A. Graham Photograph Collection

Greco-Turkish War Intelligence Reports, 1922–1923

Major A. McPherson Papers

Air Marshal S. C. Strafford Papers

F. W. Turpin Papers

C. Vinicombe Papers

Commander O. F. M. Wethered Papers

Istanbul Research Institute, Istanbul

Photograph and Map Collection

Library of Congress, Washington, DC

Mark Lambert Bristol Papers, Manuscript Reading Room

Frank and Frances Carpenter Collection, Prints and Photographs Division

National Archives and Records Administration, College Park, Maryland

State Department Records

Office of Strategic Services Archives

National Archives of the United Kingdom, Kew

Cabinet Office Records

Foreign Office Records

Special Operations Executive Records

War Office Records

Franklin Delano Roosevelt Presidential Library, Hyde Park, New York

Oscar Cox Papers

Ira Hirschmann Papers

United States Holocaust Memorial Museum Archives and Library, Washington, DC

Abraham and Simone Slowes Collection

Jewish Agency for Palestine Records, Immigration Department,
Office in Istanbul

Papers of the War Refugee Board

Romanian General Directorate of Passports Office Records,
1939–1944

Selected Records from the American Jewish Joint Distribution
Committee, 1937–1966

Selected Records from the Ghetto Fighters' House, 1920–1950

Selected Records from Romanian Diplomatic Missions, 1920–1950

Stanford Shaw Collection

Ellen T. Meth Collection, Wang Family Papers

Wiener Library Thematic Press Cuttings

Yapı Kredi Bank, Istanbul

Selahattin Giz Collection

NEWSPAPERS AND PERIODICALS

Baltimore Sun

Boston Globe

Le Courrier de Turquie (Istanbul)

Cumhuriyet (Istanbul)

L'Entente (Istanbul)

Journal de la Chambre de commerce et d'industrie de Constantinople (Istanbul)

Le Journal d'Orient (Istanbul)

Le Moniteur oriental (Istanbul)

Milliyet (Istanbul)

New York Times

Orient News (Istanbul)

Stamboul (Istanbul)

Tarih ve Toplum (Istanbul)

Toplumsal Tarih (Istanbul)

Times (London)

Türkische Post (Istanbul)

Vecherniaia pressa (Istanbul)

BOOKS, ARTICLES, AND OTHER SOURCES

Abravanel, Jacques. *Mémoires posthumes et inachevées de Jacques Abravanel, juif portugais, salonicien de naissance, stambouliote d'adoption*. Istanbul: Isis, 1999.

Adil, Fikret. *Asmalımescit 74: Bohem Hayatı*. Istanbul: İletişim, 1988.

———. *Gardenbar Geceleri*. Istanbul: İletişim, 1990.

Agabekov, Georges [Georgy]. *OGPU: The Russian Secret Terror*. New York: Brentano's, 1931.

Ahmad, Feroz. *The Making of Modern Turkey*. London: Routledge, 1993.

Ahrweiler, Hélène. *Byzance et la mer: La marine de guerre, la politique, et les institutions maritimes de Byzance aux VIIe–XVe siècles*. Paris: Presses universitaires de France, 1966.

Ahrweiler, Hélène, and Angeliki E. Laiou, eds. *Studies on the Internal Diaspora of the Byzantine Empire*. Washington, DC: Dumbarton Oaks Research Library and Collection, 1998.

Akçam, Taner. *From Empire to Republic: Turkish Nationalism and the Armenian Genocide*. New York: Zed Books, 2004.

———. *A Shameful Act: The Armenian Genocide and the Question of Turkish Responsibility*. New York: Metropolitan Books, 2006.

———. *The Young Turks' Crimes Against Humanity: The Armenian Genocide and Ethnic Cleansing in the Ottoman Empire*. Princeton, NJ: Princeton University Press, 2012.

Akçam, Taner, and Ümit Kurt. *Kanunların Ruhu: Emval-i Metruke Kanunlarında Soykırımın İzini Sürmek*. Istanbul: İletişim, 2012.

Akçura, Gökhan. *Gramofon Çağı*. Istanbul: OM, 2002.

———. *İstanbul Twist*. Istanbul: Everest, 2006.

Akgüngör, Sedef, Ceyhan Aldemir, Yeşim Kuştepeli, Yaprak Gülcan, and Vahap Tecim. "The Effect of Railway Expansion on Population in Turkey, 1856–2000." *Journal of Interdisciplinary History* 42, no. 1 (Summer 2011): 135–57.

Akhmedov, Ismail. *In and Out of Stalin's GRU*. Frederick, MD: University Publications of America, 1984.

Aksakal, Mustafa. *The Ottoman Road to War in 1914: The Ottoman Empire and the First World War*. Cambridge: Cambridge University Press, 2008.

Alexandris, Alexis. *The Greek Minority of Istanbul and Greek-Turkish Relations, 1918–1974*. Athens: Center for Asia Minor Studies, 1983.

Alexandrov, Vladimir. *The Black Russian*. New York: Atlantic Monthly Press, 2013.

Allen, Henry Elisha. *The Turkish Transformation*. Chicago: University of Chicago Press, 1935.

Andrew, Christopher, and Vasili Mitrokhin. *The Sword and the Shield: The Mitrokhin Archive and the Secret History of the KGB*. New York: Basic Books, 1999.

Andreyev, Catherine, and Ivan Savický. *Russia Abroad: Prague and the Russian Diaspora, 1918–1938*. New Haven, CT: Yale University Press, 2004.

Arslan, Savaş. *Cinema in Turkey: A New Critical History*. Oxford: Oxford University Press, 2011.

Atabaki, Touraj, and Gavin D. Brockett, eds. *Ottoman and Republican Turkish Labour History*. Cambridge: Cambridge University Press and Internationaal Instituut voor Sociale Geschiedenis, 2009.

Aurenche, Henri. *La mort de Stamboul*. Paris: J. Peyronnet, 1930.

Avriel, Ehud. *Open the Gates!* London: Weidenfeld and Nicolson, 1975.

Azak, Umut. "Secularism in Turkey as a Nationalist Search for Vernacular Islam." *Revue des mondes musulmans et de la Méditerranée* 124 (Nov. 2008): 161–79.

Balakian, Grigoris. *Armenian Golgotha: A Memoir of the Armenian Genocide, 1915–1918*. New York: Alfred A. Knopf, 2009.

Balard, Michel. *La Romanie génoise (XIIe–début du XVe siècle)*. 2 vols. Rome: Ecole Française de Rome, 1978.

Bali, Rıfat N. *1934 Trakya Olayları*. Istanbul: Libra, 2008.

———. *American Diplomats in Turkey: Oral History Transcripts (1928–1997)*. Istanbul: Libra, 2011.

———. *Bir Türkleştirme Serüveni (1923–1945): Cumhuriyet Yıllarında Türkiye Yahudileri*. Istanbul: İletişim, 1999.

———. *The First Ten Years of the Turkish Republic Thru the Reports of American Diplomats*. Istanbul: Isis, 2009.

———. *The Jews and Prostitution in Constantinople, 1854–1922*. Istanbul: Isis, 2008.

———. *Portraits from a Bygone Istanbul: Georg Mayer and Simon Brod*. Istanbul: Libra, 2010.

————. *Les relations entre turcs et juifs dans la Turquie moderne*. Istanbul: Isis, 2001.

————. *The Turkish Cinema in the Early Republican Years*. Istanbul: Isis, 2007.

————. *The "Varlık Vergisi" Affair: A Study of Its Legacy*. Istanbul: Isis, 2005.

Balkanstaaten und Konstantinopel (Meyers Reisebücher). Leipzig: Bibliographisches Institut, 1914.

Bankier, David, ed. *Secret Intelligence and the Holocaust*. New York and Jerusalem: Enigma Books and Yad Vashem, 2006.

Barlas, Chaim. *Hatsalah bi-yeme sho'ah*. Lohame ha-geta'ot: Bet Lohame ha-geta'ot, ha-Kibuts ha-Me'uhad, 1975.

Barsley, Michael. *Orient Express: The Story of the World's Most Fabulous Train*. London: Macdonald, 1966.

Beevore, J. G. *SOE: Recollections and Reflections, 1940–1945*. London: Bodley Head, 1981.

Behrend, George. *Grand European Expresses: The Story of the Wagons-Lits*. London: George Allen and Unwin, Ltd., 1962.

————. *The History of the Wagons-Lits, 1875–1955*. London: Modern Transport Publishing, 1959.

Benezra, Nissim M. *Une enfance juive à Istanbul (1911–1929)*. Istanbul: Isis, 1996.

Beyoğlu in the 30's Through the Lens of Selahattin Giz. Istanbul: Çağdaş Yayıncılık/Galeri Alfa, 1991.

Bibesco, Princess G. V. [Marthe]. *The Eight Paradises*. New York: E. P. Dutton, 1923.

Blasing, Mutlu Konuk. *Nâzım Hikmet: The Life and Times of Turkey's World Poet*. New York: Persea Books, 2013.

Bloxham, Donald. *The Great Game of Genocide: Imperialism, Nationalism, and the Destruction of the Ottoman Armenians*. Oxford: Oxford University Press, 2005.

Boyar, Ebru, and Kate Fleet. *A Social History of Ottoman Istanbul*. Cambridge: Cambridge University Press, 2010.

Braham, Randolph L. *The Politics of Genocide: The Holocaust in Hungary*. 2 vols. New York: Columbia University Press, 1981.

Braude, Benjamin, and Bernard Lewis, eds. *Christians and Jews in the Ottoman Empire*. 2 vols. New York: Holmes and Meier, 1982.

Bridges, Sir Tom. *Alarms and Excursions: Reminiscences of a Soldier*. London: Longmans Green, 1938.

Brigg, E. W., and A. A. Hessenstein. *Constantinople Cameos*. Istanbul: Near East Advertising Co., 1921.

Brockett, Gavin D. "Collective Action and the Turkish Revolution: Towards a Framework for the Social History of the Atatürk Era." *Middle Eastern Studies* 34, no. 4 (Oct. 1998): 44–66.

———. *How Happy to Call Oneself a Turk: Provincial Newspapers and the Negotiation of a Muslim National Identity*. Austin: University of Texas Press, 2011.

———. *Towards a Social History of Modern Turkey: Essays in Theory and Practice*. Istanbul: Libra, 2011.

Brodsky, Joseph. *Less Than One*. New York: Farrar, Straus and Giroux, 1986.

Brook-Shepherd, Gordon. *The Storm Petrels: The Flight of the First Soviet Defectors*. New York: Harcourt Brace Jovanovich, 1978.

Bumgardner, Eugenia S. *Undaunted Exiles*. Staunton, VA: The McClure Company, 1925.

Busbecq, Ogier Ghiselin de. *The Turkish Letters of Ogier Ghiselin de Busbecq, Imperial Ambassador at Constantinople, 1554–1562*. Edward Seymour Forster, trans. Oxford: Clarendon Press, 1968.

Cagaptay, Soner. *Islam, Secularism, and Nationalism in Modern Turkey: Who Is a Turk?* London: Routledge, 2006.

Çelik, Zeynep. *The Remaking of Istanbul: Portrait of an Ottoman City in the Nineteenth Century*. Seattle: University of Washington Press, 1986.

Çetin, Fethiye. *My Grandmother: A Memoir*. London: Verso, 2008.

Christie, Agatha. *An Autobiography*. New York: Dodd, Mead, 1977.

———. *Come, Tell Me How You Live*. New York: Dodd, Mead, 1946.

———. *Murder on the Orient Express*. New York: Berkley Books, 2004 [1934].

Churchill, Winston. *Great Contemporaries*. London: Thornton Butterworth, 1937.

Clark, Bruce. *Twice a Stranger: The Mass Expulsions that Forged Modern Greece and Turkey*. Cambridge, MA: Harvard University Press, 2006.

Conquest, Robert. "Max Eitingon: Another View." *New York Times Book Review*, July 3, 1988.

Constantinople. Washington, DC: Bureau of Navigation, Navy Department, 1920.

Cookridge, E. H. *Orient Express: The Life and Times of the World's Most Famous Train*. New York: Random House, 1978.

Cornwell, John. *Hitler's Pope: The Secret History of Pius XII*. New York: Viking, 1999.

Criss, Nur Bilge. *Istanbul Under Allied Occupation, 1918–1923*. Leiden: Brill, 1999.

Dağdalen, İrfan, ed. *Charles Edouard Goad'ın İstanbul Sigorta Haritaları*. Istanbul: İstanbul Büyükşehir Belediyesi, Kütüphane ve Müzeler Müdürlüğü, 2007.

Dalal, Radha Jagat. "At the Crossroads of Modernity, Space, and Identity: Istanbul and the Orient Express Train." Ph.D. dissertation. University of Minnesota, 2011.

Dallin, David J. *Soviet Espionage*. New Haven: Yale University Press, 1955.

De Amicis, Edmondo. *Constantinople*. Stephen Parkin, trans. Richmond, UK: Oneworld Classics, 2010.

De Paris à Constantinople (Les Guides Bleus). Paris: Hachette, 1920.

Deal, Roger A. *Crimes of Honor, Drunken Brawls, and Murder: Violence in Istanbul under Abdülhamid II*. Istanbul: Libra, 2010.

Deleon, Jak. *Pera Palas*. Istanbul: Istanbul Otelcilik ve Turizm Ticaret, n.d.

———. *The White Russians in Istanbul*. Istanbul: Remzi Kitabevi, 1995.

Deringil, Selim. *Turkish Foreign Policy During the Second World War*. Cambridge: Cambridge University Press, 1989.

Deutscher, Isaac. *The Prophet Outcast. Trotsky: 1929–1940*. London: Oxford University Press, 1963.

Dos Passos, John. *Travel Books and Other Writings, 1916–1941*. New York: Library of America, 2003.

Doumanis, Nicholas. *Before the Nation: Muslim-Christian Coexistence and Its Destruction in Late Ottoman Anatolia*. Oxford: Oxford University Press, 2013.

Downes, Donald C. *The Scarlet Thread: Adventures in Wartime Espionage*. London: Derek Verschoyle, 1953.

Draper, Theodore H. "The Mystery of Max Eitingon." *New York Review of Books*, Apr. 14, 1988.

Duben, Alan, and Cem Behar. *Istanbul Households: Marriage, Family, and Fertility, 1880–1940*. Cambridge: Cambridge University Press, 1991.

Duke, Vernon. *Passport to Paris*. Boston: Little, Brown, 1955.

Dünden Bugüne İstanbul Ansiklopedisi. 8 vols. Istanbul: Türkiye Ekonomik ve Toplumsal Tarih Vakfı, 1994.

Dunn, Robert. *World Alive: A Personal Story*. New York: Crown, 1956.

Dwight, H. G. *Constantinople: Settings and Traits*. New York: Harper and Brothers, 1926.

Eastman, Max. *Great Companions*. New York: Farrar, Straus and Cudahy, 1959.

———. *Heroes I Have Known*. New York: Simon and Schuster, 1942.

Edib, Halidé Adivar [Halide Edip Adıvar]. *Conflict of East and West in Turkey*. Lahore, Pakistan: Shaikh Muhammad Ashraf, 1963 [1935].

———. *Memoirs of Halidé Edib*. Piscataway, NJ: Gorgias Press, 2004 [1926].

———. "Turkey and Her Allies." *Foreign Affairs* 18, no. 3 (Apr. 1940): 442–49.

———. *Turkey Faces West*. New Haven, CT: Yale University Press, 1930.

———. *The Turkish Ordeal*. New York: The Century Co., 1928.

Edmonds, James E. *The Occupation of Constantinople, 1918–1923*. Uckfield, UK: Naval and Military Press, Ltd., 2010.

Edwards, George Wharton. *Constantinople, Istamboul*. Philadelphia: Penn Publishing Company, 1930.

Eissenstat, Howard Lee. "The Limits of Imagination: Debating the Nation and Constructing the State in Early Turkish Nationalism." Ph.D. dissertation. University of California, Los Angeles, 2007.

Ekmekçioğlu, Lerna. "Improvising Turkishness: Being Armenian in Post-Ottoman Istanbul (1918–1933)." Ph.D. dissertation. New York University, 2010.

Ekrem, Selma. *Unveiled: The Autobiography of a Turkish Girl*. New York: Ives Washburn, 1930.

Eldem, Edhem. "Istanbul, 1903–1918: A Quantitative Analysis of a Bourgeoisie." *Boğaziçi Journal* 11, nos. 1–2 (1997): 53–98.

Eldem, Edhem, Daniel Goffman, and Bruce Masters. *The Ottoman City between East and West: Aleppo, Izmir, and Istanbul*. Cambridge: Cambridge University Press, 1999.

Ellison, Grace. *An Englishwoman in a Turkish Harem*. London: Methuen, 1915.

Emiroğlu, Kudret. *Gündelik Hayatımızın Tarihi*. Ankara: Dost, 2001.

Encounters at the Bosphorus: Turkey during World War II. Krzyżowa, Poland: "Krzyżowa" Foundation for Mutual Understanding in Europe, 2008.

Evliya Çelebi. *Narrative of Travels in Europe, Asia, and Africa, in the Seventeenth Century*. Joseph von Hammer, trans. 2 vols. London: Oriental Translation Fund of Great Britain and Ireland, 1834.

———. *An Ottoman Traveller: Selections from the Book of Travels of Evliya Çelebi*. Robert Dankoff and Sooyong Kim, trans. London: Eland Publishing, 2010.

Farson, Negley. *The Way of a Transgressor*. London: Victor Gollancz, 1935.

Findley, Carter Vaughn. *Turkey, Islam, Nationalism, and Modernity: A History*. New Haven, CT: Yale University Press, 2010.

Finefrock, Michael M. "Ataturk, Lloyd George and the Megali Idea: Cause and Consequence of the Greek Plan to Seize Constantinople from the Allies, June–August 1922." *Journal of Modern History* 52, no. 1 (Mar. 1980): D1047–D1066.

Fink, Anna. *Colorful Adventures in the Orient*. Austin: n.p., 1930.

Finkel, Caroline. *Osman's Dream: The Story of the Ottoman Empire, 1300–1923*. New York: Basic Books, 2005.

Fortna, Benjamin C., Stefanos Katsikis, Dimitris Kamouzis, and Paraskevas Konortas, eds. *State-Nationalisms in the Ottoman Empire, Greece, and Turkey: Orthodox and Muslims, 1830–1945*. London: Routledge, 2013.

Fortuny, Kim. *American Writers in Istanbul: Melville, Twain, Hemingway, Dos Passos, Bowles, Algren, Baldwin, Settle*. Syracuse, NY: Syracuse University Press, 2009.

Frantz, Douglas, and Catherine Collins, *Death on the Black Sea: The Untold Story of the Struma and World War II's Holocaust at Sea*. New York: Ecco, 2003.

Freely, John. *Istanbul: The Imperial City*. London: Penguin, 1996.

Friling, Tuvia. *Arrows in the Dark: David Ben-Gurion, the Yishuv Leadership, and Rescue Attempts during the Holocaust*. 2 vols. Madison: University of Wisconsin Press, 2005.

———. "Nazi-Jewish Negotiations in Istanbul in Mid-1944." *Holocaust and Genocide Studies* 13, no. 3 (Winter 1999): 405–36.

Fromkin, David. *A Peace to End All Peace: The Fall of the Ottoman Empire and the Creation of the Modern Middle East.* 2nd ed. New York: Henry Holt, 2009.

Gatrell, Peter. *A Whole Empire Walking: Refugees in Russia During World War I.* Bloomington: Indiana University Press, 1999.

Gervasi, Frank. "Devil Man." *Collier's,* June 8, 1940: 17, 49.

Gibbon, Edward. *The Decline and Fall of the Roman Empire.* 6 vols. London: Dent, 1962.

Gilles, Pierre. *The Antiquities of Constantinople.* John Bell, trans. Ronald G. Musto, ed. 2nd ed. New York: Italica Press, 1988.

Gingeras, Ryan. "Last Rites for a 'Pure Bandit': Clandestine Service, Historiography, and the Origins of the Turkish 'Deep State.'" *Past and Present* 206, no. 1 (2010): 151–74.

———. *Sorrowful Shores: Violence, Ethnicity, and the End of the Ottoman Empire, 1912–1923.* Oxford: Oxford University Press, 2009.

Göçek, Fatma Müge. *The Transformation of Turkey: Redefining State and Society from the Ottoman Empire to the Modern Era.* London: I. B. Tauris, 2011.

Goebbels, Joseph. *Die Tagebücher von Joseph Goebbels.* In *Nationalsozialismus, Holocaust, Widerstand und Exil, 1933–1945.* De Gruyter Online database.

Göksu, Saime, and Edward Timms. *Romantic Communist: The Life and Work of Nazım Hikmet.* New York: St. Martin's, 1999.

Göktürk, Deniz, Leven Soysal, and İpek Türeli, eds. *Orienting Istanbul: Cultural Capital of Europe?* London: Routledge, 2010.

Goodrich-Freer, Adela. *Things Seen in Constantinople.* London: Seeley, Service, and Co., 1926.

Greene, Graham. *Orient Express* [*Stamboul Train*]. London: Penguin, 2004 [1932].

———. *Travels with My Aunt.* New York: Bantam, 1971.

Greenfield, Robert. *The Last Sultan: The Life and Times of Ahmet Ertegun.* New York: Simon and Schuster, 2011.

Greer, Carl Richard. *The Glories of Greece.* Philadelphia: Penn Publishing Company, 1936.

Gritchenko, Alexis. *Deux ans à Constantinople*. Paris: Edition Quatre Vents, 1930.

Gül, Murat. *The Emergence of Modern Istanbul: Transformation and Modernisation of a City*. London: Tauris Academic Studies, 2009.

Gülersoy, Çelik. *Tepebaşı: Bir Meydan Savaşı*. Istanbul: İstanbul Büyükşehir Belediye Başkanlığı Kültür İşleri Daire Başkanlığı Yayınları, 1993.

Guttstadt, Corry. *Turkey, the Jews, and the Holocaust*. Cambridge: Cambridge University Press, 2013.

Güven, Dilek. *6–7 Eylül Olayları: Cumhuriyet Dönemi Azınlık Politikaları ve Stratejileri Bağlamında*. Istanbul: Tarih Vakfı, 2005.

Güvenç-Salgırlı, Sanem. "Eugenics as a Science of the Social: A Case from 1930s Istanbul." Ph.D. dissertation. Binghamton University, State University of New York, 2009.

Handbook for Travellers in Constantinople, Brûsa, and the Troad. London: John Murray, 1893.

A Handbook for Travellers in Turkey. 3rd rev. ed. London: John Murray, 1854.

Hanioğlu, M. Şükrü. *Atatürk: An Intellectual Biography*. Princeton, NJ: Princeton University Press, 2011.

Harington, General Sir Charles. *Tim Harington Looks Back*. London: John Murray, 1940.

Hayal Et Yapılar/Ghost Buildings. 2nd ed. Istanbul: PATTU, 2011.

Hemingway, Ernest. *Dateline: Toronto: The Complete Toronto Star Dispatches, 1920–1924*. William White, ed. New York: Charles Scribner's Sons, 1985.

Heper, Metin, and Sabri Sayarı, eds. *The Routledge Handbook of Modern Turkey*. London: Routledge, 2012.

Herbert, Aubrey. *Ben Kendim: A Record of Eastern Travel*. 2nd ed. New York: G. P. Putnam's Sons, 1925.

Hikmet, Nâzım. *Human Landscapes from My Country*. Randy Blasing and Mutlu Konuk, trans. New York: Persea Books, 2002.

———. *Poems of Nâzim Hikmet*. Randy Blasing and Mutlu Konuk, trans. New York: Persea Books, 2002.

Hildebrand, Arthur Sturges. *Blue Water*. New York: Harcourt, Brace and Company, 1923.

Hirschmann, Ira A. *Caution to the Winds*. New York: David McKay, 1962.

———. *Life Line to a Promised Land*. New York: Vanguard Press, 1946.

———. "Palestine as a Refuge from Fascism." *Survey Graphic* (May 1945): 195–98, 265.

Hirschon, Renée. *Heirs of the Greek Catastrophe: The Social Life of Asia Minor Refugees in Piraeus*. Oxford: Clarendon Press, 1989.

———, ed. *Crossing the Aegean: An Appraisal of the 1923 Compulsory Population Exchange Between Greece and Turkey*. New York: Berghahn Books, 2003.

Hirst, Samuel J. "Anti-Westernism on the European Periphery: The Meaning of Soviet-Turkish Convergence in the 1930s." *Slavic Review* 72, no. 1 (Spring 2013): 32–53.

Histoire de la République Turque. Istanbul: Devlet Basımevi, 1935.

Hoffmann, Peter. "Roncalli in the Second World War: Peace Initiatives, the Greek Famine and the Persecution of the Jews." *Journal of Ecclesiastical History* 40, no. 1 (Jan. 1989): 74–99.

Holquist, Peter. "'Information Is the Alpha and Omega of Our Work': Bolshevik Surveillance in Its Pan-European Context." *Journal of Modern History* 69 (Sept. 1997): 415–50.

Hovannisian, Richard G., and Simon Payaslian, eds. *Armenian Constantinople*. Costa Mesa, CA: Mazda Publishers, 2010.

Howard, Harry N. *The Partition of Turkey: A Diplomatic History, 1913–1923*. New York: Howard Fertig, 1966.

İmparatorluk Başkentinden Cumhuriyet'in Modern Kentine: Henri Prost'un İstanbul Planlaması (1936–1951)/From the Imperial Capital to the Republican Modern City: Henri Prost's Planning of Istanbul (1936–1951). Istanbul: İstanbul Araştırmaları Enstitüsü, 2010.

İnalcık, Halil, with Donald Quataert, eds. *An Economic and Social History of the Ottoman Empire*. 2 vols. Cambridge: Cambridge University Press, 1997.

İnan, Süleyman. "The First 'History of the Turkish Revolution' Lectures and Courses in Turkish Universities (1934–42)." *Middle Eastern Studies* 43, no. 4 (2007): 593–609.

Ioanid, Radu. *The Holocaust in Romania*. Chicago: Ivan R. Dee, 2000.

Işın, Ekrem. *Everyday Life in Istanbul: Social Historical Essays on People, Culture and Spatial Relations*. Istanbul: Yapı Kredi Yayınları 2001.

İstanbul Telefon Türk Anonim Şirketi. *Telefon Rehberi*. Istanbul: Matbaacılık ve Neşriyat T.A.Ş., 1934.

İstanbul Ticaret Odası. *Adres Kitabı, 1955.* 2 vols. Istanbul: I.T.S.O., 1955.

İstanbul Ticaret ve Sanayi Odası. *Adres Kitabı, 1938.* Istanbul: I.T.S.O., 1938.

———. *Adres Kitabı, 1941.* Istanbul: I.T.S.O., 1941.

İstanbul Belediyesi. *İstanbul şehri rehberi.* Istanbul: Matbaacılık ve Neşriyat Türk Anonim Şirketi, 1934.

Jacques Pervititch Sigorta Haritalarında İstanbul/Istanbul in the Insurance Maps of Jacques Pervititch. Istanbul: Axa Oyak, 2000.

Jeffreys, Elizabeth, with John Haldon and Robin Cormack, eds. *The Oxford Handbook of Byzantine Studies.* Oxford: Oxford University Press, 2008.

John XXIII, Pope. *Journal of a Soul.* New York: Image Books, 1980.

Johnson, Clarence Richard, ed. *Constantinople To-Day, or The Pathfinder Survey of Constantinople.* New York: Macmillan, 1922.

Kasaba, Reşat. *A Moveable Empire: Ottoman Nomads, Migrants, and Refugees.* Seattle: University of Washington Press, 2009.

———, ed. *The Cambridge History of Turkey, Vol. 4: Turkey in the Modern World.* Cambridge: Cambridge University Press, 2008.

Kazansky, Konstantin. *Cabaret russe.* Paris: Olivier Orban, 1978.

Kedourie, Sylvia, ed. *Turkey Before and After Atatürk.* London: Frank Cass, 1999.

Kemal, Orhan. *In Jail with Nâzım Hikmet.* Bengisu Rona, trans. Istanbul: Everest Publications, 2012.

Kenez, Peter. *Civil War in South Russia, 1919–1920.* Berkeley: University of California Press, 1977.

Kerslake, Celia, Kerem Öktem, and Philip Robins, eds. *Turkey's Engagement with Modernity: Conflict and Change in the Twentieth Century.* Basingstoke, UK: Palgrave Macmillan, 2010.

Kévorkian, Raymond. *The Armenian Genocide: A Complete History.* London: I. B. Tauris, 2011.

Keyder, Çağlar, ed. *Istanbul: Between the Global and the Local.* Lanham, MD: Rowman and Littlefield, 1999.

Kinross, Lord [Patrick Balfour, baron Kinross]. *Europa Minor: Journeys in Coastal Turkey.* London: John Murray, 1956.

Klein, Holger A., ed. *Restoring Byzantium: The Kariye Camii in Istanbul and the Byzantine Institute Restoration.* New York: Miriam and Ira D. Wallach Art Gallery, Columbia University, 2004.

Klein, Holger A., Robert G. Ousterhout, and Brigitte Pitarakis, eds. *Kariye Camii, Yeniden/The Kariye Camii Reconsidered*. Istanbul: İstanbul Araştırmaları Enstitüsü, 2011.

Knatchbull-Hugessen, Hughe. *Diplomat in Peace and War*. London: John Murray, 1949.

Koçu, Reşad Ekrem. *İstanbul Ansiklopedisi*. 11 vols. Istanbul: Koçu Yayınları, et al., 1946–1974.

Kollek, Teddy, with Amos Kollek. *For Jerusalem*. New York: Random House, 1978.

Komandorova, N. I. *Russkii Stambul*. Moscow: Veche, 2009.

Konstantinopol'-Gallipoli. Moscow: Rossiiskii gosudarstvennyi gumanitarnyi universitet, 2003.

Kuban, Doğan. *Istanbul, An Urban History: Byzantium, Constantinopolis, Istanbul*. Rev. ed. Istanbul: Türkiye İş Bankası Kültür Yayınları, 2010.

Kuruyazıcı, Hasan, ed. *Batılılaşan İstanbul'un Ermeni Mimarları/Armenian Architects of Istanbul in the Era of Westernization*. 2nd ed. Istanbul: International Hrant Dink Foundation Publications, 2011.

Laiou, Angeliki E., ed. *The Economic History of Byzantium: From the Seventh through the Fifteenth Century*. 3 vols. Washington, DC: Dumbarton Oaks, 2002.

Le Corbusier. *Journey to the East*. Cambridge, MA: MIT Press, 2007 [1966].

Levy, Avigdor, ed. *Jews, Turks, Ottomans: A Shared History, Fifteenth Through the Twentieth Century*. Syracuse, NY: Syracuse University Press, 2002.

Lewis, Bernard. *The Emergence of Modern Turkey*. 3rd ed. New York: Oxford University Press, 2002.

———. *Istanbul and the Civilization of the Ottoman Empire*. Norman: University of Oklahoma Press, 1963.

Libal, Kathryn. "Staging Turkish Women's Emancipation: Istanbul, 1935." *Journal of Middle East Women's Studies* 4, no. 1 (Winter 2008): 31–52.

Lockhart, R. H. Bruce. *Comes the Reckoning*. London: Putnam, 1947.

Macartney, C. A. *National States and National Minorities*. Oxford: Oxford University Press, 1934.

———. *Refugees: The Work of the League*. London: League of Nations Union, 1931.

Macmillan, Margaret. *Paris 1919: Six Months That Changed the World.* New York: Random House, 2002.

Mallowan, Max. *Mallowan's Memoirs.* New York: Dodd, Mead, 1977.

Mamboury, Ernest. *Constantinople: Tourists' Guide.* Constantinople: Rizzo and Son, 1926.

Mango, Andrew. *Atatürk.* New York: Overlook, 1999.

Mango, Cyril. *Byzantium: The Empire of New Rome.* New York: Charles Scribner's Sons, 1980.

———. *Materials for the Study of the Mosaics of St. Sophia at Istanbul.* Washington, DC: Dumbarton Oaks Research Library and Collection, 1962.

Mango, Cyril, and Gilbert Dagron, eds. *Constantinople and Its Hinterland.* Brookfield, VT: Aldershot, 1995.

Mannix, Daniel P., III. *The Old Navy.* Daniel P. Mannix IV, ed. New York: Macmillan, 1983.

Mansel, Philip. *Constantinople: City of the World's Desire, 1453–1924.* London: John Murray, 2006.

Mardor, Munya M. [Meir Mardor]. *Strictly Illegal.* London: Robert Hale, 1964.

Massigli, René. *La Turquie devant la guerre.* Paris: Plon, 1964.

Mazower, Mark. *Hitler's Empire: How the Nazis Ruled Europe.* New York: Penguin, 2008.

———. *Salonica, City of Ghosts: Christians, Muslims, and Jews, 1430–1950.* New York: Vintage, 2006.

Milliken, William M. "Early Christian and Byzantine Art in America." *Journal of Aesthetics and Art Criticism* 5, no. 4 (June 1947): 256–68.

Mills, Amy. *Streets of Memory: Landscape, Tolerance, and National Identity in Istanbul.* Athens: University of Georgia Press, 2010.

Mintzuri, Hagop. *İstanbul Anıları, 1897–1940.* Istanbul: Tarih Vakfı Yurt Yayınları, 1993.

Morgan, Janet. *Agatha Christie: A Biography.* London: Collins, 1984.

Moysich, L. C. *Operation Cicero.* London: Allan Wingate-Baker, 1969.

Mufty-zada, K. Ziya. *Speaking of the Turks.* New York: Duffield and Co., 1922.

Musbah Haidar, Princess. *Arabesque.* London: Hutchinson and Co., 1945.

al-Muwaylihi, Ibrahim. *Spies, Scandals, and Sultans: Istanbul in the Twilight of the Ottoman Empire*. Roger Allen, trans. Lanham, MD: Rowman and Littlefield, 2008.

Nabokov, Vladimir. *Speak, Memory*. Rev. ed. New York: G. P. Putnam's Sons, 1966.

Nansen, Fridtjof. *Armenia and the Near East*. New York: Da Capo Press, 1976 [1928].

Neave, Dorina L. *Twenty-Six Years on the Bosphorus*. London: Grayson and Grayson, 1933.

Nelson, Robert S. *Hagia Sophia, 1850–1950: Holy Wisdom Modern Monument*. Chicago: University of Chicago Press, 2004.

Newman, Bernard. *Turkish Crossroads*. New York: Philosophical Library, 1952.

Neyzi, Leyla, *İstanbul'da Hatırlamak ve Unutmak*. Istanbul: Tarih Vakfı Yurt Yayınları, 1999.

Nicol, Graham. *Uncle George: Field-Marshal Lord Milne of Salonika and Rubislaw*. London: Reedminster Publications, 1976.

Nicolson, Harold. *Sweet Waters: An Istanbul Adventure*. London: Eland, 2008 [1921].

Norwich, John Julius. *A Short History of Byzantium*. New York: Knopf, 1997.

Ofer, Dalia. *Escaping the Holocaust: Illegal Immigration to the Land of Israel*. New York: Oxford University Press, 1990.

Ökte, Faik. *The Tragedy of the Turkish Capital Tax*. London: Croom Helm, 1987.

Olson, Robert W. "The Remains of Talat: A Dialectic between Republic and Empire." *Die Welt des Islams* (new series) 26, no. 1/4 (1986): 46–56.

Orga, Ateş, ed. *Istanbul: A Collection of the Poetry of Place*. London: Eland, 2007.

Orga, Irfan. *Phoenix Ascendant: The Rise of Modern Turkey*. London: Robert Hale, 1958.

———. *Portrait of a Turkish Family*. London: Eland, 2002 [1950].

Osman Bey [Vladimir Andrejevich]. *Les femmes en Turquie*. 2nd ed. Paris: C. Lévy, 1878.

Ostrorog, Léon. *The Angora Reform*. London: University of London Press, 1927.

———. *The Turkish Problem: Things Seen and a Few Deductions*. London: Chatto and Windus, 1919.

Pallis, A. A. "The Population of Turkey in 1935." *Geographical Journal* 91, no. 5 (May 1938): 439–45.

Pamuk, Orhan. *Istanbul: Memories and the City*. New York: Knopf, 2004.

Patenaude, Bertrand M. *Trotsky: Downfall of a Revolutionary*. New York: HarperCollins, 2009.

Pears, Edwin. *Forty Years in Constantinople*. New York: D. Appleton and Co., 1916.

———. *The Life of Abdul Hamid*. London: Constable, 1917.

Peirce, Leslie P. *The Imperial Harem: Women and Sovereignty in the Ottoman Empire*. Oxford: Oxford University Press, 1993.

Pelt, Mogens. *Tobacco, Arms, and Politics: Greece and Germany from World Crisis to World War, 1929–1941*. Copenhagen: Museum Tusculanum Press, 1998.

Phayer, Michael. *The Catholic Church and the Holocaust, 1930–1965*. Bloomington: Indiana University Press, 2000.

———. *Pius XII, the Holocaust, and the Cold War*. Bloomington: Indiana University Press, 2008.

Pirî Reis. *Kitab-ı bahriye*. Robert Bragner, trans. 4 vols. Istanbul: Historical Research Foundation, 1988.

Pope, Nicole, and Hugh Pope. *Turkey Unveiled: A History of Modern Turkey*. Rev. ed. New York: Overlook Press, 2011.

Poynter, Mary A. *When Turkey Was Turkey*. London: George Routledge and Sons, Ltd., 1921.

Price, G. Ward. *Extra-Special Correspondent*. London: George G. Harrap, 1957.

———. *The Story of the Salonica Army*. New York: Edward J. Clode, 1918.

———. *Year of Reckoning*. London: Cassell, 1939.

Procopius of Caesarea. *Procopius*. H. B. Dewing, trans. 7 vols. Cambridge, MA: Harvard University Press, 1954–1961.

Raeff, Marc. *Russia Abroad: A Cultural History of the Russian Emigration, 1919–1939*. Oxford: Oxford University Press, 1990.

Rakı Ansiklopedisi: 500 Yıldır Süren Muhabbetin Mirası. Istanbul: Overteam Yayınları, 2010.

Reisman, Arnold. *Turkey's Modernization: Refugees from Nazism and Atatürk's Vision*. Washington, DC: New Academia Publishing, 2006.

Rendel, George. *The Sword and the Olive: Recollections of Diplomacy and the Foreign Service, 1913–1954*. London: John Murray, 1957.

Report of the Rescue Committee of the Jewish Agency for Palestine. Jerusalem: Executive of the Jewish Agency for Palestine, 1946.

Reynolds, Michael A. *Shattering Empires: The Clash and Collapse of the Ottoman and Russian Empires, 1908–1918*. Cambridge: Cambridge University Press, 2011.

Righi, Vittore Ugo. *Papa Giovanni XXIII sulle rive del Bosforo*. Padua: Edizioni Messaggero, 1971.

Robinson, Paul. *The White Russian Army in Exile, 1920–1941*. Oxford: Clarendon Press, 2002.

Rogan, Eugene, ed. *Outside In: On the Margins of the Modern Middle East*. London: I. B. Tauris, 2002.

Rosenthal, Gérard. *Avocat de Trotsky*. Paris: Éditions Robert Laffont, 1975.

Rozen, Minna. *A History of the Jewish Community in Istanbul: The Formative Years, 1453–1566*. Leiden: Brill, 2010.

———, ed. *The Last Ottoman Century and Beyond: The Jews in Turkey and the Balkans, 1808–1945*. 2 vols. Tel Aviv: Tel Aviv University, 2002.

Rubin, Barry. *Istanbul Intrigues*. New York: Pharos Books, 1991.

Runciman, Steven. *The Fall of Constantinople, 1453*. Cambridge: Cambridge University Press, 1965.

———. *A Traveller's Alphabet: Partial Memoirs*. London: Thames and Hudson, 1991.

Russell, Thomas. *Egyptian Service, 1902–1946*. London: John Murray, 1949.

Schwartz, Stephen, Vitaly Rapoport, Walter Laqueur, and Theodore H. Draper. "'The Mystery of Max Eitingon': An Exchange." *New York Review of Books*, June 16, 1988.

Sciaky, Leon. *Farewell to Salonica*. Philadelphia: Paul Dry Books, 2003.

Scipio, Lynn A. *My Thirty Years in Turkey*. Rindge, NH: Richard R. Smith, 1955.

Scognamillo, Giovanni. *Bir Levantenin Beyoğlu Anıları*. Istanbul: Metis Yayınları, 1990.

Second Section of the General Staff on the Western Front. *Greek Atrocities in Asia Minor, First Part.* Istanbul: Husn-i-Tabiat, 1922.

"Sefirden Sefile": Yapı Kredi Selahattin Giz Koleksiyonu. Istanbul: Yapı Kredi Yayınları, 2004.

Serge, Victor, and Natalia Sedova Trotsky. *The Life and Death of Leon Trotsky.* London: Wildwood House, 1973.

Service, Robert. *Trotsky: A Biography.* Cambridge, MA.: Harvard University Press, 2009.

Sharapov, E. P. *Naum Eitingon: Karaiushchii mech Stalina.* St. Petersburg: Neva, 2003.

Shaul, Eli. *From Balat to Bat Yam: Memoirs of a Turkish Jew.* Istanbul: Libra Kitap, 2012.

Shaw, Stanford J. *The Jews of the Ottoman Empire and the Turkish Republic.* New York: New York University Press, 1991.

———. "The Population of Istanbul in the Nineteenth Century." *International Journal of Middle East Studies* 10, no. 2 (May 1979): 265–77.

———. *Turkey and the Holocaust.* New York: New York University Press, 1993.

Sherrill, Charles H. *A Year's Embassy to Mustafa Kemal.* New York: Charles Scribner's Sons, 1934.

Shissler, Ada Holland. "Beauty Is Nothing to Be Ashamed Of: Beauty Contests as Tools of Women's Liberation in Early Republican Turkey." *Comparative Studies of South Asia, Africa, and the Middle East* 24, no. 1 (2004): 107–22.

———. "'If You Ask Me': Sabiha Sertel's Advice Column, Gender Equity, and Social Engineering in the Early Turkish Republic." *Journal of Middle East Women's Studies* 3, no. 2 (Spring 2007): 1–30.

Shorter, Frederic C. "The Population of Turkey after the War of Independence." *International Journal of Middle East Studies* 17, no. 4 (Nov. 1985): 417–41.

Smith, Douglas. *Former People: The Final Days of the Russian Aristocracy.* New York: Farrar, Straus and Giroux, 2012.

Snyder, Timothy. *Bloodlands: Europe Between Hitler and Stalin.* New York: Basic Books, 2010.

Sperco, Willy. *Istanbul indiscret: Ce que les guides ne disent pas.* Istanbul: Türkiye Turing ve Otomobil Kurumu, 1970.

———. *Istanbul: Paysage littéraire*. Paris: La Nef de Paris, 1955.

———. *L'Orient qui s'éteint*. Paris: Editions Baudiniere, 1935.

———. *Turcs d'hier et d'aujourd'hui*. Paris: Nouvelles éditions latines, 1961.

Sphrantzes, George. *The Fall of the Byzantine Empire*. Marios Philippides, trans. Amherst: University of Massachusetts Press, 1980.

Stone, Norman, and Michael Glenny. *The Other Russia*. London: Faber and Faber, 1990.

Sudoplatov, Pavel, and Anatoli Sudoplatov. *Special Tasks: The Memoirs of an Unwanted Witness—A Soviet Spymaster*. New York: Little, Brown, 1994.

Suny, Ronald Grigor, Fatma Müge Göçek, and Norman M. Naimark, eds. *A Question of Genocide: Armenians and Turks at the End of the Ottoman Empire*. Oxford: Oxford University Press, 2011.

Tanpınar, Ahmed Hamdi. *The Time Regulation Institute*. Maureen Freely and Alexander Dawe, trans. New York: Penguin, 2013.

———. *A Mind at Peace*. Erdağ Göknar, trans. New York: Archipelago Books, 2008.

Tekdemir, Hande. "Collective Melancholy: Istanbul at the Crossroads of History, Space, and Memory." Ph.D. dissertation. University of Southern California, 2008.

Teteriatnikov, Natalia B. *Mosaics of Hagia Sophia, Istanbul*. Washington, DC: Dumbarton Oaks, 1998.

Thompson, Laura. *Agatha Christie: An English Mystery*. London: Headline Review, 2007.

Tischler, Ulrike, ed. *From "Milieu de mémoire" to "Lieu de mémoire": The Cultural Memory of Istanbul in the 20th Century*. Munich: Marin Meidenbauer, 2006.

Tittmann, Harold H., Jr. *Inside the Vatican of Pius XII: The Memoir of an American Diplomat during World War II*. New York: Doubleday, 2004.

Toledano, Ehud R. *The Ottoman Slave Trade and Its Suppression, 1840–1890*. Princeton, NJ: Princeton University Press, 1982.

Tolstoy, Vera. "The Compensations of Poverty." *Atlantic Monthly* (Mar. 1922): 307–10.

Tomlin, E. W. F. *Life in Modern Turkey*. London: Thomas Nelson, 1946.

Toprak, Zafer. "La population d'Istanbul dans les premières années de la République." *Travaux et recherches en Turquie* 2 (1982): 63–70.

Topuzlu, Cemil. *80 yıllık hâtıralarım.* Istanbul: Güven Basım ve Yayınevi, 1951.

Toynbee, Arnold J. *The Western Question in Greece and Turkey.* 2nd ed. New York: Howard Fertig, 1970 [1923].

Treadgold, Warren. *A History of Byzantine State and Society.* Stanford, CA: Stanford University Press, 1997.

Trotsky, Leon. *Leon Trotsky Speaks.* New York: Pathfinder Press, 1972.

———. *My Life.* New York: Charles Scribner's Sons, 1930.

Tuganoff, Moussa Bey. *From Tsar to Cheka: The Story of a Circassian Under Tsar, Padishah and Cheka.* London: Sampson Low, Marston and Co., 1936.

Türkiye İstatistik Yıllığı: 1950. Ankara: T. C. Başbakanlık İstatistik Genel Müdürlüğü, n.d.

Ülgen, Fatma. "'Sabiha Gökçen's 80-Year-Old Secret': Kemalist Nation Formation and the Ottoman Armenians." Ph.D. dissertation. University of California, San Diego, 2010.

Üngör, Uğur Ümit. *The Making of Modern Turkey: Nation and State in Eastern Anatolia, 1913–1950.* Oxford: Oxford University Press, 2011.

Urgan, Mîna. *Bir Dinozorun Anıları.* Istanbul: Yapı Kredi Yayıncılık, 1998.

Van Heijenoort, Jean. *With Trotsky in Exile: From Prinkipo to Coyoacán.* Cambridge, MA: Harvard University Press, 1978.

Volkogonov, Dmitri. *Trotsky: The Eternal Revolutionary.* New York: Free Press, 1996.

Von Papen, Franz. *Memoirs.* New York: E. P. Dutton and Co., 1953.

Vryonis, Speros, Jr. *The Mechanism of Catastrophe: The Turkish Pogrom of September 6–7, 1955, and the Destruction of the Greek Community of Istanbul.* New York: Greekworks.com, 2005.

Webster, Donald Everett. *The Turkey of Atatürk.* Philadelphia: American Academy of Political and Social Science, 1939.

Weisband, Edward. *Turkish Foreign Policy, 1943–1945: Small State Diplomacy and Great Power Politics.* Princeton, NJ: Princeton University Press, 1973.

White, Charles. *Three Years in Constantinople; or, Domestic Manners of the Turks in 1844.* 3 vols. London: Henry Colburn, 1845.

White, T. W. *Guests of the Unspeakable.* London: John Hamilton, 1928.

Whittemore, Thomas. "The Rebirth of Religion in Russia." *National Geographic* (Nov. 1918): 379–401.

Wilmers, Mary-Kay. *The Eitingons: A Twentieth-Century Story*. London: Faber and Faber, 2009.

Woodall, G. Carole. "'Awakening a Horrible Monster': Negotiating the Jazz Public in 1920s Istanbul." *Comparative Studies of South Asia, Africa, and the Middle East* 30, no. 3 (2010): 574–82.

———. "Sensing the City: Sound, Movement, and the Night in 1920s Istanbul." Ph.D. dissertation. New York University, 2008.

Woods, Henry F. *Spunyarn: From the Strands of a Sailor's Life Afloat and Ashore*. 2 vols. London: Hutchinson and Co., 1924.

Woolf, Leonard S. *The Future of Constantinople*. London: George Allen and Unwin, Ltd., 1917.

Wrangel, Peter Nikolaevich. *The Memoirs of General Wrangel*. London: Duffield and Co., 1930.

Wyers, Mark David. *"Wicked" Istanbul: The Regulation of Prostitution in the Early Turkish Republic*. Istanbul: Libra, 2012.

Yalman, Ahmed Emin. *Turkey in My Time*. Norman: University of Oklahoma Press, 1956.

———. *Turkey in the World War*. New Haven, CT: Yale University Press, 1930.

Yıldırım, Onur. *Diplomacy and Displacement: Reconsidering the Turco-Greek Exchange of Populations, 1922–1934*. London: Routledge, 2006.

Zürcher, Erik J. *Political Opposition in the Early Turkish Republic: The Progressive Republican Party, 1924–1925*. Leiden: E. J. Brill, 1991.

———. *Turkey: A Modern History*. New rev. ed. London: I. B. Tauris, 1998.

———. *The Unionist Factor: The Role of the Committee of Union and Progress in the Turkish National Movement, 1905–1926*. Leiden: E. J. Brill, 1984.

———. *The Young Turk Legacy and Nation Building: From the Ottoman Empire to Atatürk's Turkey*. London: I. B. Tauris, 2010.

RECORDINGS

One of the earliest sources for this book was the album *Istanbul 1925* (Traditional Crossroads, 1994), the work of the violinist and sound engineer Harold G. Hagopian, who accessed the original metallic masters of Columbia recordings from the 1920s and re-created an audible world that few people remembered ever existed. His Traditional Crossroads label has gone on to issue several other period recordings, including the haunting *Women of Istanbul* (1998), where I first listened to Roza Eskenazi, and two volumes of Udi Hrant's early work. More recently, Ian Nagoski has cataloged the musical world of the "Ottoman diaspora" in America after the First World War on the album *To What Strange Place* (Tompkins Square, 2011).

The rerelease of old recordings is a booming business in Turkey, and at the center of it is Kalan Müzik, a company that has reissued a trove of Greek, Armenian, and other music of Istanbul's minority cultures, as well as the forgotten art of Turkish tango and *bel canto*. I first heard the voice of Seyyan on Kalan Müzik's *Seyyan Hanım: Tangolar* (1996). The same company's *Kantolar: 1905–1945* (1998) is an introduction to the light music of the Istanbul stage.

INDEX

Turkish historical figures who are generally known by their first
names rather than by their surnames are alphabetized accordingly.

Page numbers in *italics* refer to illustrations.